ISBN 978-1-390-96136-2
PIBN 11011919

1 MONTH OF
FREE
READING

at

www.ForgottenBooks.com

By purchasing this book you are eligible for one month membership to ForgottenBooks.com, giving you unlimited access to our entire collection of over 1,000,000 titles via our web site and mobile apps.

To claim your free month visit:
www.forgottenbooks.com/free1011919

English
Français
Deutsche
Italiano
Español
Português

www.forgottenbooks.com

Mythology Photography **Fiction**
Fishing Christianity **Art** Cooking
Essays Buddhism Freemasonry
Medicine **Biology** Music **Ancient**
Egypt Evolution Carpentry Physics
Dance Geology **Mathematics** Fitness
Shakespeare **Folklore** Yoga Marketing
Confidence Immortality Biographies
Poetry **Psychology** Witchcraft
Electronics Chemistry History **Law**
Accounting **Philosophy** Anthropology
Alchemy Drama Quantum Mechanics
Atheism Sexual Health **Ancient History**
Entrepreneurship Languages Sport
Paleontology Needlework Islam
Metaphysics Investment Archaeology
Parenting Statistics Criminology
Motivational

THE LIFE

OF

ST. CHARLES BORROM

THE LIFE

OF

T. CHARLES BORROMEO

CARDINAL ARCHBISHOP OF MILAN

From the Italian of

JOHN PETER GIUSSANO

PRIEST AND OBLATE OF ST. AMBROSE

WITH PREFACE

BY

HENRY EDWARD CARDINAL MANNING

ARCHBISHOP OF WESTMINSTER

VOL. II.

BURNS AND OATES

LONDON	NEW YORK
GRANVILLE MANSIONS	CATHOLIC PUBLICATION SOCIETY CO.
ORCHARD STREET, W.	BARCLAY STREET

1884

CONTENTS.

BOOK V.

VOL. II.

BOOK VI.

BOOK VII.

Contents.

BOOK VIII

BOOK IX.

LIFE OF ST. CHARLES BORROM

—o—

Book F.

CHAPTER I.

ST. CHARLES AGAIN MEETS WITH OPPOSITION IN
ECCLESIASTICAL JURISDICTION.

1578.

THE fame of the saint's charity and labours durin
plague spread far and wide, earning for him ack
ledgments from distant kings and princes, and
pelling the calumnies of those who misinterpre
ıctions even of good men.   A certain Cardinal, hı
 ad occasion to observe this, said: "The Cardin
·anta Prassede has now cleared up, once for al
doubts of those who chose to misunderstand hir
he has given a proof they cannot gainsay of the cl
which burns in his heart, by putting his own li
jeopardy for the sake of his people."   Those
entertained ill-will against him—for God always
mits ill-will against the just in order to try their ı
—were now put to silence, and even when they ı

not acknowledge his saintly character, there remained nothing which they could take hold of as matter for their censures.

There was a fair promise, therefore, that out of the common calamity there would arise an era of peace and forbearance; and that the bickerings about ecclesiastical jurisdiction, which even yet crippled the action of the Church courts, would be clean forgotten. So, indeed, thought all, including the Crown officers, who deemed that this was the least return they could make to the Cardinal for all the toil and anxiety he had undergone.

But the enemy of mankind was excited against the servant of God in proportion as he was more fully appreciated, and could not endure that he should be left at peace. He cast about, therefore, to set up some new calumny to disturb him, if that were possible. Such is the lot of the just in this life, as it is written, "Many are the afflictions of the just." [1] The further a man advances in the path of perfection, the greater are the obstacles he has to surmount, in proportion as the degree of glory prepared for him in heaven is also greater. The saint had indeed already encountered a large measure of suffering, but God designed to bestow upon him a brighter crown, and therefore permitted a heavier cross to be laid upon him.

The Governor of Milan had from the time of his accession to office behaved towards the Cardinal with mistrust, which arose no doubt from the fact of the excommunication of his predecessor, and the remon-

strances he had brought upon himself on accou
his absence from his proper sphere of duty. Nor
there wanting evil counsellors ever ready to fost
will by way of ingratiating themselves. There
also some among the officers of the Crown who
malice against the Cardinal on account of his ref
who would rather have been left in their old evil l
—his saintly example being a thorn in their si
as is said in the Gospel, "He who walks in dar
hateth the light."[1] Two of these in particular
among the Governor's most intimate advisers, and
an especial dislike to St. Charles because he ha
several occasions reproved the scandalous licen
their lives. Yet they did nothing openly against
but cloaked their devices under a show of zea
what was just and right, in which they succeede
better that one of them had formerly been int
with the saint, who had been known to speak of
in terms of commendation. I do not say this in
way to vindicate St. Charles, whose motives no
would venture to call in question, not even in his
day; but in order to show that the Governor
really deceived in his opinion of the man, and
the opposition arose from a very small section o
King's ministers, the great majority of whom were
minded persons, and well affected towards the Card
as was also their royal master. What wonder if
were some who were ill-disposed among so la
number of upright and conscientious persons, s
there was a Judas even in the college of the Apos

[1] John iii. 20.

The city had hardly been declared free from the contagion, when the vexed question of the limits of the Archbishop's jurisdiction was again mooted by the Governor. Matters of this kind relating to other dominions of the Catholic King were about to be submitted to the judgment of the Holy See, when the Governor seized the opportunity of opening up his suit. In pursuance of this purpose he sent an envoy to Rome to conduct the proceedings in his behalf, little doubting the cause would be decided in his favour, as his advisers led him to expect. He selected for the mission a certain doctor, whom he knew to be unfavourably disposed to the Cardinal's claims. This person was recommended to him by the two adversaries of the latter already mentioned, and was, in fact, their creature. To his commission they superadded instructions, with several unfounded complaints against the saint, to be laid before the Sovereign Pontiff, wishing, by means of these accusations, to weaken his credit with His Holiness, thereby to obtain the readier hearing for their view of the question of jurisdiction, and above all to neutralise his power of enforcing the reforms so obnoxious to them. Among other things, he was to accuse the Cardinal of having endeavoured to exempt ecclesiastics from the observance of the ordinances made by the Governor and municipal authorities for the regulation of the city during the pestilence, alleging that it belonged to himself to give orders respecting the quarantine in all that concerned them. Then he was to pretend—though there was no foundation

whatever for the allegation—that great mischie
accrued from the freedom with which ecclesi
armed with the Cardinal's permission, passed
one part of the diocese to another without the
sary quarantine from the office of public h
This is enough to show the spirit of his acc
since we see them imputing these measures t
as faults. Such is the strength of passion
can blind men so that they call good evil, an
good; and such the mischief that arises wher
counsellors have the ear of a ruler, and induce
under the plea of upholding right, to do all m
of injustice.

But this was not all. To give a more colo
appearance to their inventions, they had recou
the base artifice of representing that all the
of Milan were aggrieved by the restrictions arbit
as they alleged, laid by the Cardinal upon
liberties. They endeavoured accordingly to
the support of the Council of the city for their
plaints, but it was only a very slender mir
misled by worldly interests, who would afford
any sanction, and the whole city was highly
nant when the intrigue was made public. The
of accusation were, that he had prohibited
amusements and balls on holidays, allowing n
but religion to be then attended to; that h
reserved to himself the sole power of giving a
tion for a great number of sins; that he had abc
the custom of allowing the use of meat on th
Sunday of Lent; that he had closed up all th

entrances of the churches, and revived the obsolete
practice of dividing men from women in the congregation, and had set up wooden partitions for that
purpose; and that he introduced the observance of
the festival of the Martyrs Gervasius and Protasius,
to which they had never before been accustomed.

It would seem, however, that, with all their malice,
his enemies still perceived that these charges were at
best but frivolous, if indeed they did not in making
them run the risk of calling attention to the wisdom
and piety of his decrees. They sought, therefore, to
find something more tangible to lay hold to his prejudice. For this purpose they instituted a searching
inquisition not only into the acts of the Cardinal himself, but also into those of his rural deans; and sent
for the deputies of many towns and districts, and
examined them, in many cases using threats, in the
hope of discovering something which might be used
against him. But in this they were foiled, for all
that was to be learnt was that the ministers of the
Cardinal were diligent in their duties and in enforcing
discipline. Such result, instead of changing their purpose, was received by them only with disgust.

Fertile in resources, the Governor then bethought
himself of another expedient. Fancying that the
reforms the Cardinal had so vigorously carried out
among the religious orders were likely to be as dis-
tasteful to some of them as those effected in the city
were to himself and his party, he caused it to be exten-
sively circulated among them that if any had cause
of complaint personally against the Cardinal, or in any

matter affecting their Order, they would do well themselves to declare it, as he was ready to take their cause and support them with the weight of authority at Rome as well as in Milan. He had miscalculated in this, for among the great bod the religious, who appreciated the piety of the s and gladly accepted his reforms, were certain mem who chafed at what they considered innovations u the laxity they had once enjoyed. These, it will readily believed, did not remain silent when they the promise of countenance and support in so hig quarter. In the month of August of the year be the saint had called all the heads of religious ho before him, on purpose to inquire whether the dec of various Bulls of Pius IV., Pius V., and Gregory X were observed by them, when he told them pla that he should have felt himself bound to report matter to the Holy See if he had found any ne gence in their observance. With the natural shr ing of our nature from discipline, it is scarcely ma of surprise that a certain number came forward swell the Governor's budget of complaints. T were some communities of nuns also that joined outcry against regulations which had pressed seve upon them as well as others.

Such were the ways in which the emissary of Governor tried to bring the Cardinal into discr He did not fail to urge his allegations with all address he could command, backing them with memorials of the disaffected religious, and not hes ing to amplify them where the naked truth appe too frivolous to be made a ground of serious accusation. But the Pontiff was not thus to be deceived. He at once remarked that every matter of complaint against the Archbishop was, rightly considered, deserving of praise, and tended to prove his wisdom in the government of his diocese. It was perfectly clear, therefore, that the whole was a plot of the enemy of mankind to entrap him, an outburst of his malice against St. Charles in revenge for the numbers who had been delivered from his snares by the labours of the saint. At the same time the Holy Father was struck with indignation that any persons, calling themselves Christians, should have been found to listen to such suggestions when they involved so great an injustice towards their good pastor; and that at a time when he had been ready to sacrifice his life for them, and had actually spent his whole energies in their service, thus rendering him cursing instead of blessing— an inconceivable piece of ingratitude. To give unmistakable evidence of his abhorrence of conduct so base, he took no other notice of the charges than to send a statement of the whole matter to St. Charles himself, in order to acquaint him with the sentiments of his flock—for the Pope did not know that their apparent concurrence had been surreptitiously obtained—and that he might see how little they could be depended upon.

On receiving the statement, St. Charles was not a little grieved to find that his enemies had suffered themselves to be caught in the snares of Satan, and lamented the scandals that might result from their conduct, as well as the dishonour they had

offered to God. He sent for some of the princ⁣
people of the city, who had been eye-witnesses
his whole course of conduct and fellow - worl
during the pestilence, and consulted with them u
this business. They were beyond measure disgus
and assured him, that however boldly the name
the people had been used, they were altogether :
from any knowledge of the affair. At the s⁣
time they begged him to keep silence, for if the ma
came to the ears of the people, their resentment wc
be so unbounded that they would of a certainty t
some signal vengeance on the authors of it.
from seeking such a triumph, their pastor, with g
charity, determined not so much as to notice it, sin
writing to the Pope to thank him for his goodi
in treating the matter as he had done, and rende⁣
such explanations as he was now able to furnish.

Page 2.—The Governor of Milan.

Don Antonio de Guzman, Marquess of Ayamonte, entered upo⁣
office in October 1573. St. Charles writes of him to Mgr. Castelli
went to-day to pay a visit of compliment to the new Governor.
received me in his ante-chamber, where we had to converse in p
before all who were there. I do not know whether this is pride or Sp
etiquette in a first visit, or because he was afraid I had come to :
some demand of him."—Letter of October 7, 1573, vid. *Sala Docun*
etc., tom. iv. p. 528.

Page 4.—A certain doctor.

Giacomo Riccardi, a native of Lodi, presented the Governor's men
to Pope Gregory XIII. in May 1579.

CHAPTER II.

INCREASED AUSTERITIES — CORRECTION OF ABUSES —
INSTITUTION OF THE STATIONS OF THE SEVEN
CHURCHES—THE FIFTH DIOCESAN SYNOD.

1578.

WHILE St. Charles was content to take no steps
to vindicate himself from the charges brought
against him, he was far from passing over the
matter without drawing some spiritual profit from it.
He entertained no doubt that God had permitted it
for a good purpose, and he applied himself in earnest to learn His design. He called to mind the
examples of the Apostles, and the Bishops, Ambrose,
Basil, John Chrysostom, and others, who, in doing
their duty, and in asserting the authority of Holy
Church, bore without quailing persecution, exile, and
death. Yet, however much they were wronged, they
never wearied or fainted under the burden laid upon
them, but laboured more strenuously to approve
themselves valiant soldiers of Jesus Christ, the captain of salvation. These considerations strengthened
him to advance more vigorously in the path of reform,
notwithstanding the disappointment of his hopes, the

door opened for all manner of evil habits, the neg
of the decency of God's service, and the dishonour d
to His House, leading him to think that God wo
punish the city and people with new chastisement.

In the midst of his affliction he derived consolat
from the piety of the Governor's wife, who being l
self full of the fear of God, never let slip any op
tunity of urging her husband and her sons to remem
the respect due to the Archbishop, and to observe
precepts. She exerted all her influence also to
them to abstain from profane diversions on festiv
in which certain men now indulged, on purpose
bid defiance to the saint. Her good offices ava
little more than the fatherly admonitions of the (
dinal himself in softening their hearts and turn
them to obedience. Though all else failed, he c
tinued to pray for them, that their eyes might
opened and the mist of passion taken away.

To his prayers he added increased austerity of
continuing the same fasts and penances which he
adopted during the plague, hoping thus to obtain g
for his persecutors. When Mgr. Castello of Rim
who had previously been his Vicar-General, besou
him to moderate this rigour, now that the pestile
had ceased, he replied, with humility, " I thinl
ought rather to increase than to diminish it, si
though the plague is stayed, the cause of its inf
tion remains. I look for some fresh scourge by rea
of the sins and offences which yet abound in
city."

The stumbling-blocks which his enemies labou

to throw in his way were thus made by him stepping-stones to a higher degree of perfection. He indeed never rested, but when he had carried through one measure of reform, he immediately took another in hand.

There is a collegiate church in Milan, dedicated to the proto-martyr St. Stephen, which at this time had but six Canons and a Provost in residence, with but a slender stipend for their maintenance. Owing to this small endowment it was impossible fittingly to celebrate the Divine offices, the church being one of the most spacious as well as the most ancient in the city, and the Cardinal was accordingly desirous of increasing the revenues and the number of Canons. During the visitation he had noticed another collegiate church of St. John the Evangelist, at Pontirolo, on the outskirts of his diocese, bordering on the Venetian territory. Pontirolo was a straggling village of no importance, containing only a few scattered dwellings, which were the resort of outlaws from both states. The turbulence of these men kept the Canons in continual peril of their lives, and their extortions created great scandal. With the sanction of the Holy See and the consent of the Canons, he transferred this foundation to St. Stephen's at Milan, and put in their place a secular priest, suppressing three canonries in order to provide him with a sufficient support. There remained twenty-four prebends, which the Cardinal reduced to eighteen, that there might be a proper maintenance for each. To these he added a theological prebend, thus duly providing for all needs. .

It was suggested to him about this time that
were relics of several saints in different parts o
cathedral which were not honoured as they oug
be. There were, among others, the body of St. D
sius Marianus, twelfth Bishop of Milan, who di
exile in Further Cappadocia, whither he was ban
by the Emperor Constantius, the abettor of the .
heresy; of St. Aurelius, an Armenian Bishop,
brought to Milan the body of St. Dionysius i:
time of St. Ambrose; the ashes of St. Pelagia, ·
and martyr; and some of the bones of St. Julian, B
St. Charles collected and enclosed them in ꜰ
shrines, and placed them in the crypt, which h
previously restored, spending a great part of th
and night in prayer before them. At the same
he had some others, viz., the heads of St. Max
martyr of the Theban legion; of St. Thecla, virgi
martyr; of St. Monas and Galdinus della Sala,
dinal Priest of St. Sabina and Archbishop of ?
placed in silver shrines that they might be expos
the veneration of the people and carried in proces
Among abuses which he set himself to remed
the want of reverence among the people for
places. He admonished them seriously on accoᵤ
the disorders which often happened at the time ᵤ
indulgences, and issued an edict requiring that
and women should visit the churches separatel
minding them of the special privilege he had obı
for them from Rome, viz., the indulgence of the
Churches, and appointing a public pilgrimage to
on the feast of the Visitation of Our Lady.

On this occasion he wrote a pastoral letter, showing the antiquity of these stations, the object for which they were instituted, the value of the indulgences attached to them, and the importance of visiting them; exhorting his people to be earnest in making these visits, and to treat holy places with veneration, especially on account of the Blessed Sacrament and the precious treasures of relics which they contained.

At the close of this year he held his fifth diocesan synod, not only to satisfy the obligation of his office, but also to have an opportunity of meeting all his clergy together after the afflictions of the plague, calling upon them for signal fruits of gratitude for their deliverance in the salvation of souls. This synod sat three days, and on each day he addressed the assembled clergy in terms more moving than was usual even with him. On the last day in particular he spoke of the obligations of the parish priests, and denounced the negligence of those who are wanting in the requirements of their sacred office. The eyes of many overflowed with tears of compunction, and that this was no mere passing fervour was shown by the steady resolution that was taken by a considerable number, not only to devote themselves more seriously to the salvation of souls, but also to offer themselves to him under a particular obedience in the Congregation of the Oblates, upon the foundation of which he was at this time deliberating. Many wholesome regulations were laid down by this synod for the furtherance of his reforms, and besides these public labours

audiences, finally dismissing the clergy much e
and consoled.

Another measure he took in hand was to i
the Canons of the metropolitan church to uni
gether with himself in a community life.   I
his perpetual maxim that a Bishop was bou
aspire to nothing less than apostolic perfectio
used even to say that the episcopal order presu
a state of more eminent holiness than that of cloi
religious.   This was always his guiding princip
to work it out more effectually he had always l
his eyes the example of some Bishop illustrio
sanctity in the Church of God, as a model and
for all his actions.   Thus he was always striving
the attainment of more and more perfection.   I
with this intention that he sought to revive the a
custom [1] of the Bishop living in community wit
Canons.   A season of rejoicing for the cessati
the plague, that united all classes in a common
seemed to him an appropriate time to join aga
this practice of fraternal charity.   He called to
the Canons, whom he always regarded as his bre
and opened his heart to them, exhorting the
return with him to this custom of the early Cl
to have one common purse as brethren, he h
being willing to lead the way.   He showed
that it was in perfect conformity with their
of Canons, which implied that they were re

---

[1] Mgr. Bascapè, Bishop of Novara, in his Life of St. Charles, r
letters of Pope Eugenius III., elected in 1145, which show that
Pirovano, the then Archbishop of Milan, lived in common w
Canons.

priests, bound to live by rule, as brethren of the Lord, according to the usage of the times when the title was first conferred upon them; that they were of all the clergy the nearest to the Bishop, and that they ought, therefore, to be specially united to him, not only in heart and will, but also in their mode of life.

While the whole body of the Chapter concurred in these opinions, a small number only offered to adopt them. The rest thought that there were too many obstacles in the way of carrying them out, and they were a majority. Rather than that it should lead to any contention, the Cardinal yielded, recognising, as was his wont under all circumstances, the hand of God directing him. At the same time he was too well convinced of the benefit such an example would have upon the rest of the clergy to let the matter drop altogether, so after he found all endeavours to conform the opinions of the present Canons to his own plans unavailing, he determined to found a new congregation of priests, and to give them a rule of common life.

Page 15.—He called together the Canons.

Four of the Canons of the Duomo joined the Congregation of the Oblates of St. Ambrose, viz., Jerome Rabbia, Giovanni Fontana, afterwards Bishop of Ferrara, Ottaviano Abbiato Forrero, and Giovanni Battista Caina, who was Dean of the Chapter. Vid. *Oltrocchi.*

CHAPTER III.

THE COMPANY OF THE CROSSES; COLLEGE OF SAN
SOPHIA AND THE HOSPITAL OF MENDICANTS.

1578.

WE have already spoken of the altars which
erected in the public streets, to enable the pe
to hear Mass during the time they were kep
their houses by the regulations of quarantine.
would seem that they had conceived a great dev
towards these altars, and the saint thought it w
be a means of perpetuating their gratitude for
deliverance to foster this feeling. He set up, there
in those places, the standard of the Holy Cros
keep alive a perpetual memory of the Passio
our Lord, and to fortify the city in every part
that bulwark of our salvation against the assaul
the enemy; to make Milan a religious city, si
on every side with the sign of the cross, to re
its inhabitants constantly of the obligations of
calling as Christians. He had crucifixes placed
pedestals of stone, with an iron railing to pre
the crosses and altars to which they were atta
with greater reverence. In order that the dev

might not die away, he instituted a company or confraternity of pious persons of the neighbourhood in
which each crucifix was erected, with a rule and offices
of their own, and put them under the direction of the
oblates of St. Ambrose. They were to join together
every evening in public prayer each before their own
crucifix, and to go in procession every Friday evening
at the Ave to the cathedral to visit the relic of the
Holy Nail, and assist at a discourse on our Lord's
Passion.

This work was fruitful in benefits to souls, particularly in the treasures of indulgences obtained from
the Holy See for its members. It was not, however,
suffered by Satan to flourish without opposition, for
the King's ministers set themselves against it on the
plea that the Cardinal intended to exempt all these
places from the royal jurisdiction, but they did not
succeed in effecting any interruption of his plans. In
saying that they especially promoted the glory of God
we need only mention the fact of so large a number
of voices being raised evening by evening in public
thanksgiving to God throughout the city, of so many
men united in procession every Friday to honour the
Mysteries of the Passion. These confraternities are
now thirty-six in number in Milan alone, besides those
scattered throughout the diocese, and twenty-five other
pious associations which joined them in their religious
exercises.

Among other charitable works of St. Charles,
during the time of the plague, of which we have
not yet spoken, was the protectory he extended over

young girls, who being left orphans and des
stood in some risk of losing virtue and reput
With the assistance of some pious persons
especially of a member of the Sant' Agostino f
a conventual father of the Order of St. Franc
was enabled to gather them all into a place of s
Though the pressure of the terrible time was p
would not forsake them, but resolved to o]
retreat for them, where they might be safe fro:
perils and scandals awaiting them in the world.
this purpose he hired a commodious building,
a chapel and garden attached, called St. Mary
Angels,[1] close to St. Calimero, where he estab
them under the invocation of the Holy Ghos
title of Santa Sophia, committing the direction (
internal affairs of the house to the Ursuline
and its temporal concerns to a Chapter compos
laymen and ecclesiastics, who governed the
according to a rule prescribed by the saint.
proved one of the greatest benefits conferred b
upon the city, as it afforded at all times an a:
for poor girls exposed to temptation in the '
from which they were not only preserved, but,
over, brought up in the fear of God, and ultin
provided for in good situations or in the cl
according to their vocation.

There was another work of charity, which
out of his former provision for the plague-str
We have before spoken of the place of refu

---

[1] Which had originally belonged to the Humiliati, and after
the Theatines.

gave to a great number of destitute persons in the
palace of Vittoria, who, now that the danger had
passed away, expected to be dispersed, though many
of them had lost their homes and their all, and knew
not whither to go.　Their pastor, however, could not
bear to send them away, but resolved to convert this
temporary resort into a permanent hospital for mendicants of both sexes.　He had before this time noticed
the wretched condition of these outcasts, who grew up
uninstructed and uncared for, driven by their poverty
to gambling and stealing and all manner of shameful
modes of obtaining their livelihood, besides wandering
about the churches begging and distracting people at
their prayers, and that others were led to join them
out of mere idleness.　However degraded they might
be in the world's estimation, to his eye they were
souls created by God to live with Him in Heaven,
and redeemed by the precious Blood of His only Son.
The Stella convent, in the suburb of the Porta Vercellina, being vacant, he fixed upon it as the most
convenient place for these outcasts, as it not only
had a chapel attached, but afforded accommodation for
the separation of the sexes.　He appointed a priest
to take charge of their spiritual needs and to instruct
them, and nominated a committee to attend to their
temporal concerns, contributing largely to the funds
by his own alms, and urging others to do the
like.　He obtained from the Holy See a Plenary
Indulgence for Trinity Sunday, on which day he
instituted a special procession to kindle the devotion
of the people more abundantly towards this hospital,

———

Hospital of Mendicants.

and to induce them to liberality in their alm
support.   By his rule, all destitute persons, ·
natives or strangers, were admitted, and he p
upon the public authorities thenceforward to :
begging from door to door and in the churches.

CHAPTER IV.

THE VENERABLE CONGREGATION OF THE OBLATES OF ST. AMBROSE.

1578.

EIGHTEEN years' experience in the government of his See had taught St. Charles the impossibility of making the progress he desired in establishing discipline and order in his colleges, seminaries, and other foundations, without the assistance of efficient ministers and fellow-workers, who being disengaged from trammels of secular affairs should be free to carry out his measures for their good government. The dangers to which those parts of his diocese that bordered on heretical states were exposed, urgently called for such a body of men, as did also the want of priests in the outlying and mountainous districts.

To supply these requirements he resolved to found a congregation of secular priests, who should be united under himself as members of the body to their head, and be always in readiness to execute promptly whatever work he appointed them to do. He intended that they should restore a perfect pattern of ecclesiastical discipline, serving God purely for the sake of His

glory without seeking their own interest, and 1
together in common as brethren in the Lord.

Having taken counsel with God in prayer, acco
to his wont, he made choice of certain ecclesi;
who appeared to him most fitted for his new inst
out of those who had offered themselves after hi;
course at the last Synod. Having thus got toget
good number, he laid the foundation of his new
gregation on the 16th of August, 1578, the fee
St. Simplicianus, Archbishop of Milan, and plac
under the protection of our Blessed Lady an
Ambrose, Doctor of the church and patron of the
giving it the title of the Congregation of the Ol
of St. Ambrose. It afterwards received the app
and confirmation of the Supreme Pontiff Gr
XIII., who granted to it privileges of indulgenc
perpetuity, and some ecclesiastical revenues rema
over from the suppressed Order of the Frati Hum
St. Charles assigned for its first establishmen
Church of the Holy Sepulcre, which had belong
some titular Canons, who had long ceased to 1
there, together with some adjoining houses whi
bought of the pious Society of the Rosary, ·
afforded all the means for the exercise of their min
He made choice of this place because it was sit
in the very heart of the city—a convenient ba
operations for all parts—and because it was
frequented by the people out of devotion to the
Sepulcre and other mysteries of the Passion, ·
were there commemorated in sculpture. It had a
been the custom to have priests at this church t

the Rosary, visit the sick poor, and employ themselves·
in the work of souls.

When St. Charles first came to Milan, he found at
this church Father Gaspar Belinzago, and others with
him, whose zeal and devotion in the service of God
might be said to have kept alive the light of faith at
a time when piety was at a low ebb in the city. This
Father had been called to a better life about three years
before the foundation of St. Charles' institute, amid
the regrets of all the people, who held him for a saint.
Some of his priests joined the new congregation, among
whom was Father Francis Crippa, a man of apostolic
spirit, greatly esteemed for his sanctity, who was the
confessor of Ludovico Moneta. The spirit of primitive
piety which animated this little band of priests had
no small share in St. Charles' selection of their house,
as he himself bears testimony in the constitutions of
this congregation, by saying that he hoped it would
be hereditary in their house and perpetually kept up
among them.

The rule which he gave them is to be found at
length in the "Acts of the Church of Milan." The
leading features of it are that the oblates should be
under the obedience of the Archbishop, taking the
simple vow of obedience at his hands on entering the
congregation: that they should be united to him as
the members of a body to their head, sharing in his
spirit, his zeal, and his desire for the glory of God and
the salvation of souls: that they should in all their
actions breathe a spirit of piety, and aim at that religious perfection which should prove them worthy of

such a union. It should be their especial office to
the Archbishop in the government of his diocese,
to co-operate with him in all his functions and off
and particularly in his visitations. They should
ready at all times to go out like apostles upon
mission which he might entrust to them, especiall
places which, on account of their remoteness and
accessibility, were often left destitute of spiritual a
also to take temporary care of parishes during va
cies, to discharge the duties of urban inspector
rural deans: to direct colleges, seminaries, school
Christian doctrine, Confraternities of the Cross
give the spiritual exercises to those preparing for 1
Orders, and in general to be ready to preach, admin
the sacraments, and undertake other pious work
which they might be called. He directed that
the devotions which were usual at Santa Mari;
Vallicella, the Church of the Oratory in Rome, sh
also be practised at the Church of the Holy Sepul
a custom which was very advantageous in gai
souls and giving pious occupation to many per
who had leisure.

All these intentions were fully carried out, an
see at this day more than two hundred priests bel
ing to this institute; many with the degree of De
in Theology, and all of singular holiness of
their united labours working great benefits in
diocese. We cannot be far wrong, therefore, in rec
ing this work among the labours of the saint that
greatly blessed in the spiritual vineyard of the Ch
He divided the oblates into two classes. The

were to remain permanently at St. Sepulcre's without holding any cure which bound them to residence, so that they might be free to exercise any ministry that might be required of them. Those of the second order were to be distributed in different parishes of the city or diocese, and bound to residence.

Though they were by this arrangement sometimes separated from one another, in order to keep them united in spirit, so that they should all feel themselves part of the body, keep alive the spirit of the institute, and grow continually in virtue, he divided the congregation into six *consortia* or companies, two being established in the city, and four in other parts of the diocese, to each of which he gave a Superior and a spiritual Prefect. Each of the companies were to meet once a month, those in the city at St. Sepulcre's in presence of the Archbishop, those in other parts of the diocese, sometimes in one place, sometimes in another, presided over by the Superior-general, or at least by the Superior of the particular company. These associations were to be opened by reading the rule of the congregation, after which the members were to confer upon the mode of its observance, upon their progress in the spiritual life, and upon the means of advancing souls in the way of salvation. The president was to exhort them to perfection, and two members of the congregation were to preach in public to the people on some profitable topic. This practice not only kept up a spirit of union and brotherly love among all the members, but afforded a means of continually infusing into them anew the mind and intention of

their head, the Archbishop, so as to reproduce
multiply his efforts for the benefit of the souls o!
people in every part of his diocese.

The love which he bore to the oblates was
manifest, for he always called them his sons,
treated them as such. He chose out a little ce.
St. Sepulcre's, where he often went to stay with t
and behaved with such humility as if he had been
of the least of them, following all the observance
the house. He was always pleased to be there,
spoke of it as one of his greatest enjoyments, and
to say that it ought to be the special recreation o
Archbishop of Milan. If any of them fell ill, he
not content with simply visiting them, but w
attend upon them himself with every sign of
lively interest he took in their well-being. In
year 1580, a priest of the house named John]
Stoppano, at the present time archpriest of Mazzo ir
Valtellina, was seized with a mortal sickness. V
the saint heard of it, he went to see him without
of time, and installed himself at the bedside of
dying man, attending him by day and by night, :
he had been infirmarian, through all the crisis o!
sickness, till it had reached the last stage, an
seemed about to deliver up his soul to his M
But the saint who foresaw keenly the loss which
death of such a priest would prove to the dic
besought God for his recovery so earnestly tha
obtained it. When great surprise at this cure
shown, " You do not know," he said, " the value o!
life of a good priest."

It was part of the design of St. Charles to found other houses of his congregation in all the principal cities and towns of his diocese, similar to that of St. Sepulcre, as we see by the rule which provides that a number of the oblates should be in readiness to be sent to other places, to act as eyes, by which he might learn the wants and necessities of his flock. He was prevented, however, by death, from carrying out this extension of the institute; but he annexed to it a congregation of laymen, and gave them a rule of their own. They were, while continuing to live in their own homes, to occupy themselves in good works, particularly in giving instruction in Christian doctrine. Besides this, he instituted a congregation of matrons, also attached to the church of the Holy Sepulcre, with the title of Company of the Ladies of the Oratory, for whose guidance he prescribed rules and works of piety. He endeavoured to enlist in this band the ladies of the principal families of the city, who otherwise would be likely to spend their time in vain amusements and other evils of idleness. He wished thus to lead them to frequent the Sacraments, to attend the sermons and to keep alive in their minds the Passion of our Divine Redeemer.

CHAPTER V.

PILGRIMAGE TO THE HOLY WINDING-SHEET AT TU

1578.

THE Passion of our Divine Lord might be said to ?
been the particular devotion of our saint. Thu
cherished a great reverence for all its sacred ins
ments, as we have seen in the case of the Holy]
He had often expressed a desire to visit the]
Winding-sheet, in which the sacred body of our]
reposed in the sepulchre. When he saw his pe
wasted by the pestilence, he resolved to make a
grimage to the place where it was preserved, in c
to beg God to have mercy on his flock.

This precious relic of the winding-sheet of
Lord is preserved at Chambery, in Savoy, whei
was held in great honour by the dukes of that
vince, who watched over it as a precious heirl
entrusted by the hand of God to the keeping of t
house. It was brought from Jerusalem in the cru
in which Godfrey de Bouillon was made King
Jerusalem, and was held for many generations in
family of the Lusignans, Kings of Cyprus. In
cess of time it came into the hands of Mar;

Carma, wife of Hector Lusignan, who took refuge in France when the Turks overran Greece in 1457. She travelled safely as far as Chambery, which was at that date the residence of the Dukes of Savoy, and was affectionately received by the reigning Duke, Louis, and Anna Lusignan his wife, herself a sister of John the last King of Cyprus, and a relative of Margaret. During her stay in that city, God was pleased to show by miracles that this was the very winding-sheet of our Saviour, upon which the Duchess Anna was moved with so great a devotion towards it, that she earnestly entreated her cousin to make her a present of the treasure. But Margaret, whose veneration for it was no less sincere, replied that she would rather part with everything she possessed in the world than with this, and soon afterwards set out on her journey northwards.

The devotion of the Duchess Anna was, however, to have its reward, as the relic she so ardently desired at last came into her hands. For Margaret had hardly reached the outskirts of the city when it was found that the mule which carried it could not be made to go on, though beaten with many stripes. Margaret took this as a manifestation that the relic was to remain in the custody of her relatives, and consigned it accordingly to their keeping. The Duke and his consort, not wanting in gratitude for this favour, with public prayers and processions, laid it up in a chapel of their palace prepared to receive it, and erected into a collegiate church by Pope Paul II.

veneration of the faithful, many of whom, inclu
kings and princes, made pilgrimages to visit
Among the rest came Francis I. of France.
prince being in danger of defeat from the Swiss fo
at Melegnano, about eight miles from Milan, mac
vow that if he should gain the victory, he would n
a pilgrimage to the holy relic. Immediately the
turned in his favour, and though his army was v
nigh cut to pieces, he was left master of the field
the 15th June, 1516. He withdrew soon afte
Lyons, and then, in accomplishment of his vow, v
on foot to Chambery, to venerate the relic, concei
at the same time a great desire to possess it. '
came to be so well known, that when he was enga
in hostilities with the Duke of Savoy, fourteen y
later, it was removed for safety to Vercelli in P
mont. In the reign of Francis's son, Henry II.,
inherited his father's desire, when in November, 1 !
war was waged in Piedmont, Brissac, the comman
thought he could not carry back a more accept
trophy to the King than the holy winding-sheet ;
after making his way to the place where it was k
he was miraculously impeded from advancing bey
the threshold, and forced to retire. When peace
restored the relic was brought back to Chambery
Duke Emanuel Philibert in 1560.

To return to our history. The Cardinal reso
when his diocese was free from pestilence to fulfil
intention of visiting Chambery in order to rer
thanks for this great mercy before the precious r
He determined to make the journey on foot, tho

he had to cross difficult passes through the mountains. Duke Emanuel Philibert, inheriting the pious disposition hereditary in his house, was a warm admirer of the saint, and was glad when he heard of his intention, to have an opportunity of paying him respect. He would not allow St. Charles to make such a journey on foot, but transferred the relic to Turin, on the other side of the mountains, in a solemn procession, in charge of the Archbishop of Turin and four other Bishops. The Duke came to meet them on foot, following it to the Church of St. Laurence, where it was deposited. He then sent his secretary, Francis Lino, to Milan, to inform the Cardinal of this translation, and to invite him to satisfy his devotion at Turin, begging him to take up his quarters in his palace, in order that he might be free to devote his whole attention to him.

After concluding a league with the Swiss ambassadors which he had been negotiating, he sent his secretary to invite him again, and to defray all the expenses of the saint's journey. The Cardinal carried out his intention of going on foot in pilgrim's garb, choosing twelve members of his household to accompany him, together with Father Francesco Adorno, S.J., to give the spiritual exercises during the journey. The day before they set out, he assembled all the pilgrims in his private chapel, and one of their number addressed the rest in presence of the whole household upon two points, viz.: devotion towards the holy relic they were going to visit, and penance for their sins, exhorting them to suffer no other thoughts to occupy their minds.

A time-table was drawn up for the pilgrims th
things might be done to edification. They we
rise every morning at four o'clock, each priest w
say Mass, and the others were to go to communi
the Cardinal's Mass, and say the offices of prime
terce; they were then to begin the day's journe
peating the Itinerary, then two hours of mental p
and the Rosary aloud with a meditation on
mystery. If there should be any more time
before they reached the next halting-place, it w
be spent in saying certain psalms and in spiritual
versation. On their arrival at the place when
were to rest, they were to go at once to the cl
and after spending some time in prayer, to say
and none on their knees, and then take their refe
which consisted of Lenten fare. While they
at table, a spiritual book was read. Afterwards
made a visit to the church to make a thanks
and say vespers, and then continued their jou
giving two hours to mental prayer and recitin;
penitential psalms and other devotions to fill uj
time, no part of which was without its proper oc
tion. In the evening when they arrived at the
where they were to pass the night, they went to
church and said compline. After the evening
tion they met again for a spiritual conference upo
meditations of the past day, and Father Adorno
out the points for the following day. Then af
quarter of an hour's examination of conscience
Cardinal sprinkled them with holy water, and

withdrew for the night, each saying matins by himself at his own convenience.

The meditations were arranged with the same fore-thought. The distance between Milan and Turin is about ninety miles, and it was divided into four days' journey. The meditation of the first day was upon the pilgrimage of our Divine Lord through this world, while He was preaching the Gospel, healing the sick, and delivering souls from the bondage of sin. That of the second day, upon the pilgrimage sufferings and persecutions of the apostles; on the third day, the pilgrimage of poor mortal men through this world; on the fourth, the proper way of adoring the holy Winding-sheet, and the edification to be derived from contem-plating the marks of those wounds which the Son of God endured for our salvation.

They set out from Milan on the 6th October, 1578, which was a Monday. Early that morning all the pilgrims assembled in their habit in chapel, where the saint said Mass, and gave communion to all who were not priests, as they each said their own Mass. Vested in full pontificals, he gave them his benedic-tion, and a pilgrim's staff to each. They went to the city gate in procession two by two, the Chapter of the cathedral accompanying them, and the Cardinal, at-tended by a great number of the clergy and people, bringing up the rear, all singing the Gradual psalms. On arriving at the Porta Vercellina, leading to Ver-celli, the Cardinal put on his purple habit, in accord-ance with the pilgrim's character, with the rochet and mantelletta over it. He then embraced his Canons

with great affection, receiving from them the kis
peace amid many tears, and having blessed all
people, set out on the road to Novara, follo
strictly the rule we have given above. The
stage was Sedriano, about fourteen miles from M
at the house of the parish priest, and the same e
ing they came to Trecà, in the diocese of No
another fourteen miles. Here the inhabitants
out to meet them in procession, a mile outside
town, with torches in their hands, and the doors
windows of their houses lighted up. As the
passed along, the people ran together round
thinking themselves happy if they could touch
garment; fathers and mothers bringing their little
in their arms to crave his blessing. They passed
night at the monastery of the Franciscan friars,
the saint read aloud while his companions su
taking nothing himself but an apple, as he conti
to keep his daily fast. The following morning al
people flocked to hear his Mass, though he sa
before daybreak; great numbers going to commu
including all the principal inhabitants, who had
pared for it the night before in the Sacramer
Penance.

After this he set out for Novara, in spite of
and the people there were equally ready to do hc
to his arrival. The Bishop was ill, but the V
general, Canons, and gentry came to beg hin
lodge with them. But he went straight to
church, where a musical service with the organ
arranged, and continued his journey through

rain, which had already drenched his garments; but the most earnest entreaties could not stay him, as it was not then more than two o'clock in the day, and he counted on accomplishing a considerable part of his journey before nightfall.   He pushed on therefore to Camairano, where he had his clothes dried; and after taking refreshment, started for Vercelli, with the intention of finishing another stage, but the rain had made the roads impassable and effectually hindered further progress.   The Bishop, Mgr. Francesco Bonomo, with his Canons and the principal inhabitants, came out to meet him some distance from the city, and when he came to the River Sesia he perceived on the opposite bank a multitude of people waiting for him to cross, looking like an army drawn up in array.   At the gates the clergy escorted him to the cathedral, with lighted torches, as evening had set in, and while the saint was saying compline, the organ was played, and the relics preserved in the church were exposed solemnly on the high altar for their veneration.   He passed the night at the Bishop's palace, where the Marchese Federigo Ferrerio, majordomo of the Duke of Savoy, met him, to welcome him and attend him during the remainder of his journey, Vercelli being situated on the border of the duchy.   No words could convey an adequate idea of the joy of the people at beholding the saint, hearing his Mass, and receiving his benediction.

At Vercelli the number of pilgrims received a notable increase, as the Bishop of that place, together with some

of his Canons and other pious persons, resolved to fol
the Cardinal to Turin on foot. This day's journey
long and the roads rough, so that they arrived at t
lodging wearied and way-worn. But the saint wo
not take any refreshment that night, and rose at
usual early hour to resume his journey. About e
miles from Turin he was received by Mgr. Girol
della Rovere, Archbishop of the city, afterwards of
dinal, with other dignitaries sent forward by the D
Having chosen a shady spot, they dined together ·
the pilgrims seated on the ground, to the great con
of the Cardinal, who was never better pleased t
when he was ill-served.

After the refection the Archbishop of Turin retur
to the city, that he might come out in state with
clergy to receive the Cardinal, a mile without the w
followed by the Duke's body-guard. A little fur
on they met Cardinal Guido Ferrerio, who gave
saint an affectionate greeting, and accompanied him
rest of the way on foot; about a quarter of a mile f
the city came the Duke and the Prince of Savoy, his
with their suite. They gave the Cardinal a he
welcome, embracing him and giving every testimon
their veneration. The whole party continued their
into the city in the following order. First walke
the court of the Duke, next the pilgrims,[1] walking
and two with much recollection, showing by t
devout bearing evident tokens of the spirit of hum

---

[1] Francesco Adorno, Jacopo Croce, Antonio Seneca, Lodovico Mo
Francesco Bernardino Crivello, Giovanni Battista Caimo, Otta
Abbiato Ferrero, Giovanni Pietro Stoppano, Girolamo Castano, (
Brunetto, Giovanni Pietro Biumo, Giulio Omato, and two others.

and penance which animated them. Then came St. Charles with the Duke on his left hand, the Cardinal Ferrerio with the Prince of Savoy, the Archbishop of Turin and other bishops, and the ducal guard on either side, multitudes of people bringing up the rear. It was a heart-stirring spectacle of humble pilgrims attended by royal pomp and circumstance.

A salvo of artillery announced the arrival of the procession at the gates, which brought out all the rest of the inhabitants to witness the entry. As was usual with the saint, his steps were first directed to the cathedral, after which he visited the Church of St. Laurence, where the sacred relic which he had come to venerate reposed, before which he remained a long time in prayer.

When he rose from his knees, the Duke led him to his apartments next to the palace, the same that had been assigned to Henry III. of France when he came from Poland. St. Charles wished the Cardinal of Vercelli to remain with him, as they were united not only by family ties, but also by friendship of long standing. The saint endured to be treated in this fashion to please the Duke, who was beside himself for joy at being permitted to entertain so honoured a guest, not allowing him, in the great reverence he bore him, to have the trouble of coming to visit him, but at the least word or gesture he was at the Cardinal's side and would gladly have waited upon his person. In testimony of his joy he proclaimed a public holiday of three days, during which the people were entertained with spiritual exercises.

It pleased God to try His holy servant in this и
and suffer him to be treated with this external sl
We must not imagine that these things afforded
in themselves any gratification. He would l
reckoned himself to be better served, had he l
in a poor hut, than surrounded with all the state
pageant of the palace. A scanty repast of herbs wo
have been more to his taste than the costly vio
placed before him. But while he felt no complace
he knew how to gain both pleasure and profit f
them, taking them as the simple expression of
affectionate disposition on the part of the Prince
order to converse upon matters which he dextero
improved to his spiritual benefit, for he knew
those in high station do not often find any to ad
them in such way. But our Lord was pleasec
grant him a favour, which was far more to his m
as it gave him the opportunity of doing penance for
sake, viz., great suffering in one foot. The many n
of bad roads he had traversed had caused blisters
the soles of his feet, and in having them cut
an unskilful barber, he received a severe wound wi
took many days to heal. He endured this suffe
with fortitude, and did not omit any of his v
to the churches or other necessary walking, notw
standing the pain it caused him. It was ino
to him a cause of rejoicing, as it gave him an op
tunity of tasting some of the sufferings endured
our Divine Redeemer, which were brought to
mind by the contemplation of the linen cloth, wi
had received the impress of His most sacred wou

His precious blood, and the whole of His suffering form.

On the morning after his arrival at Turin, which was a Friday, and therefore especially dedicated to the Passion, the Cardinal again went early to San Lorenzo, spending a long time in prayer before the sacred relic, and said Mass, surrounded by a great concourse of people, who came to hear it and receive communion at his hands. Afterwards the Duke expressed a wish to dine with him, and in the meanwhile had the relic removed to the cathedral and spread upon a large table, where all the pilgrims could see it conveniently. In the afternoon the Archbishop of Turin, in his pontifical vestments, attended by the Canons bearing lighted torches, reverently uncovered it in presence of all.

The pilgrims could not restrain their tears as they gazed upon the precious memorial of the sufferings of the Son of God, and traced out the marks where the thorns had pierced His Sacred Head, and where the spitting had defiled His Divine Countenance, where the nails had torn His hands and feet, and the lance entered into His side, and blows and bruises lacerated His body in every part. The saint did not rest satisfied with this outward adoration, but entered into the depths of woe which overwhelmed the Sacred Heart of Jesus, of which these were but the tokens. This contemplation awakened his tenderest sympathy, and though he took great pains to conceal his emotion, he could not prevent his tears from falling and bearing witness how those sufferings were graven on his heart.

Before he left the church, the relic being so c
veniently placed, he satisfied his devotion to the
by kissing it, and particularly the marks of the sac
wounds.

On the following morning he again visited it
San Lorenzo, whither it had been taken, said
Mass, and remained some time in prayer befor
He asked the young Prince Charles to dine with :
that day, and had the Bible read, while they v
at table, according to his custom. He took occas
from the part of Holy Scripture they had read, viz.,
Book of Macchabees, to enter into conversation v
the Prince, and was glad to find him well acquair
with the Sacred Scriptures, so that he formed a l
opinion of his understanding, and entertained m
affection for him. It was then arranged 1
the relic should be carried in procession to
cathedral the next morning, that it might be seen
the people, and a station of forty hours' devo
observed before it, according to the Milanese
also that the saint should sing the Mass, and prea
It was found, however, that the function attrac
such crowds of people from distant parts that
cathedral could not hold them all. It was, theref
agreed to adjourn to the Piazza del Castello
spacious place, where all could see it easily. A p
form was erected there, and early in the morn
the relic was transported thither in state, acco
panied by the two Cardinals, the Archbishop of Tu
Joseph Parpaglia, Archbishop of Tarantasia, and

Bishops,[1] preceded by the clergy, the Duke, Ottavio Santa Croce Bishop of Cervia, the Apostolic Nuncio, Prince Charles, the orders of knights, and the people.

As soon as the Cardinals and Archbishops had mounted the platform, they unfolded the sacred cloth, and raised it three times before the eyes of the people, so that all might behold the impress of the sacred Body of our Lord. It was a sight so moving that the whole assemblage, at the spectacle of what the Son of God had suffered for them, rent the air with cries of sorrow and contrition.

It was then conveyed to the cathedral, where it was laid in an elevated place in the sight of the people, and a station of forty hours' devotion begun; the clergy and people from all parts keeping up the watch by night and day, the knights of St. Maurice and St. Lazarus, in the robes of their order, assisting. Every hour a discourse was addressed to the people, three of which fell to the share of the saint, one to the Cardinal of Vercelli, others to the Bishops who had taken part in the function, and the remainder to the theologians and regular clergy of the city. The Duke and his son set an example of devotion; as they not only often visited the relic, but were more than once seen in tears. During this station St. Charles went to visit the bodies of the holy martyrs, Solutor, Adventor, and Octavius, citizens of

---

[1] Viz., Lodovico Grimaldo of Venza, Hippolyto de Rossi of Pavia, Giovanni Francesco Bonomo of Vercelli, Cesare Gromio of Aosta, Cesare Ferrerio of Savona, and Giovanni Maria Taparello of Saluzzo.

Turin, preserved in the Jesuit Church, where also said Mass.

The Duke, understanding that a number of heret from the mountain districts and valleys had co to join in the celebration, attracted by the reputat of the Cardinal, thought it might be beneficial prolong the station through another day, and t discourses should be directed for their especial bene This idea was put in execution, and the saint preacl again at the close of the station. The next morn he again returned to visit the relic, and delive another discourse, celebrated Mass, and gave H Communion to the Prince and others. Later in day the pilgrims paid their visit, the saint remain on his knees, his eyes intently fixed on the relic, if he had not power to withdraw them from it. Duke invited him to dinner the next day, when received him with royal honours, and spent m than two hours with him in private conversation, Cardinal advising him on the things of his s the government of his subjects and of the heretics particular, who had overflowed into parts of dominions from the French provinces. His adm tions bore fruit afterwards, in regulations made staying the further progress of heresy.

Having now accomplished all the objects he had view in going to Turin, St. Charles asked the Dul leave to return, which was granted with great rel tance; for his affection towards the saint has gre increased since he had seen him personally, and perienced the sweetness of the spirit that breathed him. When the hour for his departure came, he called the Princes, Charles and Amadeus, his sons, and all three bent their knees before him and begged his blessing with tears in their eyes. The saint struck with their humility would have made them rise, but the Duke told him frankly they would not move till they had received his benediction. Having received it, the Duke said: "Now I have good confidence that my affairs will prosper, since I have received the blessing of God at the hands of so illustrious a Prince of the Church." He then bade his sons, first in French, and then in Italian, always to look upon the Cardinal as their father, and to honour and obey him as such, and to beg him to take them for his children; which request they immediately made with much grace and affection. Their prayers were answered, for the Duke died within two years, and Prince Charles on succeeding to the government was very grateful for the fatherly advice of the saint. As soon as St. Charles heard of the Duke's death, he sent the Prince a Dominican father of Perugia, whose learning and discretion were well known to him, as his confessor. The young Duke returned his affection and always looked up to the Cardinal as his father, and after his death used all his interest with the Holy See to obtain his canonisation, offering at his tomb a candelabrum of eleven lights to burn perpetually before it.

The example of humility and devotion set by these princes greatly edified all present, many of whom were moved to tears, to see renewed in these later times the ancient spirit of faith and piety with which kings and

emperors were wont -to honour the Bishops of
Church—the successors of the apostles and dispen:
of the treasures of heaven. The example and prea
ing of St. Charles was not only a consolation to
city of Turin, but greatly instructed and edified
The devotion inspired by his sanctity prompted
noble matron to use great exertions to become
possessor of the staff which had served the saint
this pilgrimage, and to treasure it as a precious h
loom.

Thus was God pleased to comfort His servant w
these testimonies of affection, at a time when his s
was afflicted by the perversity of certain among
own flock, and to strengthen him against new assai
which the devil was preparing against his return.

CHAPTER VI.

1578.

THE contemplation of the relic he had visited left upon the mind of the saint so lively a sympathy for the sufferings of our Lord that he resolved, before returning to Milan, to visit the holy mountain of Varallo to meditate in private on the mysteries of the Passion, commemorated there in little chapels distributed over the mountain.

Having taken leave of the Duke, who accompanied him a considerable distance on his way, he set out for this place, taking with him only six of his companions and Father Adorno his confessor. He was accompanied also by the Cardinal of Vercelli, as he wished to visit on his way the relics of the saints preserved at the Abbey of St. Michael, belonging to the latter. He said Mass there and passed the greater part of the day in prayer before them, continuing his journey the next morning.

Varallo is situated in the diocese of Novara, in the valley of Sesia, bordering on Switzerland. About a

hundred years before, a Franciscan Father, a nativ
Milan, of the noble family of the Caimi, had bui
church in honour of our Lady on one of the lofty p
of this district, and many little chapels dedicated to
mysteries of the Life and Passion of our Divine L
one of which was copied from the Holy Sepulcr
Jerusalem, which the father had visited. The site
retired from the noise and turmoil of the world, w
in itself it was picturesque and well adapted for
purpose of holy contemplation. The principal mys
gives it the general name of the Sepulcre of Var
but beside the large church, which was served
Franciscan friars, there are thirty-eight chapels w
are portrayed all the mysteries of the Life, Death,
Resurrection of our Saviour in figures of the si
life, embellished with paintings. Its first founder
moreover enriched it by a number of precious relic

It was two o'clock in the day before St. Ch
arrived at this place, and he had not broken his
but before taking anything he visited the diffe
chapels for meditation, of which Father Adorno
him the points. As evening drew on, he withdre
take his refection of bread and water, and then retu
again to the chapels till after midnight, though
weather was very cold. He then took two hours' re
a chair, and at five o'clock in the morning resume
devotions; then, after having said his Mass, he a
allowed himself a small portion of bread and w
and continued his journey to Milan, renewed in fer
of spirit and with a firm determination to begin a
to serve God with greater energy than ever.

This same year God was pleased to permit that his
Catholic Majesty, Philip II., should be tried, to prove
his patience, with many sorrows. Besides the troubles
in his Flemish provinces, within three months he
sustained four severe losses both in his public and
private relations. The first was the death of his
nephew Sebastian, King of Portugal, who having gone
with his army against the Mahomedans in Africa, fell
in a disastrous defeat in which all the leaders and
most of his troops were either cut to pieces or taken
prisoners, among whom were the Bishops of Coimbra
and Oporto, the flower of his nobility, and a great
number of persons of consideration of different nations.
The King of Spain in particular, lost many valiant
soldiers whom he had sent to attend King Sebastian.
Soon after this, he lost another nephew, Wenceslaus of
Austria, his sister's son, and brother of the Emperor
Rudolph, a youth of great promise to whom he was
much attached, and whom he always kept near him
at his court. About the same time died in the prime
of life, his brother, Don John of Austria, who after
his victory of Lepanto, had been entrusted with the
government of Flanders, where he died waging war
with the rebels. Death also deprived him of his son
Ferdinand, who had been recognised as his successor on
the throne, and had given ground for hope that he would
inherit his father's good qualities.

These poignant sorrows, though they followed one
another so rapidly, and though they struck so closely
home, cutting off his fairest earthly hopes, did not
deprive his soul of its constancy and conformity to the

will of God. He accepted the blows at His han
with resignation like Job, turning to Him in a chil
like spirit, and praying Him not to abandon him
his tribulations, but to change them into blessings bo
for himself and his subjects.

He wrote to the lieutenants of his different state
informing them of his affliction, and begging them
root out sin and everything displeasing to God fro
their provinces, and to join with their people in pray
to appease His anger and to obtain mercy for H
Church.

The Governor of Milan sent this letter of the Kin
to St. Charles, that he might co-operate with him
carrying out his wishes. The Saint was greatly co
soled by the King's Christian spirit, since it was man
fest that however sharply he had been wounded l
his bereavements, he felt dishonour done to God mo
deeply still, and strove earnestly to drive out sin fro
among his people. He thought the letter would mov
the Milanese to renewed fervour, and therefore had
translated and published, together with a pastor
letter from himself. It ran as follows :—

Letter of Philip II., King of Spain, to the Governor
of Milan.

" Since it has pleased Almighty God to call to Hin
self on the 18th of this present October, Ferdinar
our firstborn son, to our great affliction both o
account of his virtues and being heir to our kingdon
we have thought it well to inform you of this our los

and to assure you that bitter as it is, we have received it as coming from the hand of God, with entire conformity to His most holy will, rendering thanks for His mercies in taking him to Himself. We beg you also in a Christian spirit, not to make in any part of our kingdom or dependencies, either in public or private, any outward mourning, but that instead you should call upon the people to join in devout processions and public prayers to render thanks to God for this signal favour, and to beseech Him in all humility not to visit our sins and offences upon us. And that we may do this more worthily, and that He may be moved to turn His eyes of mercy on the affliction of His Church and people, let it be our task and yours, as our ministers, to endeavour to drive out sin, whereby His Divine Majesty is day by day dishonoured, so that His wrath may cease, His holy will be done, and His glorious name praised and magnified by all His creatures."

St. Charles entered deeply into the King's sentiments, sharing alike his grief for the losses he had sustained and his desire to improve them in the way he had set forth. He wrote both to him and to the Queen, to express his sympathy, and published a pastoral, dated December 13, 1578, calling upon the people to join in fervent prayer to Almighty God for the intentions of his majesty.

He instituted prayers throughout the city, beginning with the Forty Hours' Exposition of the Blessed Sacrament at the cathedral, carrying it on at all the other churches, and had processions in the different parishes,

Prayers for Philip II., King of Spain.

and an hour's prayer offered in all collegiate
parochial churches on festival days after Ves
and ordered the Collect for the King to be sai
every Mass.   To this he added exhortations to t
to join in more abundant almsgiving and to inci
their fasts, striving by every means in their po
to appease the anger of God and to move Hir
spare their sovereign and his children, to bestow i
them every blessing, spiritual and temporal, to su
all the needs of the Church, and to have mercy on
souls of the deceased princes.

The readiness with which the clergy and pe
responded to these appeals testified to their loy
and affection for their king ; and the evidence of
sincerity of the Saint's sympathy is found in
earnestness with which he called upon all to
in these intercessions and added to his own pena
and prayers.

Note on page 48.—" Sebastian of Portugal."

This defeat was in the battle of Alcazarquivir on the 4th of A
1578.

CHAPTER VII.

1579.

WE have already spoken of various ways in which the new Governor lent himself to the designs of the perverse faction by reviving the vexed question of ecclesiastical jurisdiction, and not shrinking even from unworthy means in order to injure the saint's credit and procure a decision against him at Rome. We have seen how unfounded were their aspersions upon his loyalty to the crown of Spain, so that the whole was clearly the work of the father of lies.

There was worse, however, to come. The Governor opened up again the whole dispute in the matter of jurisdiction, and this in the face of the proof the King had so lately given of his favour and the opinion of the Marquis of Alcanisio,[1] a gentleman of irreproachable character, who, having lately returned to Milan from a mission to Rome, declared without reserve that the King had the highest veneration for the Cardinal, and that it was ludicrous to suspect him of harbouring any disloyal designs. The Governor seems to have

[1] A son of St. Francis Borgia according to Speciano.

taken pleasure in thwarting the Cardinal in petty
harassing ways. Thus, as the carnival season of
year 1579 approached, he gave out that he would
glad to see the people indulge in the diversions
spectacles which the Saint had laboured to super
by more serious and holy recreations.

St. Charles had hoped that the King's letter, wl
he had published, would wean the people f
these amusements, but now he saw his expectat
blighted by the encouragement lavished in high q
ters upon these amusements. Yet he did not give
hope of doing good or his determination of withst
ing evil, even when aware of the organised systen
opposition planned by the Governor and his frie
It was quite clear that nothing could be more opp
to the mind of the King or to his expressed de
than to dishonour God by scandals during the carn
season, bringing danger to many souls, so tha
would have been competent for him by virtue of
King's letter to have prohibited such offences ur
penalties. Nevertheless, after mature considerat
he resolved to proceed first by way of charity be
having recourse to what might seem harshness.
circulated, therefore, a pastoral letter, dated 22d]
ruary 1579, warning his people of the snares sp
for them in terms of fatherly affection, pointing
how the sinful amusements he sought to abolish v
repugnant to their Christian profession, and remin
them of the mercies of God in their deliverance f
the plague, and of the ingratitude of provoking
anger by the commission of new follies and

"What was this indeed," he said, "but to call down upon themselves fresh chastisement? If they had no regard for God's honour, or for the grief of their King, who was at that moment mourning the loss of his firstborn and other relatives, at least let them have regard to his letter, which begged them to put away all scandals and occasions of sin, to unite in prayer and works of holiness, and to tread all impiety beneath their feet." He spoke, in conclusion, of the little book he had begun, setting forth the special mercies and favours of God in delivering them from the pestilence they had just passed through.

This pastoral was no less fruitful than usual, but at the same time it failed to win the compliance of the Governor and those for whom it was especially designed. They seemed rather to have hardened their hearts more obdurately against his paternal reproofs. Going on from bad to worse, they were promoting the desecration of the first Sunday of Lent by masques, public balls, and tournaments in direct contravention of the Cardinal's decree in his provincial council, already accepted by the people as a precept of obligation, which could not, therefore, be transgressed without giving grave scandal and committing mortal sin. When St. Charles had satisfied himself that this was no vain threat, but that preparations were already made for giving effect to it, he perceived the time was come to exert the strong hand of authority. Remembering that he was chief pastor of the flock, he knew that when he saw the wolf coming, it behoved him not to flee like a hireling, but to stand

his ground manfully even unto blood. It being p
that his former overtures of mildness were disregar
he published an edict in which after proving
obligation of Christians to sanctify holy days anc
time of Lent to avoid the dissolute games and s
tacles prohibited by the laws of the Church and e
cially by the Council of Trent, he forbade every
of whatsoever condition or dignity to hold jousts, 1
or other profane spectacles both on the first Sur
and in the rest of Lent during any part of the
and also on all other Sundays and festivals of obl
tion throughout the year during the hours of di
service at the cathedral under pain of excommui
tion, to be incurred *ipso facto* both by those actu
taking part in them and by those instituting or
moting them, with absolution reserved to himself :
persons co-operating in the same or being present
curring the same penalty to be incurred also *ipso f*

By this means the contemplated irregularities 1
effectually checked, for the fear of the Church's
sures was too general to render it possible to
ceed further with the preparations commenced.
Governor was greatly vexed to find his purpose chec
and declared that the Cardinal had published
edict to mortify him and put him to shame before
people. Having made up his mind to this conclus
it was in vain that the Saint sought to disabuse
by means of mutual friends, or to convince him
he had acted according to the obligations of his past
office. Far from yielding to these representations
suffered himself to be led entirely by ill-intentio

persons, including some religious of no very edifying spirit, and with their co-operation fomented fresh anxieties for the Cardinal.

There were some religious, who understood little about the obligations and difficulties of the episcopate, being without experience, and yet taking upon themselves to censure and abuse the Cardinal's proceedings in public and without reserve, and even from the pulpit. One preacher was especially notorious for these animadversions. When it was reported to St. Charles, he would take no steps to close his mouth, but left it entirely in God's hands, giving the same answer which David in his humility gave to the curses of Semei, that God had permitted it, and he would not resist Him. Some persons of consideration, however, represented to him that he was letting the matter go too far in allowing the preacher such license, that it was a public scandal, which might prove injurious to many souls. Even then the Saint opposed him with nothing but his own meekness and forbearance, and left it to his superiors to admonish him. The preacher did not, however, yield as yet, when at last the Inquisitor, Father Angelo of Cremona, full of zeal for God's glory, acknowledged that he could not allow him to go on with impunity, and represented to the Cardinal that the mischief that might accrue was one of Satan's devices for the introduction of heresy, by weakening the consideration of the people for the dignity and authority of their pastor. Mgr. Jerome Federici, Bishop of Lodi, who happened to be staying in Milan,

supported these arguments, adding that though
might be a Christian duty to excuse and pass o'
personal insults, it ceased to be so when these insu
were directed against episcopal authority, which v
a breach of the apostolic laws and constitutions,
which it was forbidden to censure a bishop in pub
according to the words of Holy Scripture,[1] "Tou
not my anointed, and do no evil to my prophe[
Yielding to this reasoning, St. Charles suffered them
take the steps they deemed necessary for the honour
God and the interests of justice.   Upon which t
Father Inquisitor and the Archbishop's Vicar-Gene
took together the necessary information, and havi
examined the preacher, forbade him to preach
future without permission, and required him, to cc
fine himself to the house of his order.   A report
their acts was sent to Rome.   The preacher v
afterwards restored to his liberty by the Cardin
of the Holy Office, after having done penance a
been inhibited from preaching for some years.
this sentence he submitted obediently, and was aft
wards noted for the regularity of his life and t
excellence of his sermons.

[1] I Paral. xvi. 22.

Page 56.—One preacher was especially notorious.

This was Father Giulio Mazzarino, S.J., a native of Sicily, and u·
of the celebrated Cardinal of that name, who preached the Lent of 1
in the Duomo, attracting the favourable notice of the Governor,
Marquess of Ayamonte. The Father was invited by the latter to pre
the next Lent in his chapel, and having accepted the invitation with
reference to the permission of the ordinary, received orders to pre
elsewhere. He then attacked the Cardinal openly in his sermons,
even accused him of preaching heresy in the pulpit.

CHAPTER VIII.

FOUNDATION OF THE CONVENT OF CAPUCHIN NUNS OR POOR CLARES OF SANTA PRASSEDE.

1579.

WHILE the servant of God was harassed by these trials, our Lord vouchsafed to favour him with a great spiritual consolation in the foundation, about this time, of a convent of nuns who sought after great perfection. These sisters embraced the rule of St. Clare, which binds them to observe a perpetual Lent, to sleep upon boards covered only with a single blanket, to rise in the middle of the night for matins, to chastise their bodies with disciplines, not to see or speak with secular persons, even near relations, to wear an ash-coloured habit of coarse cloth next to their skin, to go barefoot like the Capuchin friars, to observe with great exactness the three vows of religion, to be assiduous day and night in prayer, and in the exercise of all Christian virtues. A rule indeed of great bodily severity, but full of spiritual consolations !

A lady, Martha Piantanida by name, had gathered together in her house, five years before, a number of maidens who desired to lead a spiritual life, under the

direction of the Regular Clerks of St. Paul. Our Lor
inspired them now with a resolution to devote them
selves to Him in a stricter way. They according
applied to the Cardinal to place them under the con
ventual rule of St. Clare.

Nothing pleased him better, for he had long de
sired to see a convent of these religious establishe
in Milan, and he promised, therefore, to satisfy the
wishes without delay. Having further examined then
and found them steadfast in their determination, h
gave them enclosure in the house they then occupie
having had it arranged for the purpose, intending ult
mately to build them a church and convent, accordin
to the rules laid down by himself in his book of " In
structions on Ecclesiastical Buildings." He appointe
a certain number of pious persons to undertake th
supervision of the building, and bought a site we
adapted for the purpose, affording ample space for a
the necessary offices, garden, and cloister, and sur
rounded with a wall which at once enclosed th
convent and protected it from being overlooked b
surrounding houses. He contributed largely himse
to this foundation in its beginning and during his life
it is now completed, and, allowing for the simplicit
and poverty required by the rule, it may be said to b
one of the most commodious convents of Milan. A
the Saint set great store by this foundation, an
reckoned it among his most important works, h
opened it with solemnity, with the view also of mak
ing the institute known to the people, that they migh
be liberal in alms for the daily support of the nun

since they could not hold any property either individually or in common. After mass on Low Sunday, April 26, 1579, he blessed the habits of the nuns and clothed eighteen of them in the presence of a large concourse of both regular and secular clergy and lay people. After the clothing he laid a large cross upon the shoulders of each and a crown of thorns on their heads, after the example of Him whom they had chosen for their spouse, and thus they went in procession to their new convent. St. Charles gave them the rule of perpetual enclosure under the guidance of four nuns of the same order whom he had summoned from Perugia. At the same time he blessed and laid the first stone of a new chapel for their use under the invocation of Santa Prassede, granting a plenary indulgence to all who assisted in virtue of a brief which he had obtained from Rome. He made a decree that this convent should always remain under the Archbishops of Milan. The blessing of God has manifestly rested upon this work, which has gone on increasing to this day, now counting more than fifty nuns, among whom are daughters of the noblest families of Milan, who have passed from a life of ease to one of seemingly intolerable austerity. But though their rule is severe externally, the grace of God compensates abundantly for all their mortifications, that they not only bear them cheerfully, but rejoice in them in the joy of the Holy Ghost. So edifying has been their mode of life that they have always been looked upon as examples of perfection, and their prayers are constantly asked by the people in all necessities and trials. The odour of

their sanctity has spread far and wide, and the peo[
of Pavia and Cremona have applied to them to est;
lish convents of the order in their own cities.

While we are upon this subject, we must not or
to mention the signal example of the Countess Coror
daughter of the Count John Baptist Borromeo, w
desirous of imitating the holy life of the Cardinal]
uncle, entered as a nun into this convent, tread;
beneath her feet the grandeurs and pleasures of t
world. Preferring the love of Christ to all the brilli;
allurements that surrounded her path in the woi
she gladly put on the rough habit and girdle of ro
devoting herself with a pure intention to the life
penance in the convent of Santa Prassede, where ;
took the name of Sister Helen. In entering it she l
desired to taste of suffering for the love of God, ;
our Lord granted her wish by sending her the he;
cross of a life-long illness, accompanied with sufl
ings so great that it might well be reckoned a mart
dom, and a perfect example of patience and c
formity with the will of God. After she had b
thus tried and refined in His love for three years ;
three months, He called her to receive the reward
glory she had merited, leaving behind her a gr
reputation for sanctity. Among her virtues n
was perhaps more remarkable than her spirit of o
dience, which was exemplified even after her de;
Though the nuns had closed her eyes, they afterwa
found them open on several occasions, until the Mot

---

[1] She was heiress to her father's property, having only a married si
Hippolyta, wife of Count Alberico Belgiojoso.

Abbess, Sister Jeronima of Perugia, placing her hand upon them, said, " My daughter, as you have always been most obedient during life, so now obey me and close your eyes." No sooner said than done : she closed them as if she had heard her words, and it was taken by all the sisters, not only as an effect of her spirit of obedience, but as an evidence that her soul had entered upon her heavenly rest.

CHAPTER IX.

FIFTH PROVINCIAL COUNCIL—TRANSLATION OF TH
RELICS OF ST. NAZARIUS.

1579.

ALTHOUGH the decrees of the Fourth and last .
vincial Council had not yet received the formal
firmation of the Holy See, as it was now three y
since its close, the Cardinal began his preparat
for holding the fifth. He desired, in particular
insert in its Acts the measures adopted by him du
the late visitation of the plague, as a guide to o
prelates and pastors in similar emergencies.

He had learnt by experience that at such ti:
if men are not prepared with the knowledge
to grapple with them, they are apt to be o
whelmed with solicitude and deprived by t
anxiety of the power of forming a correct j
ment. A concise statement of all his regulat
may be found preserved in the second part of
Acts of this Council, which was held early in :
of the year 1579, having been attended by
bishops of the province as usual. Many other
ful decrees were also published concerning the def

of the Catholic faith, the reverence due to holy seasons and places, and the reform of discipline.

. The bishops assembled on this occasion took occasion to renew the representations they had made to the Saint in the last Council three years before, concerning the mortifications he practised, which they thought to be excessive, when the government of the province and the cavils against his ecclesiastical jurisdiction were taken into account. They were' afraid lest he should endanger his health and be unequal to continuing labours which so greatly benefited the Church at large. To himself it seemed as if his penances could never be rigorous enough to counterbalance the sins of his people in the sight of God. In order not to appear attached to his own will, or regardless of their opinion, he yielded so far as to use a paillasse, which was quilted tight, so as to give less ease than loose straw would have afforded, and for his covering he had a coarse counterpane of canvas, and a straw pillow completed the bed on which the Saint took his rest during the remainder of his life.

While the bishops, who had come up to the Council, remained in Milan, St. Charles deemed it was a fitting occasion to give solemnity to the translation of the bodies of St. Nazarius and other saints which reposed in the church dedicated to that martyr, called the Basilica of the Apostles.[1] It received the name of St. Nazarius when the

---

[1] So called because St. Simplicianus brought some relics of St. Peter and Paul from Rome, when he succeeded to the See of Milan.

body of that saint was placed there by St.
brose. The canons of this church had determ
more than a year before to improve and restore
fabric, and it therefore became necessary in confor
with the decrees of St. Charles to remove the be
of the saints deposited there. Search was first i
for that of St. Nazarius, which was found about s
or eight feet beneath the pavement in a marble si
phagus, the bones alone remaining. The saint i
himself to verify the relics, and remained in pi
before them till midnight with his canons, and ar
them Mgr. Charles Bascapè, by whom all the partic
are given at length in his life of the saint. He
the most satisfactory evidence of identity, sufficie
refuting those who have said that the body was ti
lated to Metz by Grodegand, Bishop of that city, ir
year 775, in the pontificate of Paul I. In
manner, beneath the altar of St. Peter, under
cupola of the church, was found a small silver sl
with different mysteries of the passion worked i
it, containing, wrapt in a veil, a small circular v
with the relics of the holy Apostles. At the same
were brought to light the bodies of four canoi
Archbishops, Venerius Oldrado, Glycerius Landr
Marolus, and Lazarus Boccardio, who instituted
Litanies on the three Rogation days in Milan.
the right, on the Gospel side, was found the body o
Oldericus, Bishop of Aosta, and in one of the cha
that of St. Matronianus the hermit. All these i
were laid up in shrines prepared for the purpos
a place of honour until the time when the transla

could be made with the solemnity which the presence of so many prelates warranted.

When the church had been restored, the saint gave orders that it should be fittingly adorned, and that tapestries should be hung along the streets through which the procession would pass. The day before, together with several of the Bishops, he had replaced in their shrines the holy relics, which diffused around a delightful fragrance. In the procession all the clergy in Milan assisted with burning tapers in their hands, the Cardinal and Bishops in pontifical vestments bearing the shrines upon their shoulders. At the close the relics were all laid upon the high altar except the body of St. Oldericus, which was placed under a new altar in the north aisle, where there had formerly been a side door, and that of St. Matronianus, which was restored to the chapel under his invocation.

This translation kindled the devotion of the people towards these saints, so that the church was much frequented by the faithful, especially the Chapel of St. Oldericus, on account of the frequency with which graces were obtained by his intercession.

CHAPTER X.

SIXTH DIOCESAN SYNOD—DEDICATION OF THE ?
CHURCH OF ST. FIDELIS—FOUNDATION OF
HOUSE OR DEPOSITORY OF ST. MARY MAGDALEN.

1579.

THE labours of the Provincial Council were no soc
brought to a close than the Saint began to prepare
the next Diocesan Synod, which he had never omit
except when he had been legitimately prevented,
then he had always asked for the permission of
Supreme Pontiff to transfer it to another season, s
not to break through the order of the Council
Trent. This year he called together his clergy for
12th of June, when, besides fulfilling the appoir
duties, he laid down certain decrees, and laboure
kindle more and more zeal for the salvation of s
in the hearts of his priests, impressing this upon t
particularly in three discourses full of the Spirit
God.

At its close he gave to all the priests who des
it the usual audiences, and was asked by the Je
Fathers to dedicate their new Church of St. Fid
Accordingly, on the 24th of June he went thither

cessionally with the Chapter of the cathedral, and removed the bodies of the martyrs St. Fidelis and St. Carpophorus from the altar of the old church, where he had placed them three years before, and transferred them solemnly to the new edifice, preaching to the people upon the imitation and glories of the holy martyrs. At the close of the procession he sung Mass, the first celebrated in the church, and gave communion to great numbers of persons. Afterwards the old building was demolished and the fathers removed to the new church, although not as yet entirely completed.

The zeal of the Saint kept him ever on the watch for new occasions of benefiting his people and procuring for all the means of attaining eternal life. At this time he had before his mind particularly the case of those unhappy women, who, in giving themselves over to a life of sin, not only lose their own souls, but draw multitudes of others to perdition, thus infinitely multiplying the dishonour done to God. He found two houses already established in the city for their relief: first, a convent where they made a religious profession with the three solemn vows under the name of the " Convent of the Crucified ; " secondly, the house of St. Valeria, where a rule without vows is observed. He fostered and encouraged these two institutions by his alms and counsel; but they did not suffice to receive all who presented themselves, nor did the House of Succour[1] he had founded make up for the deficiency. He determined therefore to establish a

---

[1] Book II. chap. xvii.

new house capable of receiving all who should m
application with the recommendation of the Ar
bishop.

Four years before he had made a small beg
ning by hiring a house for the purpose, and 1
finding it had fully answered his expectations,
made a permanent foundation under a legal ins
ment, and gave it a rule for its temporal and spirit
government, appointing a committee of twelve m
bers, two ecclesiastics and the rest laymen, to man
its affairs. This house was called the " Deposito
and he placed it under the protection of St. M
Magdalen, on whose festival these arrangements v
completed. He provided it with a confessor
ordinary, whose charge was to deliver these p
creatures from their sin, and to put them in the 1
of salvation, confiding the internal government
pious women of sufficient experience. He gave
the name of the Depository, to signify that it
intended as a temporary abode from which the
mates might either enter the marriage state, or dev
themselves in the Convent of the Crucified, or am
the penitents of St. Valeria, or adopt any respecta
calling in the world.

This good work was never lost sight of by
Charles, being aided by his alms from time to ti
and has been blessed by being the means of sav
many souls.

CHAPTER XI.

CHAPTER OF THE FATHERS OF CONGREGATION OF ST.
PAUL, AND OF THE BROTHERS OF ST. AMBROSE
AD NEMUS.

1579.

AMONG the institutions of Milan none is more worthy
of mention than the Venerable Congregation of the
Regular Clerks of St. Paul, commonly called Barnabites. It was founded in this city about the year
1530 by three priests, viz., Antonio Maria Zaccaria
of Cremona, and Bartholomew Ferrari and James
Antony Morigia, both of Milan. All three belonged
to noble families, but withdrew from the world to
devote themselves to the service of God in a life of
perfection, and to labour for the salvation of souls.
They were soon joined by others who shared their
zeal and devotion, and were ultimately formed into
a Congregation under the authority of the Holy See.
They received the name of Barnabites from the
church dedicated to St. Barnabas, which they served
in Milan. Under the blessing of God their Congregation increased both in numbers and in the fruits of
their labours, and soon spread to other cities of Italy.
Their work was to hear confessions, to preach to the

people, and to hold themselves at the disposition
the Bishops in their pastoral labours.

This Congregation has produced many excel
priests; among them two particularly eminent
piety. First, Father Alexander Sauli of Ge
Bishop, first of Aleria, in Corsica, afterwards
Pavia. Of his virtues I can speak with confide
as they were intimately known to me throug]
long course of years, and won him the sin
esteem and attachment of St. Charles. When
passed to a better life, so great was the reputa
of his sanctity that the people ran in crowds
touch his bier with their rosaries. His tomb in
cathedral church of Pavia has never ceased to
visited by numbers of clients anxious to obtain
intercession, the fruit of which is testified by
votos placed in grateful remembrance.

The other was Father Charles Bascapè, of a n
Milanese family, whose name has already been n
tioned, and will frequently appear in the course
this history. When in the College of Advocates
Milan, St. Charles recognised his talents, and n
him Canon in Ordinary of the cathedral, employ
him in various way in his diocese. Believing l
self to be called by God to a more perfect life
entered the Congregation of St. Paul, in which he s
rose to the highest offices.[1] It is to his labours
we owe the history of the life of our Saint in L
which we have endeavoured to reproduce in t]
pages in the vulgar tongue.

---

[1] He was afterwards made Bishop of Novara by Clement VIII.

When this Congregation had increased in numbers and importance, their original constitutions, which were very brief, required to be revised. In order that all might be done with exactness, the permission of the Holy See was obtained that St. Charles should preside over their deliberations. Under his auspices the work was brought to a conclusion, and afterwards received the approbation of Gregory XIII. in a special Bull. Great harmony and mutual esteem had reigned from the first between these fathers and their Archbishop, and this issue of their labours gave him great joy. He always warmly acknowledged their merits, employing them in the various offices of the diocese, living in great intimacy with them, and often withdrew for a time from his public duties for spiritual retirement at St. Barnabas, and other houses of their Congregation; while they, on their part, were always most devoted to him, and ready to lend themselves to all his wishes.

Soon after this he was asked to perform the same office for the brothers of St. Ambrose *ad nemus*, whose monastery is situated in the environs of Milan. They were about to hold a General Chapter, and applied for the permission of the Apostolic See to that effect. With his assistance rules were made for the government of the institute, which had been founded by three Milanese of good families, viz., Alexander Crivello, Albert Besozzo, and Antonio Pietra Santa, who had devoted themselves to a life of seclusion in the midst of a wood, whence the church still retains the name of St. Ambrose *ad nemus*, or " in the wood." It was dedicated to St. Ambrose in the first instance

The Brothers of St. Ambrose.

because that saint used to frequent the spot for c
templation and retirement. The fame of these ?
recluses drew numbers to follow them, and in pro
of time they grew under Apostolic sanction int
Regular Congregation, using the Ambrosian Rite w
the name of the house where they had their i
foundation. Other houses of the same Congrega
were subsequently founded in different places, and t]
first fervour having somewhat slackened, St. Cha
gladly embraced this opportunity of quickening tl
in the true spirit of religious perfection. Overl
dened as he was with many duties, he counted not
cost when it was a question of promoting what he
most at heart, viz., the revival in religious commu
ties of discipline and ancient observance.

CHAPTER XII.

1579.

As the entire cessation of the plague now gave him some little liberty, St. Charles resolved to continue the visitation of the province, which he had begun at Cremona and Bergamo, taking Vigevano next in order, which, being a small diocese, would not require him to be long absent from his own see. Having given notice of his intention, the citizens of Vigevano prepared to receive him with every mark of honour. Setting to work with his accustomed energy, he gained in a few days a good knowledge of the needs of the diocese; nor did he return without having endeavoured, by preaching daily to the people, to quicken them in the fear and love of God, and giving them an opportunity of approaching the Sacraments. He provided also for the worthier celebration of the Divine offices in the churches, and by these and other blessings conferred upon them, so endeared himself to all the people that they have always held his memory in

veneration. Neither has this feeling passed away w
time, for we have lately seen the people of this c
come in solemn procession to visit the Saint's tor
accompanied with trumpets and choirs of musicia
Among the offerings which they brought with th
was a banner on which was represented, in e
broidery, the city of Vigevano begging for the prot
tion of the Saint.

From Vigevano he went on to visit some parts
his own diocese, where great havoc had been ma
among the flock by disobedience to the decrees of
synods. The opposition shown by the Governor
his measures of reform, and the encouragement giv
by him to licentious amusements, had not escaj
notice, and afforded a pretext to dissolute persons
give themselves up to such pastimes. Nor had th
any respect to the commands of their Archbish
since they reckoned that the example of their bett
was sufficient excuse for themselves to set them
nought. In this way the old scandals and abuses
public balls and other profanities, on Sundays a
holidays, had again crept into many places. To su
a pass had this spirit gone that during the Cardina
visitation—a time when it was customary for all
put business and pleasure aside, and frequent
Sacraments—certain persons dared to hold great pul
festival on a holy day of the Church, using force a
violence to those who wished to avail themselves
the means of grace, in order to prevail upon them
join them. Distressed as he was at this scandal,
would not at first visit it with the penalties he mi;

have used, knowing that the mischief took its origin from a higher source, and he hoped by patient endurance to restore order by pacific measures.

When men in high places set the example of contempt for their spiritual rulers and the laws of the Church, it cannot be expected that the common people should not indulge in similar excesses. This is one way in which God chastises the sins of princes by making them react upon themselves. The license which they have themselves taught the people in reference to moral and ecclesiastical precepts soon accustoms the latter to the disregard of civil laws also, and thus are sown seeds of revolt which ultimately bear their fruit in outbreaks of the populace and overthrow of governments. The secular arm will not long continue to be obeyed where respect has ceased for that spiritual authority which is the reign of God Himself upon earth.

In the meantime it became clear to St. Charles that it would not be possible to make himself personally acquainted with the whole province, and that it was undesirable to absent himself any longer from the capital. With the consent of the Pontiff, therefore, other visitors were appointed to finish the work, Brescia only being reserved for his own supervision besides those he had already visited.

In pursuance of this arrangement, His Holiness appointed the Bishop of Famagosta to undertake the rest of the work, after finishing the visitation of Milan itself. Mgr. Francesco Bosso, Bishop of Novara, was to take Lodi in charge, and Mgr. Giovanni Francesco

Bonomo, Bishop of Vercelli, to undertake the visitai
of Novara. At the request of St. Charles, howe
these dispositions were subsequently altered so
that Mgr. Bonomo was appointed for the visitatior
Como instead of Novara, because Como afforded
scope for the exercise of his zeal, both on accoun
its size, and because it extended some distance into
territory of Switzerland and the Grisons, from wl
parts heresy had spread into the valleys of Chiave
and Valtellina, while the Bishop of Como, being a
and infirm, was unable to grapple with the increas
evil. Although Como did not belong to the eccles
tical province under the saint's jurisdiction, yet
nearness was sufficient to establish a claim upon
charity. The Bishop of Vercelli, knowing his prude
would not set out on this mission without first resor
to him for advice on the difficult matter of trea
with the people of Switzerland and the Grisons.

St. Charles had before this brought about
establishment of a Nuncio Apostolic to these p
for the promotion of the Catholic faith, a mis
which was greatly needed, for ecclesiastical affair:
those states were at this time by no means flourisb
Finding that the Bishop of Vercelli had conducted
visitation of Como with great prudence, the Saint
posed him to the Holy See as a fit person for
Nunciature. Gregory XIII. immediately made
desired appointment, and gave him as his Aud
Marcantonio Bellini, who was afterwards Canor
Ordinary and Chancellor of Milan, and at the pre
moment Bishop of Bobbio.

The Bishop of Novara filled the office of Nuncio for
two years, during which time, aided by the counsels
of St. Charles, he did good service to the Church in
reforming the clergy, introducing the observance of the
decrees of the Council of Trent, and effecting many
other improvements, to the great satisfaction of His
Holiness, who next employed him as Nuncio to the
Emperor in the year 1581, and intrusted to him the
delicate commission of deposing Gebhard Truchses,
Archbishop of Cologne, together with the Provost and
some of the Canons who sided with the Bishop, and of
assembling the Chapter for the election of a new prelate.   In this business he also succeeded, and under
his auspices the suffrages were given in favour of a
good Catholic prelate, Ernest, son of the Duke of
Bavaria.   Another work which he found means to
accomplish, was to send the notorious heretic, James
Palæologus, for trial at Rome.   When he had been
about three years at this post, he was sent by the
Pope, with the title of Apostolic Nuncio, into the Low
Countries, which at that time stood in great need of
such assistance, on account of the heresies which had
made havoc there.   He laboured there for two years,
and was called away in the midst of his toils at Liege
on the 26th February 1587.   He left all his property
at his death to the Monte di Pietà, founded by himself
at Vercelli, in order to imitate his master St. Charles,
whose memory he has celebrated in some Latin verses
on the wonderful preservation of the Saint, by whom
he had been consecrated Bishop, and who renounced
in his favour the abbacy of Nonantula.   Since this

time the Holy See has always continued to send
Nuncio to Switzerland, who has been received w
every mark of honour.

St. Charles' exertions in behalf of Swiss Cathol
did not end here. He this year laid the foun
tion of a college for Swiss priests in Milan, a w
which had long occupied his thoughts, and formed
subject of consultation with the Holy Father.
well knew that there was no means of promoting
Catholic faith so effectual as the provision of prie
sufficiently well instructed to teach the mysteries
religion, who should by their life and conduct elev
and edify their flock. Of such there was gr
lack, and total absence, moreover, of the means
supplying the deficiency. This he felt most urgen
with respect to the territory of the Grisons, wh
Satan had contrived almost entirely to obscure
light of truth. The civil authorities had prohibi
any but Swiss ecclesiastics from entering the count
and as heretical opinions reigned at Coira, where
only seminary was, no fresh priests could be ordain
In this way the authorities reckoned they should i
short time cut off religion at its source. Meanti
the people, being deprived of pastors, were driven
attend the preachings of false teachers, from wh
they imbibed pestilent doctrine, which they had
the wit to gainsay, and thus their souls day by (
fell a prey to the enemy. The scheme was undenia
well devised, and might have ended in total loss
faith, had not God in His mercy raised up St. Cha
and enabled him to repair the mischief.

Such was the origin of the Swiss or Helvetian College founded by the Saint in this year, 1579. In drawing up its rules he received every faculty and privilege from the Holy See. In the first instance he made the full number of students to be forty, of whom half were to be Swiss, and half natives of the Grisons, the perpetual administration of the college being reserved to the Archbishop of Milan for the time being. The internal direction he gave to the Oblates of St. Ambrose, with rules like those of his own seminary, the students attending the schools of the Jesuit Fathers in the College of Brera, founded also by himself. He obtained for them from Cardinal Alessandrino the house and church of the Holy Spirit, which had formerly belonged to the Umiliati. He subsequently removed it to a more salubrious situation in a convent, the nuns of which he, by Apostolic authority, transferred and united to the sisters of Santa Maria al Cerchio.

In this foundation, the Supreme Pontiff and many of the Cardinals helped him liberally with alms. He afterwards assigned to it the revenues of two benefices which fell in to him, one at Monza, the other at Novara, and not long afterwards the benefice of St. Anthony at Pavia also. Within a year and a half he procured from his cousin Cardinal Altaemps, Bishop of Constance, a grant duly secured under an Apostolic Bull of the benefice of Mirasole near Milan, with the stipulation that four-and-twenty youths of the diocese of Constance should be maintained in the college during his life, and fourteen during the lives of his two immediate successors.

By these means he provided the college with a fi
income of eight hundred crowns. A commission of
ecclesiastics was appointed by him for the administ
tion of these revenues. It was his good pleasure tl
I, John Peter Giussano, the writer of this work, sho
be of this number, and this office made me well
quainted with the affection he bore the students a
his solicitude for them as future propagators and o
fenders of the faith. He obtained from the Holy S
several privileges to be exercised by the Archbisho
of Milan in its favour; such as permission to ord:
its members after three years of study, for which p
pose he created certain titles annexed to the chapel
the college, upon which he could ordain them as if
were their diocesan, also a faculty to confer the deg
of Doctor of Theology on those who had finished th
course of philosophy and theology, so that being du
invested with the character of priests and the deg
of doctor there should be no further impediment
the way of their at once going out to work in
vineyard in obedience to their several bishops,
before admission to the college they were required
take an oath that at the close of their studies tl
would devote themselves to labour in their own coun
—the object for which the college was founded.
obtained also certain indulgences for such of its me
bers as should be enrolled in a confraternity of
Blessed Virgin attached to the college.

This pious work of our saint has abundantly answe
his intentions, and continually supplies Switzerland a
the Grisons with pastors sound in doctrine and blamel

in life, by whose labours heresy has been quelled and discipline restored. We shall have occasion to speak hereafter of some of the more immediate results with which these labours have been crowned, and which will abundantly prove that this foundation has been of great advantage to those states and an effectual bulwark of our holy faith on this frontier of Germany.

Book VI.

CHAPTER I.

1579.

WHEN the Governor of Milan, who was alread
judiced against our Saint, saw his favourite pro
removed in the middle of his Lenten course of ser
as he had himself requested the General of his
to allow him to preach, he felt much annoyed,
ing that the Cardinal had done it on purpose to
him. As usual, there were not wanting evil coun
to confirm him in this opinion and to urge him to
his resentment. Besides the efforts made by so
the fathers of the order to prove to the worl
the Cardinal was in the wrong, the Governor h
had written to Rome complaining bitterly of th
in which he had been treated, and begging th
hasten their decision, and to take into conside
some other charges formerly brought against the
He used all his influence at the Roman Co

partisans and others to spread injurious reports and to diminish the reputation of the Cardinal.

As the decrees of the Fourth Provincial Council of Milan were awaiting confirmation at that time, there were not wanting some who openly found fault with them, and strove in every way to lessen their authority, saying that so much liberty ought not to be allowed to the Cardinal. The spiritual edifice, that the watchfulness of the servant of God had raised up in so many years, was thus imperilled by the malice of Satan. Besides the evil reports spread in Rome, additional efforts were made to defame him in Milan. It was repeated that he was a man void of prudence, that he was disliked by many, that the King of Spain had desired his ambassador to have him removed, and had directed the Governor to proceed against him with strong measures. Other like rumours were industriously spread abroad by his enemies, in the hope that, on his going to Rome, he would not be allowed to return. These lies had a bad effect upon men of the world, who, as if freed from all restraint, thought themselves at liberty to do as they liked without any regard to the laws of the Church.

Mgr. Speciano, in reporting this state of affairs from Rome, wrote that he was no longer able to obtain audiences as formerly; that he thought it expedient that the Cardinal should come in person and defend his cause before he should be attacked with greater violence. The good pastor thereupon perceived that he was in a difficult position, and although he had never hitherto gone to Rome on account of intrigues

against himself, and had left such matters to
decision of the Holy See, yet considering that in
case discipline was endangered, involving loss of s
and detriment to religion, he judged it necessary to
but kept his resolve secret for a time lest his ener
should work mischief.

As he was visiting the district of Desio at this t
he summoned his ministers and the visitors of
diocese, making known his intention and his rea
for keeping it secret. They begged him by no me
to go on such a journey at that time—the first w
in August, but to defer it to a less inconven
season. While preparing to start after the feas
the Assumption, news was brought to him that I
Domenico Bollano, the Bishop of Brescia, was dy
Upon which he instantly started for that city
arrived in time to administer the last sacrame
assisting him to make a good death, and then c
brating Mass for the repose of his soul. On the f
of the Assumption, he sang High Mass in the cathe
of Brescia, and gave Holy Communion to about
thousand persons.

From thence he went to Mantua to consult v
his widowed sister Camilla, on family affairs, and
received with great kindness by the Duke of Man
On leaving by way of Bologna for Rome, he was as
by his attendants where he meant to stop on
road, in order that they might give notice ol
" Where the Lord wills," he replied, giving them
understand that he wished no preparations to be n
for him, but was content to put up with any inc

venience he might encounter. It so happened that he had to take shelter that night in a poor priest's house, where there was only one room on the ground-floor.

As he was well aware that the storm which was threatening him was stirred up by the enemy of mankind to hinder the salvation of souls, he saw that he stood in great need of assistance from God in order to overcome all difficulties. To this end he resolved to retire for a while to the hermitage of Camaldoli, in order to treat with our Lord alone on the matter. This retreat is situated in the Apennines, between Tuscany and the Romagna, in a wild district where the roads were bad. While he was riding thither through the mountains, he was overtaken by night in a part unknown to him ; and as he was passing a little church dedicated to St. Michael, the priest living there heard the tramp of horses' feet, and going out, cried, "Stop, stop!" At this the Cardinal stopped, and the priest coming up, asked where he was going. On his replying to Camaldoli, the priest said he could go no further that night, but must stay with him, as the roads were dangerous, and not safe even in the day-time. The Saint took his advice, and remained with him, though there was but small provision for supper, and only one poor bed to lie on. After eating a little food he withdrew to the church, where he remained all night in prayer, allowing his attendants to take it in turns to pray with him, while the rest slept upon straw, in order not to deprive the poor priest of his bed. The next morning he proceeded

on his way, and had scarcely gone half a mile w
on passing a precipice, Julius Omato, his train-be
slipped over it, his horse falling over at a bound,
they heard no more of him. Omato, however,
caught in his fall, the Cardinal having given him
blessing as he went over, and he was rescued witl
injury, which was considered a miracle worked by
through the prayers of the Saint. On their arriva
Camaldoli that morning, after the Cardinal had
Mass, he retired to one of the cells, keeping no
with him but Moneta and a secretary, sending
rest on to Loreto. He continued for some days
fasting, prayer, and contemplation with God. Nor v
his prayers offered up in vain, for all his undertak
were wonderfully blessed.

. Owing to his long retreat, the report was sp)
that he had abandoned the world and had becom
hermit in a fit of despair, but this was not belie
by well-disposed persons.

From Camaldoli he went to Mount Alvernia, wl
the glorious St. Francis received the stigmata from
Lord, giving himself there up to the contemplatioi
heavenly things, and meditation on the seraphic s)
of St. Francis, and the flame of love that burnt in
heart. In this retreat he not only gained new ferv
but likewise a strong desire to suffer every kin(
opposition for the love of God. Renewed in s)
he then went on to the holy house of Loreto, b
warmly received by Francis Mary, Duke of Url
as he passed through his territory. Out of devo
he went on foot from Fossombrone to Loreto, a

tance of not less than fifty miles, with his spirit intent upon God, meditating, praying, and saying psalms the whole way; if he occasionally spoke, his conversation was always upon holy things. He was visited by the Archbishop of Urbino, who accompanied him to Loreto, the roads by which they went being full of pilgrims who crowded from all parts to see him. On his arrival in the evening he went at once to the shrine, and remained there all night in prayer. The next morning being the Nativity of our Blessed Lady, one of the principal feasts there, he sang Mass and preached with such fervour on the love of God, whose only begotten Son had taken flesh for our salvation in that poor little room and had dwelt there in poverty and humility many years, that he drew tears from the eyes of all present. He gave communion to many, and filled the people who thronged thither with no small degree of wonder and edification, every one thinking there was more of divine than human in him. He accepted an invitation of the canons who practised community life after the custom of early times, and dined with them in their refectory.

From Loreto he went on to Rome, where he was looked for both on account of the report of his sanctity and of the wonders that had occurred during the plague at Milan. Many cardinals, prelates, and nobles went to meet him, so that the road from the Porta del Populo to the Ponte Molle was filled with crowds of people. It was most striking to see the general eagerness manifested to do honour to so distinguished a member of the College of Cardinals.

CHAPTER II.

1579.

ON his arrival in the city, St. Charles alighted at
titular house of St. Praxedes, intending to visit
Peter's and the Scala Santa the first thing next n
ing.　He was prevented doing so by the Card
and others who flocked to visit him, and the]
who was then at Frascati, sent a special messeng
beg him to take up his abode in the palace o
Cardinal his nephew at that place.　This reque
his Holiness not only gave the Cardinal the sati
tion of being admitted to his presence, but also
opportunity of speaking upon the matters which
brought him to Rome, and about all his trou
showing how, through the efforts of his enemie
the decrees of his Fourth Provincial Council had
censured by those who had been deputed to r
them, not a single decree having been left as it s
The Pope, knowing the goodness of his intentions
beyond measure displeased that he should have

treated in this way. He directed the decrees of the Council to be brought to him, and went through all in the Cardinal's presence, spending four hours a day in the revision. The Saint passed the time almost without sleep, as he prepared over night the documents to be placed before his Holiness the following day. The Pope seeing plainly the artifices of the devil to frustrate the good works of the servant of God, commissioned St. Charles to send in his name to the Cardinals of the congregation for the revision of provincial councils, wishing to know their reasons for censuring the decrees which his Holiness approved of. Mgr. Seneca, as being experienced in the business of councils, presented the request of his Holiness to the Cardinal de Sens, one of the congregation of revision, who showed him a packet of papers, written by different persons upon this subject. The Cardinal was then given to understand that there was no foundation for these censures, and whence all the opposition had arisen. Seeing the calumnies, in so many words, he said—" I cannot account for this ; these documents cannot be trusted. Cardinal Borromeo is a member of our college, and is like an angel from heaven ; it would be a blessing for the Holy See if there were a dozen Cardinals like him. I have an only nephew, who is to start to-morrow morning for France, whom I kept here till the Cardinal arrived in order that he might obtain his blessing, which I consider will be of great service to him."

The Pontiff was glad to hear of this reply of the Cardinal de Sens, and to see the deceits of Satan

brought to light. With apostolic authority he c
firmed all the decrees of the said Council, and
those of the Fifth, which the saint had brought v
him. He also invited him to breakfast at his ta
during his stay, and one day he went expressly to l
his Mass, and see his vestments, which he hand
with particular devotion.

St. Charles then returned to Rome to visit
churches and holy places, the Pope's house having k
during those eight days like a monastery, all striv
to keep the rules. Cardinal Guastavillani, the Po
nephew, even directed his household to wear
Borromean livery out of compliment to the Sa
Every one in Rome was much edified by his humil
two of the Cardinals who had not known him v
but had been set against him by others, after see
him, became his most warm friends. His ener
were lowered in reputation in the same proportior
it became clear that they had been moved only by
passions.

He received much kindness from his brother (
dinals, and used to invite them to dine with hir
St. Praxedes, having, according to his custom, spiri
books read during the meal, which pleased them gre
on account of the benefit they derived from the p
tice; he, on the other hand, relaxed in some degree
ordinary rigour and abstinence to suit himself to t
way of living. He asked to his table also many o
prelates and gentlemen, striving to instil into t
affections for spiritual things, and to incite them
his discourse to devotion and piety, setting them

example himself by the fervency of his prayers, and visits to the churches, whither he went on foot. He spent the whole of Christmas night in watching and prayer, going, after the midnight Mass at St. Peter's, to Santa Maria Maggiore, where he remained in the Chapel of the Manger till daybreak, returning thence to St. Peter's for the Pope's Mass. On the feast of St. Sebastian he passed the whole night in prayer in the subterranean crypt in the church dedicated to that saint, and did the same at Tre Fontane in the church called Scala Coeli, where the bodies of ten thousand martyrs repose.

So great was the devotion of the Roman people to him that they rushed out to see him as he passed through the streets, and many knelt down to show him reverence; the churches were filled where he said Mass, and as many desired to receive Holy Communion from him, he was asked by the Oratorian Fathers to officiate at a general Communion in the Chiesa Nuova, their church. Such an unusual concourse of people came together that an account of it was printed, with a likeness of the Cardinal. He was asked to preach, but declined to do so except in his own titular church of St. Praxedes, where a great gathering of people went to hear him, many of the nobility of both sexes frequenting the church in order to receive Communion at his hands, although it was at some distance from the city.

During this sojourn in Rome he had a good opportunity of doing much with the Pope for the benefit of the whole Church, as well as for his own diocese in

particular. He obtained the revenue of the Abbe
Caravaggio for his Seminary, and that of St. An
of Pavia for the Swiss College. The Pope was q
satisfied with him, finding that he had been acc
for the good he had done; and accordingly appro
by word of mouth, and afterwards by writing, of
his decrees for the sanctification of festivals,
against profane balls, tournaments, and other sin
dissolute amusements. These regulations, indeed,
so pleasing to His Holiness that he was wishfu
draw up a general constitution or code of them fo
Christian people, but for some particular reasons
project was not carried into execution.

St. Charles on this occasion urgently appealed f
decision on the controversies about jurisdiction,
which also the King of Spain had made applica
through the Marquis Alcagnizio, who was at R
for the purpose; but as it was an affair that requ
time, it was left to the judgment of His Holiness,
in the meantime, availed himself much of his advic
important matters, to the great benefit and advan
of all both in public and private. The Bishop
Italy especially had recourse to his good offices, m
coming to Rome for the purpose.

While the Saint was engaged in this way, Satan
not idle in Milan, for being in doubt whether
servant of God would not return in triumph with
his decrees confirmed by the Pontiff, he made it
business to suggest to the Governor through the med
of his evil counsellors that it would be a good thin
send ambassadors to Rome to oppose the Cardinal,

prevent such confirmation if possible, otherwise that
the Cardinal would be sure to gain the day. The
Governor called together the Council of the city, presiding himself as grand chancellor, in order to decide
matters according to his own will. From this meeting
were absent many of the principal decurions,[1] and those
who did attend, partly from interested motives, partly
because they had not the courage to make any opposition, were induced to elect the creatures of the Governor for the embassy, one of whom was his chief
counsellor, who opposed the Cardinal so much. When
this proceeding was made known it caused great displeasure in the whole city, as every one took it ill as
being unable to show their resentment. The people
complained that their city, which had always been
most loyal to their archbishops, should now be compelled
to send envoys to oppose so holy a pastor, to whom
they were under infinite obligations. The Cardinal
was immediately informed of these measures, and received a copy of the letter of instructions which the
ambassadors were taking with them. He was deeply
grieved, not on his own account, but because his enemies
allowed themselves to be so blinded by their passions,
and that the city should be supposed to consent to an
injustice so damaging to its reputation; for although
in nowise blameworthy, yet the report of what had
been done in its name would be bruited abroad.

These envoys left for Rome in the beginning of the
year 1580, causing much talk throughout the country.
A rumour was spread about by the evil disposed that the

---

[1] The sixty members of the Council were so called.

Cardinal would not return again to Milan, and i
far gained belief that even in Rome it was consid(
to be certain, for it was said that the Pope would n
him Cardinal-Vicar.   On being asked by one of
household if this report were true, the Saint rep
that he would rather resign the cardinalate than al
don the souls which God had committed to his cha
Satan thought it would be to his advantage to spi
such a report, but as some good religious report,
rumour was of great benefit to the city of Rome,
no sooner was it noised abroad, than about a d(
notorious courtesans took their departure without w
ing for the publication of a decree, so high was
reputation for virtue and sanctity.

The Pope in the meantime had gone to Palo on
sea coast where he sent for the Saint, who wishe(
give His Holiness information of the embassy, to n
excuses for the city and point out the author of
mischief.   They had various discussions togethei
to the best way of receiving and dismissing the env
A letter was written to them, and it was decided
the Cardinal should leave Rome immediately after t
arrival, the Pope commissioning him to pass thro
Venice to conclude important business with
republic.

Before leaving Palo, the saint wrote to Nic
Galerio, Canon of Padua, his vicar-general at Mi
to have the edicts again published, especially thos(
the sanctification of festivals, and the observanc(
the first Sunday of Lent, in order that the pe
might not think they had been suppressed, and

they were at liberty to renew their bacchanalian disorders at the next carnival.

Hearing of the arrival of the envoys, he returned
to Rome together with His Holiness, and brought his
household the next day for the Pope's blessing. Having
obtained an audience for the ambassadors at the same
time, he introduced them himself to the Pope, explaining to His Holiness the high position they held in the
service of His Catholic Majesty. With the Pope's
blessing he then retired, leaving them at liberty to
accomplish their mission without prejudice. On the
next day there was a consistory, at which he attended,
and there took leave of all the cardinals, not to lose
time by visiting them at their dwellings. The consistory being ended, he rode to the house of the Cardinal
of Vercelli, in the Borgo, near St. Peter's, and there
received the visit of all the sacred college, and of the
ambassadors themselves, who were displeased at his
departure, considering that it was a slight to themselves, when another would have stayed to defend
himself. They prevailed upon the Cardinal of Como
and Alciato to try and induce him to remain, saying
that he appeared to have little consideration for the
city of Milan, which they represented, the more so as
they protested that they desired nothing more than
the accomplishment of his wishes. They had a wily
motive in saying this, in order to detain him, that by
his presence in Milan he might not prevent a relaxation of his edicts, which they had planned in case of
his absence; and moreover, because they had boasted
that they would keep him in Rome, and that he should

never go back to Milan. He heard this request
great humility, and replied that he had great
tion for his city, that he wished to start under
circumstances, leaving them more at liberty for
mission, that he would offer them no opposition
submit entirely to the decision of His Holiness,
ever orders he might give.

The poor men did not know that their bus
had been already considered and decided, and
they were to receive the due reward of their pres
tion. We see clearly here how Satan blinds the
men of the world who devote themselves to pc
without piety and the fear of God, and leads the
commit egregious mistakes to their own prejudice
dishonour. Such was the case of these envoys,
became a byeword among the people under the
of "Carnival ambassadors." The Saint did not
to waste time in discussion with them, but too!
leave with kind words, and quitted Rome that mo
for Venice.

Note on page 90.—" The Cardinal of Sens."

Nicholas de Pellevé, Professor of Canon Law in the Univer
Bourges, made Cardinal by St. Pius V. in 1570, Archbishop of
afterwards of Rheims. Was present at the later sessions of the (
of Trent. Died 1594, at Paris.

Note on page 91.—" Cardinal Guastavillani."

Philip Guastavillani, Cardinal Deacon, 1574; died 1587.

CHAPTER III.

THE Saint was quite as much honoured on his departure as he had been on his entrance into Rome, being accompanied by many cardinals, prelates, and great numbers of people who followed in sorrow as if their father was leaving them taking the heart of every one with him. When he reached Florence, he was heartily welcomed by the Grand Duke Francis, who considered himself as his son. He remained there a few days to transact important business. He was compelled to satisfy the devotion of many who wished to receive communion, which he gave them at the Church of the Jesuit Fathers. So great were the numbers that he had difficulty in finishing in one morning. He praised the piety of the Florentines, but found fault with the fine dresses of the ladies.

From thence he went to Ferrara, sending his chamberlain before him, in order not to take the Duke Alphonso d'Este by surprise, as he wished to stay a short time there. It was in the month of February, when all were preparing for the carnival;

but the Duke, when he heard that the Cardinal wa:
his way, withdrew the permission which he had gi
for the commencement of festivities, and forbade
masking and other pastimes while the Cardinal
mained there. He then went to meet him, and rece:
him with great joy, treating him as a royal guest du
the three days of his stay, which were spent
the Saint in visits to the churches, in preaching
giving communion to many thousand persons,
duchess herself with all her ladies setting the exam
All were astonished to see such a change all at (
on the arrival of this servant of God, the days se
ing like those in Holy Week.

At his departure for Venice, the Duke accompa
him to the vessel which he had placed at his disp(
secretly ordering another to follow with every
paration and provision for supper, for the Card
was sailing by night. As soon as he discovere(
knowing that many of the Duke's household wer(
board, he gave orders for supper to be served, in o
not to take them any further. Early in the mor:
he reached Chioggia in the Venetian territory, w.
he said Mass in presence of the whole population.
entered Venice privately, alighting at the hous(
the Papal Nuncio. He had hardly arrived when
report of it was spread throughout the city, and sh(
came the Doge in the Bucentaur, accompanied by
senate, to visit him, in especial compliment to :
The Venetian Republic, always noted for its sple
receptions, seemed determined to keep up its rep
tion for magnificence, receiving him in grand style,

supplying him with everything at their own expense. During the nine days of his stay he had more than twenty persons at his table every day; not that he liked it, but because he did not wish to refuse the favours conferred by the state, and knew how to accommodate himself to all times, places, and circumstances, and to reap spiritual gain from them. Many of the principal men accompanied him to visit the Doge, and found, to their astonishment, that all the roads were crowded with people, and all the canals with gondolas, so that they could hardly make their way; he could scarcely mount the stairs of the palace for the multitudes anxious to behold him, even the roofs being crowded. The Doge and senate welcomed him with honour and affection, and then withdrew to treat of the business of his commission from the Pontiff. The complimentary visits required by his rank and position being over, he went to visit the churches and sacred relics in which the city abounded, and was presented with some of great value, which he took with him to Milan.

There were in Venice at this time about sixteen bishops and church dignitaries, who, although they did not before appear in clerical attire, now were all seen as bishops and prelates in the proper habit of their rank, the people being greatly surprised at so unusual a sight, remarking that so many priests had never been seen in Venice before, as hitherto they had not been publicly known as such. He particularly urged the clergy of the city and a congregation of regulars who have a college there to adopt the square clerical

berretta instead of the round one. The bishops
exhorted to reside at their sees and not to abs
themselves without good reason, and he asked
Holy Father to send orders to that effect. By requ
he gave general communion at the Jesuit church,
preached at the wish of the Patriarch and Apost
Nuncio; and although it was the Thursday after Se
gesima Sunday, commonly called " Giovedi grasso,"
crowding of the churches was so great that it seer
like Easter Day, not a single person being seen wit
mask in public.

When invited to visit the arsenal, he at first
clined, considering it a mere matter of curiosity au
loss of time, but on being shown the inscription c
the entrance, " For the defence of the Catholic fai
and told that it ought to be seen by every pious ;
son, he gave way and went over the whole place, be
pleased to see such a store of arms and ammunitior

As he had proposed to make a visitation of Bres
a city in the dominions of Venice, he asked
authorities to forward his wishes, which they w
glad to do. From the willingness of the Venetians
give up their worldly amusements, in order to att
to piety and devotion during the few days he had b
in their city, he anticipated great benefit would a
from an Episcopal visitation, and wrote strongly
His Holiness, asking him to send thither the Bis
of Verona, Augustine Valerio, after he had finis
the visitation of Dalmatia.

He took his departure from Venice on the
of Quinquagesima Sunday, accompanied by m

dignitaries, among whom was the Bishop of Padua, Frederick Cornaro, afterwards Cardinal, with whom he stopped the following day, preaching in his cathedral, and giving communion to a great number of persons.

From Padua he went on to Vicenza, where he was met by the Bishop and inhabitants, who begged him to stay till the following day, which was Tuesday, the day of the carnival, in order that they might all make a spiritual carnival by going to confession and communion. He entreated them to excuse him, as he had to be at Milan on the following Saturday to keep the first Sunday of Lent there, promising them that at Mass on the morrow he would give them a discourse, and communion to all who were prepared for it. The priests had to remain in the confessionals all night hearing the confessions of the people, who filled the cathedral in the morning to hear his Mass and sermon and to go to communion, seeming entirely to forget that it was carnival day.

As his friend the Bishop of Verona was still absent on his visitation in Dalmatia, he determined to proceed without stopping there, as he was pressed for time. But a prelate who saw him passing through, went in haste to the gate to warn the soldiers on guard to raise the drawbridge and not allow Cardinal Borromeo to pass over. To the Saint's entreaties to be allowed to pass that evening, it being about five o'clock, the porter replied that he had orders not to open it to any one under pain of death. In the meantime the lords of the city and a great concourse of people came with complaints at his hurrying away so

quickly, without blessing the city by his prese
Although he made many apologies, and begged to
allowed to continue his journey, they would not yi
so that he was obliged to go back and stay at
Bishop's house. So great was the delight of
people when they heard of his consent, that it q
drove from their minds the carnival in which t
had all been occupied shortly before. The next
being Ash Wednesday, he said Mass before daybr
and gave the blessed ashes to the people; and a
was still dark when he finished, he was escorted
of the city on the road to Brescia by torchlight.

The Brescians being apprised of his coming, v
comed him with all honour and reverence as the A
bishop of the province. He stayed three days
make arrangements for the visitation of the city
diocese which he wished to hold shortly. Here
began to hear the voices of his beloved Milanese, v
were impatiently expecting him, notwithstanding
false reports of his enemies as to his never ag
returning. He had no sooner passed Martinengo t
he met many of his flock who had set out to n
him.

There was a still greater demonstration in the ev
ing at Triviglio, where he passed the night; for all
inhabitants rushed out to see him, tears falling f
their eyes for joy, the church bells being rung a
for a festival. When he left in the morning, all
people accompanied him on the way, praising God
his happy return.

When he reached Pozzolo, twelve miles from Mi

he found entire confraternities and schools meeting him in procession ; the nearer he came to the city, the greater was the concourse, so that he was obliged to go slowly for the crowds—every one seeking to touch his garments, his boots, or his mule, tears flowing from all eyes so abundantly that they would have melted a stone ; for the people, not being able to express their joy, made their eyes supply the defect of their tongues. It was considered wonderful that his mule, at other times so restive, seemed then to sympathise with the people, letting them touch and press against him without kicking. Among the rest was a lady who went out two miles to meet him, who no sooner saw him than, forgetting decorum and the danger to which she was exposed, cast herself at the mule's feet, sobbing aloud out of the fulness of her heart. Seeing these extraordinary marks of affection, the Saint could scarcely refrain himself from tears.

As he approached the city gates all the bells of the churches rang out as a sign of his arrival, and men and women, old and young, of every condition, went forth to meet him. The streets were soon so full of people that they crushed and stifled one another, not without damage to the shopkeepers, who could not keep them off, not even with naked weapons.

The saint had great difficulty in reaching the cathedral, and much more in getting to his own house. Tears were shed in floods, and voices were heard crying, " Our Cardinal is come, who was never to return, as they said ; it is not true that the Pope has made him his Vicar-General at Rome ; we shall hear his

sermons again, we shall receive Holy Commu
from his hands, we shall have the consolation ol
blessing."

These were the words spoken by the Milanes
the general rejoicing, showing how false were
calumnies of his enemies, who had said publicly,
in writing and by word of mouth, that he was h
and disliked. At length he reached the cathedral,
returned thanks to God for his happy return ; and ;
giving his blessing to his beloved flock, he with(
to his apartments to receive the Governor, senate,
magistrates the next day.

Note on page 100.—" Sixteen Bishops."

The Saint enumerates them in a letter to Speciano at Rome.
Patriarch of Aquileia says that he cannot go back to his See on ac
of the controversy about the pallium. . . . The Bishop of Feltri ;
that the Supreme Pontiff has given him leave of absence. . .
Bishop of Chioggia says he cannot live in his diocese on account
poverty. . . . Laibach and Spalatro allege that their Sees have no
of them. . . . Concordia, Cydonia, and Belluno plead ill health.
Traou and Curzola law suits. . . . Torcello the nearness of his See.

Note on page 101.—" The Arsenal."

The famous show-place of Venice. The keel of a war vessel wa
there and finished within a day for the delectation of Henry III. of F
in 1573. When the Prince of Saxony visited it in 1740 a galley was
and launched in an hour's time.—Stirling Maxwell's *Don Jo(
Austria*, i. p. 360.

CHAPTER IV.

EVENTS AT MILAN: DISMISSAL OF THE MILANESE ENVOYS
BY THE POPE.

1580.

IT must not be supposed that St. Charles was allowed
by Satan to remain long at peace, God suffering it to
be so, lest public applause should give rise to self-
complacency, and that continual mortification might
lift him to a higher degree of sanctity. As the envoys
met with delays in Rome, in order to assert their claims
more vigorously, and to show that the decrees were
not accepted in Milan, letters were despatched by them
to the Governor, begging him to order the festivities
and tournaments as usual on the first Sunday of Lent
in order to assert their rights. The Governor accordingly invited many knights and gentlemen of the city
to take part in them, feeling sure of having an imposing celebration. Among the Milanese, however,
who had been extremely displeased at the embassy
sent to Rome, no one could be found to transgress the
orders of the Cardinal, or again to profane the Sunday.
The Governor, in order to avoid the shame of a defeat,
and to carry out the request of the ambassadors, ordered

one of the captains to bring up his company from P
where they were in garrison, to tilt in the games.
was done in spite of the penalty of excommunic:
incurred *ipso facto*, as before mentioned.

When the Saint on his arrival heard of the G
nor's preparations, he directed that the usual ge:
communion should be announced in the cathedral
other churches of the city, in order to gain the ple
indulgence. He was himself in the church at an
hour, and having said Mass, gave communion tc
people, and did not finish till two o'clock in the
though he was assisted by the canons who gave
munion at different altars, he could scarcely satisf
multitude, and would willingly have continued till n
fall had he not been obliged to stop short to sing Ves
The communion being ended without any rest, he
Pontifical High Mass, and then ascended the p
to preach, the people thronging the cathedral to
flowing.

In that address, which was the most earnest I
heard from him, he was particularly affected on g
the people the blessing of the Supreme Pontiff,
explaining the importance of the benediction of
Vicar of Christ, and in bestowing it he made u:
the words of Moses in blessing the people of Isra
God's name: "Blessed shalt thou be in the city
blessed shalt thou be in the field," [1] &c., whicl
uttered with such feeling that no one could re
from tears.

But in the square outside, combatants in n

[1] Deut. xxviii. 3.

were incurring the penalties of the Church in the presence of the Governor and his family. At this very
moment trumpets sounded so loudly that they echoed
through the cathedral, drowning the Cardinal's voice.
I was present at the time, and afraid that this uproar
would disconcert him, narrowly watched him; but he
only stopped and raised his eyes to heaven, and continued
his sermon with greater fervour. The offices on that
day did not end till the Ave in the evening, the Saint
having been in the church from twilight to twilight
without leaving it, thronged as it was all day long.

This incident wounded him to see how little heed
was paid to the censures of the Church, purposely
defied to the scandal of the public, to God's dishonour,
and to the destruction of those poor souls who in the
hardness of their hearts were publicly encouraged to
incur them. He was more deeply pained, as the evil
was prompted by one who ought to have worked with
him and aided in the spiritual government of a state
whose King was so zealous for the salvation of his
subjects. Holding the place of God as pastor, he felt
compelled to take measures to prevent such scandalous
excesses in future, and accordingly after due consultation he denounced, by word of mouth and writing, all
those who had taken part in the tournaments or had
ordered or encouraged them, as well as those who had
been present at them, and forbade them to enter the
churches, that all who had committed so grievous a
sin should be anxious to free themselves from the
censures they had incurred. The result was that
those who had been induced to be present at the

tilting-match, and among them some of the Gover:
family, begged for absolution from the excommuj
tion. Some of the combatants likewise did the s
and because they had asked for absolution wit
the Governor's leave, were put in prison by hin
was also the printer of the notices of excomm
cation for printing the same. The Governor's
declined to go on the Sunday, though she had
present the previous evening, and as one who had
fear of God before her eyes reproached her husk
begging him not to allow such a scandal to take pl
she had likewise entreated her sons not to be pre
but they paid little heed to her admonitions.

There was a Spanish Capuchin monk, Father I
preaching at that time in the cathedral, who repr
the Governor in private, and exhorted him to con
how grievous a sin it was to despise the prelat€
the Church and treat their censures with disdai
the source of every evil, of heresies, and the rui
kingdoms. In a sermon he publicly denounced
sin, and reproved those confessors who, in orde
gain the favour of princes, foster their evil inten
though contrary to ecclesiastical discipline. " If t
religious," he said, " who have the direction of
sciences, possess the Spirit of God and would
their chief pastors all would be well, and we sh
not see such scandals among Christian people a
behold nowadays ; for they would then strive to
men united in loyalty to their rulers and obediei
their commands."

I remember that when this zealous Father e:

his reproof, he said that his habit and profession bound
him to speak the truth, and that if he should be beaten
to death for it as soon as he left the pulpit, he should
consider it the greatest gain he could receive in
this life. His words produced a good effect, for the
prisoners were immediately released; and the Apostolic Jubilee being then published, the guilty were
absolved from the censures; which was all their pastor
desired, viz., to lead men to acknowledge their sins and
amend their lives. However, this did not save the captain
of the tournament from punishment for his defiance of
the Church; for, being within a few months thrown into
prison for certain misdeeds, he found means of escaping
to Lugano in the Swiss territory, and there was unfortunately murdered—a warning to all to reverence
their pastors and take heed to their censures.

In the meantime the ambassadors in Rome were
making every effort to obtain a decision in their favour;
but His Holiness proceeded with circumspection, consulting persons of experience, and noting down with
his own hand the reasons and replies that inclined
him to sanction the Cardinal's decrees, which finally
as Vicar of God he approved and confirmed as to
be observed by all. This answer displeased the
ambassadors, who found themselves disappointed in
their hopes and obliged to go back in disgrace. They
uttered loud complaints, saying that the Milanese
ought not to be forced more than any others to obey
laws that were not observed elsewhere, not even in
Rome itself. The Pope paid no attention to these
murmurs, except that in Rome he prohibited the custom

of running races and other games during the carni
and went himself to make the visits of the se
churches, accompanied by the cardinals, in order
set good example, and to take away all cause of c
plaint from the ambassadors, to whom he gave leav
departure with his apostolic blessing, and a brief
reply to the city in the following terms :—

"POPE GREGORY XIII.—Beloved children, he
and the apostolic blessing. From your letters rece:
at different times, and from the statement of your
bassadors, we have learnt everything relating to
decrees of our beloved son Charles, Cardinal of
Praxedes, your pastor, that you wished us to kr
and which you deem important for the city and
vince. You do well to recognise his integrity
zeal for the glory of God in restoring and maintai
ecclesiastical discipline, for in this way you are bea
your witness to his virtue, and by rejoicing in tl
manifest your piety and fear of God. 'They who
thee shall see me,' says the Prophet; and this
will bring you to share in the same crown as :
pastor, according to the promise of God to Abrah
'I will bless those who bless thee, and I will c
those who curse thee.'

"Although your opinion and that of all good
gives us no reason to suppose that your pastor w
make any order contrary to right and justice, ye
take in good part the complaints you bring befor
and commend you for informing us of them and
mitting them to our judgment as children devote
this see and beloved by us.

" In compliance with your request, having examined
with the greatest care all the questions propounded,
we consider that the observance of the decrees will be
of great benefit to you, and we exhort you to obey
them with a ready mind, not only refraining from
opposing them in any way, but with all your power
aiding to carry them into execution, as we have
explained to the Cardinal himself. We are aware
that they may appear somewhat hard at first, but with
good will, which every one should pray with confidence to obtain from God, they will become sweet
and easy. Narrow and strait is the way to heaven
when we look at our fallen nature, but in the grace of
God the yoke of the Lord is easy. When habit is
joined to a willing mind, those things will be found
light which at first seemed heavy. Above all, the
great charity of your pastor ought to console you, who
only looks to the salvation of the flock committed to
him by God, valuing it more than his own life, as you
have clearly seen. Place yourselves, therefore, in his
hands, which you have found in times of danger ever
ready to be employed for your salvation, disposing
yourselves to obedience to a pastor who loves you so
much, and be assured that in so doing you are fulfilling your duty and acting in a manner most pleasing to
God, and will enjoy that peace of Christ our Lord
which we all so earnestly desire."

The ambassadors, knowing the tenor of this brief,
would not present it themselves for very shame: it
was sent by other means, and was not opened till the
year 1602, when it was placed in the hands of Mgr.

Antonio Albergato, Bishop of Bisceglia, at one t
Vicar-General of Milan, who was collecting docum(
for the canonisation of St. Charles, by Giulio Ce:
Coiro, collegiate doctor of Milan, Vicar provisiona.
the time the brief was sent from Rome, in order (
it might be inserted in the process as an additi(
evidence of the sanctity of the servant of God.
copy of it was sent, which was read in the counci
the city to the great consolation of all its memb
who loved and revered their holy Cardinal, and wis
all his orders to be obeyed. It was afterwards p
lished throughout the city to the great joy of all (
had been displeased by the doings of the Envoys[1] (
had brought reproach upon the city without faul
its own.

We may see in this way how the wiles of Satan
defeated by the hand of God, and that although
permits tribulations to fall upon His servants,
in the end He makes known to all their sanct
Wretched are those who, blinded by the same devi
are led to persecute their pastors who serve God (
all their hearts; they end their lives miserably, (
leave behind them but a sorry memory. Happy,
the contrary, will be those bishops and pastors of s(
who do not lose heart amid difficulties and opposit
in reforming their flocks; for those who labour wit
right intention are never abandoned by God.

---

[1] The two envoys, or "carnival ambassadors," were Count P
Antonio Lonato and Camillo Trotto, both creatures of Ayamonte.

CHAPTER V.

VISITATION OF THE DIOCESE OF BRESCIA, DEATH OF THE
GOVERNOR OF MILAN, SEVENTH DIOCESAN SYNOD.

1580.

AFTER the beginning of Lent, St. Charles returned to
Brescia to begin his visitation. He took with him
but eight assistants, in order not to lay too heavy a
burden upon the city. The people made great preparations to receive him, having raised triumphal
arches and decorated the streets with royal magnificence. He was welcomed by the Bishop and clergy,
together with the nobility and people of the city,
with such demonstrations of universal joy as testified
the delight of the citizens. The Saint began with a
solemn High Mass in the cathedral, when he explained
to the people the object and importance of the visitation, entreating all to strive to obtain due benefit from
it, and gave communion to great numbers of people,
finishing the visitation in Holy Week. He went back
to Milan for Palm Sunday and Easter Day, and at
that time paid a visit to the Governor, hoping it might
be productive of benefit to him by leading him to
acknowledge his wrongdoings in the matter of the

ecclesiastical censures, so great was his desire to
his soul. It seemed that the Governor was trou
at this exhortation, for raising his eyes to heaven
is too much," he said, "to require of the Milanese
is not done elsewhere?" thus showing what a
impression had been made upon his mind, tha
should be so indisposed to obedience. Yet as
lieutenant of the Catholic king,—who was so des
that all his subjects should fear God as good (
tians, shown by his letter on the death of his ε
son,—he ought to have been glad to aid the .
bishop in banishing abuses which led to many
and in helping men along the road to heaven.

The Governor thanked the Cardinal for his pat
admonitions, and paid him more honour than
at his departure, as if he had a presentiment that
would be his last visit; for he shortly afterwards
an attack of fever, which carried him off in a few
at the time the Saint was on his way to Br
Learning that he was on his deathbed, the Car
returned with all speed and found him in his a
breathing with great difficulty, as if he could
die. His struggles ceased, to the astonishmei
the bystanders, with the arrival of the Cardinal,
assisted him to make a good death, and afterv
said Mass for the repose of his soul, and accomp
his body to the grave, preaching upon death and
wretched condition of human things.

Before he went back to Brescia he held his se·
diocesan synod on the 20th of April, and thou
lasted three days as usual, there were no decrees ɪ

but those of the fourth and fifth Provincial Councils
were read which he had brought with the Papal confirmation from Rome. At this synod he delivered
four sermons to the clergy, a perfect compendium of
discipline and good observance. To the usual mental
prayer he daily added a prayer for the kingdom of
Portugal, for which intention he also had a general
procession on the 26th of September following, to
obtain the blessing of God and deliver it from war and
tumult.

He then spent some time in continuing his visitation of Brescia, as it was a large and populous diocese,
but was frequently interrupted by other business to
which he had to attend; he was not in consequence
able to finish it until the following year, 1581. He
first visited the city, banishing all abuses and bad
customs, and introducing a wholesome reform in discipline, which he did not find difficult on account
of the good-will of the people, who were so devoted
to him that they gladly obeyed his slightest wish.
Wherever he went, he was followed by great numbers
of people, some kissing his garments, others touching
him with their rosaries as is the custom with the relics
of the saints.

His fatigue was great in giving communion, both on
account of the devotion of the people and a plenary
indulgence granted at the time, there being as great
a concourse as at the season of a jubilee.

Discovering that there were in the Castle of Brescia
the bodies of four sainted bishops, and that of St.
Dominator in particular, which were not receiving the

honour due to them, as access to the fortress was
permitted, he thought it better to transfer them to
cathedral in accordance with the wish of the peo
Permission was asked of the government at Ver
where there was a long discussion of the subject;
although they were unwilling to deprive themselve
such treasures, the authority of the Saint prevaile
far that they could not oppose his wishes. He 1
made the translation with great solemnity to
cathedral, where the people could more convenie
have recourse to their intercession.

He also endeavoured to settle the question of
relics of SS. Faustinus and Jovita, martyrs and
tectors of the city, in order to put an end to a 1
troversy between two religious bodies, each claim
the possession of them for their church. The ca
was tried, but as it took much time, was not decic
however, the relics are supposed to be preserved
the church of the Cassinese congregation of Bene
tines.

This diocese includes the important valley ca
Camonica, extending to the confines of the territor,
the Grisons, many parts of which, being wild
uncultivated, are difficult of access, and in a bad s
as regards morals and the worship of God. The cle
especially observed no discipline, and set a very
example, sorely needing correction. But the Vene
rulers doubted whether the Saint's visit might not l
to disturbances, the inhabitants being so ill-dispo
They therefore wrote to the Pope, begging him
desire the Cardinal not to visit the valley him

but to send some prelate from their own dominion. His Holiness replied that as the Cardinal had great prudence, he left it to his decision. St. Charles, knowing the state of the valley, where, on account of the neighbourhood of heretics, greater freedom was allowed from fear of insurrection, decided not only to visit the district himself, but to spend some time there, in order that he might be able to do more good among those poor souls. Making his visitation, therefore, in the spirit of compassion, he endeavoured to show the clergy and people how little their lives were conformed to the laws of the gospel, and that the churches were not treated with the respect due to the houses of God. So great was the efficacy of his words in addition to the holiness of his life, that a general conversion took place; all his decrees were obeyed, and the sacraments received with such devotion that he often said he never had greater consolation. They strewed his path with flowers to show the love they bore him, and he had such influence among them, that many of the clergy who had grown old in open concubinage and other sins, which from custom were thought nothing of by the people, came freely to his feet to disclose their wounds, determined to save their souls. The Saint willingly received them with these signs of true amendment, and absolved them from these grievous sins. Such cases were so frequent that the Cardinal, astonished at the confidence they placed in him, asked them what had moved them to confess their iniquities, of which he had no knowledge. "We desire," they said, " to change our lives and to be reconciled to God,

for we could not find a better time, nor a fathe
pastor more merciful, who seeks not money, nor
nor milk as others, but only the salvation of our s
The good pastor was greatly consoled by this ge
and thorough conversion, saying that he had
made a more satisfactory visitation.

A remarkable circumstance happened as he
passing through Plano in this valley, where the p
were under interdict and forbidden to enter the cl
because they refused to pay the usual tithes t
Bishop. As the Cardinal passed through, they a
out to see him, wishing to get his blessing; b
placed his hand on his breast and would bless
of them. Deeming they were deprived of a
treasure, they ran after him, weeping and cryin
pity, begging him not to leave them without gra
the boon. As he wished them to acknowledge
fault, he paid no attention to them, telling the
obey their Bishop and pay their tithes. He after
sent Mgr. John Baptist Centurione, Bishop of Ma
in Corsica, who accompanied him in this visitati
learn his method of discipline, to exhort them
their duty, promising his blessing on his return.
prelate was an eloquent preacher : his sermon
such an effect upon the people that they pai
tithes, and the Bishop freed them from the interc

The Cardinal stopped there on his return t
Mass, when he preached to them and gave ther
blessing they desired.

CHAPTER VI.

IN THE VALTELLINE: STATE OF THE CATHOLIC
.ITH IN DISTRICTS INFECTED BY HERESY.

1580.

Grison district, bordering on the Camonica
s the Valtelline, where there is a church
l to our Blessed Lady, called Santa Maria of
 place of great resort in those parts, a con-
ncourse of the faithful flocking thither from
arts on account of the graces received from
ugh the intercession of His Holy Mother.
harles, having great devotion to our Lady,
 to visit this church as it was only fifteen
tant. He wished at the same time to make
on of the district, which was much infected
 heresy of Calvin, in order to try what he
 to root it out, and to make the way easy for
)p of Como, to whose diocese it belongs. He
:en on the subject to the Supreme Pontiff,
 therefore full authorisation. The people of
earing that he was travelling in those parts,
)ys to beg that he would by no means fail to
a, and to favour them with a discourse, assur-

ing him that he would be very willingly listened
even by the heretics themselves. Before he set (
he asked permission of the Bishop of Como to pre:
the word of God, and in a short cassock, with a s
in his hand like a pilgrim, he started with his att
dants, spending the whole time in vocal or mer
prayer, according to his custom during such journe;

He was so carried away by his fervour of spirit t
the others could not keep up with him unless some (
begged him to slacken his pace, and withal the road (
very difficult over a mountain called Zappelli[1] d'Aur:

On his way he beheld the sacred images disfigu
by the heretics, which grieved him much, and he
so ardent a desire to teach them better that on me
ing some peasants on the road he stopped to instr
them in Christian doctrine, exhorting them with infir
charity to live as good Catholics. When he ente
the valley he was met with great honour by the peo
of Tirano, especially by one of the chief persons
the place, Bernard Lambertengo, who, kneeling at
Saint's feet, humbly asked his blessing, and would
rise till he had received it, the Cardinal finding a, d
culty in giving it as he was not in his own jurisdict:
He begged the Saint to stay at his house, or at leas
dine with him the next day; but, the Cardinal re
ing that he must remain at the priest's house, he t
his refusal to heart, saying that some misfortune m
be falling on his house since it was unworthy to
blessed by his presence. Mgr. Centurione, moved
his tears, made him rise with the promise that

---

[1] Little spades or hoes.

Cardinal would come to him after visiting the church, where he remained in prayer a great part of the night before the miraculous image of our Lady, without taking any rest after so long a journey.

In the morning the mayor of the place, who was one of the heads of the province, paid his respects to him. A difficulty was made, however, about receiving him, as he was a heretic, but at the instance of the Catholics the objection was waived. With the usual compliments the mayor placed himself and the valley at the disposal of the Saint in the name of the authorities, and begged him to ask some favour. To which the Cardinal responded, that he desired nothing but the salvation of his soul. The mayor then through an interpreter said that he wished to speak to him in private, and on being taken aside hinted that he was well aware of his wretched state, and desired to return to the Catholic faith, that he would have done so before but for human respect, finally asking leave to hear his Mass. The Cardinal commended his good intentions, and begged him to put them into execution while there was time without regard to any one; as to his Mass, he could not give permission, but he might hear his sermon. On the mayor suggesting that there would be many heretics present, the Saint replied, that as he did not know them, he could not forbid them.

The report of the visit spreading throughout the valley, all the people of the place and the neighbouring mountains flocked to him, heretics as well as Catholics. He said Mass in our Lady's Church on Sunday the feast of St. Augustin, and after the Gospel

preached from the pulpit wearing his mitre, to ￼
astonishment of the congregation, who had never bef
seen a Cardinal. He began his sermon with th
words : " I am here in this pulpit with the permiss
of your pastor, the Bishop of Como," in order to sh
the respect that should be paid to prelates. The p
port of his discourse was to confirm Catholics in ￼
faith, and to enlighten heretics concerning the Cath
doctrines and the errors of false teachers. Many
ceived communion at his Mass; and as he sorrov
much over the needs of these parts, the greater ￼
his joy at finding faith there. Complying with ￼
request of Lambertengo, he went to his home, wh
among those who waited was a son of the house, thirt￼
years of age, deaf and dumb from his birth, who ser￼
the Cardinal, and made signs of displeasure if he s
any one else attending to him, showing such devot
ness that surprised every one.

The Saint was visited by many who entreated ￼
to remain a while in the valley, assuring him that
his presence and his sermons he would do great go
especially as the heretics were glad to see him ￼
did not forbid his stay, although there was a pul
decree prohibiting any foreign ecclesiastic, and e￼
the Bishop of Como, from any ministrations with￼
the permission of the authorities. He was not, h￼
ever, able to stay longer, having to finish his visitat
at Brescia before he returned to Milan, where imp
tant business was awaiting him on the Feast of ￼
Lady's Nativity; he therefore took leave of them ￼
returned to Valle Camonica.

CHAPTER VII.

CONTINUATION OF THE VISITATION OF THE DIOCESE
OF BRESCIA.

1580.

WHEN he had finished in Camonica, the Saint went on
to the Trompia valley, where he was well received, and
laboured with the same success as in other places.

From thence he passed on to the Sabbia valley,
where he spent many days in the salvation of souls
that anxiously awaited him. Going to the shore of
Lake Garda, he made his pontifical entry into Salò,
where he made a long stay, preaching and administering the sacraments, endeavouring to put an end to
long-standing feuds by reconciling those who were at
variance, and establishing peace among them. Hearing
that there was a very poor parish in the diocese,
situated amid the mountains, where the roads were
difficult, extending to the diocese of Trent, he was
anxious to make his way thither, hoping to find an
opportunity of doing good; and while passing through
that wild country, the mountaineers assembled from
every part to see him, as if something miraculous had
appeared among them, not so much on account of his

reputed sanctity, as because they had never before se
cardinal or prelate in those barren mountains. On l
return, when visiting Liano, he was told that near tl
church of that place there was a stone chest, with
which were some bones held in great veneration as tl
relics of saints. The general report was that on tl
night before the feast of St. Peter's chains, there issu
miraculously from these bones such a quantity
water that it filled the chest, and although mar
people of the neighbourhood came in·crowds to vis
the church, and to fetch away some of the wate
considering it miraculous, still it never diminished, tl
chest always remaining full. The Cardinal, who he
the relics of the saints in veneration, taking ca
to have them recognised and held in due reveren
wherever he found any,[1] set about investigating the
origin, but could ascertain nothing for certain. I
therefore began to suspect some trick, so to find o
the truth he directed the chest and the bones to l
wiped dry, and left in charge of three trustwortl
priests on the night the water was wont to flow. *
no sign of water appeared, it was clear there was son
deception. To prevent a recurrence of this, he he
the bones and the chest that held them buried, th
they should no longer be venerated, which increase
the general reverence for the Saint as one who he
the Spirit of God with him.

Of this a proof was afforded on two other occasio
—the first while he was visiting the district of Casti

---

[1] This gave rise to the saying that "Cardinal Borromeo would neith
let the living nor the dead be at rest."

lione delle Stiviere, a populous part of the country belonging to the Marquis Gonzaga. In the month of July 1580, he was invited by the Marquis to lodge in his palace of La Rocca. But being on visitation, he would not depart from his custom of taking up his abode in priests' houses only, and stopped in the arch-priest's house, where many gentlemen went to call upon him. Among them was a youth of twelve years of age, Luigi, the eldest son of the Marquis Ferrante Gonzaga, brother of the present Marquis Francesco. Discovering in this boy, through the divine light with which he was endowed, signs of great virtue, and that he would one day be a saintly priest, he had long private conversations with him upon the things of God: as Luigi, although so young, was intelligent and well-disposed, he endeavoured to impress upon him the perfection of the spiritual life, and the way to serve God well. Finding that he had not yet made his first communion, he exhorted him not only to do so as soon as possible, but also to receive frequently that heavenly food as the proper nourishment of the soul, and the only means of loving God and being united to Him. He gave him, too, a short rule for preparing for that holy duty, so as to reap abundant fruit. He recommended him frequently to read the Roman Catechism, which he had had printed, in order to learn the ecclesiastical style of Latin, and what was more to the purpose, the salutary doctrine contained in it. It was a singular favour from God that this devout child should have such an opportunity of disclosing his thoughts, and all the interior graces infused into him by God to such

a holy man. The youth received his warnings a
paternal instructions with a firm determination to
guided by them, and God bestowed grace so abundan
upon his soul at his tender age, that he was batl
in tears on approaching the sacraments of confess
and holy communion. He made such progress in
spiritual life, that of his own free will he renoun
all the delights of the world and his paternal estai
to which, as eldest son, he was heir at his fath
death, and entered the Society of Jesus, where
advanced so rapidly in perfection that when he d
at twenty-three years of age, he left behind a h
opinion of his sanctity. As his death was followed
many miracles wrought by God through his intercessi
the Holy See allowed his life to be published with
title of Blessed in the fourteenth year after his dece
by a brief of the Supreme Pontiff, Paul V., r
reigning.

At this time he put into execution a pious wish
had entertained of visiting Roano. He had previou
discovered in Count Frederick Borromeo, his cou
who is now Cardinal, great virtue and ability, and
slight inclination for a good life. According to te
mony quoted in the preliminary examination of
life of the Saint, St. Charles foresaw through a sup
natural light that this Count Frederick would w
the ecclesiastical habit and be a great prelate in
Church of God. The Saint resolved, therefore,
undertake the care of his education, as since the de
of his father, Count Giulio Cesare, the youth had b
left in charge of his mother, Marguerita Trivi

Borromeo, and Count Renato, his elder brother. As
the saint never did anything of consequence without
taking the advice of others, he consulted with Moneta
and Seneca, who were with him in his visitation, and
took this step not from any motives of near relationship, but because he foresaw that the youth would
become a priest, and one day a great benefactor of
the Church of Milan, and that he would some time be
its Archbishop.   Both Moneta and Seneca approved
of his intention, and urged him by all means to carry
it into effect.   As Count Frederick was then studying
at Bologna, he sent for him, and upon his expressing
his intention of becoming a priest, he gave him the
cassock and the tonsure with his own hand.   After
having examined him in spiritual things, he sent him
to study at the Borromean College in Pavia, giving
him as a guide in spiritual matters, a priest who was
a doctor of theology.   Frederick finished his course of
sacred theology there, and applied himself to the study
of the Greek and Hebrew languages with great profit,
as is well known to all.

Nor was the Cardinal's prediction a vain one, for
Frederick became as distinguished in learning as he
was in virtue.   Having been raised to the Cardinalate
by Pope Sixtus V. in his twenty-second year, he was
made Archbishop of Milan when thirty years of age
by Clement VIII., showing in that office how he had
profited by the example and teaching of his saintly
cousin.   Aware of the great responsibility of the Episcopal dignity, and considering himself unworthy of it
although imposed upon him by the Vicar of God, he

made every effort to escape it. Although His I
ness earnestly entreated him to undertake it,
employed persons of influence to persuade him to
so, and in particular his confessor, the Blessed Pl
Neri, a man of great sanctity of life, he could
bring himself to take the burden upon his shoul
without an express command from the Supreme Poi
But the greater the repugnance he felt at undertal
so weighty a charge, the greater was the joy of
Milanese when they heard the news. It seemed
if God had restored to them the saintly Archbis
deceased in the person of his living cousin, so g
was the rejoicing throughout the city. When
made his pontifical entry into Milan on the 28tl
August, 1595, the feast of St. Augustin, the conco
of people was greater than had ever been known,
devout people imagining they saw their saintly Card
restored to life again; and he has always been
sidered as a living relic of that holy Pastor,
trained him to his own spirit and virtues.

When the Saint had finished his visitation, he sta
at Tosculano on Lake Garda to draw up the ordinal
and decrees he had made. In the meantime prep:
tions were made for the translation of the body of
Herculanus, Bishop of Brescia, then reposing in
parish church of Maderno, a short distance off. W
ing to celebrate it with all possible solemnity,
invited all the clergy of the neighbourhood, toget
with two Bishops, viz., Francesco Cittadino, Bis
of Castro and Giacomo Rovellio of Salò, Bishop
Feltro. Before the ceremony the Saint fasted on br

and water, and as usual passed the preceding night in prayer.

We must not omit to mention, that having found the diocese of Brescia infested by four companies of banditti under well-known captains, who made great havoc among the inhabitants and travellers, not only carrying away their goods but often taking their lives, he felt an ardent desire to rescue the souls of the robbers and to deliver the country from such a plague. As there existed a mortal enmity between the captains of these companies, he undertook by means of letters and by word of mouth to reconcile them and establish peace. To bring them to a knowledge of their wretched state, he took an opportunity of conversing with Bertazzolo in Salò, with Sala in Asola, and also with the others, Chierico and Avogadro, with some good result.

It was surprising to see the great respect these lawless people paid to the Saint, and that they not only reverenced him but also rendered prompt obedience to his directions, not venturing to remain in church with their weapons, and laying them aside on going into his presence. One day when he was visiting a populous part of the country he chanced to meet Count Ottavio Avogadro, one of them, together with his band, who were all under an interdict, when the captain begged the favour of being allowed to hear his Mass and sermon. The Saint consented on condition that no one should carry arms in church. The Count ordered all his band to remain outside and he alone entered the church, for his personal security taking

his weapon with him, but laying it upon the
with his foot upon it out of obedience.

As the Cardinal was returning from Bres
Milan, he reached Martinengo about eight o'cl
night, and finding all the gates shut for fear of b
he was obliged to take shelter at an inn outsi
walls, where some of these outlaws had occupi
the rooms. Hearing of his arrival, they cleare
the best rooms for the Saint and his attendan
gave him a hearty welcome; at which he was
pleased, hoping to have an opportunity of ef
some good. He told his people to get their s
and go to bed, for he himself had found othei
more to his taste, meaning the conversion of
wretched men. Having retired to his room h
for their leader, and then for all the rest, one b
and they, laying down their arms, knelt down
him, and with all confidence gave him an acco
their unhappy state. With all charity he be
them to amend their lives, promising them ai
protection if they would but abandon their
ways. His words had such effect that thei
hearts were softened and filled with compu
and thus he passed the night in labouring fo
salvation. Calling them together the next m
he addressed them again to confirm them
promises they had made overnight. At his dej
they wished to accompany him on his way to
but that he would not allow, but took leave o
with his blessing. A great compassion for the
deeply impressed upon his heart, and he long con

to think and speak of some means of rescuing and directing them in God's ways. This affair was reported throughout Martinengo and other places, on account of the Cardinal's kindness to men accustomed to rapine and murder.

It was on this visit to Brescia that Jerome Luzzago, a gentleman of that place, having had proof of the Cardinal's sanctity, became so attached to him that he could not leave him, but accompanied him through the city and diocese. He was accustomed to use every means of obtaining what was left of the daily bread and water taken by the Saint, and was glad to be allowed to carry some of his clothes in his journeys. Hearing of his good qualities, St. Charles sent for him, and gave him leave to carry his cloak. This affection continued ever after, as was shown by the interchange of friendly offices between them. In the year 1602 he and his son Alexander came on purpose to visit the tomb of the Saint, and left many votive offerings there. During their long and frequent prayers there, Alexander was taken ill, and died at the Jesuit College of St. Fidelis; where Cardinal Frederick Borromeo assisted at his funeral, together with a great assemblage of clergy and people, on account of the general opinion of his holy life, devout persons touching his body with their rosaries. There was good reason for this reverence; for, among others, I have myself known him in Milan for nearly a year, and as he often came to see me, I had an opportunity of observing his sanctity.

The fruit of this visitation of the Cardinal was very

great, as were likewise his labours and fatigues.
rooted out many abuses and offences, both among cl‹
and laity, and introduced good discipline in their st
Mgr. Marino Georgi, the present Bishop of Bresci‹
a letter addressed to Cardinal Frederick Borro‹
dated October 1, 1608, begged him to assembl
Provincial Council in order to send a petition to
Supreme Pontiff to promote the canonisation of
Charles, in the name of the whole province of M‹
and bears his testimony in the following terms:—

"This church of Brescia was brought to a be
state of discipline by the labours of this most ‹
man, and furnished by him with excellent rules
decrees, which, on my appointment as Bishop, I fc
to be as beacons, and as the column of fire which ‹
before the Israelites by night."

Cardinal Morosini, who was also Bishop of Bre
was wont to say that his whole diocese was regul
by the holy decrees of Cardinal Borromeo, and tha
found his people so willing in their observance of t
that to trespass against them was considered a sin

CHAPTER VIII.

SETTLEMENT OF THE CAPUCHINS AND THE FATHERS OF THE SOCIETY OF JESUS IN SWITZERLAND.

1580.

AMID the multiplicity of his affairs the Saint always retained in his mind a recollection of Switzerland and its spiritual needs. As he was well aware how much good the Capuchin monks did among the people by the example of their lives, their continual prayers and sermons, full of apostolic zeal, he exerted himself to introduce them into that country after having assisted in founding several monasteries of the Order in his own diocese. He first consulted with some of the heads of the Cantons, and induced them, by means of Mgr. Bonomo, the Apostolic Nuncio, to ask the favour of the Supreme Pontiff and the General of the Order; and as he had himself spoken of the needs of that country to the authorities when he was in Rome the preceding year, they obtained their desire. On Ascension Day, 1580, he sent, at his own expense, Father Bormio, a good religious, together with John Ambrose Fornero and another, to the Catholic Cantons, to found there a house of the Order. They were

kindly received by Colonels Lusio and Rolli, friei
of the Cardinal, and faithful to the Holy Aposto
See. These Fathers built a church and monastery
Altorf, and they induced others to follow their examp
so that they now have thirteen monasteries, w
numerous members, and more than thirty preache
who have laboured with signal effect in rooting out t
heresies that were creeping into the Cantons. Wis
ing that they should also hear confessions, in order
be of greater assistance to the people in the dea1
of good confessors, the Saint appealed to the Pope
dispense them from the rule of not hearing the confe
sions of seculars, which favour was promptly granted
His Holiness, and was of great benefit to the people

In like manner he introduced the Fathers of t
Society of Jesus, in order to increase the number
good priests, and to bestow upon the country t
advantage of schools and well-trained masters. T
colleges were founded, one at Lucerne, the other
Fribourg, with public schools, which were bulwai
against the introduction of heresy into Italy.

CHAPTER IX.

MISSION OF FATHER CHARLES BASCAPÈ TO SPAIN—
A NEW DIFFICULTY AS TO ECCLESIASTICAL JURIS-
DICTION.

1581.

ST. CHARLES at this time was still suffering from the
determined opposition of the secular power to his rights
and jurisdiction, in restoring discipline, and reforming
his people. He was well aware that the intention of
the King of Spain was most upright, that he was far
from wishing wrong to be done to the Church; that,
on the contrary, he was desirous that all her rights
should be respected, and that all his subjects should
live in obedience to the Divine precepts under Holy
Church and her prelates. Accordingly the Saint felt
sure that his Majesty would not only remove all
impediments, whenever the truth should come to his
ears, and he should be rightly informed as to his own
intentions, but that he would also assist him to the
best of his power in his undertakings.

Although he had endeavoured to make this clear
to his Majesty through the medium of the Apostolic
Nuncios, and not altogether without result, yet his

wishes were not entirely fulfilled, owing to the
that these affairs were treated together with o
business, and so had not been sufficiently impre
upon the King's mind, especially as they had tc
conveyed through other persons, who were gu
only by human prudence and policy. He there
thought it expedient to send a religious person,
was well informed on every matter, who would c
municate with the King, plainly and sincerely,
word of mouth, mentioning persons and giving reas
in order that the King, seeing how affairs were gc
might take measures to remove all obstacles to
spiritual progress of Milan. This purpose being
proved by prudent persons whom the Saint consu
he chose Father Charles Bascapè of the Barnabite
regular clerks of St. Paul, now Bishop of Novara
this mission, having had long experience of his
cretion and tact in the management of affairs.
judged it necessary to send him before the arriva
a new Governor, in order that ill-disposed per
might not put a false colouring on matters, as (
had done before with former Governors. Ha
given the Father all necessary credentials toge
with a present for the King, viz., a relic of the l
of one of the holy Innocents enclosed in a suit
shrine, he sent him to Portugal where the King was
gaged in war. He took the opportunity of sending
with Cardinal Riario, the Apostolic legate despatc
by the Pope on important affairs to the King of Sp
Thus the mission was kept secret in order that
malignant should have no opportunity of interferi

We must not omit to state that after the departure of Father Bascapè, the Cardinal had a new grievance as to his jurisdiction, notwithstanding the expectation that upon the death of the Governor all troubles would cease. The provincial government rested, until a new appointment was made, in the hands of Sanchio de Guevarra, the Prefect of the Castle, a pious man who had been much displeased at the action of the late Governor against the Church. It was generally thought that there was a good understanding between him and the Cardinal, as he had at the suggestion of the Saint prohibited certain comedies as injurious to Christian morality. The state of things was therefore quiet; persons, however, were not wanting who strove to make difficulties as they had done before between this deputy and the Cardinal.

Nothing interrupted the agreement between them until the following circumstance occurred. The Cardinal had delegated Mgr. Giovanni Fontana, his Vicar-General and Archpriest of the cathedral, now Bishop of Ferrara, to make the visitation of the Great Hospital of Milan, according to the decree of the Holy Council of Trent, sess. 22, chap. viii., which directs Bishops to visit all hospitals and other institutions, which are not immediately under the protection of temporal princes. When about to commence the visitation, the Royal Assessor,[1] who was one of the Saint's principal adversaries, ordered all the accounts of income and management to be concealed, and directed the lay deputies not to submit to the visitation under the pretext that

[1] Pietro Antonio Lonato, one of the "carnival ambassadors."

the hospital was under the protection of the Ki
This was a mistake, for according to its foundation
is governed by eighteen deputies, two of whom w
to be always ecclesiastics; and as they might
changed from year to year, they were chosen by
Archbishop, and acted conjointly with the ot
persons qualified for the appointment. These
puties cannot make any contract nor alienate ι
property without the presence and sanction of
Archbishop or his Vicar-General, whence it is cl
that the government is in the Archbishop's har
and that he has the authority and right to visit
Mgr. Fontana, finding such opposition, tried every ρ
sible means to come to an understanding consistent w
the rights of the Archbishop. But when no heed ·
paid to him, he then deemed it necessary to have recou
to the authority of the Church, and threatened all ν
prevented the visitation with excommunication.
order to escape such censure the deputies immediat
yielded, which they would have done in the beginn
had they not been hindered. The Assessor, who 1
concealed the books, not dreading the penalty
excommunication, and persevering in his intention
give trouble to the Cardinal, refused to make his s
mission. Consequently Mgr. Fontana was compel
to excommunicate him by name, and had the not
thereof publicly exposed. He refused even then
come to terms, and took no heed of the public censu
asserting that he was privileged and exempt as be
a Knight of the Cross. His cause was tried in Ro
where judgment went against him, and he was ρ

nounced duly excommunicated. He did not fail to make a disturbance, and wrote about the matter to Spain, whither Father Bascapè had not yet arrived, thinking to excite the King and the Royal Council against the Cardinal. But Mgr. Filippo Sega, Bishop of Piacenza, afterwards Cardinal, was then Nuncio Apostolic to the King of Spain, and much attached to St. Charles, so warmly defended his episcopal rights that the Assessor was obliged to give up the books he had concealed, and to acknowledge that the powers and privileges of visitation belonged to the Archbishop. Thus was the opponent of the Saint put to confusion, after all his ill-will to his pastor, who had conferred signal benefits upon him. God allowed him to fall into disaster in the end, and he was obliged to humble himself, and sue for the Cardinal's protection. He probably did not act with an upright intention, for returning home one day from business, without any illness he was suddenly seized with a fit, in which he fell to the ground dead, losing his speech and his life almost at the same time.

CHAPTER X.

FATHER CHARLES BASCAPÈ reached the city of Badaj
on the confines of Portugal, where the King w:
on the 4th of August, 1581. Although living
retirement, and not usually granting audiences,
account of the war, yet on hearing that an eccl
siastic had come from Italy on business, the King w
pleased to admit him. The third day after his arriv.
he presented to his Majesty St. Charles' letters a
the relic he brought with him, begging for anoth
audience before the new Governor should be sent
Milan, that he might make known all that he h:
been commissioned to say by the Cardinal. The Ki
accepted the gift on his knees, kissing it with devotic
and returned many thanks to the donor, granting t
request of an audience.

Three days after the Father returned, and explain
that he had been sent by the Cardinal of St. Praxed
to inform the King of the state and needs of t
Church at Milan, begging him not to commit its affa:
to Governors possessing merely political prudence, b

to those who were known to be religious men. He
described the upright intentions of the Cardinal, and
his prudence in his pastoral office, without entering
into discussions as to jurisdiction, as the decision was
referred to the Roman Pontiff, but explaining all that
the Governor and his friends had done to hinder good .
discipline and the discharge of spiritual duties. The
King promised to bear in mind what the Father said to
him, and to consult those upon whom he could rely,
sending him to Father Diego Clavesio, a Dominican,
his confessor. This was a great consolation to Father
Bascapè, as he hoped to bring the affair to a happy
issue. Nor was he disappointed, for the Dominican
reported favourably to the King, who decided in the
Cardinal's favour.

When Father Bascapè was about to return to Milan,
two events happened to retard him. First, the serious
illness of the King, which nearly put an end to his life ;
next, the death of the Queen, who, being within two
months of her confinement, was seized with premature
pains of childbirth, ending in her decease. This was a
great grief to the King, who was much attached to her.

Father Clavesio sent a long letter to St. Charles
intimating that his mission was likely to do good,
that a man of piety and virtue was already named for
the government, viz., the Duke of Medina Sidonia, who
did not, however, come in the end. Matters turned
out well notwithstanding, for the Duke of Terra Nuova
being appointed instead, St. Charles was left in peace
and tranquillity, as there was an excellent understanding between them. It was said that this Governor had

express orders to confer with the Saint, and to
nothing whatever displeasing to him; he even resto
the castle of Arona to him, which had been taken fi
him some time before, and that too without his app
ing for it. I cannot refrain from mentioning what
Saint deigned to tell me himself on this subject:
have good news," said he, "which I know will b
great consolation to you, and that you will thank (
for it as you ought, and as I wish you to do. Hen
forth our difficulties will be at an end, we shall live
peace, and be free to attend to our pastoral cha:
His Catholic Majesty has sent a new Governor w
the express order to act in concert with us. For si
in past times the King's lieutenants have not been
good terms with us, and have caused much trouble
the result of this agreement will be peace and or
both temporal and spiritual."

There arose, in fact, no further controversy, not e
as to jurisdiction; although there was occasion:
some difference of opinion between one tribunal
another, yet they found the means of coming to
understanding without contention or disturbance.
a proof of this, I remember making a visitation o
pious institution myself which had never been visi
before. The members of the committee, who w
persons of note, would not appear until they had c
sulted the King's ministers, who replied that they :
an express order from his Majesty to forbear from :
opposition to the Cardinal in the government of
diocese, that they were not in any way to prevent
visitation, as he had undoubtedly the right to do so

A short time ago the Vicar-General wished in like manner to visit another institution, and the committee appealed for orders as to what they were to do to the Grand Chancellor, who directed them to submit. We may hereby judge how right-minded the King was, for he was no sooner informed of the truth, than he determined that the service of God and the government of the Church should no longer be interfered with, under pretext of infringing on his jurisdiction, well knowing that such a holy pastor had no wish to usurp his rights, but rather to establish them. This pious King was much attached to St. Charles, and felt grateful to him for his care of his subjects and of the Church of Milan, and showed it by especial marks of favour to the mission, and especially by desiring that all impediments in the administration of his diocese should be removed.

It is quite evident, therefore, that the troubles which the Cardinal had so long endured, in defending the rights of his Church, did not come from the King, but from his ministers only. In the Saint's life, written by Father Bascapè, he relates minutely the circumstances of this expedition, the care of the King (though unwell at the time) for himself while he was at his court, and his directions that everything he wanted should be provided, so that the courtiers were surprised, especially as he was but an Italian priest, and did not seem to be a man of such importance as to deserve these particular marks of favour, as he practised great reserve, never speaking of himself or the business he had in hand except to the King and his confessor.

CHAPTER XI.

EIGHTH DIOCESAN SYNOD—TRANSLATION OF BODIES
THE SAINTS—THE EMPRESS MARY OF AUSTRIA.

1581.

THE Saint was extremely solicitous about his clei
Besides ordinary visitations he never failed to call tl
together in synod once a year, unless something seri
occurred to prevent him, and made it his business
ascertain, by minute examination, their progress
ecclesiastical discipline. By his sermons he enc
voured to renew their spirit, and by particular dec
provided against irregularities and deficiencies.
the 12th of April, 1581, he held his eighth dioce
synod, in which he lamented some cases of n
observance of the rules of discipline prescribed
choir, and of neglect in wearing the ecclesiast
habit, according to his decrees. He charged the r
deans by word of mouth, and by a synodal letter
secure among the clergy the observance of these ru
and the sanctification of holy days by the laity.

On this occasion, assisted by his clergy, he tr
lated the bodies of Leo and Martinus, martyrs,

Arsatius, Bishop, deposited in the collegiate church of St. Stephen in Broglio. As the chapel of St. Vincent in that church was undergoing restoration, it was necessary to remove these sacred relics there deposited. In order to incite the people to great devotion, he made the translation with great ceremony on the 14th of April, having given due notice of it, that all might be present to honour the martyrs. The Saint sung Mass and preached with his usual fervour before the magistrates, nobility, and people.

It happened in the same month of April that an altar dedicated to the martyrs Basilides, Cyrinus, and Nabor, in the left aisle of the church of St. Celsus, was considered by Mgr. Famagosta, the Apostolic Visitor, to be too near the high altar, and the canons having to dig a grave near for a burial, found there a marble coffer. A report of this discovery being made to St. Charles, he went thither, together with the Bishops of Novara and Vercelli, and raising the lid, found within bones of the three holy martyrs. Having authenticated and venerated them, he placed them in an aumbry, suitably adorned, in the sacristy of the church, to be carried back to their own altar after its restoration.

The Catholic King, Philip II., having conquered and taken possession of Portugal, saw that many of the Portuguese were in an unsettled state, and inclined to the party of Don Antouio, as being a descendant of the royal family, though being illegitimate, he was incapable of succeeding to the throne. In order to pacify them, the King thought it would be well to

place the government in the hands of his sister,
Empress Mary of Austria, considering that it would
pleasing to the nation, as she was the granddaugl
of Emmanuel, King of Portugal. Accordingly, w
that Princess was on her way from Bohemia to I
tugal, in the year 1581, with her son, the Archd
Maximilian, the Cardinal, complying with the obli
tions of his position as Archbishop of Milan toward
person of her rank,[1] went suitably accompanied to m
her at Brescia, the first city in the province of Mi
that she reached on her journey.

The Empress was much consoled by this visit, a
showed St. Charles every mark of kindness, rec
mending herself to his prayers, and hoping to be a
to hear his Mass. He could not, however, comply w
her wish then, as he was intending to pay her a v
of ceremony at Milan.

The Saint took this opportunity of staying w
Signor Jerome Luzzago, his devoted friend, a fav
he had refused to grant him before when on
visitation, because he never lodged with seculars
such times. The delight of Luzzago at this fav
could not be described, so great was his joy wl
he saw entering his house one whom he loved a
esteemed so highly. I leave the reader to imag
the honour paid him during his stay, and will o
mention that his guest had no sooner left his hou
than he closed the room where he had slept, allow
no one to enter or use it any more.

---

[1] She was daughter of Charles V., daughter-in-law of Ferdinand
wife of Maximilian II., mother of Rudolph II., now reigning, sist
Philip II., our most potent King, and a lady of great piety.

the Empress was not passing through Milan, the
, thought that he could do no less than pay her
,ur at Lodi where she was to pass a night; and
> directions that the cathedral in that city should
duly prepared for a pontifical Mass, sending the
st musicians in Milan, and his master of ceremonies,
gether with rich decorations. He went to meet
er himself on her entrance into the Milanese state
it Soncino, and requested her to meet the clergy in
the cathedral of Lodi, where he intended to say the
Mass which her Majesty had desired. The Empress
thanked the Cardinal for his kindness, declining to
require the clergy to meet her, as she said it would
be unbecoming for them to be on foot when she was
in her carriage. She was therefore met by the
nobility only, and accompanied to the house prepared
for her, where St. Charles paid her a visit, spending
some time in conversation, which she appeared to
enjoy, and begged him to oblige her by saying Mass
in a private oratory, as she felt too much fatigued
by her journey to go to the church. This he promised
to do, at the same time acquainting her with the
troubles he had endured from the King's ministers,
and begged her to be his protectress, and to use her
influence with his Majesty for the removal of such
impediments. The following morning he said Mass
for her, and preached a sermon full of fervour. He
paid her another visit to take leave, presenting her
with a gold cross full of relics, a rosary from the
Holy Land, with many indulgences attached to it,
an Agnus Dei, and two spiritual books. These gifts

were highly prized by her as presented by a g
servant of God. He also made similar present
rosaries and spiritual books to the Archduke M
milian and the ladies and gentlemen of her co
from his desire to encourage them all in the
of salvation. Some of the ladies, although pre
for time, begged him to give them Holy Commun
which pious request he granted them.

CHAPTER XII.

VISIT TO VERCELLI — SECOND PILGRIMAGE TO TURIN, OUT OF DEVOTION TO THE HOLY WINDING-SHEET —THE VALLEYS OF THE GRISONS.

1581.

ST. CHARLES, after finishing his visitation of Brescia, set out for other parts, intending particularly to return to the three Swiss valleys, in order to gather the harvest of his former visits. It occurred to him, however, first to gratify a wish he had long entertained of going to Vercelli, and venerating the relics of St. Eusebius, martyr and Bishop of that city, to whom he had great devotion as a defender of the faith to the shedding of his blood in the Arian persecution, and because he had rendered great service to the Church of Milan in upholding the honour of St. Dionysius, its Archbishop, in the cause of St. Athanasius against the Arians. It was not known where the body of St. Eusebius lay in the cathedral, but when the Bishop Giovanni Francesco Bonomo was restoring it, the sacred relics were found, to the great satisfaction of all. The Saint now fulfilled his intention with great devotion as was his wont.

Finding himself at Vercelli, he took the opportu
of going to Masino close at hand, in order to pay
respects to Charles Emmanuel, the new Duke
Savoy, and to condole with him himself on the d
of his father, Emmanuel Philibert, who had pa
to a better life ten months before, though he
already sent Father Francis Adorno to fulfil
duty. The Prince was much pleased to hear of
Charles' intention, for he looked upon him as a fa
and went in great joy to meet him, and discussed
him various matters relating to the government of
states.

The Duke then invited him to go with him
Turin, in order to enjoy his society longer, and
honour that city by his presence; and as an ind
ment added that the Saint would be able to
another visit to the holy winding-sheet of our I
to which he knew the Cardinal had great devo
St. Charles accepted the invitation, and they
the visit together, in which the Duke did not
short of his father in rendering honour to his gues

The Saint then went on to the Lago Maggior
make a visitation of the three valleys. On reac
the lake he sent forward Giovanni Ambrogio For
with his horses, with directions to leave then
Magadino, at the head of the lake, and to go o
Bellinzona and keep open the great gate w
divides the valley, as he intended to pass the n
there before beginning his visit. He himself
lowed in a boat, and when he reached Magadino
beheld a great conflagration of the stables in w

in number, and among them
animal. This fire was caused
o hearing the bells ringing on
, rushed out to see him land,
alight, which unfortunately set
St. Charles arrived when the
it, threatening the adjoining build-
ed impossible to save; but on his
Agnus Dei into the flames, they
d in a wonderful manner without
chief, though all the horses perished.
he showed no signs of vexation, nor
ny complaint, but out of pity for the
se stables were burnt, presented him
d crowns to enable him to rebuild them.
ad no horses for the journey, he gladly
ot for Bellinzona, staff in hand, consider-
e of good luck that he had to travel like
d His Apostles in their journeys for the
f souls. Neither would he give up his
but persevered walking many miles a day
roads. At length he reached Mount St.
which separates Italy from Germany, when
erceived that he could hardly keep on his
m weariness, yet he was not once seen to
y rest.

as stated in the judicial process for his canonisa-
Giovanni Basso, provost of Biasca and visitor
three valleys, a holy priest, who had converted
souls to God in those parts, that when St.
rrived at his house at Airolo in Val Leventina

on foot, having walked many miles by Mount St. (
hard, he was so overcome by the heat, that he c
scarcely stand. He would not, however, enter
house to rest, or even sit down outside, but ha·
spoken to him on some business, leaning the w
against the churchyard wall, he continued his jour
over rough roads and still on foot, to Bidretto,
miles further on; where he immediately begun
duties of his visitation, as if he had just risen fro
long rest. This witness testifies to the labours of
Saint during this visitation in these words: " Of
patience in enduring fatigues, no one in the w
could form an idea, who had not seen it, for he cro
mountains by ways that perhaps had never l
trodden before, and never seemed exhausted or
patience." When he came to a place where t.
were horses enough for all his household, he made
of them. It was during this visitation that by mal
the sign of the cross he miraculously saved Guis
Cavaliere, a notary, and Bernardino Tarugi, from b
drowned in the Ticino.[1]

While visiting this valley, the Saint felt a g
desire to venerate the relics of St. Placidus, ma
and Sigisbert, confessor, which are in the church o.
Martin in Tisitis, a Benedictine abbey in the Gri
district and diocese of Chur. His wish was soon n
known to the Father Abbot, Christian Castelber
religious who had great esteem for St. Charles
account of his sanctity, the fame of which had rea
those parts. Being very desirous of receiving

[1] Book ix. chap. 2.

with honour in his own monastery, he sent a priest to pay his respects to the Cardinal and to beg him to visit them. This message was delivered to him at Giornico, in the Leventine valley; the Saint much pleased, sent his thanks to the Abbot and accepted his invitation, though he would not inform him of the time of his arrival, in order to avoid any concourse of the people, only making inquiries as to the best way by which to go.

Having finished his visitation in the Leventine, he went on to Bregno, and thence reaching Ruolo at the foot of the Mount St. Maria, he begun his pilgrimage on foot accompanied by ten of his household. By a long and difficult road he climbed to the top of the mountain the first night, and found no food but chestnuts and milk, and nothing but hay to sleep upon. In the morning he went down into the valley, praying and meditating the while with his attendants, who became so exhausted by their long and fatiguing journey at the hottest season of the year, that they from time to time threw themselves on the ground from sheer weariness; but he so cheered and encouraged them, that they at length reached Tisitis, a distance of five and twenty miles, fasting, and bathed in perspiration.

The Abbot ordered all the bells to be rung to assemble the people, and went out to meet him in procession with the bodies of the saints; St. Charles casting himself upon his knees before them with such emotion that tears flowed from his eyes, causing others to shed tears also to see a Cardinal so weary with

fatigue and so devout. It was then about two o'clc
in the afternoon, and, although fasting, he did not 1
to follow the procession which first went to the par:
church of St. John Baptist, while the Cardinal s{
prayers and visited all its altars, examining them o
by one to see if they were properly cared for and t
rubrics observed. From thence they went to t
Abbey, when all the bells were rung, with singing
psalms and hymns, which filled every one with j{
In the Abbey Church the bodies of the saints w{
placed upon the High Altar, when solemn vespers w{
sung, which were not over till nearly evening, all t
people remaining as if never tired of looking on t
Cardinal, wrapt in devotion to those sacred relics.

He was then received in the monastery by Capt{
Paul Fiurino, in the name of the commune, with {
pressions of their delight at his presence, and than
for his condescension. He remained during the nig
in prayer before the sacred relics in spite of his fatig{
In the morning he said Mass, when all the people w{
present, and although it was a week-day and harv{
time, the concourse was as great as on a festival d{
After Mass he again visited the relics which he wish
to see uncovered, and asking the Abbot for a sm
portion, he was told he was free to take whatever
pleased. He, therefore, took a small particle from ea
of the relics of St. Placidus, St. Sigisbert, and {
Emerita, V. M., at the same time noting down t
principal acts of their life, and the days on which th{
feast was kept. He then visited the altars, our Lad{
chapel, which was the oratory of St. Sigisbert, a

another chapel on the site of the martyrdom of St. Placidus. He was asked to remain at least three or four days with them, but he declined, as the nativity of our Blessed Lady, one of the principal festivals of the Cathedral of Milan, was nigh, and it was necessary for him to keep the feast there. He thanked them, and to give a proof of his good-will, he took three ecclesiastical students from the place, two for his own seminaries, one of whom, John Sacco by name, is now parish priest of Tisitis, and one for the Swiss college. He then took leave of them with a promise that, if it were God's will, he would visit them again, and remain a longer time.

CHAPTER XIII.

DEATH OF THE QUEEN OF SPAIN—THE TRANSLATIC
THE IMAGE OF OUR LADY OF SARONNO—SIXTI
LAST PROVINCIAL COUNCIL.

1581.

THE death of the Queen of Spain, Jane of Au
mother of the Catholic King, Philip III., now ha
reigning, was much felt, both by the King, her
band, and her subjects, but by none more k
than St. Charles, both from his loyalty to the
of Spain, and on her own account as a lady of
rity and virtue. He therefore celebrated her fu
with every honour due to her exalted rank.

⟩ The cathedral was hung with black cloth, di
ing the royal arms, and eulogies of the deceased
the midst, under the cupola, was a catafalque of
of gold, with a likeness of the Queen in royal 1
above her the semblance of fire, showing her s
it were on fire with charity, and going up to h
It was surrounded by statues representing th
ferent cities in the Milanese state, in mournin
the Queen. At the four corners were lofty pyi
adorned with paintings.

The funeral rites were celebrated in September, 1581, in presence of the Governor and magistrates, by the Cardinal, who preached her funeral sermon. Among other things, he mentioned an heroic act of hers during the illness of the King, her consort, when she offered her own life for his, in terms following :— "Not only did the Queen deny herself in those things which the world values, but in her love for her own life also. During her husband's sickness, considering of how much greater worth his life was than her own, she earnestly besought God to take her life in exchange for his, on account of the great loss that would ensue to Christendom if he died. Her prayers were not in vain; they ascended to heaven; God accepted the sacrifice; He gave back health to the King and called this blessed soul to Himself by death. Thus it was she desired and begged to die. Pleasing to God was her offering; the health of the King was purchased by her loss, which to her was neither hard nor bitter." Such a fact was worthy to be recorded by a saint.

After this function he had a solemn translation of the sacred image of our Lady of Saronno. Among the duties he always strove to impress upon the minds of his people was devotion to the Blessed Virgin, and veneration for her images and relics, as a means of inciting them to piety and fervour. So much the more as the devil was trying to hinder, or at least to diminish, such devotion as far as possible by means of heretics, who denied this worship, although as ancient as the Church of God. St.

Charles therefore seized every opportunity of encou
aging it in his flock.

As this image had to be. replaced on the Hig
Altar of the church which had been rebuilt, he ha
the ceremony conducted with solemnity, as th
translation of a miraculous image held in veneratio
throughout the diocese. In order to ensure th
attendance of the faithful and spiritual benefit (
souls, he obtained a plenary indulgence from Rom
for all those who after Confession and Communio
should be present on the 10th of September, 158
and at the same time published a pastoral on th
veneration due to sacred images.. This letter mad
such an impression upon his flock that great numbei
assisted at the translation, at which he himself sun
Mass, preached, and gave Communion.

He spent the rest of the year in visitation of th
city and diocese, and promoting discipline among th
clergy and laity. About this time he had the grea
pleasure of giving the tonsure to Count Ferrant
Taverna, a young nobleman of promise, who did no
disappoint his hopes, for Clement VIII. afterward
employed him in the service of the Apostolic Se
finally making him Governor of Rome, and Cardina
in the year 1604.

At the beginning of the following year, 1582, S
Charles renewed his efforts to banish the profane diver
sions of masquerades and balls on feast days, not onl
during the Divine office, but also the rest of the da
Our Lord give him the consolation of seeing obedienc
on the part of all, and the regular observance c

festivals established. During the carnival he kept the people so occupied in spiritual exercises that they had no leisure for idle pastimes. He took great pains to bring all to their Easter duties, by having note of all who were leading a bad life, of public sinners and those who had grown old in iniquity, and he desired the parish priests not to admit them to the sacraments. Thus by means of their dread of eternal punishment, the disgrace of being excluded from the sacraments, and the exhortations of their pastor, many souls were rescued from their vices to begin a new life. Among them were some of the nobility who had been living in public and scandalous sin forgetful of their salvation.

In this way the Saint pointed out to Bishops and pastors how to exercise their zeal for souls, that God had made them shepherds of their flocks to feed and guard them and heal their wounds with care, and not like hirelings to seek for the enjoyment of repose.

When Easter was over he began his preparations for his sixth and last Provincial Council, held on the 10th day of May. In addition to the usual decorations of the hall where the Bishops assembled, he placed there the pictures of all the patron saints of each diocese in the province. Beside publishing many decrees, he strove to urge the Bishops to embrace the perfect apostolic life, quoting the words of Christ our Lord to His apostles : "Take nothing for your journey, neither staff nor scrip nor bread nor money, neither have two coats." [1] He showed how these words principally applied to Bishops, the successors of the apos-

---

[1] St. Luke ix. 3.

tles, who had, like them, to despise all worldly th
and imitate their life. He pointed out the spir
weaknesses of the province, which he had noted ̀
with the proper remedies, viz., the orders and de
of the Councils, begging them, as the spiritual pl
cians of sinful souls, to apply them and to take e
possible care to see that they were fully observed
God said to Josue the guide of his people : " Let
the book of this law depart from thy mouth,
shalt meditate on it day and night, that thou m
observe and do all things that are written in it." [1]

This discourse was uttered with such earnest
that it seemed as if he were making his will; and
this would be the last Council, and these his last w
to his suffragans, as actually turned out to be the ̀

[1] Jos. i. 8.

CHAPTER XIV.

WHEN the monks of Monte Cassino were restoring
their church of St. Simplician, originally dedicated to
our Blessed Lady, it was found necessary to remove
the relics of the saints from the High Altar, which had
to be rebuilt elsewhere. St. Charles went to make
formal recognition of the bodies, finding in one shrine
those of martyrs Sisinius, Martyrius, and Alexander,
together with the bones of St. Benignus Bentius, Archbishop and citizen of Milan; in another, those of two
other Archbishops Ampelius and Gerontius, the latter
of the Milanese family of Bascapè; in the third was
the body of St. Simplician, also Archbishop and citizen
of Milan, of the Cattaneo family.

This saint was looked upon as a father by St. Ambrose, and was his successor in the government of the
church of Milan. In Rome, he had been instrumental
in the conversion of Victorinus, the orator, whose
example led many others to embrace the faith, among
them St. Augustine, who having recourse to Simplician

for instruction, received the knowledge of the t
ever afterwards looking up to him as a friend,
consulting him in the interpretation of the Holy S
tures. The fame of his wisdom spread so far that
advice was sought by a Council of Bishops in Afri

The translation of the body of this saint and of
others mentioned was made by the Cardinal du
the sitting of the Provincial Council on the Sunda
the Octave of Ascension Day, May 27, in order
it might be. celebrated with greater solemnity
usual. In addition to the Bishops of the Counci
invited Hippolyto Rossi, Bishop of Pavia, and a
wards Cardinal, and Cardinal Gabriel Paleotto, A
bishop of Bologna, on account both of their friend
and the intimate relations of the Sees of Milan
Bologna. As St. Ambrose once went to the li
city for the translation of the bodies of the mar
Vitalis and Agricola, it was but fitting that a Bi:
of the same See should assist at this translatior
Milan.

Father Seraphino Fontana, Abbot of St. Simplicia:
the suggestion of St. Charles, invited many abbots
monks of his Order to Milan for the occasion.
Cardinal himself announced the event to his
people in a pastoral letter which was read in all
cathedrals of the province, setting forth the praise
St. Simplician, and explaining the ancient custon
the churches in the veneration due to sacred re
He also published the order of the procession,
printed a little book containing the psalms and pra:
to be recited, and hymns written in honour of

A plenary indulgence was obtained from the e Pontiff for all present at the celebration, who ecommended to fast on the Wednesday, Friday, aturday of the preceding week, to ask for the in- ssion of the saints. For greater honour, for some previously, the joy-bells were rung in the city diocese, and throughout the province by permission the Bishops. The cathedral and Abbey Church of Simplician, and the streets through which the pro- ssion was to pass, were decked out with banners nd pictures describing the acts and virtues of these saints.

St. Charles passed the night previous to the cere- mony in the Abbey Church, keeping watch before the relics as usual. In the procession first went the schools of Christian doctrine, long files of companies of the cross and Disciplinants, the Regular Orders of clergy, among whom were about two hundred Bene- dictine monks, the clergy of the diocese from twelve miles round, all with lighted tapers in their hands. Then came sixteen Benedictine Abbots and nine Bishop of the province,[1] all in pontifical vestments, who carrie the relics, alternately relieving each other from ti to time. Lastly came the two Cardinals, who, with t other Bishops, bore the head of St. Simplician, wh had been found deposited in a silver shrine, still corrupt and beautiful. Over each relic was he

1 These were Cesare Gambara of Tortona, Nicola Sfrondato of C afterwards Pope Gregory XIV., Hieronymo Ragazzone of Berga vanni Delfino of Brescia, Domenico della Rovere of Asti, C Guasco of Alessandria, Vincenzo Marini of Alba, Francesco Ventimiglia, and Alessandro Andriasio of Casale.

canopy, held by members of noble families. B
the clergy were the Governor of the city, the s
and magistrates, and doctors of law, all with li
torches, together with a concourse of people so
that all the roads for ten miles round and the s
of the city were so crowded that it was diffict
pass along; every one striving to touch the holy
with their rosaries.

All this devotion St. Charles enjoyed much, s
the fulfilment of his wishes to honour the saints
a celebration such as Milan has seldom witne
and although he was so much incommoded by
crowd that his mitre nearly fell off his head, y
was filled with delight to see the devotion of his

The streets for about four miles round were ad
with tapestry, pictures, and drapery. Altars
triumphal arches were erected on the way, ever
offering their most precious possessions to do h
to the day. The Jesuit Fathers erected a spl
altar at their college of Brera, and covered their
with tapestry and inscriptions in Latin, Greek
Hebrew, in praise of the acts and glorious dea
the three martyrs and of the sanctity of St. Si
cian. At the Archbishop's house St. Charles
covered the entire front opposite the church
pictures of all the Bishops of the See, a hundre
twenty-three in number, beginning with St. Bar
the apostle, and ending with Filippo Archinto, h
mediate predecessor, with the name of each one m
upon them. It was said by the people that the Ca
would be among them one day with the title of

The palace of the City Council in the Market Square was decorated with pictures, where there was represented the signal victory gained by the Milanese over the Emperor, Frederick Barbarossa, through the intercession of the three martyrs Sisinius, Martyrius, and Alexander. More magnificent, however, than all the rest, was the church of St. Simplician itself, with hangings, symbols, and panegyrics in Latin, Greek, and Hebrew.

When the procession came to this church, and the Bishops withdrew to take a little rest in the monastery, St. Charles, without the least sign of weariness, sung Mass and preached a sermon on the imitation of the saints. Afterwards the Cardinals and Bishops remained with the Fathers to take refreshment, which was of no luxurious kind, as the Abbot wished to satisfy St. Charles and comply with the decrees of the Provincial Councils. Before their meal they all waited upon twelve poor men at dinner, the Saint serving them himself to his great delight, and seasoning the food of the body with the spiritual words of a Father for the sustenance of their souls. Whatever portion was left at the prelate's table was added to that allotted to the poor, so that they fared sumptuously.

He then appointed a station of forty hours' prayer before the relics, during which time there was a perpetual concourse of people to venerate them, and he finally placed them beneath the High Altar, after watching before them himself in prayer.

At the judicial inquiry for his canonisation Father Pio Camuzio bore witness that at the time of the

translation he held the office of sacristan, and obser
that St. Charles remained fifty hours in prayer in
church at that time. It pleased our Lord on
occasion further to manifest to the world the sanc
of the Cardinal, by enabling him to deliver with
sign of the cross one possessed by a devil.

CHAPTER XV.

TRANSLATION OF THE BODY OF ST. JOHN BUONO—NINTH
DIOCESAN SYNOD—THIRD VISIT IN COMPANY OF
CARDINAL PALEOTTO TO VISIT THE HOLY WINDING-
SHEET.

1582.

THE next day after these solemnities was the first of
the Rogation days, which are kept with fasting in the
Ambrosian rite. As the processions took a long time,
and as the Cardinal officiated, singing Mass and
preaching, the function was not ended till about
two o'clock in the afternoon, although it begun early.
All the repose he took after so much fatigue was
two hours' sleep, as he went at midnight to sing
matins with his Canons, and after laying the ashes
on the clergy and people, as is the Ambrosian custom
at that time, he joined the procession to the usual
churches with cope and mitre, which increased his
fatigue, besides fasting on bread and water and
preaching for an hour, as he had done at Mass.
Nor can it be said that he rested after his return
home, as others did, to recover from fatigues, for on
the first Rogation day he went to St. Simplician's

to arrange the relics already placed there in
order; on the second to St. Michael's to mak
formal recognition of the body of St. John F
Archbishop of Milan and native of Genoa, and
pare for its translation; and thither again, o:
third, as he intended to have the church p
down, as it was in ruins, and too near the cath
after singing vespers he placed the body in a s:
reserving the head to be encased in silver; he
spent the night in prayer, according to custom
the next day, Thursday, in solemn procession, t
lated it to a new altar in the cathedral, erected v
the side door used to be, leading to the Archbis
house. When the function was over, he woul
take food, until he had served a number of
persons to whom he gave a dinner on that day.

The ninth diocesan synod had been fixed for
Wednesday in Whitsunweek, the 7th of June.
withstanding his continual labours and fatigue
was able to find time for the necessary prepara
although he never failed in his episcopal dutie
the three days of Pentecost. On the vigil he bl
the font; on the feast of Pentecost, sang Mass
vespers and preached; on the two following day
administered confirmation in the morning, and
vespers on Whitsun Tuesday, went in processic
the hospital of St. Gregory, outside the eastern ga

While he was thus occupied, he did not
Cardinal Paleotto idle, employing him in on
another function. One day he sent him to
Sepulcre's to receive some ecclesiastics into the

gregation of the oblates; on another to St. Nazarius to confirm candidates from the district of the Porta Romana; a third day to the congregation of Christian Doctrine to preach, so that he never allowed him to lose a moment of time.

He took him also to all the sessions of his synod, at which he delivered an address in Latin to the clergy, gratifying his audience by his eloquence and knowledge of the Holy Scriptures. As he then enlarged upon the merits of St. Charles, the Saint the next day desired Domenico Ferro, a Canon of the cathedral, to thank Cardinal Paleotto for his sermons.

This Cardinal much enjoyed St. Charles' society, acknowledging that he was amazed at the fire of his charity, and the fatigues he underwent, as it seemed to him impossible for a human body to bear up against so many toils. After St. Charles' death he drew up and published an account of his sanctity and virtues. Before leaving Milan, he begged for a portion of the precious relics for his church of Bologna, seeing that Milan was rich in such treasures. He received among others, relics of St. Simplician and St. John Buono, Archbishops of Milan; and of St. Nabor and St. Felix, martyrs, together with a part of the dalmatic of St. Ambrose; all of which he placed in his cathedral church at Bologna on the feast of St. Peter and St. Paul, when he spoke of the virtues of St. Charles, as having been himself an eye-witness of them.

St. Charles had been so impressed by the likeness of our Lord, with the marks of His precious wounds,

as seen by him in the holy winding-sheet at 1
that the remembrance of it never left his mind, se
as a stimulant to his love for God, and memori
the sufferings of our blessed Lord. He felt such
tion to that holy relic, that he was not satisfied
visiting it once or twice, but invited Cardinal Pal
to go with him, that they might both share ir
grace of the pilgrimage. Setting out together,
they reached the halting-places on the road, their
visit was to the church, where they said prayers
litanies, both saying Mass in the morning b
they started again. At Novara and Vercelli, ir
province of Milan, where the whole population fl
to the church to see them, they preached with
edification. In Piedmont great honours were
to them by order of the Duke, being escorte
soldiers who fired volleys on their knees in wel
and they were met by the Duke himself outside 1
and made to take up their abode in his palace.
veneration of the holy winding-sheet, St. Charle
lowed the same order as on his first visit, havin
exposition of forty hours, and giving a discourse t
people every hour before great numbers from all 1
even those infected by heresy.

As the feast of Corpus Christi fell during this
the Duke had the procession celebrated on a gra
scale than usual, and devoutly received Holy
munion from the hand of St. Charles.

Great spiritual benefit was reaped by Car
Paleotto from his visit, and he was much rejoice
see the piety of the young Prince, to whom St. Ch

showed himself a true father by his good offices and advice before his departure. As he wished to visit Frassineto, a parish in his diocese near Casale, the two Cardinals went by water to that place, where they bid farewell to each other.

Cardinal Paleotto, on his return home to Bologna, being asked about the Cardinal of St. Praxedes, used to make answer in the words of the Queen of Saba after her visit to King Solomon. "I have beheld," said he, "with my own eyes things that far exceed all that fame has reported of him." When he visited relics and the bodies of saints departed, he would say, "I have seen a living relic, a living saint."

CHAPTER XVI.

WHEN he had finished his visitation of Frassineto
Charles went on to the mountains near the Lake
Lugano and Como towards Bergamo. This jour
was very fatiguing, as it was in the months of
and August, as well as on account of the roughnes
the roads, and the poverty of these parts. He
quently had to go many miles on foot across mo
tains where it was impossible to ride.

He began this visitation at Porlezza on Lake Lug
after passing through the Menasina valley on a
night in the pouring rain. On arriving there he fo
the people waiting for him in church, and though it
very late, and he was wet through from head to foo
did not hesitate to mount the pulpit and preach, set
no store on his own life to attend to the salvation
souls. The next morning, beside the ordinary duti
the visitation, he conferred the subdiaconate on
Camillus Sfrondato, who is now cardinal priest o
Cecilia, a nephew of Gregory XIV. and son of B
Paul of that name. Here, after watching the nigl

prayer, it was a great pleasure to him to effect a lasting peace between two of the principal persons in the district, who with armed bands fought each other to bloodshedding and death. Finding that in these parts of the mountains there were certain men [1] who made a business of imposture, going about in disguise and living by trickery and lies, he prohibited the practice under heavy penalties. The poor and those who had no means of subsistence, he aided with alms in order to put them in an honest way of getting a living. The Capuchin Fathers, who had been placed there by him, he helped in the building of their monastery by the application to that purpose of certain pious bequests which had hitherto been squandered in drunkenness and other offences against God. Attached to the parish church under a provost were several canonries of but small value, some he added to the provostship, the others he suppressed, making two prebends instead, one for an assistant priest, the other for a schoolmaster, with the obligation of a daily Mass, and teaching grammar and Christian doctrine to children. St. Charles then climbed the rugged mountain of St. Luguzzone in order to inspect the state of the church of St. Lucio. There he remained till evening; as there was no inn near he went down the opposite side of the mountain at night towards Lugano and Colla in order to visit the Capriasca valley. The way was so steep that it was said that an angel must have conducted him and his companions over those rocks and precipices. The

[1] Called Cavargnoni because they came chiefly from the Cavargna valley.

parish priest of Sonvico in the diocese of Con
whom they had recourse for torches, entreated h
remain in his house the rest of the night, wondering
he could descend the mountain in the thick dar
without an accident. But he always trusted in
and felt sure of His aid in every danger, as he
undertook such journeys rashly, but to save the
souls scattered about the mountains, where it
difficult for any priest to live on account of
severity of the climate.

It was astonishing to behold the joy of the
mountaineers in these uncivilised parts at the pre
of their Archbishop; they rushed out to see him,
ing him their Holy Father, going in procession to
him from the neighbouring villages, singing h
and litanies; they often received Communion fro
hand, and would secretly touch his vestments
their rosaries. The walking-sticks he made use of
would keep as relics, as also knives and other o
which he had touched.

Having consecrated a parish church, dedicat
St. Martin, in the Sasna valley, he left the peo
impressed with his sanctity, that the wooden
he had used on that occasion were preserved
lady, who would not allow them to be put to pr
use afterwards. They had indeed good reaso
believing in his sanctity, with clear proofs of it I
their eyes—the unceasing toils he daily under
making his way through inaccessible roads, fasti
bread and water, not sleeping in a bed at nigh
lying for two or three hours on straw, or leav

trees, and very often on the ground: his almsgiving to the poor and to churches, at times bequeathing to them the very vestments he had used, the charity he showed towards all, and the zeal that inflamed his breast for the salvation of souls.

There were other proofs of his sanctity in the cries and shouts of those possessed by evil spirits in his presence, not being able to bear the sight of the Saint; in the obedience rendered by the demons to his command, as, for instance, when giving Communion to those tormented by malignant spirits, he had only to bid them open their mouths, when the demons immediately left them, and as if ordered by God, did not venture to make any further attack. The kindness and charity of their pastor for these persons, however poor and rough, could not be exceeded by a father's love for an only son, and filled all with such affection for him, that when he left them, they parted from him with sighs and tears, as if each had lost in him the father who gave them birth.

When he had finished his visitation, he brought together the clergy of those parts at his own expense, in order to make known to them the deficiencies he had noted, and to urge upon them the observance of his decrees, and serving God more perfectly.

He then returned to Milan, to keep the Nativity of the Blessed Virgin. It was about this time that he received the news that the King of Spain had gained a victory in his campaign against Portugal, for which he returned thanks to God by a solemn procession of clergy and people.

Book VII.

CHAPTER I.

THREE years having elapsed since the Cardin
visited Rome, he now resolved to go thither, b
obedience to the decrees of Trent, and to obtain th
firmation of the decrees of his Sixth Provincial
His Holiness, moreover, was waiting for his adv
affairs of grave moment. Intending to begin his j
at the end of November, the Saint heard of the ill
Camilla, his sister, wife of Cæsar Gonzaga, and
at once for Guastalla, but on his arrival four
already dead, just as another of his sisters,
Colonna, died a few months before. Having off
at her burial, to prepare for his journey to
he withdrew to the Capuchin monastery at Sabb
where he gave much edification to the monks
austerities; not being content with conforming
severity of their rule, but lying upon boards wit
a single blanket. In obedience to the decrees
Council of Trent and of his own Provincial Syn

asked leave to start on his journey from the Dean of his Province, Mgr. Cæsar Gambara, Bishop of Tortona. The testimony of Father Lucian of Florence, a cistercian monk of Vallombrosa, gives us some account of the Saint's manner of living in Rome, as St. Charles took up his abode at their monastery in his titular house of Santa Prassede.   This Father bears witness that the Saint always said the Divine office in church on his knees, with head uncovered, together with one or two of his chaplains ; that he recited matins in the chapel of the Pillar [1] of the Scourging, being in church by four o'clock in the morning, having first given some time to mental prayer, although the place was damp and cold, and the season inclement.

Having said his office and the litanies, he made his confession every morning to Father Ludovico Moneta, and then said his Mass in the same chapel.   Many used to come to hear his Mass early as it was, both ladies and gentlemen, amongst whom was Count Olivares, the Spanish Ambassador, who used to kneel always on the bare ground, and said that he thought the Cardinal was rather an angel than a man.   Many went to Communion at his Mass with great devotion, even on week days.   He then used to give audience to all who came, if he had not to go to the Pope, as was often the case.   He then went out on business, and on his return always made a first visit to the church, and said his office.   His ordinary refection was bread and water.   On Christmas day when he

[1] A portion of the pillar to which our Lord is said to have been bound is preserved in this church.

joined the monks in their refectory, by way of
brating the feast, he added a roast thrush to his
At the dinner hour the courtyard was filled wit
kinds of poor people to whom he gave alms.   O₁
evening, about five or six, he paid another visit t
church with his household, devoting twenty mi
to mental prayer in the Chapel of the Pillar,
which he gave a spiritual conference, proposing
or four points for the meditation of the next moɪ
He habitually took but little sleep, and his beɛ
an alcove in his oratory on which he slept for tɩ
three hours at most.   He was also used to reti
a vault beneath the High Altar, where relics o
saints were preserved, and remain there duriné
night in prayer.   He persevered in these austeriti
the time he remained in Rome, till after the Epiɪ
of the year 1583.   On his departure, finding tha
sacristy of the church needed repairs, he gave ɩ
that a new one properly furnished should be bu
his expense.   This building was completed iɪ
following year, 1584, when God had called hi
his heavenly home.

During this time he did not relax in his effoɪ
do all the spiritual good possible in Rome, hav
burning desire that its prelates should be conspi
in all the Apostolic virtues to the edification c
Christian world.   Besides private offices of char
his daily life, in advising, admonishing, and encouɪ
all who stood in need of such assistance, he estab
a meeting of all the prelates of Lombardy iɩ
church of Saint Ambrose, to further the spɪ

advancement of the members, which was a school in
fact for the formation of good Bishops. Amongst
other things he arranged that every member should
practise preaching, in order to be able to minister the
Word of God with greater benefit to the people.
This Society becoming numerous, and joined by prelates
of other nations, afterwards held its meetings in St.
Peter's, and gave Cardinals and Bishops of exemplary
life to the Church, continuing to the end of the Pontificate of Gregory XIII. (1585).

The Holy Father, knowing that the Cardinal was
endowed with great prudence and with the Spirit of
God, and that he had handled successfully most difficult matters, imposed upon him at this time the
charge of accommodating a difference between two
Italian Princes. St. Charles did not shrink from the
duty, but trusting in the assistance of God, surmounted
all difficulties.

St. Charles always endeavoured to make his sojourn in
Rome prove of advantage to his own diocese, and never
quitted the city without obtaining from the Sovereign
Pontiff some spiritual graces which the Holy Father
always granted, as well as substantial favours ; among
the latter he obtained two benefices that had belonged
to the Frati Humiliati, for his seminary in the district
of Caravaggio, and in Sezzè near Alexandria for the
congregation of the Oblates of St. Ambrose, vacant by
the death of the Abbate Raphael Corte of Pavia.

The diocese of Milan was now, by the grace of God,
brought into a better condition ; abuses were corrected,
and good discipline was established. St. Charles was

thus able to govern his flock without difficulty,
had now formed a school of ecclesiastics skilled
management of ecclesiastical affairs. Full of zε
the faith, he now resolved to visit in person the
of Switzerland and the Grisons infected with l
in order to bring them back to the fold. He ob
full powers from the sovereign Pontiff to go to
places in the name of the Apostolic See, as
reformer, and delegate general to the dioceses of
Coire, Constance, and the Grisons, with faculti
all reserved cases included in the Bull in
Domini,[1] with all other faculties and privileges, s
they amounted to all but Pontifical powers to
him to do all that was necessary to free souls
sin, to restore Divine worship, and the purity c
faith in those lands.

He obtained leave of his Holiness to take h
parture in the month of January, 1583, althoug
season was inclement. Passing through Sien
Archbishop Piccolomini received him in his hous
from a wish to pay him respect, invited many
nobles of the city to assist at a grand dinner.
Saint, who especially disliked extravagance in e
astics, at last rose from table, and though it wa
ing heavily at the time, declared his intention of
ing on his journey. On the Archbishop beggin

---

[1] Viz., for the absolution of heretics and dispensation of all
larities, except voluntary homicide and bigamy; in marriages oo
in the present or the future, in the third or fourth degree of
guinity, and affinity, and in spiritual relationship; to set rigl
guilty of simony, and to confer ecclesiastical benefices *de novo*; tε
the revenues of benefices wrongfully received, and to make other
tions of the same.

not to do so, he said: " My lord, I do not wish to hurt the poor; if I remain here this evening, the poor of this city will suffer for it, as the Bishop is bound to distribute among them everything beyond his own needs."

He left the Archbishop with this paternal admonition, and went on to the place [1] where the Holy Father had commissioned him to reconcile a difference between two princes. By prayer, both public and private, he put an end to the matter, to the great satisfaction of the two principals and of the Pontiff himself.

[1] Viz., Mantua, where he had to pronounce on the nullity of the marriage between Vincenzo Gonzaga, Prince of Mautua, and Margaret Farnese of Parma. The latter finally became a Benedictine nun, entering the convent of St. Paul at Parma, and taking the name of Sister Maura Lucenia. St. Charles himself preached a sermon on giving her the habit, on October 18, and also at her profession on the 30th of the same month, 1583, both of which are extant in a Latin version in the collection of his sermons.

CHAPTER II.

DEATH OF THE PRINCE OF SPAIN—DON CARL
ARRAGON APPOINTED GOVERNOR OF MILAN—
DIOCESAN SYNOD.

1583.

ON his return to Milan, St. Charles received tidi
the death of Prince Diego of Spain, son of his C:
Majesty, at the age of ten years, a youth of gree
mise. He mourned not only his decease, bu
the loss sustained by his father, writing to the
and encouraging him to patience and thankfuln
God's mercies. The King bore up well und
affliction, forbidding all show of sorrow in his i
and leaving himself and his surviving children
hand of God to be disposed of according to Hi
pleasure. St. Charles heard with satisfaction
the King was resigned, and had a mind detached,
religious. He did not fail to correspond to the
of his Majesty, ordering for his intention three i
sions to the usual churches, in which the city
and great numbers of the people took part, an
he did not only on account of the King's reque:
because he always felt bound by ties of affect.
the Crown of Spain.

In this year, 1583, Don Carlos of Arragon, Duke of Terra Nuova, a prince of great integrity, was made Governor of Milan, with orders from the King to put himself into communication with St. Charles, and avail himself of his advice. His appointment was a great consolation to the Saint, as he hoped for peace and assistance in the government of his diocese from him. St. Charles went to meet him on his arrival, and together with his Vicar-General and Canons escorted him into the city, and was visited by him in turn with lively expressions of regard and friendship. He also ordered public prayers to implore the blessing of God upon the new Governor, and a procession of all the clergy and people to the principal churches. These supplications were not poured forth in vain, for the good effects of the rule of the new Governor were soon visible, discipline was maintained, and the promise of the King to Mgr. Bascapè fulfilled.

Between the Governor and the Cardinal there was such union and concord ·that the people of Milan boasted that they had two rulers of the name of Charles with one heart, and that the spiritual and temporal rule were centred in one to the great advantage of all, so that they lived in peace, free from bloodshed and crime, with the blessing of God in the abundance of the fruits of the earth. The judges and lawyers only suffered, having but little business.

The following incident shows the friendship between the Governor and St. Charles:—On the occasion of a cavalry review, the Governor seeing a soldier riding badly, rebuked him, and was answered by him

in a manner so contrary to discipline, that, acc
to military law, he was condemned to death.
he was led to execution, some pious persons w
acquaint the Cardinal, who was engaged at a m
of Governors of the Hospital for Beggars.   Hearin
the unfortunate man had many children, he ex
himself, and went immediately to the Governo
obtained his pardon.

In this year, 1853, Charles held his Tenth Dic
Synod, in which he published the Decrees of the
Provincial Council, exhorting his clergy not to
in their endeavours after good discipline and g
perfection.   In his first discourse at the Synod h
for his subject the history of the Jews in the ti
Esdras, after the captivity in Babylon.   When re
how they began to rebuild the Temple, the
men who had not seen the Temple rejoicing, whil
old men wept, he applied this to the spiritual
of the Church, showing that if some reform had
accomplished, yet there was rather occasion for s
when they considered how much remained to be
and how far they were from attaining the fervc
the early Church.

Agostino Valerio, Bishop of Verona, who was
after made Cardinal, was present at this Council.
was a great admirer of the Saint, calling him
" Second Ambrose," and, anxious to follow his exa
in his own diocese, wrote and published his rec
tions of the Saint for the benefit of other prelate
pastors of souls.

· CHAPTER III.

ASCONA, a town on the Lago Maggiore, belonging to
Switzerland, had given birth to one Bartholomew Pappi,
who by will in the year 1580 bequeathed his property
to found a college in his native place for the Christian
education of children. He had made the Supreme
Pontiff his executor, who appointed St. Charles as administrator of the future college, with faculties for ·
making all rules and regulations, which charge was
willingly accepted by him. He went thither in the
month of July and chose a site near a church of our
Blessed Lady, where the building was immediately
begun, so that in the next year it was opened.

He took the opportunity of visiting Brissago, a
short distance from Ascona, but just within his own
diocese, the inhabitants of which were suffering from
the plague, and supplied their wants bountifully, so
that he was obliged to borrow for his own necessities
in order to go back to Milan.

In the month of September he was apprised of the

serious illness of Charles Emmanuel, Duke of S
then lying at Vercelli, and was much distr
because he looked upon him as a son, and saw in
a great zeal for the faith; and that there wou
disturbance in case of his death, as there were
pretenders to the throne and no direct heir. Wi
delay the Saint started for Vercelli on horseback
writing to Milan and directing public prayers
said for the Duke. He reached Novara early in
morning, where he said Mass and gave Holy Comm
to many persons. He then took a carriage plac
his disposal by the Bishop, and hastened on, by
cult roads, where he was upset into the water
escaped all damage but a wetting; at which mish
did not show any displeasure, but occupied himse
overcoming the annoyance of his companions.

A countryman observing the accident bega
follow after the carriage barefoot, and wheneve
saw it endangered by the bad roads, put his sho
to the wheel, and prevented an overset, without
asked to do so. The Cardinal, out of pity, the
him, and begged him not to take so much trouble.
countryman, however, not obeying his repeated w
was at length ordered by him to stop. The
man then knelt down and said: "I follow you
lord, because you are a saint." The Cardinal
displeased at this and would not go on, wher
countryman told him all his grief with simplicity
his wife had left him, and that the matter was I
the Bishop of Vercelli. "I shall be there to-mon
said St. Charles, "and will do what I can for you

When he reached Vercelli, he went immediately to the bedside of the Duke, who was very glad to see him, and raising his hands to heaven, said from his heart, "I am cured;" convinced that the presence of the Saint had wrought his cure. The Cardinal spent half an hour in conversation upon spiritual things; pointing out that the soul ought first to be cared for, and that its infirmity is often the cause of weakness of the body. He gave public thanksgiving to God in the cathedral with the forty hours' devotion, giving Holy Communion to the Duke, and singing the Mass of thanksgiving himself before a congregation full of joy, because a prince whom they loved had been rescued from death.

Charles Emmanuel always attributed his restoration to the holy Cardinal's prayers; and years after, in 1602, he sent a public attestation of it to Milan, with an offering of a silver lamp and a thousand crowns to keep lights burning before the tomb of the Saint in gratitude for the favours received from him, and especially his recovery from this illness. "We acknowledge," in his own words, "and shall always confess, that Almighty God restored us to health through the prayers and merits of this great Cardinal."

The King of Poland, Stephen Bathory, who had succeeded to the throne upon the abdication of Henry III. of France, had conceived so high an opinion of the Cardinal's sanctity that on sending to Rome his nephew Andrew, as his ambassador, he bade him go by Milan, even if he had to go a hundred miles out of his way, to visit Cardinal Borromeo. The King wished his nephew to imitate the Saint, and take him as a pattern in the spiritual and ecclesiastical life; he had also scruples about certain benefices which he asked the Cardinal to decide for him, and if necessary to settle by appeal to Rome. The Cardinal met the ambassador in state and gave him a grand reception in his palace, and took great pains, according to the King's wish, to imbue him with the true spirit of his vocation. He invited him also to assist at High Mass at the cathedral, and surprised him by the majesty of its ceremonial, sending him on to Rome with suitable presents, and writing to him there to remind him of the lessons he had learnt at Milan. The Saint acknowledged the King's letter in the following terms:—

Letter of St. Charles to Stephen Bathory, King of Poland.

" I have received two letters from your Majesty, one of the 13th December last, and the other of the 15th July, brought by your illustrious nephew Andrew, both of which I take this opportunity of answering. I congratulate myself on the zeal of your Majesty for the Catholic faith, because to be a King is not so great a glory as to live in obedience to the King of Heaven, and to give laws to many subjects is not so high a prerogative as to keep them in obedience to the law of God, and that not by force of arms, but by the spread of His Gospel, especially in these times when wicked men fight so fiercely against Him.

" I acknowledge myself obliged by your confidence in recommending to me your illustrious nephew, and will, as far as in me lies, never be wanting in my exertions to further his spiritual well-being. I have striven in the same way to teach him the rules of ecclesiastical discipline, both by word of mouth and by writing to him at Rome; and I beg of your Majesty to urge him by your own authority to put them in practice, that by the lessons of the Church he may be enabled, young as he is, to walk in the way of perfection."

The King, when informed of the welcome accorded by St. Charles, expressed himself as very grateful for all his good-will to his nephew, who was soon after created Cardinal by Gregory XIII.

The Saint in congratulating him on his elevation, reminded him of its obligations and the necessity of satisfying them by the holiness of his life, by letter as follows: "In your present rank, you cannot, even if you would, escape the eyes of men. You have been put in this high place that your light may point out the way to those who have lost it, and shine out afar as a beacon to those who know the truth. Your office carries with it great weight and power, to recall the minds of men from sin, to keep them steadfast to their duty, and to urge them on to virtue. If to it you add watchfulness, together with the fire of charity (called zeal in Holy Scripture) and the desire of spreading the knowledge of God, it is difficult to say what fruit you may not reap."

The next year the new Cardinal left Rome to return to Poland, passing through Milan again on his way to ask St. Charles' advice and assistance. He begged him to recommend some friend to him whom he could

take as his director and spiritual guide. The S
was glad to send with him a good priest, Dome
Ferre by name, of Viterbo, a doctor of theology,
made him many presents, as well as those of
household. To the King his uncle he sent an iv
crucifix with the following letter :—

"I send your Majesty an ivory image of J
Christ crucified, that you may have Him, with wl
love you are set on fire, for whom you fight, as y
guide in warfare, your master in peace, your refug
adversity, your glory in prosperity. In His C
you must conquer, at His feet you must lay
spoils of victory. Upon Him I call, as its author
witness to my love and loyalty to your Majesty."

CHAPTER IV.

VISITATION OF SWITZERLAND AND THE GRISONS.

1583.

ST. CHARLES having been delegated by the Pope Apostolic Visitor of all the countries of Switzerland and Grisons, placed all the affairs of his diocese under the care of Mgr. Owen Lewis, his Welsh Vicar-General, who was afterwards Bishop of Cassano, so that everything might go on as usual during his own absence. He begun his visitation towards the end of the year 1583, in the Valley of Mesolcina, because religion was at a low ebb there, and needed a thorough reform, as will be seen by the condition in which he found it.

There belong to Switzerland five valleys on the Italian side of the mountains adjoining the German territory near the Rhaetian Alps, of which the chief town, Chur, is a bishopric formerly in the province of Milan, as appears by a Synodal letter written by the Archbishop St. Eusebius and the bishops of his province to St. Leo, the first Pope of that name. The first of these valleys is called Mesolcina, from a castle in the vale of Misocco, and is twenty Italian miles in

circumference and well populated. It formerly
longed to the Milanese family of Trivulzio, but
people joined the Grison confederacy. The sec
valley, Poschiavo, so called from its chief town of
same name, also belonging to the Grison league, is,
Mesolcina, in the diocese of Chur. The other
valleys are not allies but subjects of the league,
the Tellina valley, fifty miles long, containing m
rich and highly - populated districts, and the C
venna valley, equally rich and well populated. Tl
two valleys bound the territory of Milan toget
with Lake Como, into which the river Adda, flov
through the Valle-Tellina, empties itself. The
valley is called the valley of San Giacomo, borde:
on the Chiavenna, and these three are in the dio
of Como. The districts on the north side of
mountains, and in particular the city of Chur, v
infected with the pestilential doctrines of Zwingl
Luther, and Calvin, and their inhabitants hav
continual intercourse with the people of the vall
the contagion spread among the latter, so that tl
valleys became a shelter and asylum for many a]
tates, heretics, and evil-doers. These delinquents
into these retired parts of Italy to escape from
correction of the ecclesiastical courts, and to live l
of unbridled license in a secure place of refuge. T:
bad example perverted many simple persons, and
duced them to separate themselves from the E
Roman Church, the true mother of faithful Christi
and to live in whatever evil way they liked best w
out danger of being restrained by the canon law.

ecclesiastics who still retained the Catholic faith set such a bad example and led such evil lives, that they did much more harm than good to the ignorant inhabitants of those districts. Owing to all this, these unfortunate places were in the worst possible state, and in danger of entirely losing the light of faith, since heresy was making continual progress, and already some of the principal towns were all but won over to Protestantism. The Cardinal, who had not failed in watchfulness, as far as he was able, feared that the Devil might in time, owing to its vicinity, injure his own diocese of Milan. He had, therefore, an additional reason for helping this unfortunate people, viz., the preservation of his own diocese and the whole of Italy from the danger of such contagion. The valley of Mesolcina in particular, in addition to heresy, abounded in wizards and witches, who worked great mischief, through the instrumentality of the Devil, to whom the miscreants dedicated themselves. Not only did they afflict children, grown-up people, and even animals with illness by their sorceries, but even with death, and men and herds of cattle were sometimes hurled down mountain precipices. All this happened because nobody could find a remedy. The people therefore assembled a general council of the valleys this very year to deliberate how they could best provide against these evils, and resolved to apply to St. Charles, and beg him for advice and help. They accordingly sent some of the chief inhabitants of the valley on an embassy to Milan, who were received with great kindness by the Saint. He was delighted that Almighty God

had opened to him a way of devoting himself to
service of those people, so he promised them his
tection, and that he would go himself to the dis
to make fuller investigations and provision for t
needs.

St. Charles weighed well the importance of
business, and thought it necessary first of all to i
them a judge with the title of Inquisitor, to pro
against the sorcerers in a legal way. He sele
Francesco Borsatto, a juris-consult from Mantua
this office, who had only recently entered upon
ecclesiastical career, and had come to Milan st:
by the fame of St. Charles, to receive holy or
from his hand, and to learn in his school the pra
of ecclesiastical discipline. Borsatto accordingly i
to Mesolcina, made the necessary investigations,
found nearly the whole country infected with sorce
and what was worse, discovered that the Provos
the Valley, resident in the Collegiate Church
Roveredo, was the head of all the crew, the pe
having thus become a ravening wolf in the n
of his own flock. As nothing in the way of per
sion could induce these miscreants to give up t
practices, Borsatto proceeded with such gentle
that he gained all hearts, and was able to do a
wished with the people. These prudent meas
were a great help towards the visit of the Card
and as it were, a preparation and forestalmen
better things. In the meantime the Saint, knov
how cautiously he would have to proceed, and
difficulties in his way, after fervent prayer, accon

to his custom, chose various assistants in this undertaking. Among those selected for this office were
Father Francesco Panigarola, a Milanese priest, afterwards Bishop of Asti; Fr. Achille Gagliardi, a Jesuit,
a man of authority and experience; and Bernardino
Morra, his auditor-general, who was afterwards made
Bishop of Aversa by Clement VIII.

Having made all these arrangements, he set out
from Milan in the beginning of November, and took
up his headquarters at Roveredo, the principal place
of the Valley, where he was received with great
delight by the people, affording him great hopes of
effecting some good among them. He went at once
into the church and preached to a vast crowd, beginning his sermon with the story of Joseph, how he was
sent to visit his brethren to find out how they were,
and all about them; saying, that the Supreme Pontiff
and common Father of all the faithful had, in imitation of this Patriarch, sent him to visit them as his
own brethren and children. He showed them the
affection of the Holy Father, who had sent him so
far, to his own inconvenience, in the cold weather,
travelling over mountains by bad roads, with the
one object of visiting and helping them in whatever way he could, in their eternal welfare. He was
so successful in this sermon that his hearers could not
restrain their tears, and exclaimed that God had sent
him to console them, and were very grateful for his
kindness, becoming attached to him by ties of heartfelt
affection.

St. Charles began his visitation in the following

way, in order to do as much good as possible to 1
poor souls. Father Panigarola preached every n
ing on the dogmas of the Faith, to confirm the C;
lics and convert the heretics, after which the Car
said Mass and preached another sermon, for the
version of sinners, the reform of morals, and
restoration of Divine worship. After dinner I
Achille explained the catechism and taught Chri
doctrine with such clearness that the people g;
great profit as well as pleasure from it, and st
nearly all the rest of the day in church. Be
this there were many confessors who were occu
continually in hearing confessions for the daily
munion of the faithful, which the Cardinal ga\
his Mass. Although all this took place on \
days, and the people belonged to the working-cl;
for the greater part field labourers, yet they left e
occupation to attend these spiritual exercises.
St. Charles was aware that good example in his
person as a Bishop would do more towards ga;
souls than words, especially with a peasantry ar
whom were heretics grown old in error, wit
the light of faith. During the whole time of
visitation he devoted himself to prayer with ;
assiduity, and fasted every day on bread and \
except on feast-days, only eating once in twenty
hours, according to his custom. His household fi
likewise, although it was only Advent, which ca
them some inconvenience owing to the scarcit
fasting-food in those regions. The Saint was
than usually liberal in almsgiving, and paid all

expenses of the visitation out of his own pocket, without being the slightest burden to the people in any way. He had brought a large sum of money from Milan for this purpose, it being his custom to say that a prelate's liberality to the poor and the Church was a most efficacious means of aiding his people spiritually and converting them to Almighty God. He slept only a few hours upon a little straw and bare planks, chastised his body with disciplines, and bore the cold with patience, although sharp and piercing, among the mountains covered with snow. For this reason the peasants of those parts live in rooms with stoves, but the Saint would never make use of them. On the contrary, he would not allow his room to be warmed at all, and would never go near the fire, according to his custom, though he was but scantily clad, and only wore a single garment thread-bare and old. He did more good by this mode of life and self-denial than by anything else, as the people, seeing such austerities combined with such zeal for their salvation in a Cardinal of Holy Church, had their eyes opened to the light, this being quite the contrary of what apostates and heretical preachers had told them about the lives of Cardinals and prelates. Indeed, his manner of life converted many more sinners, and even heretics, than all his sermons.

When Borsatto had finished his examination of those suspected of dealing in magic, he gave a full report to St. Charles, who, knowing that these kind of people are very difficult to deal with, owing to their close friendship with the Evil One, tried every possible means,

with much patience and the assistance of his pri
to bring them to repentance and a new life. His e
tions were not in vain, as many of them were
verted; on one occasion a hundred and fifty per:
abjured their errors, went to Confession, and recei
Holy Communion from the Saint. Eleven old wor
however, ringleaders of the rest, who seem to 1
given themselves entirely up to the Devil, and
longer deserved mercy on account of their sins aga
the Divine mercy, remained obstinate in their crin
and as nothing could move them, were finally har
over to the secular power and punished by the fla
The Provost of Roveredo, the head of the whole
showed the same obstinacy. Notwithstanding all
efforts of the Cardinal and his priests to convert 1
nothing could bring his hard heart to repentance.
was necessary, therefore, to degrade him publicly f
his office, a course of action which moved the Card
to tears, to whom it was very painful to do anyt!
contrary to his natural tenderness, even in the inter
of justice. He preached a sermon full of sorrow
this occasion, in the presence of the culprit. "Sec,
children," he began, "the decision of Holy Church
regard to those of her ministers who have rend
themselves unworthy of their holy calling." He t
showed how the Church, as a tender mother, ab:
such severity. St. Charles noticed particularly du
this visitation that the destruction of souls in t!
districts was in great measure owing to the evil 1
of ecclesiastics. He found two apostate monks li·
publicly as if married, with wives and children,

having compassion on their wretched state, with paternal kindness tried to bring them to repentance. The unfortunate men, struck by his clemency, threw themselves at his feet with tears in their eyes, and besought him to take pity upon themselves and these poor women and children. St. Charles, delighted at gaining over these souls, replaced the monks in religious observance in their monasteries, and sent the women and children to asylums in Milan. He suspended other priests of evil lives, and banished others from the country. One, however, who showed signs of amendment, the Saint had well trained in discipline at Milan, and eventually he turned out well. Exemplary ecclesiastics, Jesuits and others, were put in the places of these bad ones, and Giovanni Pietro Stoppano, of the Congregation of the Oblates, was made Provost over all. By this means the spiritual necessities of these valleys were supplied, and these priests were maintained partly at his own expense and partly through the funds granted him by the paternal charity of Gregory XIII.

The Cardinal spent much time in this way, teaching and instructing the people in the truth. He showed great patience towards certain women of low class, some of whom were extremely obstinate and impertinent in their answers, but he overlooked all this in his anxiety to gain them to God. Many heretics belonging to the best families of the valley were converted, and abjured their errors, and were received back into the Church. The chancellor of the valley who lived at Misocco, who had been most obstinate at first, was converted, and so altered in his disposition,

that after having abjured and denounced his h
he publicly burned all the books and writings
him by Calvinistic preachers. The Cardinal di
same himself with many other heretical books ᛫
he found, making a bonfire of them one night
meadow : in their stead he distributed good ones ᛫
he procured from Milan at his own expense. He
out many instances of invalid marriages, contɪ
within degrees prohibited by the Church withou
vious dispensation, many usurers of the worst sor
many persons who had incurred ecclesiastical ceɪ
and committed excesses, all of which he set riɡ
virtue of the powers granted him by the Supreme
tiff, delivering many souls from sin to God. Hᛁ
fittingly restored the celebration of Divine worshi
the ornaments of the churches, as he found everʝ
in a neglected state.

. During this visitation he did not fail to go ɪ
church dedicated to our Blessed Lady in the
of Calanca on the top of a mountain. Althoɪ
was an ascent of four miles, up a bad road, wit
snow lying deep on the ground, he journeyed thɛ
foot, and said Mass and preached to the semi-s
inhabitants of the region to confirm them iɪ
Catholic faith. He administered the sacrame
baptism several times in full pontificals, to exciɪ
people to a greater reverence for it, and to sho
priests what respect they should pay to holy t
He reconsecrated several churches in which hɛ
had been buried, and made many regulations fᴄ
service of God and the welfare of souls. In

he reformed the whole valley thoroughly in a truly miraculous way. In consequence of this his fame spread through all the adjacent territories, even beyond the mountains, where it seems to have had a good influence on heretics, as the inhabitants of the valley of the Rhine, all Protestants, sent ambassadors to him in secret to beg him to pay them a visit, promising him to let him say Mass, preach, and do what he liked. St. Charles was greatly rejoiced at seeing the wonders worked by Almighty God in the hearts of the ignorant who had been deceived by false prophets. After receiving them kindly he promised them, if possible, a visit at a future time, as he was not able just then to grant their request, having no one with him who knew the language of the country.

Page 199.—" The Provost of Roveredo."

This was the Rev. Domenico Quattrini, Provost or Rector of the Church of St. Victor. In a letter to Bernardino Morra, dated November 28, 1583, St. Charles writes : "Please inform the Bishop of Chur that Domenico Quattrini has been found guilty of most flagrant crimes. . . . On his own confession he used to take part in dances of devils in priestly vestments with the holy chrism in his hands, and said Mass every day, though he kept in his house a woman who lived with him as his wife, obstinately showing no sign of sorrow or repentance to the last."

CHAPTER V.

NEGOTIATION OF MONSIGNOR BERNARDINO MORRA AT
—VISIT TO BELLINZONA AND ITS NEIGHBOURHOO

1583.

As St. Charles desired the good effects of his vi
Mesolcina to be lasting, and religion to be kept
so as to spread into the rest of the land for the r
of souls, he saw it would be necessary to ma
permanent provision for the ministers of the Ch
as these benefits would chiefly depend upon '
Hearing, therefore, that the authorities of the co·
were just then holding their diet at Chur, he res
to send an envoy to confer with them about its
tual necessities, and to beg them no longer to ι
apostates or strange religious of evil lives into
territories, as such persons caused the perditic
souls through their corrupt example ; and to
the people to provide themselves with good pι
foreigners if necessary, notwithstanding the prc
tion which existed to the contrary. He chose ¹
signor Bernardino Morra for this mission, a mι
great prudence and decision of character, who]
short time previously resigned his post of civil ɪ

trate, and embracing the ecclesiastical state, had entered the Cardinal's household.　He sent Giovanni Ambrogio Fornero with him as an interpreter, and gave them a letter to the Bishop of Chur, full of fatherly counsel, mingled with rebuke, for his negligence in his pastoral duties, exhorting him with ardent affection to have a greater reverence for his office, and to provide more diligently for the salvation of his flock, by residence in his diocese, and preventing the ravages of the Evil One.

In crossing Mount St. Bernard they lost their way, in spite of their guide, and could no longer see any trace of a path amidst the snow piled up around them. They were therefore in a very sorry plight, as they did not know which way to go, amid desert places and intolerable cold.　Fornero, who knew more about those mountains than the others, made Monsignor Morra and the guide stay with the horses while he went on foot towards the Rhine, where the snow came up to his waist.　As he went on through these solitudes, full of fear at the thought of the risk which they ran, a little dog suddenly appeared before him, though not a trace of a human being was to be seen, and as if it had been sent, led him to a bridge over the Rhine, where he procured men to make a path through the snow with shovels, and where he was also able to buy provisions.　They then fetched Monsignor Morra, who had become very ill from the cold, down from the mountain, and their strength having been renewed by restoratives, they proceeded happily on their way.　One Friday they happened to be passing the night in the district of Tosana, which had lost the faith. At supper-time, the host put both meat and abstinence food on the table, as is the custom in those countries where there are as many heretics as Catholics, for every one to take what he preferred. But the guests, who had heard that Monsignor Morra came from Cardinal Borromeo, felt such respect for him that not a single heretic ate meat in his presence that evening. The host began to converse with Fornero about the Cardinal's holiness, and boasted that he had received his blessing. And when Morra replied that it would do him no good, as he was of a different religion, the heretic rejoined that next time he hoped to receive it with profit, hinting thereby at his conversion. The people in those parts were all looking forward to St. Charles' coming with gladness, and were already making arrangements for mending the roads and meeting him in state ; even the heretics were well disposed for conversion at his bidding, so highly did they esteem the sanctity of this servant of God. When Morra reached Chur he made his negotiations with the authorities assembled in diet, who treated him respectfully enough, though most of them were Protestants, owing to their regard for St. Charles. Not only did they listen willingly, but readily granted all his requests, except the admission of foreign priests into their territories.

While Monsignor Morra was fulfilling his embassy, the Cardinal left the valley of Mesolcina about the beginning of December, leaving the inhabitants very anxious to see him again, and proceeded to visit

Bellinzona in the diocese of Como, but in temporals under Swiss jurisdiction. Although this place was not infected with heresy, it was sadly deficient in morals and virtuous living, since the ecclesiastics of the district lived in a lax manner, and some had even incurred ecclesiastical censures through having obtained benefices through unlawful means. There were many invalid and illegally contracted marriages among the people, and the temporal rulers were in mortal sin owing to their usurpation of the ecclesiastical jurisdiction, and had incurred excommunication.

St. Charles employed the same method as at Mesolcina, and so touched the hearts of the people that they readily discovered to him their bad state and their hidden sins, like sick people on the arrival of a physician reputed to be able to cure all diseases. He devoted several days with great patience and charity to the salvation of these souls, not only in Bellinzona, but also in the neighbourhood, and performed marvellous conversions by daily sermons and administration of the sacraments, freeing poor sinners from the bonds of sin, and absolving those who had rebelled against the ecclesiastical power, and making them promise to refrain from similar excesses for the future. He erected a scholastic prebend at Bellinzona to provide for the instruction of children in Christian doctrine and to keep them from heresy. He was intending to found a college for the youth of those regions in Misocco, and had already purchased a large house for this purpose, when death carried him off before he had time to carry this project into execution.

Father Achille Gagliardi, at the Saint's sugge
wrote a catechism of Christian doctrine for the ꞵ
of those regions, in which religion was explained
the greatest clearness, published the following
1584. Having finished this spiritual harves
Cardinal returned to Milan to keep Christmas
to feed his flock with spiritual food and the
Sacraments.

CHAPTER VI.

FALSE REPORTS OF THE HERETICAL PREACHERS IN THE
GRISONS, EFFORTS OF CHARLES IN FAVOUR OF THE
CATHOLICS OF THOSE PARTS.

THE influence which St. Charles had acquired over the authorities of the Grisons would have sufficed to induce them to concede all that was necessary to bring the league to their ancient obedience to the Roman Church, and to purify them from their heresy, as he had made a beginning already. But the enemy of souls, the persecutor of this servant of God, and hinderer of all his good works, rose up to harass him by means of the preachers, as the teachers of heresy were called. These men being apostates and fugitives from the bosom of Holy Church, feeling certain they would be hunted from the country after Monsignor Morra had left Chur, held council among themselves, and described the Cardinal's visit to the Valle-Mesolcina in a most invidious and unjust way to the members of the diet, making out that he had usurped their jurisdiction. Under plea of zeal for the interests of the state, they asserted that the inhabitants of Mesolcina deserved to be punished as rebels and violators of the confe-

deracy, alleging that they had, contrary to law, in
an inquisitor of heresy (meaning Borsatto), a
ceived a Cardinal, who was an ally of Spain, to
they had given for his residence a building which
serve for a fortress. They further declared this w
way to break their treaty with France, and unit
in common cause with Spain against them, and
accused St. Charles and his friends of being des
men, who would soon deprive them of their libe
they did not quickly take measures against s
catastrophe. With these wily arguments they no
managed to have the chief inhabitants of Mes
imprisoned and punished, but also procured an
ment against St. Charles (and this was their chief
forbidding him to enter the country. By this :
they felt assured of their own position, and es
the risk of banishment themselves. These te:
are much esteemed by heretics, because they m
to keep themselves in favour, with craft and adu
flattering the self-love of their followers, and le
them in the broad way of perdition, and are, the:
cherished by the enemies of the Cross of Christ
this way Luther, Calvin, Zwinglius and others t
doctrines quite different from those of the apostle:
liberty of conscience, freedom to sin, a life accord
the flesh, and everything contrary to the law of
and the Church. On this account they have had
berless followers, as our fallen nature is naturally ε
disposed, and apt to run along the broad road to hell
heretical ministers being highly thought of, the au
ties of the league were not loth to listen to them, espε

as they were careful to discuss political matters, which touched many interests in those parts. Although there were many Catholic members of position in the confederacy, who were well enough disposed towards St. Charles, and anxious for the propagation of the Faith and the extirpation of heresy, yet as the heretics outnumbered them in votes, it was determined that those who had received the Cardinal into the Valley of Mesolcina should be prosecuted. Many of them were therefore, as guilty persons, shut up in prison at Chur. The members of the Grison League were angry at this injustice, and undertook the defence of the sufferers, saying that to them alone belonged the decision of the case, on account of their belonging to themselves, and not to the other two leagues, to whom the people of Mesolcina were not subject, but only allied. The Cardinal, who had heard all this with great pain, did not fail to do everything in his power to help the accused, and sought the aid of the Swiss Catholic cantons through their ambassadors. By this means he obtained the liberation of the prisoners without any punishment, and everything he had done in the valley remained unaltered. The Catholics were so encouraged by this that they took heart to defend the Faith and the discipline the Saint had taught them, if necessary, by arms, and at the risk even of their lives.

The Cardinal, who knew that these mishaps were caused by the devil, in order to prevent the conversion of the heretics deceived by his false ministers, did not like to give up his visitation. In order to overcome these difficulties, as he was desirous that the Catholics

should be free both to provide themselves with good
priests from any country they thought best, and to be
visited by their Bishop (at his convenience) and by the
Holy Apostolic See, and that no more apostates or other
vagabonds should to admitted to the cure of souls and
the administration of the Sacraments, as in the past.
One of the most efficacious means employed by him
for this object was that he prevailed upon the Swiss
Catholics to send ambassadors to the Grisons, when they
were holding a Council, to persuade them to grant their
vassals liberty in everything concerning the Catholic
Faith, and to protest on behalf of all the Catholic cantons, that if this freedom were not granted, as was only
fitting and according to the stipulations of their con-
federation, they would no longer help them in time of
need. This measure would certainly have had the most
beneficial result, and, supplemented by other steps,
would certainly have enabled the Cardinal to overcome
all obstacles, and effect his intention of converting those
districts to the Faith, and thereby gaining innumerable
souls, if Almighty God, in His own good providence,
had not called the Saint to Himself, just at the time
when he was about to carry his purpose into execution,
and continue his visitation.

When the Catholics of the other valleys heard of
the good St. Charles had done in the Mesolcina, and
that he had even found means of liberating the
prisoners, and that the valley had been provided with
good priests, owing to his protection, they sent to him
secretly to acquaint him with their condition, that
they were oppressed by heretics, and harassed in the

practice of their faith, that they were famishing after the things of God, asking for bread, and having no one to break it to them. Therefore they implored him, by the mercy of God, to vouchsafe to take them under his protection, and console them with his presence, or at least to send them good priests to instruct and help them to save their souls. The Cardinal, who had no greater desire than this, promised to help them as soon as he could; and as things were not sufficiently settled to enable him to visit them in person, he sent them some good priests in the meantime. In the months of February and March, of 1584, he dispatched Fathers Francesco Adorno, S.J., and Domenico Boverio, of the Congregation of St. Paul, to Chiavenna, a populous place, in extreme need of help, by reason of heresy, which abounded in the district, and to Poschiavo. He also sent Marc Aurelio Grattarola,[1] of the Congregation of the Oblates, to Plurio, another populous town of the same valley. These priests did great good by their sermons, and administration of the Sacraments, by teaching Christian doctrine, and above all, by their holy lives, to the delight of good Catholics, who ran with avidity to learn about the things of God, even coming from distant parts of the country for this object, so that it was easy to see how they had longed for such graces. When the preachers saw that their first plot to prevent St. Charles sending aid to the valleys had not been successful, but that, on the contrary, he was sending fresh priests to

[1] This Father was afterwards instrumental in beginning and completing the cause of the canonisation of the Saint, which cost him ten years of continuous labour.

other parts of the country, they went back to Chur, and tried to raise the suspicions of the diet by saying that the Cardinal was trying to win over the districts on their side of the mountains to the Crown of Spain, as they had formerly belonged to the States of Milan, and his Catholic Majesty still claimed them as his due. They reminded them that the famous general, Giovanni Giacomo de Medici, had formerly attempted the same enterprise, and had taken the territory of Chiavenna and Morbegno in Valtellina, and they urged that this Cardinal, his nephew, entertained the same designs, as he was sending spies all over the valleys under pretext of helping the Papists (as they called the Catholics); they further asserted that the priests we have mentioned were spies of the Cardinal, and made such crafty complaints against them, and especially against Boverio and Grattarola, that they greatly alarmed the minds of the heretics, who determined to imprison and punish them. Not content with poisoning the minds of the nobles, these preachers tried to excite the Protestant part of the peasantry against the Fathers. Indeed the Valle-Bregaglia, which had become entirely Protestant, was on the point of taking up arms to march to Chiavenna to put Father Adorno in prison, when he made his escape, forewarned by the Catholic party. Father Boverio was summoned to Chur and put in prison, and though he was found innocent, they would not release him till he had promised to leave the country. Fifteen of the chief nobles of the three leagues, most of them heretics, came to Grattarola, and summoned him to appear before them at Chiavenna, meaning to imprison and punish him severely for the charges brought against him by the preachers, who had declared he was a spy of Cardinal Borromeo, that he had entered the country contrary to the laws, that he preached false doctrine, that he was inciting the Catholics to rebellion, that he had published the Gregorian calendar, which had not as yet their sanction, with other false accusations. As he was innocent, he was not afraid of appearing before them, and defended himself so well against these charges, that the nobles understood the injustice of the accusations brought against him. One of them, the Governor of Plurio, a Catholic, helped him greatly in the matter, by bearing testimony to his uprightness, and exposing the duplicity of his enemies. His innocence being thus recognised, the nobles allowed him to return to Plurio without imprisonment or fine, and gave him permission to resume his ordinary ecclesiastical duties. This affair was of great consolation to the Catholics, but gave offence to the heretics, who thought he ought to have been condemned to death. It is, therefore, to be conjectured that the nobles, now that they were disabused of the suspicions the preachers had instilled into their minds, under the pretext of state interests, would neither have prevented the Cardinal's visitation, nor interfered with his policy, as they now looked upon him as a holy man.

CHAPTER VII.

THE LAST YEAR OF ST. CHARLES'S LIFE.

1584.

ALTHOUGH St. Charles had the reformation of Ca
and the conversion of heretics in Switzerland
his mind, it is none the less evident that he wa:
cipating the approaching close of his life. Nc
did he predict it, or at least hint at it, but two
last occasions on which he appeared in publi(
what he felt. One was the convocation of all h
cials, diocesan visitors and rural deans, and the
his eleventh and last diocesan synod. He was
tomed to say that it was not enough for a Bis
make decrees for the government of his dioce
that he ought also to find means of carrying the
execution. He therefore summoned all his rural
sixty in number, to Milan, after the Feast
Epiphany, and lodged them in his own house,
he opened the Congress, which sat for three
About this time he was attacked by erysipelas
leg, which was a great trouble to him, and con
him to remain in bed. Notwithstanding this, .

not curtail his usual labours, but had a couch made up in the audience-chamber, on which he lay and transacted business, clad in his usual costume. First of all he explained his object in gathering them together, which was to find out whether all his decrees were fully observed; if not, the causes of their non-observance, and the best way of carrying them out in future. As long as the meeting lasted he would attend to no other business, but even spent part of the night preparing and collecting materials for discussion. He had compiled a manuscript volume, in which all the decrees of the Councils were briefly entered, each one under its proper heading. This he kept in front of him and read from beginning to end, inquiring at every fresh heading how the rules were kept, and noting down every new proposition and conclusion.

He next considered the abuses remaining among clergy and people, and settled upon the best means of removing them. This Congress seems to have included a general examination of all the wants of the diocese, and of the necessary means of supplying them. St. Charles had its decisions published in a volume and presented to the clergy at the next synod, when he gave orders to have them carried into execution. All this shows he knew he was giving the last finishing-touch to the work of reform in which he had so strenuously laboured for so many years, and that he was about to depart, having finished the task appointed him by Almighty God.

During this Congress he showed in another way his fatherly love for his clergy and his presentiment that

he should soon have to leave them, for he gave am
faculties to all the ecclesiastics of his diocese, throu
a special privilege obtained from Rome, for absoluti
from all censures, and dispensations from all irregul
rities incurred in the administration of the Sacramen
He licensed special confessors both in town and count
for this object, and gave great consolation to the cler
who saw in it a clear proof of their Bishop's love for the

Only one thing now remained for him to do,
satisfy his desire of removing every imperfection fro
his people, and bringing them to a perfect observar
of a holy life. He had always extremely disliked t
Carnival, and thought it highly unbecoming for ratio
Christians (chosen by Almighty God as His o'
peculiar people, and bound to employ their streng
and time in His service) to give themselves over
the animal enjoyment of the senses, and lose mu
time in worldly pastimes, foolishly allowing themselv
to be led away by the evil custom of the world
commit follies, just at the time when Holy Church
inviting her children to weep over their first parer
sin, in their transgression of God's commandmer
and to prepare themselves to keep the sacred fast
Lent. He had, indeed, already done away with simi
profanities on Sundays; but this year he wished
abolish them entirely, even on week-days, and indu
his people to occupy themselves in holy things a
spiritual exercises worthy of their Christian professi
He therefore held the following services during t
three weeks immediately preceding Lent. First,
ordered public devotions every Sunday and feast-d

in the cathedral and other collegiate churches, consist-
ing of litanies and other prayers, and points of meditation, read aloud, to enable the people to learn the
practice of mental prayer. Secondly, he ordered processions of the clergy and people in each of the six
quarters of the town, to the seven stational churches,
every day during Septuagesima Week. The Saint
attended all these processions himself at the head
of his clergy, and preached sermons against vanity
and worldly dissipation; which functions were very
popular and attended by great crowds. Indeed, the
holy Archbishop's influence and exhortations had a
marvellous effect on the Milanese, who not only gave
up their ordinary Carnival amusements, but even their
lawful business and occupations, to attend these services; ladies and gentlemen of high rank behaved in
the same devout way. In the third place, St. Charles
invited all the inhabitants of Milan to receive Holy
Communion from his hands on appointed days in the
different churches belonging to the several quarters of
the city; and, in addition, there was a general Communion on Quinquagesima Sunday, which gave him
great fatigue, owing to the number of persons to whom
he gave Holy Communion, it being more like Easter
than an ordinary Sunday. Fourthly, he ordered that
devotions in St. Sepulcre's should be held every afternoon during these three weeks, to occupy the people
during the latter part of the day.

He selected the most eloquent preachers in the
diocese to give the two first discourses; the third he
took himself, and in it he recapitulated all that had

been previously said with great skill, and added fresh subject-matter of his own. The nobility attended in numbers, and the Cardinal quite succeeded in changing worldly dissipation into spiritual exercises.

As the Saint wished these devotions to do much good, he announced them himself, pointing out how displeasing to God were the grievous sins committed at the instigation of the devil, in profane amusements at that holy season, and besought all his people to fly these excesses, and devote themselves, like true Christians, to things which would help them to save their souls, and acquire the treasure of eternal salvation. Besides this, he sent to all his parish priests to give the same directions to their flocks at the Masses of Obligation, with his Pastoral Letter on the mysteries of the holy season of Septuagesima, and to exhort the people to make use of the advantages offered them. It is, therefore, not to be wondered at that the people attended the services in great numbers, since the Saint had made such exertions in their behalf.

On this occasion, just before the commencement of these devotions, one of his priests happened to remark to the Saint, in course of conversation, that he did not think much good would come of them; as the people would surely never give up the amusements they had enjoyed from time immemorial to attend services hitherto unknown at that season of the year. St. Charles retorted that this was not the case, and that the devotions would do much good according to *his* ideas on the subject. He then went on to say, that if the world and the devil were so anxious to invite people to sin, he, as Bishop and pastor of his flock, felt all the more bound to do his utmost to prevent this harm, by giving his people the opportunity of devotion in place of the sensual pastimes offered them by the world. He affirmed that, as many, hearing the voice of the world, follow it and give themselves up to its service, so in the same way many would at the voice of their pastor forsake worldly vanities, if only he did his part in the way of assistance and watchfulness. He added that the example of the good always acted beneficially on the lukewarm, that if the devout had devotions to attend, they would invite others to go with them ; that many persons would be ashamed to appear openly wanting in piety with such good example before their eyes; in short, that the Word of God was always profitable and fruitful, that it was precisely at the time of the greatest worldly profanity and temptation that a pastor should do his utmost to prevent evil effects by means of sermons and public devotions, and that when a Bishop saw souls perishing around him, and his people drawing down the wrath of God upon their heads, it was his duty to induce the good to have recourse to prayer and penance, to appease the Almighty, and move Him to compassion for sinners. Such were the holy Cardinal's reasons for beginning the Septuagesima devotions, as he explained them himself to the priest who doubted their efficacy, and we can therefore see from the Saint's own words how ardent were his love and zeal for the welfare of souls, and how carefully he sought every means of guiding them safely in the way of salvation.

CHAPTER VIII.

FOUNDATION OF THE CHURCH OF OUR LADY OF RHÒ·
OF A CONVALESCENT HOSPITAL—ELEVENTH Aï
LAST DIOCESAN SYNOD.

1584.

ABOUT eight miles from Milan, in the parish of Rl
was a little wayside shrine, on the walls of which w
painted a representation of Our Lady with the de
Christ in her arms. The peasantry held this shrine
great veneration, as it had in former days been the sce
of miraculous occurrences. Towards the end of Api
1583, a report was spread that Our Lady had on
more performed miracles through this holy pictu:
and crowds of people from all parts of Lombarc
came to visit and bring offerings to the shrine. Whi
the Cardinal, hearing of this, had made the requisi
investigations, and consulted the Holy Apostolic Si
he visited the spot in person, and determined to bui
a church in honour of the Immaculate Mother
God near the shrine, and not only this, but also
establish a college of priests there for the bett
observance of Divine worship and convenience of ti

faithful who flocked thither in such numbers. Pending
the necessary arrangements for the foundation, he
installed a suitable staff of priests to attend to the
spiritual wants of the place and take care of the
offerings of pilgrims.

On revisiting the place, about a month afterwards,
he found the pilgrims had increased in number, and
the offerings brought by them had amounted to a
large sum. Part of this sum he invested in landed
property, to maintain the ministers of the new church,
and the rest he reserved for the building fund, deter-
mining that the same plan should be observed for
the future with the alms given by the faithful, as he
disapproved of churches being built without sufficient
revenues to keep them up properly.

He had a magnificent design drawn out by the
architect Péregrino; bearing in mind that rich gifts
were likely to be brought by pilgrims, not only at that
time, but in the future; and his conjectures proved
true, though many at first were of a contrary opinion.
Some persons indeed openly expressed their astonishment at his wishing to build a church large enough
to be a cathedral in that little spot. The Saint's
answer was as follows: " I wish to give future generations a worthy object on which to lavish the alms
which will be given here, and all must agree that
churches should be built conformably to the designs
of Divine Providence, and not according to the dictates
of human prudence." As St. Charles wished the
building operations to be well managed, he gave the
regulation of everything to a company of gentle-

men, ecclesiastics and laymen. On the seventh of March, 1584, he laid the foundation-stone himself, with solemnity. He then handed over the church to the Oblate Fathers of St. Ambrose, as a collegiate house for priests, to serve the church and devote themselves to the saving of souls by preaching and the administration of the Sacraments.

St. Charles' love for the poor and needy was perpetually urging him to find fresh means of relieving their necessities. Just about this time he undertook the foundation of a Convalescent Hospital, for poor invalids who had left the great Hospital, which was famous both on account of its size and the many buildings in connection with it, where the sick, even if they were foreigners, were taken in and treated with the greatest kindness. But as many of the convalescent patients had not enough money on leaving the hospital to provide themselves with proper nourishment, and in consequence often suffered relapse and died, the Saint thought it would be well to found a Convalescent Home, where invalids would be kept till they had completely regained their strength and were capable of supporting themselves in the usual way. He therefore chose a committee of noblemen to superintend the erection and internal management of the Home, and then selected a suitable site, and began to buy the furniture at his own expense. All was going on well, when the Saint's death put a stop for the time being to the undertaking; but as Almighty God did not wish His servants' wishes to remain unfulfilled, He inspired Monsignor

Gasparo Visconte, the Saint's immediate successor, to give a piece of ground to the Fathers of St. John of God for the purpose, and the Convalescent Hospital erected by them was afterwards a source of great benefit to the poor.

Another fact which shows us that St. Charles felt his life was drawing to a close, was his convoking his eleventh and last Diocesan Synod after Easter, towards the middle of the month of April. In this we may say, he made, as it were, his last will, and left a rich inheritance to his clergy in the volume compiled at the preceding conference of his' rural deans, read and published before the Synod, and we may well say it contained every possible instruction for the perfect reformation of the diocese. Indeed, the volume was the greatest treasure he could have left behind him, because it embraced and contained the sum of all the discipline he had taught, and because it showed the practical means of observing it perfectly. He preached four most zealous and affectionate sermons on this subject. It seemed as if he were giving his last instructions and advice to his clergy, and that his heart was so inflamed with charity and love, that he would have given, as it were, his flesh to feed his beloved children. Indeed, he said quite plainly in his first address, that he did not think he should be able to hold another Synod. It is not necessary for us here to discuss at length the matters which the Saint spoke of in his discourses, suffice it to say that his tenderness and fervour melted the hearts of his hearers to such a degree that they felt ravished into an ecstasy.

Indeed, each one present felt an inward joy seemed like the foretaste of heaven itself, toge with sorrow and repentance for his past faults negligences, and a resolution to begin afresh to s after perfection.

It was easy to see that the Saint was soon to e into eternal bliss, as he was on fire with Divine just as if he were already in the light of Paradise was therefore not to be wondered at that his w had a marvellous effect upon his audience. Whe spoke of the spiritual destitution of the Grisons, the dearth of good priests in those territories, mar the clergy present at once offered themselves as sionaries, without a thought of themselves or t own interests.

About this time Guglielmo Gonzaga, Duke of Mar invited St. Charles to honour with his presence nuptials of his son, Vincenzo, with Margherit Medici. But the Saint would not accept the in tion, because the wedding-day fell on the Feast of Invention of the Holy Cross, on which day he arranged to have a procession of the Holy Nail, had invited the Bishop of Verona (who had created a Cardinal the year before) to Milan to a at the function, as he had often done before in days before his elevation to the Cardinalate. W he was busily engaged in making preparations for festival, and the reception of the Bishop of Vero messenger arrived late one Sunday evening to him Monsignor Giovanni Delfino, Bishop of Bre was dying. St. Charles, although he had beer day in church, mounted his horse at once, and made his appearance the following morning in the sick man's room, after a journey of sixty miles. After having consoled the dying prelate and prepared him for death, the Saint gave him the last Sacraments and assisted him in his agony. After his death, St. Charles sung a Requiem Mass for him, and preached to the people, as was his custom on such occasions; this kept him at Brescia till the Wednesday evening. As the following day was the festival of the Holy Cross, he posted all night and reached Milan the next morning at eight o'clock, when he immediately set about composing his sermon for the occasion. He then paid a visit to the Cardinal of Verona, who had come to Milan by his invitation, and asked him to preach at Vespers to the people; after which he went straight to the cathedral, where he sung the High Mass and preached, and then assisted at the long and fatiguing procession, carrying the relic of the Holy Nail himself. Not satisfied with all this, he presided at Vespers and Compline the same evening, and made the Cardinal of Verona give the people a solemn blessing in his stead; so it was nearly dark by the time everything was over. St. Charles afterwards entertained the Veronese Cardinal several days, occupying him in good works for the glory of God and the benefit of souls.

CHAPTER IX.

A COLLEGIATE CHURCH ESTABLISHED AT LEGNANO.

1584.

AFTER the departure of the Cardinal of Verona from Milan, St. Charles began his usual summer visitation of the diocese for the last time. His ardent charity on this occasion was like a brilliant light which shines its brightest when about to be quenched for ever. Every one saw by his appearance and words that he was all on fire with the love of God, as he seemed to be more in heaven than on earth, and more like an angel than a human being. This naturally caused a great excitement in the people, who pressed from all parts to see and hear him, and receive Holy Communion from him; indeed, they followed him wherever he went more than on former occasions. It is not to be wondered at, therefore, that his visits were productive of great good. Several important works were undertaken by the Saint during this progress, among which we may mention his erection of a collegiate church at Legnano. Although this was a populous place of considerable consequence (where Perego, a former Archbishop of Milan, had built a palace for

himself and his successors in the time of Pope Celes-
tine IV.), it was very badly off in spiritual things.
Although there were five hundred families, and more
than two thousand communicants, it only possessed one
priest, and as the river Olona divided the parish, it
was difficult for some of its inhabitants to get to
Mass and the Sacraments. St. Charles found just the
opposite of this in the district of Parabiago, where
there were only seven hundred communicants, but
which boasted of a collegiate church with a Provost
and five Canons, though the Provost alone lived there
and served the church, there not being sufficient
revenue and suitable houses for the Canons. The Saint
resolved to transfer the collegiate church to Legnano,
as being a more important place, as well as being in
greater need of spiritual provision; besides, by this
plan, he saw the Canons would be enabled to keep
residence. He carried this into effect in the month of
August 1584, and placed a curate and coadjutor at
Parabiago instead. He then raised the parish church
of San Magno at Legnano into a collegiate church,
where he fixed a Provost and three Canons, on whom
he imposed the duty of residence, and ordered all
(except the Canon Theologian) to devote themselves
to parochial labours. Another Canon was sent to serve
the church in the hamlet of Legnarello, which had
hitherto been neglected, and the Saint directed him to
live there and keep the Blessed Sacrament in the
church. By this means he provided, at one stroke, for
the greater spiritual benefit of three places.

Busy as the Saint was in these diocesan visits which

were productive of so much good, he did not scruple.
to interrupt them when he had to attend to sacred
functions or other important business; indeed, he went
twice to Milan this summer to consecrate two Bishops
of his province. These were Ludovico Michaelli,
Bishop of Alba, a city of Monferrato, and Ottavio
Paravicino, Bishop of Alessandria, who had been
Nuncio to Switzerland and the Grisons, created Cardinal by Gregory XIV. St. Charles had a great respect
for the latter, and after he had consecrated him Bishop,
entertained him for several days, and treated him with
peculiar affection.

CHAPTER X.

BEGINNING OF THE CAPUCHIN NUNS OF ST. BARBARA AT MILAN — VISIT TO NOVARA, VERCELLI, AND TURIN.

1584.

ONE of the Saint's chief works in the last months of his life was his foundation of the Convent of Capuchin Nuns or Poor Clares of St. Barbara, in Milan. Although he did not live long enough to finish the foundation himself, we may well believe that in heaven he took a peculiar interest in the work, and helped it to a happy consummation. There were living in Milan, in 1584, a merchant, Annibale Vestarino, and his wife, Giovanna, who having no children, resolved to spend their wealth in some good work which would be pleasing to God, and profitable for their souls. The lady consulted her confessor, who advised her to help poor maidens to lead lives of piety and retirement from the world, those especially who had no means of accomplishing their holy desires. Giovanna devoted herself to this work, so that she soon gathered together a company of women, and placed them in a house, formerly a convent of Augustinian nuns, which she had bought from the religious for this work. She trained them in the exercises of the spiritual life under rules of her own framing, assisted by a confessor appointed by St. Charles, and a committee of lay persons, who helped her in the domestic management of the institution. After a time, the maidens wishing to serve God with greater perfection, resolved to take vows and become nuns, and accordingly, with the consent of their confessor, communicated their desire to Giovanna, who gave her sanction to the scheme, making only one condition, viz., that they should not embrace any rule of which she herself did not approve. They then asked the Cardinal to give them the veil, who having duly considered the matter, and given much time to prayer, on the 3d of September, said Mass for them and gave them Holy Communion. After having examined them well, he felt convinced of their true vocation, as they all were unanimous in their desire of embracing the rule of poverty, and willing to leave the form of the habit, and all other matters, entirely in his hands. He accordingly proposed the first Rule of St. Clare for their acceptance, as being one of great poverty and austerity, and promised to give them the habit—a great consolation to the twenty-seven young aspirants to the religious life, as it exactly corresponded with their own wishes. Giovanna, however, did not approve of the rules she had framed herself being laid aside, although they were novel, imperfect, and disliked by the postulants. St. Charles had to employ all his powers of persuasion and argument to induce her to accept the Rule of St. Clare, in which he was at last successful, and the good lady placed the management of the affair unreservedly in his hands. The Cardinal then ordered the deed of the foundation to be prepared, and other necessary arrangements to be made, so as to enable him to give the postulants the habit, and enclose them as soon as possible. In the meantime he went to pay his accustomed visit to the Seminary and the Swiss College, where he sang High Mass on the Feast of the Nativity of Our Blessed Lady, and gave his last solemn blessing to the people. While he was preparing to hold the September ordinations, news reached him one evening that Monsignor Francesco Bosso, Bishop of Novara, was on his deathbed, and anxious to receive his benediction. The Saint, on hearing this, set out on the same day, the 18th of September, leaving a suffragan Bishop to hold the ordination; but although he travelled with the greatest speed, he did not reach Novara in time to see the Bishop alive. As the Saint had earnestly desired to give the dying man a testimony of his friendship, by assisting him in his last moments, he complained bitterly that no one had told him of the Bishop's critical state in time. All he could do was to preside at the obsequies of the departed prelate, on which occasion he preached and exhorted the people to pray earnestly for the soul of their pastor, and for the appointment of a holy successor to the See. He ordered processions to obtain this last favour from heaven, and gave instructions to the Chapter of the cathedral on the management of the diocese before the appointment of the new Bishop.

Guido Ferrerio, Cardinal of Vercelli, a relative and intimate friend of St. Charles, happened to be at Messerano at this time, and hearing the Saint was at Novara came to see him, and informed him that their common relative, the Marquis of Messerano, was dangerously ill. They went together to see him, to the great consolation of the dying man, who begged St. Charles, as a great favour, to give him Holy Communion. The Saint not only granted his request, but prepared him to make a holy death. The two Cardinals then went on to Vercelli, where Gregory XIII. had deputed St. Charles to dispatch diocesan business, as the Bishop, Monsignor Giovanni Francesco Bonomo, was at that time acting as Nuncio at the Court of the Emperor. St. Charles stopped ten days there, and not only accomplished the Papal commission, but also succeeded in quelling violent feuds among the chief men of the place, which had arrived at such a pitch as to threaten the city with danger. The people of Vercelli recognised the greatness of the benefit conferred on them by St. Charles, and came in a body to thank him for his charity. Many of the neighbouring bishops and prelates came to see him during his stay, among the number Cardinal Vincenzo Lauro, Bishop of Mondovi, in Piedmont, who came with an invitation from the Duke of Savoy for St. Charles to visit him at Turin. The Prince wished to receive the Saint's congratulations on his approaching marriage with the Infanta Catharine of Spain. St. Charles, to whom this monarch was particularly dear, accepted the invitation, not only because he wished to gratify Charles Emmanuel, but also be-

cause he would once more have an opportunity of seeing the Holy Winding-Sheet of our Lord. The three
Cardinals therefore proceeded to Turin, where they were
received and entertained with great honours by the
young Prince. St. Charles was so overcome with devotion at the sight of the Holy Winding-Sheet, that it
seemed as if, aware that it was for the last time, he
could hardly tear himself away. On his taking leave
of the Duke, the latter besought him to return to Turin,
to bless his nuptials as soon as the Infanta should
arrive. St. Charles gave an unsatisfactory answer, and
when urged by the Duke to grant his request, finally
replied, that perhaps they should never meet again, referring to his approaching death. Charles Emmanuel
records this incident in the process of the Saint's canonisation in the following words :—

" The said most illustrious and venerable Cardinal
came in the month of September, of the year 1584, to
Turin, to venerate the Holy Winding-Sheet of our
Lord Jesus Christ, and for the sake of seeing us. This
happened shortly before our journey to Spain to conclude our marriage with the Infanta Catharine, daughter
of the King. On our beseeching the Cardinal to bless
the nuptials on our return, he replied in an ambiguous
manner, as if declining our request, but finally said,
' perhaps I shall never be able to see you again.' I
paid, however, no attention to the words at the time ;
but when in the ensuing month of November, news
was brought me of his death, to my great sorrow, those
last words of his recurred to my mind, and I saw that

he had said them inspired by a spirit of prophecy and conscious of his approaching end."

The Duke felt all the more certain of the fact as he knew St. Charles would not otherwise have refused him a favour he so earnestly desired. Other persons have also declared the Saint foretold that his end was very near in a conversation with a relative of the deceased Bishop Bosso, at Novara, couched in terms which correspond with those he used to the Duke. Father Francis Panigarola, in his sermon delivered at St. Charles's funeral, declared that he had heard him repeatedly say that he should die that year.

Antonio Seneca, who accompanied him in his visitation in the preceding month of August, feared he must suffer greatly from the hot sun beating upon his head, on which he wore his Cardinal's hat in addition to his berretta, and tried to induce him to wear something lighter. The Saint replied in a marked manner, "Seneca, it will not be for long," adding that nothing is too heavy to bear for the love of God, if it comes in the way of duty. We may here observe that the Saint, having to give his blessing to the persons he met on the road during his journey through his diocese, never liked to be without his hat and berretta out of respect to his office. When the Saint left Turin he intended to go straight to Varallo, but on reaching Chivasso that same evening, news was brought him of the death of the Marquis of Messerano. Immediately he turned back, and went to celebrate his requiem, and console the widowed Marchioness and her afflicted family.

CHAPTER XI.

SPIRITUAL EXERCISES AT MONTE VARALLO—SUBSEQUENT
ILLNESS—THE COLLEGE OF ASCONA.

1584.

THE holy Cardinal was accustomed every year to make
a retreat and annual confession in retirement, and in
this, the last year of his life, he selected Monte Varallo
for this purpose, doubtless led by his devotion to the
Passion of our Blessed Lord, as on this mountain there
were little chapels containing representations of the
mysteries of the Passion.   On his arrival at Varallo
he sent for Father Francis Adorno, to act as his director
during the Retreat.   Although St. Charles made his
Retreats at all times with great fervour, it seemed on
this occasion as if he were redoubling his efforts in
devotion and austerity of life.   We can easily imagine
that he was impelled by a strong desire of preparing
for his approaching death, and that Almighty God
wished him to bring his good life to a good end.   He
began by dismissing nearly all his attendants, and such
as remained he forbade to come near him under any
pretext whatever.

He chose a little cell for his room, in which he

arranged a plank with a coarse blanket, without straw, to serve as a bed. He slept but little, and not content with observing his accustomed fast on bread and water, he gave himself such disciplines that his shirts were saturated with blood and his body much lacerated, as was discovered after death. During the first days of his Retreat he passed seven hours out of the twenty-four in meditation, and visited the little chapels every night with a small lantern in his hand. In the early morning, long before daybreak, he went, candle in hand, first to Father Adorno's room, and then to the apartments of his attendants, to rouse them from sleep, as they were all following the spiritual exercises with him. So great, however, was the reverence he paid Father Adorno, that he would tread most softly for fear of waking him abruptly, and would always incline his head as he passed him. About this time, towards the middle of October, two young Milanese clerics, students in the seminary, came to visit Mount Varallo, out of devotion, it being their vacation time. While they were going round the chapels, they suddenly came upon St. Charles kneeling, rapt in prayer, to their great astonishment, as they had thought him still at Milan. They visited him, out of respect, when he had gone back to his cell, and the Saint, who loved them like a father, received them with great kindness, and invited them to follow the Retreat with him. We may observe here that Father Adorno gave the points of meditation, and each person chose the chapel he liked best for his own private prayers, but that all met together at fixed hours for conferences and prayer to keep up their mutual fervour. The Cardinal did not fail to visit the two young ecclesiastics every morning, to wake them up and light their candles, and this paternal kindness seems to have had a good influence on their careers. One of them, Alfonso Oldrado, became a famous preacher, and afterwards joined the Capuchins, wishing to lead a more perfect life, but died during the first fervour of his novitiate. The other, Cesare Besozzo, spent several years in labours for souls, and died a holy death on his return to Italy after a pilgrimage to Jerusalem and the Holy Land.

St. Charles made his general confession on the fifth day of the Retreat, with such compunction, fervour of spirit, and tears, that the confessor himself could not refrain from weeping. The previous night he had spent eight hours in prayer on his knees, motionless and with nothing to lean on, and yet the time seemed to pass only too quickly for him.

The following day he was obliged to go to Arona, to confer with the Cardinal of Vercelli on some unavoidable business, but he returned as quickly as possible to Mount Varallo, and continued his Retreat with increased austerity, knowing his time was short, like an industrious husbandman who redoubles his labour when he sees the sunlight fading and the day drawing to a close. Father Adorno and others attest that he seemed quite withdrawn from the things of earth, and that, in spite of his habitual humility, which induced him to hide the spiritual favours with which he was filled, he could not help showing during this Retreat the wonderful union his soul enjoyed with God. He seemed in an ecstasy when he said Mass, and very often his tears flowed with such abundance that he was incapable of speech. Bernardino Morra, Bishop of Aversa, deposed that he had seen him with his face beaming with light during the celebration of the Divine Mysteries, and that it seemed to him to proceed from the interior illumination of his soul, which was so soon to shine with unveiled glory in his heavenly fatherland.

St. Charles' two favourite chapels on Mount Varallo were those of the Prayer in the Garden and the Holy Sepulchre, where he made even longer meditations than in the other shrines. This no doubt came from his mind continually dwelling on his own approaching end, as well as from his ardent desire to depart and be united with his Lord, a desire which Almighty God soon vouchsafed to gratify, as on the 24th of October he was seized with an attack of fever. He kept this, however, carefully concealed from all around him, and persevered all the more diligently in his prayers and exercises. But on the 26th, two days later, a second attack supervened, a proof that the fever was tertian. He therefore told Father Adorno what was the matter with him, and when ordered by that good priest to moderate his penances and shorten his prayers, obeyed with the greatest humility. He consented to partake of some bread, boiled in water, without salt or season-ing, at his meals, and he allowed some straw to be placed on the plank that served him for a bed. He also gave himself a little recreation between his medi-tations, such as, for instance, going round all the chapels and giving directions for their restoration and embellishment. All this time he continued saying his daily Mass, even on the days of the fever, which seemed to abate its violence at that hour. On the 28th, a third attack came on and left him very weak, but the vigour of his mind got the better of the weakness of his body, and he resolved to return to Milan to keep the Feast of All Saints, which was drawing near. First of all, however, he determined to go to Ascona, to complete the foundation of the college, all preliminary matters having been satisfactorily arranged for its establishment.

He gave orders, therefore, to his servants to descend the mountain, but while they were on their way down he returned to the chapel of the Holy Sepulchre, where he soon became engaged in prayer, as if he could not bear to say a final farewell to it. His attendants had not noticed that he had left them, and were therefore obliged to return to seek him, and make the round of the chapels before they could ascertain where he was. He accompanied them on foot down the mountain, but on reaching Varallo was persuaded to mount on horseback, and in this way at length reached Arona, his birth-place, after a journey of eighteen miles, on the 29th of October. In spite of the lateness of the hour, he at once ordered a boat, wishing to go the same night to Ascona, on Lake Maggiore, fifty miles from Arona. His cousin, the Count Renato Borromeo, brother of the Cardinal Frederic Borromeo afterwards Archbishop of Milan, who was then residing at the Castle of Arona,[1]

---

[1] He was a royal Privy Councillor, and Captain of the King's Bodyguard.

begged St. Charles to spend the night with him; but the Saint declined, on the plea that he was obliged to return to Milan for the festival of All Saints. One of his attendants having observed that he could put off the foundation of the College of Ascona to a more convenient time, he replied that he was obliged to go thither at once, as later it would be impossible. He embarked at seven o'clock at night, after a slight repast of bread-soup at the priest's house, where he had alighted in order to avoid the comforts he would have enjoyed at his own castle. On entering the boat, he knelt down and recited the prayers for travellers, the litanies, and for the departed, with those of his household who were with him. He then turned to the boatmen and asked them if they said any special prayers before they embarked every day, and made them promise to say for the future the "Our Father," the "Hail Mary," and the "Creed" before beginning their day's work; and then and there got the men to say these prayers aloud after him, and made them a little spiritual discourse, showing how necessary it was to do the holy will of God alone, and to endeavour to lead lives of perfection, caring little for human affairs and temporal interests. He also spoke much about death, and how men ought to be always well prepared for it, and that, for his part, he should be glad to depart to a better life, and that he did not belong to a long-lived race. One can easily see he well knew all about his approaching death; yet strange to say, none of his attendants attached any importance to his words, probably because no one would have supposed Almighty

God was about to deprive the Church of so great a saint at the very time when he seemed to be doing wonders for the conversion of heretics and the propagation of the Faith.

St. Charles then lay down on a bench to rest a little, but rose again at one o'clock to say matins on his knees, with his attendants, after which he spent an hour and a half in mental prayer. At six o'clock he reached Canobbio, where he landed, and went straight to the house of the Rev. Provost, where he continued his meditation till it was broad daylight. He then recited Prime and Tierce, went to Confession, and said Mass with particular devotion, after which he breakfasted on a little soup, and then re-embarked and went straight to Ascona, in spite of wind and weather. His haste was partly owing to his anxiety to send off some of his priests to Switzerland and the Grisons, on mission work. The plague was then raging in Ascona, but notwithstanding this, the Cardinal went to pray and preach a sermon in the church. After this he publicly opened the college in person, chose a rector to take the management of the place, and would have had some boys examined for admission, but for the prevalence of the plague. Hearing that at the neighbouring town of Locarno so many persons were dying of the plague that the cemetery could not contain them all, he resolved to go there and consecrate a fresh cemetery out of pure charity, as Locarno was neither in his diocese or province, though his office of apostolic delegate empowered him to do so. But on finding that his mitre had been left at Arona, he gave up this project, not wishing to perform any function in an unauthorised and unrubrical way.

A fourth attack of fever had come on at Ascona during the opening of the college, so after his business was over, he returned to Canobbio as quickly as possible. He found a bed ready for him, but he ordered it to be taken away, and lay down on a little straw, wishing to continue the rigours of his penance. The fever ran high for some hours, and not wishing to waste time, he sent for the Capuchin Fathers of the place, and conversed with them upon the life and virtues of St. Francis. The conversation happening to turn upon the holiness of Pius V., St. Charles, who had known that Pontiff intimately, and been a witness of the marvels of his pontificate, praised him highly, and said he looked upon him as a saint. After the paroxysms of the fever had abated, the Saint thought he could continue his journey, and after taking some porridge, wished to re-embark in order to reach Milan for the Feast of All Saints. When, however, the risk of travelling by night in his state of health was represented to him, he desisted from the attempt, and took some repose.

He was found long before daybreak next morning praying in his room, where he recited his Office and prepared himself for Mass, which he said early, after having made his confession in the Church of the Pietà. He was so weak after so many hours on his knees, that he could not make the genuflexions without help. Notwithstanding all this, he insisted on fasting all day, because it was the Vigil of All Saints, taking only a spoonful of lemon juice in obedience to the doctor's orders. When he entered the boat to go back to Arona, he once more recited the prayers for travellers, and litanies, and made the boatmen say the Roman litanies [1] with him. He then preached a little sermon on the solemnity of All Saints with such fervour that tears came to the eyes of all his hearers, after which he gave out points of meditation on the same subject. After all present had spent about an hour in mental prayer, he began again to discourse with such ardour of charity that it seemed as if he wished to make a saint of each member of his audience. All the rest of his journey was spent in furthering the salvation of souls. He even sent some more priests from Arona to Mesolcina to help the poor people there. Just before landing, he said once more the litanies and the remainder of the Divine Office on his knees, notwithstanding his weakness and suffering. His cousin, Count Renato, met him at Arona, and wished to take him to his palace, where rooms had been prepared for him, but St. Charles would not agree to this, but said as an excuse that he wished to spend the night at the house of the Jesuit Fathers, on account of the spiritual advantages he would enjoy there. He passed rather a quiet night, but rose at two o'clock in the morning, and prayed till four. He then said the Divine Office, made his usual daily confession, and prepared for Holy Mass, which he said at seven o'clock. As it was All Saints' Day, many persons received Communion from his

---

[1] The Roman offices were in use at Arona.

hands, among whom were all the Jesuit novices of the college. This was his last Mass and last Episcopal function. He remained some time in the church after his own Mass was over, to hear the Mass of the Rector, Father Simeone Arpi, kneeling all the time. As this was the day of the return of the fever, his doctors advised him not to travel, but to drink a certain quantity of warm barley-water, and to sleep as much as he could, in order to bring on perspiration. This time the attack came on more violently than ever, and, indeed, the fever never again left him. He wished to say Mass on Friday, All Souls' Day, but his weakness was too great to permit him to do so. Nevertheless, he went to the church to hear Mass, after which he made his confession and received Holy Communion with the greatest devotion; he then recited the Divine Office on his knees.

He afterwards, having partaken of a slight refreshment, went by boat and canal to Milan, which he reached the same day, accompanied by his cousin, Count Renato, who never left him again till he died. A litter had been sent to meet him, about two miles from Milan. He entered it, and reached the Archiepiscopal palace towards evening. He was welcomed on his arrival by his relations, Count Annibale d' Altaemps, with his son Gasparo, and Fabrizio da Correggio, who were then staying in the house and awaiting his arrival. They surrounded his litter, and St. Charles embraced them all most affectionately. While he was ascending the steps of the palace, he gave particular instructions to his steward to take care of one of his grooms who had been taken seriously ill. The Saint then insisted on going as usual to his chapel to say his usual prayers, after which he was forced to go to bed, being hardly able to stand on his feet from exhaustion. Although he was entirely resigned to the will of God, and his soul was quite prepared for its journey to another life, if such should be the pleasure of Divine Providence, he nevertheless thought himself bound to use human means of recovery. He therefore sent at once for a doctor, and gave him an account of the progress of his malady, telling him to apply the necessary remedies, and only stipulating that nothing should interfere with his spiritual exercises.

CHAPTER XII.

ST. CHARLES' HAPPY DEATH.

As the hour approached for St. Charles' departure from this world, his mind and heart became more and more absorbed in God. He was more careful than ever about the perfection of every little daily action, asking Father Adorno's advice, and obeying him most scrupulously. The following morning after his arrival in Milan he took the breakfast ordered by his physician, and then sent for his chaplains, wishing to say the Divine Office with them. When, however, he was informed that this would be too much for him, owing to his high state of fever, and that he should only listen without joining in the prayers, he submitted to this decision on the bidding of Father Adorno. Accordingly, his chaplain, Girolamo Castano, afterwards Canon of the Cathedral of Milan, recited the Divine Office, followed by the Office of the Dead, kneeling at his bed-side, and the Saint listened with great attention and devotion.

The Passion and Death of our Lord were so engraven in his heart, that he only seemed happy when meditating on them; so now that he was unable to indulge in mental prayer, he wished to have pictures of those holy mysteries before his eyes. He accordingly had his bed removed to the audience-chamber, commonly called the " Chamber of the Cross," where an altar was made up, facing the bed, with a picture of the Burial of Our Lord over it. Another picture of the same mystery, which was brought down from his little oratory under the roof, was placed at the head of his bed, and one representing the Prayer in the Garden was placed at its foot, so that wherever he turned delineations of the Sacred Passion met his eyes. Father Francis Panigarola had that morning preached in the cathedral at the Mass of the Holy Spirit, sung for the magistrates of the city on the day of the opening of their tribunals. St. Charles, who had a great affection for that Father, on account of his virtues and talents as a preacher, sent for him after the sermon and conversed with him for some time on spiritual things pertaining to the service of Almighty God. Father Panigarola was astonished at seeing so many pictures of the Passion in St. Charles' room; the Saint noticed his surprise, and said: " It gives me the greatest possible comfort and consolation when I am ill, to contemplate the mysteries of the Passion of our Lord, especially the Agony in the Garden, and the Burial."

When the physicians, after a careful examination of the patient, pronounced the illness to be a severe one and his life to be in danger, they were anxious to call in another doctor for a consultation, but when the chaplains asked the Saint's leave for this, he would not allow it till he had obtained his confessor's per-

mission, as well as that of Father Lewis Moneta, and
even then only on condition that he should not 'be
disturbed in his spiritual exercises. He had made up
his mind to hear Mass and receive Holy Communion
in his chapel, the following morning, Sunday; but
Fathers Adorno and Moneta dissuaded him from this,
saying that it would be very dangerous, and that he
could go to Communion in his own room, leaving his
bed for the purpose. Father Adorno even offered to
say Mass in the sick-room, at the altar which had
been put up, but the Saint would not allow this, as it
was not a consecrated place. And when the Father
replied that a Bishop's house was holy in itself, St.
Charles answered, that even if this were the case, he
would not give such an example to others, and said he
would go to the chapel if he could possibly manage it.

The doctors came back in the afternoon and were
pleased when they found the fever abated, which they
considered a good sign. When the Cardinal was told
of this, he did not manifest the slightest token of joy,
but merely said: "May the will of God be done."
It was not long, however, before the fever returned,
accompanied by great drowsiness, and when the doctors
came back and felt his pulse, they declared his strength
was failing fast, and that he had but a few more hours
to live. This unexpected news filled the hearts of
all present with dismay. Father Adorno at once
approached the Cardinal's bedside and informed him,
weeping bitterly as he did so, that his last hour was
come: he then asked him if he would like to receive
the Holy Viaticum. St. Charles eagerly replied in

the affirmative, and gave orders for the Arch-priest
of.his cathedral, Monsignor Giovanni Fontana, after- .
wards Bishop of Ferrara, to bring It to him.   At
this moment the Canons of the cathedral came to see
him, not knowing how ill he was.   When they saw
his weakness they all knelt down in tears to ask
his blessing, but he was already too far gone to
speak a word.   They went back therefore to the
cathedral to have the Blessed Sacrament exposed for
their Archbishop's recovery, and then returned to the
palace accompanying the Arch-priest who brought the
Holy Viaticum.   Count Annibale Altaemps and his
son, Count Renato Borromeo, and all the household
had in the meantime repaired to the sick-room and
were kneeling round the bed, hoping to obtain the
benediction of the dying Saint.   St. Charles feebly
moved his fingers, wishing to raise his hand to bless
them, but he was too weak for the effort, and it was
necessary to assist him to make the sign of the cross.
When the Arch-priest and Canons arrived with the
Blessed Sacrament, St. Charles made signs that he
wished to rise from his bed to receive the Holy
Viaticum on his knees, as he had intended doing in
the morning, but his weakness rendered it impossible.
They put on his rochet and placed his stole round
his neck, which he would not omit to kiss, and he
then received the Blessed Sacrament with the utmost
devotion of which his weakness was capable.   On
being asked if he wished to receive Extreme Unction, he made signs in the affirmative, and during
the administration of the holy oils he tried to make

the responses. Immediately afterwards the agony of death came on, and his attendants remembering they had heard him often say he wished to die in sackcloth and ashes, like the Bishops of the early Church, asked Father Charles Bascapè to clothe the dying Saint in a hair-shirt, and sprinkle blest ashes over him. In this garb, a fitting conclusion of his life of continual penance and mortification, St. Charles expired. The room was full of priests and officials of the household, some recommending the departing soul to God, in the words of the Roman ritual, and others reading the Passion. Father Adorno had stood to the last by St. Charles' bedside, crucifix in hand, suggesting pious aspirations, but his voice was often drowned by the tears and sobs of all around. When it was perceived the Saint had become insensible, groans and lamentations burst forth from all without restraint, and it would have moved a heart of stone to witness the sorrow of his attendants and friends, who had lost their beloved pastor without being able to show him the last token of their affection or hear a parting word of counsel from his lips.

The causes of this grief were manifold. Some mourned the injury which his death would bring to the Church in general, and the diocese in particular; others bewailed the relaxation in discipline they foresaw would follow his decease, some wept for their own private interests, but all combined in lamenting the loss of a father. The grief of his household and personal friends was heart-rending to behold. When the news of the sad event spread through the city the whole place was in commotion. Notwithstanding the lateness of the hour many of the inhabitants rushed to the palace to see their Archbishop, and many others went at once to the churches to offer up prayers in his behalf. The schools of Christian Doctrine and the Confraternities of the Cross went in procession in the middle of the night to the seven churches chanting sorrowful litanies and psalms for his recovery. Many persons ran about the city calling out, " Pray, pray for our Pastor's recovery ! " while others went along the streets scourging themselves, clad in sackcloth, and barefoot. Indeed the whole town resounded with weeping and lamentations. The news soon penetrated the convent walls, and there was hardly a nun who did not spend the night before the Blessed Sacrament in prayer for so illustrious a benefactor. Strangers seemed to feel the universal grief as much as the Milanese themselves. The crowd of people outside the palace had become so great that it was found necessary to post the Governor's Swiss Guards at the entrance to keep order. The Duke of Terra Nuova himself went at the head of the senate and magistrates to visit the dying Saint, but on finding him insensible, could only mingle his tears with those of the other mourners. His death agony lasted from four P.M. till seven o'clock, but it was an agony so calm and peaceful that it more resembled a deep slumber than anything else. At about seven o'clock the Saint expired, his eyes fixed upon a crucifix, and smiling so sweetly that he seemed like an angel. Father Charles Bascapè performed the pious office of closing the eyes of the departed; and when this was over, the sobs and tears of all present broke forth with redoubled vehemence.

The lamentations resounding from all parts of the city when the people heard the tolling of the cathedral bells, and those of the other churches, cannot be described. Voices were heard screaming for mercy in the streets, just as if Milan had been sacked and destroyed. It was necessary to guard the doors of the palace with armed men to prevent the influx of the crowds that rushed from all directions to gaze on their dead Archbishop. At one time nocturnal tumults were apprehended, so great was the sorrow that reigned in the city.

St. Charles died on the night of Saturday, the 3rd of November, 1584, at the age of forty-six years, one month and one day. Divine Providence had enabled him to imitate the great Bishop, St. Martin, in his death, just as he had copied his virtues in his life. For St. Martin had also suddenly lost his health and strength during a temporary absence from home on ecclesiastical business, and in spite of the ever-increasing fever that consumed him, would never consent to omit or even interrupt his prayers, vigils, and austerities. And even when he was actually dying, in spite of his eighty years and physical weakness, the aged Saint refused, as his biographer, Severus Sulpicius, relates, to lie on a common straw mattress, but insisted on breathing his last on his usual couch of sackcloth and ashes.

CHAPTER XIII.

HIS BURIAL.

WHEN the Saint's body had been laid out, those who paid him the last rites, from the filial love they felt for him, could not be restrained from kissing and bathing it with their tears. There was left of him nothing but skin and bone, his shoulders were scored by the strokes of the discipline, his flesh was worn rough and sore by his hair-shirt, and in the middle of his back was a mark of the shot of the arquebuse. White vestments were put upon the body, which was placed in the chapel, where watch was kept by his household and the Office of the Dead recited, although they considered it certain that his soul had gone to heaven, and they had already, in this belief, begun to possess themselves of relics as of a saint, one taking his rosary, others the Agnus Dei that hung from his neck, his skull-cap, his alb, the discipline and hair-shirt stained with his blood, his books, pictures, and vestments, and even the straw upon which he lay.

The next morning being Sunday, the whole city, like one family, was in mourning as for a father. Nothing was heard but sobs and lamentation, and both men and women in the streets saluted each other with floods of tears. In the churches that morning might be seen priests who had to break off their masses, and preachers their sermons, for their tears, and the congregations joined perforce in their grief, as if each one had lost a father, a mother, or son, or daughter. Nothing was spoken of but their sudden loss, at a time when no one expected it. There were many who said that heaven had suffered violence—that God was bound by the penances and prayers of his servant to take him away in good time from earth, without allowing his flock to obtain longer life for him.

All the Sunday the doors of the Archbishop's home had to be kept closed for fear of accident, so great was the concourse of people; the streets and squares overflowed with the multitudes desirous of venerating his sacred body. The doors were thrown open on the Monday morning, after a strong barrier had been placed round the bed on which it lay. The anxiety of every one to behold him could not be told ; the wall of the chapel had to be taken down to make an issue for the continuous stream. No one could have imagined such love for their Pastor in his flock, coming from far and near, and putting their lives in jeopardy to catch sight of him, so that many were not able so much as to kiss his sacred form, but only to touch it with their rosaries and objects of devotion. All were shedding tears, all were crying out, " Oh Father of all," " true Pastor," " holy Archbishop ; " widows and orphans lamented their only support and refuge. Those who had never let fall a tear for their own sorrows, cried their eyes out, but were filled with joy again to look upon his face with a smile upon his lips in token of his happy lot. In the meantime, many priests were reciting the Office of the Dead, one body of clergy after another taking it up alternately both night and day.

At this time was published the will made by the Saint at the time of the plague, and dated 9th Sept., 1576, when he had made up his mind to risk his life for his flock. In it he ordered his body to be buried in the cathedral under the pavement just before the steps up to the choir, the most trodden and frequented part, with this inscription in Latin :—

CHARLES, CARDINAL OF THE TITLE OF ST. PRAXEDES,
ARCHBISHOP OF MILAN,
COMMENDING HIMSELF TO THE PRAYERS
OF THE CLERGY, PEOPLE, AND DEVOUT FEMALE SEX,
WHILE LIVING CHOSE THIS PLACE FOR HIS MONUMENT.

He directed that there should be six lights only round his bier, that three dirges should be sung, and a thousand masses said for his soul, and an annual requiem in perpetuity on the anniversary of his death, unless it should fall on the day fixed for the requiem in commemoration of his predecessor, viz., the 3rd of November, in which case his anniversary should be kept on the 4th. As he actually died on the 3rd, many thought that the day of his death had been revealed to him. To the cathedral he bequeathed plate and vestments to the value of many thousand crowns, to the Chapter and Canons in ordinary his library, with the exception of his manuscripts and sermons bound up in

many volumes, which he left to Mgr. Giovanni Francesco Bonomo, Bishop of Vercelli, from whom they
came into the hands of Cardinal Frederic Borromeo,
now living. To some of his intimate friends he gave
certain pictures and objects of devotion, and legacies to
others, making the great Hospital of Milan his re-
siduary legatee, without recognising his relatives at all,
except as to his patrimonial estates, which went to the
Counts Borromeo, his uncles and cousins, showing how
great was his detachment from all earthly affections.
He directed that wherever he might happen to die his
body should be buried in Milan, a final testimony of
his love for the Church, his spouse.

On the Wednesday morning his requiem was sung
with great pomp by Nicolo Sfrondato, Cardinal Bishop
of Cremona, afterwards Pope Gregory XIV., who came
on purpose to officiate. The Bishops of Alessandria,
Vigevano and Castro, the Chapters of all the collegiate
churches, the secular and regular clergy, the confraternities and pious schools of the city assisted, meeting
at the Archbishop's house with candles in their hands.
On the arrival of the Canons in the chapel where the
body was lying the following anthems were sung:

"The joy of our heart is ceased, our dancing is
turned into mourning; the crown is fallen from our
head; woe to us because we have sinned, therefore is
our heart sorrowful, therefore are our eyes become
dim."[1] " He pleased God and was beloved, and living
among sinners he was translated. He was taken away
lest wickedness should alter his understanding, or

---

[1] Lam. v. 15.

deceit beguile his soul; being made perfect in a short space, he fulfilled a long time; for his soul pleased God, therefore he hastened to bring him out of the midst of iniquities." [1]　Then the procession started, in order as before.　After the body went Count Frederic Borromeo, now our Cardinal and Archbishop, between Count Renato, his brother, and Count Annibale di Altaemps, the Vicar-Generals of the diocese, and the rest of the household, two and two, all in long black mantles from head to foot.　The Governor, the Senate, Magistrates, the Colleges of Doctors of Law, the gentry, and multitudes from all the towns and villages round about, all the places of business and shops being shut throughout the city out of respect, while the streets and squares, windows and roofs, were crowded all the way of the procession for half a mile.　When the people saw their beloved Pastor on the bier, in the bitterness of their grief they raised their voices to heaven with cries for mercy, ever in deeper and deeper grief.　The Cardinal of Cremona in vain tried to stay his tears, the sky itself seemed to lament, the sun was hidden in clouds, and a light rain like dew began to fall, as the body took its way to the cathedral.　Cries and groans resounded from those who were possessed by evil spirits at the sight of the Saint's body, so that it seemed to be the end of the world: it was deposed on oath, by an eye-witness, in the process of the canonisation, that some who were tormented by spirits were freed from them.　There seemed to be no end or bounds to tears and lamentations, which increased the

[1] Wisd. iv. 10.

more men called to mind the greatness of the loss not only to their own city, but to all Christendom.

The bier was carried by the Canons in ordinary, the clergy singing the psalms and litanies for the dead, the people kneeling in reverence while the Saint's body passed. In the cathedral a strong barrier had been made round the catafalque, for its protection against the devotion of the people pressing on to kiss the holy body, which they were only allowed to touch with their rosaries during the rest of the day.

The mass of requiem was sung by the Cardinal of Cremona, with much interruption of the universal grief. Father Francesco Panigarola preached the sermon with so much feeling that he drew fresh tears from the eyes of his hearers, dwelling principally on the five chief virtues manifested in the Saint, viz., his ardent love for the church committed to his care, his holiness of life, his prudence, pastoral solicitude, and fortitude. After being left as long as possible to satisfy the devotion of the people, the body was then placed in the Medici chapel, which was inclosed by strong iron railings for safety. It was then buried at dead of night, when the doors of the cathedral were shut, being placed in a leaden coffin within a strong one of wood, resting on an iron grating, and laid in the spot which he had chosen.

CHAPTER XIV.

APPEARANCES OF THE SAINT—ESTABLISHMENT OF THE
.CONVENT OF POOR CLARES.

FATHER ADORNO, who remained with the Saint as his
spiritual director till he drew his last breath, then
went to his own quarters at San Fedele, but was unable,
from sorrow, to obtain any sleep till daybreak. On
falling asleep for a short time he saw the Cardinal
shining in glory, and said to him, "How is this? I
thought you were dead." The Saint replied, "The
Lord killeth, and the Lord giveth life.[1] It is well with
me, and you will soon follow me." The Father was
much consoled by this dream, and told it to his friends,
and in the pulpit, and the prediction was soon verified.
Within a few months after, going to Genoa his native
place, he fell ill and passed to a better life, leaving
behind him the reputation of a saint.

The author of this life also saw, in a dream, the
Saint soon after his death all bright and joyous, in
Cardinal's robes; and upon his asking, "What is the
matter, my lord?" "Take comfort," the Saint replied;
"it is well with me, for I am in Paradise," and dis-

[1] 1 Kings ii. 6.

appeared. Twice again he was seen in like manner after his death, in which the Saint predicted that Pope Gregory XIIL would die within six months, and also certain disorders that would come upon the diocese. As these events actually came to pass, they led to the belief that these were really appearances of the Saint, and not merely due to the imagination.

The death of the Cardinal was a great grief to the community of Santa Barbara,[1] as it interrupted his arrangements for their establishment under the rule of St. Clare. They, however, trusted to God and the protection of the Cardinal in heaven to complete the work he had begun on earth, notwithstanding the opposition of their benefactress, the Signora Vestarina, to their adoption of that rule. It was her intention that they should remain as at first established by herself. In consequence of this disagreement it was drawing towards the close of the year 1585, before anything was done. At that time Mgr. Gasparo Visconte[2] was appointed by Gregory XIII. Archbishop of Milan. The community then renewed their application to him for approval of their new rule, which the Signora Vestarina as far as was in her power opposed, going so far as to use threats as to what she would do, but was not able to move the postulants from their determination. They had recourse to fervent prayers and penances, making the Cardinal their protector, carrying his picture in processions, and openly

---

[1] See Chapter x.
[2] Formerly lecturer in the university of Pavia, and auditor of the Rota at Rome.

invoking his aid in prayers, viz.: "O holy Cardinal,
do for us now what you were not able to complete
for us in your life, and help us with your protection."
On Michaelmas Day the Signora informed them that
if they would not give in to her wishes, she would
not allow them to live any longer in her house. They
were much troubled by this threat as they did not
like to go against her wishes, but at the same time
were resolved to abide by the rule of St. Clare.

One day after the Angelus, when they were turning to the picture of the Saint hanging on the wall
in their workroom, and praying for his help, Mgr.
Fontana, the Vicar-General, came to their door, asking
if they were in any difficulty, because while in his
room at the Archbishop's house he had heard a voice
three times utter the words, "Rise and go to St.
Barbara, for the sisters there have need of you."
The mother-superior, Francesca Landriana, afterwards
abbess, explained to him the difficulties in the way
of their vocation, and the threats of the Signora. The
Vicar-General promised them his co-operation in fulfilling the Saint's intentions and their own wishes,
provided they stood firm.

They received additional encouragement from another
visit the same day from the Penitentiary of the Cathedral, Canon Luigi Boccalodio, one of the committee
who managed their affairs. "I was riding," he told
them, "from the monastery of St. Mark to the Archbishop's house, when my mule, as I passed the end of
this street, turned towards this house, and would not
be pulled away in spite of every effort I could make

to do so. I then gave him the rein, and came imagining you might stand in some need of me."

It was thought that the hand of God was here, and the consequence was, that after a council in the Archbishop's house, all difficulties were overcome, and on the 4th October, 1585, the foundation of the institute was completed, to the glory of God and advantage of the city.

CHAPTER XV.

THE grief felt by all good men at the death of the Saint was universal, not only in Milan, but wherever he was known throughout the world. His loss was particularly felt by the Catholics of Switzerland and the Grisons, to whom he had been a father and protector. When Pope Gregory XIII. received the news he exclaimed, " Extincta est lucerna in Israel," " A lamp is put out in Israel ; "[1] and in the first consistory held after his death, he pronounced him the greatest ornament of the Sacred College. In the diary of Francesco Mocante, the Pope's master of ceremonies, under the date of November 7, 1584, we find the Saint referred to in the following terms : " All in Rome are grieved at his death on account of his innocent and exemplary life, his unwearied exertions in the correction of abuses, his charity, piety, and perseverance under difficulties."

Cardinal Sirleto wrote the following eulogium upon him : " Charles Borromeo, imprisoned in the body while his soul was in heaven, seemed to have nothing

---

[1] 2 Kings xxi. 17.

of the flesh in him save the outward appearance. In appearance he was a man, by grace an angel. He was a model of Christian piety, a mirror of the office of Bishop and Cardinal, a strong defence against the wicked.

"He was a shining ornament of the Church of God. He was in life and holiness as salt, as a light by his learning and preaching, a city of defence on the hill of Sion, a burning lamp of the Gospel. He had the faith of a martyr, for he desired but had not the lot of martyrdom. In wisdom a Doctor of the Church, in his life a Confessor, he ruled with the discipline of a Pastor.

"In innocence he was like Abel; in uprightness as Noe; in faith as Abraham; an Isaac in obedience; a Jacob in labour; a Joseph in chastity; a Moses in meekness; a David in humility; in zeal, Elias; a workman that needed not to be ashamed, rightly handling the word of truth, undertaking nothing save for the glory of God; with soul so established in him that he never could be overcome; in one word, a treasure-house and home of every spiritual gift.

"This faithful servant having done his work, was glad to appear before the face of God during the celebration of the solemnity of All Saints, at a time sad for us, but happy indeed for himself. As he had always been zealous for the honour of the saints, and had imitated their virtues, it was fitting that he should be presented by the vast multitude of the saints before the throne of the Most High, when by God's grace he could say of the work committed to his charge, 'Lord, Thou hast given me five talents; lo, I have gained other five.'"

His flock, inconsolable for his loss, did not forget him. They visited his tomb, and had prayers and masses said for him, although they were sure that his soul enjoyed eternal bliss. His clergy were not behindhand, in all the collegiate churches hung in black, solemn masses were sung for his repose, the confraternities and pious societies uniting in these last offices, even in the furthest and remotest valleys, where all entertained a lively remembrance of their pastor.

The devout female sex also, to whose prayers the Cardinal had particularly recommended himself, collected offerings, and had masses said for him, going in procession to the seven churches with his picture beneath the crucifix. They formed a society and called it the Company of Ladies of Santa Prassede, to have an annual mass said, and the procession of the churches held every month for the repose of his soul, the schools of Christian doctrine joining with psalms and hymns, and visiting his tomb with great devotion. This custom was kept up till the year 1601, when the mass of repose was changed by order of the Pope to one of thanksgiving.

CHAPTER XVI.

THE VENERATION PAID TO THE SAINT AFTER HIS DEATH.

THE strong belief in the sanctity of the Cardinal, entertained both by the people of Milan and elsewhere, was increased by his holy death. The confidence in his intercession grew day by day; he was adopted generally as a particular patron, and his pictures and images were multiplied so rapidly that there was hardly a house or shop in Milan without some memorial of him. This devotion to him was not limited to grown-up persons who had seen or known him while living, but was conspicuous also in the young, who lisped his name in their prayers, and took him with loving hearts for their father in heaven.

His name was held in such reverence that many used to uncover when they heard it mentioned, and it was given in baptism by parents to their children in order to put them under the Saint's protection. This veneration was increased by the fame of the miracles worked at his intercession. Many persons began to keep the anniversary of his death, and to use his name in the litanies in private. The devotion has now been

publicly authorised since the year 1601, by letters
of Cardinal Baronius, confessor of Pope Clement VIII.,
directing that the anniversary mass of repose should
be changed for a solemn commemoration of the Saint,
to be celebrated on the day of his death. The people
of their own accord immediately kept the day as a
feast of obligation, whence we may believe that their
hearts were moved to it from above. In testimony of
their love and veneration they adorned their houses
with pictures, tapestries, and lights, without any orders
or suggestions from authority, and erected altars in
honour of the Saint in different parts of the city, and
had a general illumination at night-time, with processions to visit his tomb in the cathedral.

These celebrations used to attract a great concourse
of people, so that Cardinal Frederick Borromeo felt
himself bound to try and check them in some degree,
as the Saint, his cousin, was not as yet formally
canonised. The people, however, did not obey his
wishes, but continued their observance of the anniversary, and directions were sent to him from Rome to
allow them liberty to venerate the Saint according to
their wishes. The day was then kept, not only by
all the people, but by the magistrates, senate, and
gentry, and no servile work was allowed to be done on
it, as on holidays of obligation.

CHAPTER XVII.

GENERAL ESTIMATION OF THE SAINT.

UPWARDS of thirty-one volumes [1] of letters, addressed to St. Charles by eminent persons from all parts of Europe, give proof of the general high opinion of him. From the collection of his letters published by Giovanni Botero,[2] one of his secretaries, it may be seen that the foreign Catholic princes, especially those of Germany, had a great reverence for his character, unknown as he was for the most part, except by report.

The Protestants also were fain to acknowledge his virtues. As an instance, a Franciscan friar was once thrown into prison by a certain Protestant prince. The Provincial of the Order, to obtain his release, laid before the potentate many letters of recommendation from persons of authority, and among them one from Cardinal Borromeo. The prince put most of them aside, but on seeing the Cardinal's letter, raised it to his lips, and said, "From respect to him I will grant you this favour, and for no one else; he certainly deserves it. The prisoner is free."

---

[1] Preserved in the library of the Oblates at San Sepolcro in Milan.
[2] Book II., 15, in a letter addressed to a certain Wolfgang *Ham-astiense.*

A letter in the same collection from Mary Queen of Scots, who was imprisoned and put to death by Elizabeth Queen of England, shows how that unfortunate princess valued the prayers of the Saint in the midst of her afflictions.

When Henry III., King of France, heard of the Saint's death, he said, " If all Italian Bishops were as holy as Cardinal Borromeo and the Apostolic Nuncio,[1] lately deceased, I would propose no more Frenchmen for the vacant Sees, but would have them all Italians."

Philip II., King of Spain, felt the loss of St. Charles, and kept his portrait before him in his chamber of audience. Being asked once by the Bishop of Cremona[2] what he thought of Cardinal Borromeo, with a full recollection of the Saint's controversies with the different Governors of Milan, he replied, " I consider him a holy man, and should thank God if I had Bishops like him in all my dominions."

Philip III. of Spain, his son and successor, urged on the canonisation of the Saint, both by writing to the Holy Father himself, and by means of his ambassador at Rome.

Alessandro Farnese, Duke of Parma, famous for his achievements in Flanders, earnestly recommended himself and all his undertakings to the prayers of St. Charles, as certain to bring him success.

Pope Pius IV. recognised the wisdom and prudence

---

[1] Giovanni Battista Castello, Bishop of Rimini, Nuncio Apostolic in France, who died in 1583.

[2] Cesare Speciano, then Nuncio Apostolic at Madrid.

of his nephew, and entrusted [1] to him, young as he was, the entire management of affairs, so that he was looked upon as another Pope.

In the course of this history we have had many evidences of the opinion of St. Pius V., and indeed the ample faculties bestowed upon him by that Pontiff for the administration of his diocese sufficiently attest it. In one place St. Pius describes Charles as "a man of innocence, of extraordinary piety and sincerity of mind." In another, as "steadfast in prayer and purity of life."

Gregory XIII. honoured him as a saint, bestowed upon him full pontifical powers for his diocese and for the visitation of other places, and speaks of him as "a worthy member of the Apostolic College, who held his life as nought when souls were to be saved, of wonderful solicitude and uprightness, blessed with manifold graces from the hand of God."

Sixtus V., as an acknowledgment of his merit, conferred a Cardinal's hat upon his cousin, Frederic Borromeo, when but two-and-twenty years of age, and in one of his Briefs commended St. Charles' "extraordinary piety, wisdom, and holiness of life."

Gregory XIV. called the Saint "a second Ambrose."

Clement VIII. would have canonised him twenty years after his death, referring his cause to the Sacred Congregation of Rites, in his Brief of April 24, 1604, and in a rescript of his own hand, in answer to the instance of the city of Milan, he directed the Cardinal

---

[1] See the Brief addressed to his nephew, "*Cum nos ingravescente jam aetate nostra.*"—*Bullarium Romanum.*

of Como "to proceed with all diligence and caution in the case, as warranted by its importance and the dignity of the person of the Cardinal Charles, so eminent in the Church of God, that there is no part of the world which has not been reached by the report of his sanctity."

The canonisation of St. Charles was the first business taken in hand by Leo XI. He directed Francesco Penia, Dean of the Rota, senior judge in the cause, to bring it to a conclusion, as his days were few. He would not, on that account, allow Cardinal Frederic Borromeo to leave Rome, and was intending to build a church in the city, in honour of the Saint, and to make it a Cardinal's title. As he died after a pontificate of seven-and-twenty days, he was not able to effect his purpose. Before he was elected Pope, he wrote the following letter concerning the canonisation :—

"Alessandro de Medici, Cardinal of Florence, to the Sixty Lords of the Council of Milan.

" RIGHT WORSHIPFUL MY LORDS,—I was intimate with the late Cardinal Borromeo of holy memory, and had full knowledge, not only of his innocency of life and spiritual works, but also with my own eyes had evidence of his Christian virtues, and can, therefore, truly affirm, that I never knew a greater servant of God. It has given me great pleasure to hear of the honours paid to his remains, and of the devotion with which his anniversary is kept in your city. Be assured that I will do all that in me lies to urge on the canonisation of a Cardinal who has deserved so well of the Holy See."

Pope Paul V. showed no less good-will in promoting the cause of one whom he had personally known. He gave it the first hearing at the instance of the Sacred College, placing it before the process of St. Francesca Romana; and at length brought it to its completion amid the joy of the Christian world.

Many of the Cardinals of Holy Church have written in praise of St. Charles' virtues. Agostino Valerio, Cardinal Bishop of Verona, himself a man of learning and holiness, published a compendium of his life,[1] as having enjoyed the privilege of intimate acquaintance with him, calling him "a second Ambrose," and writes of him as follows : "He was a man of God, according to the testimony both of Pius V. and Gregory XIII. To the well-born he was a pattern of virtue, to his brother Cardinals an example of true nobility. To great cheerfulness he joined a constant punishment of the flesh, and a continual study of the Holy Scriptures. In business he was of indomitable energy, with great consideration for others. Full of interior joy, he despised death, and risked his life for his flock. His sermons were the fruit of his meditations, and won many souls. In the decrees of his Synods, he taught the way of Christian discipline both to high and low."

Gabriel Paleotto, Cardinal Archbishop of Bologna, celebrated for his learning and holiness, calls the Saint "a new kind of relic in the body of a living man, a

---

[1] Vita Caroli Borromei, Verona, 1586, pp. 72.

tabernacle containing a divine and holy spirit. A pattern of ancient discipline, a mirror of innocence, dwelling-place of all virtues, a model of episcopal dignity ; setting a fresh example day by day of watchfulness, of pastoral solicitude, of a desire for heavenly things, and a distaste for those of earth, of continual labour, of unusual abstinence, and of invincible constancy. He was an illustrious Prelate, shining like a sun, a most holy Cardinal, a pattern for Bishops of our time." [1]

Cardinal Sirletto, beside the eulogium [2] before quoted, gives the following testimony to the Saint : "Blameless of life after the manner of the ancient fathers." [3]

Cardinal Cesare Baronio, of the Oratory of St. Philip Neri, celebrated for his learning and holiness, entertained a great veneration for St. Charles. In a letter to Cardinal Frederic Borromeo, he called him "a second Ambrose, whose memory is in benediction, whose early death, lamented by all good men, inflicted a great loss upon the Church. He has gained a heavenly country, and an eternal reward."

Cardinal Silvio Antoniano, in his book on education, calls him, "a most vigilant pastor, and bright light of the Church."

Again in a letter to Cardinal Andrew Bathory, he says : "But a little while ago we saw that great servant of God, an image of the olden time, an example of temperance, another Ambrose, Charles Borromeo,

---

[1] In his book on the Administration of the Church of Bologna.

[2] P. 264, vol. ii.

[3] In his book on the Successors of the Apostle St. Barnabas.

the Cardinal of Santa Prassede, Archbishop of Milan who, born in high station, but more illustrious for virtue, lifted by the hand of God to that lofty place, nephew of a sovereign Pontiff, not only filled the province of Milan with the sweet odour of Christ, but like a burning light shone before the whole Church."

Gabriel Fiamma, Bishop of Chiozza, a preacher of note, says of St. Charles:[1] "He was a holy prelate, an angel upon earth, whose life of perfection we may praise without being able to imitate. In his discourses, in his humility and charity he brings before us St. Basil, St. Chrysostom, and St. Gregory; in his mortifications, St. Hilarion and St. Antony; in his fortitude St. Athanasius and St. Hilary; in his industry, St. Cyril, St. Jerome, and St. Paulinus. He was a living pattern of Bishops, a teacher of the faithful, a helper of the afflicted, a scourge of hardened sinners, a curb of the lovers of pleasure, a reviver of ecclesiastical discipline."

Francesco Panigarola, Bishop of Asti, a celebrated preacher, in his sermons enlarges on the holiness of the Saint. Having lived on terms of intimate friendship with him, he describes the austerities of his life as so great that it was miraculous that he should have been able to live on. He relates that when he himself used to kiss his hand before preaching, he always found it cold as ice, even in summer-time, as if his body were dead and his spirit alone alive.

Carlo Bascapè, Bishop of Novara, wrote a history[2]

---

[1] In notes on the life of St. Herbert, Archbishop of Cologne.

[2] De Vita et rebus gestis Caroli S.R.E. Cardinalis tituli S. Praxedis Libri Septem. *Carolo a Basilica Petri praepos. gen. cong. clericorum regul. S. Pauli auctore.* Ingolstadt, 1592, pp. 371.

of the Saint's life, which is highly esteemed by all who knew him, as a testimony to his sanctity.

Giovanni Francesco Bonomo, Bishop of Vercelli, has left behind him a Latin poem on the Saint, entitled *Borromeis.*

Paolo Fosco, Bishop of Serno, in his book on "Visitation," bears witness how highly he himself valued St. Charles, and how greatly he was esteemed by others. "The city of Milan," he says, "rejoices in the holiness and wisdom of Charles Borromeo, her Archbishop, so illustrious for sanctity."

Antonio Seneca, Bishop of Anagni, a prelate very high in the good opinion both of Pope Clement VIII. and Paul V., the present Pontiff, and most intimate with the Saint during eight years that he was a member of his household, in his MS. work on the "Visitation of a Diocese," says, "Charles did perpetual violence to nature, most vigilant as he was and unwearied in watching over his senses, a model of holy living, a blameless pattern of evangelical life, a bright mirror of spirituality purified from passion and appetite. He joined prudence to simplicity, justice to mercy, a great heart to humility, severity to meekness, gravity to modesty, and discretion to zeal. He did not scatter or fleece the flock, but was a true shepherd. In the defence of his people and of the liberties of the Church he was like a stronghold, a pillar of iron, a wall of brass. Vigilant in rooting out vice, benevolent in correction, just in judgment, loving in punishment, patient of human weakness, quick to avenge disobedience, his justice was united with kindness, his severity with gentleness and peace. He was a diligent guardian of wholesome discipline both in priests and people."

Father Achille Gagliardi, a theologian of the Society of Jesus, quondam provost of the professed house of San Fedele, also an intimate friend of the Cardinal, and one of his assistants in the conversion of Protestants in the Mesolcina valley, in one of the duly attested and registered documents of the process of canonisation writes : " Though there are many ways of attaining to sanctity in the Church of God, they may be reduced to two, viz., the active and the contemplative way. Those who have been famed for sanctity have taken either the one or the other path, but very few have made use of both ways. If we find one who has done so, it is not a case of ordinary occurrence, according to the testimony of Abbot John, *Cassian, chap. viii.* It is a great thing even that a man should be perfect in one way, but difficult and almost impossible, I should say, for him to attain to a high standard in both."

In another place he says : " If this standard has been reached in very rare instances by few persons, they exceed the conditions of ordinary virtue, and reach beyond and above human nature, and are not to be included in general rules, nor quoted as examples, but their cases are to be considered miraculous."

From his daily intercourse with Charles during the last four years of his life, he knew him, he continues, to have been called by God to perfection in both the above ways, living as he did always among men, and to have been conspicuous for those virtues which are peculiar to either way, attaining to such a degree of perfection that is not so much to be imitated but rather held to be miraculous.

"His virtues indeed were so great that the fame of them spread throughout the world, and it is the universal judgment of men that he was a saint. The force of his example was so great that he turned the bad from the error of their ways, and gave such strength to the good that they never grew weary. Like the loadstone draws to itself the hardest iron, so in him divine grace subdued the minds of men. Not only those who conversed with him, but even those at a distance, were moved by this grace, for many on hearing only of his virtues received an interior strength to imitate them. I have had experience of this myself in many cases, and acknowledge myself to have been astonished, feeling that the hand of God was working by him, and infused into his soul such an attractive power over men's hearts that led them to imitate him by a certain supernatural sympathy, the action of which I am unable to explain. He was not gifted with eloquence, but was rather brief and short in word, not desirous of pleasing in conversation, but somewhat austere, nevertheless with a few words spoken in so low a tone that they could hardly be heard, he used to persuade, move, and as it were compel those who listened to do his will, so that no one could say him nay. Just as when we look at something wonderful and do not know its cause, we say as the philosophers do, that it is effected by some secret power: thus when we see with wonder that vice was overcome and virtue strengthened, we must acknowledge that this Saint was endowed with a divine grace, which enabled him to work such miracles, like the Apostles, 'the Lord working with him and confirming the word with signs that followed' (St. Mark xvi. 20).

"This then is the greatest proof we can have of the fulness of sanctity in him, viz., that miracles were worked by him. When we look at his works, we see in him so many different virtues that enabled him to bring about effects so different. How then can we deny that there was in him something divine? The looks and gestures, the words and deeds of Charles, seemed all stamped with the seal of the Divinity and Humanity of Christ, as if He Himself had left upon him His mark.

"There came into my mind, when I looked on him, that live coal, by which the prophet Isaias [1] was touched within and without, and the white counter of the Apocalypse,[2] especially as I saw that this holy man was entirely intent upon God and was possessed by an unquenchable desire of promoting His kingdom, and that from him, as from a living fountain, flowed a perpetual stream of thoughts, words, and deeds, to His glory.

"I affirm the truth of all this *coram Deo* in the presence of God: and that the love of truth alone forces this confession from me. I assert indeed that my words are much less than the truth, and testify to it with the most solemn oath that I can make."

So much for the witness of Father Achille Gagliardi, with whom Fr. Francesco Adorno entirely agrees. The latter used to say that God usually sends to His

---

[1] Isaias vi. 6.   [2] Apocal. ii. 17.

Church in times of need men of extraordinary sanctity, and that the Cardinal was one of these messengers. When the Arian heresy arose he sent St. Ambrose and St. Augustine, in like manner St. Dominic and St. Francis in the time of the Albigensians. When this good Father was almost out of his mind through grief at the Saint's sudden death he cried out, *Non est inventus similis illi, qui conservavit legem Excelsi.* (Eccles. xliv. 20). " There was not found the like to him, who kept the law of the Most High."

No wonder that Catholics in England, as we read in the processes of the canonisation, have published his life as an example of holiness for the confusion of heretics who fain would disparage Catholic prelates in that unfortunate kingdom. In like manner French, Spanish, German, and Polish authors have celebrated his praises, in order to make known the Saint in the purposes of Divine Providence to all nations and tongues.

The Evil One, however, envious of the reputation of St. Charles, has endeavoured to diminish his glory. For this end he made use of certain religious men, two examples of which only out of many shall be quoted. The first was one who did not live a good life according to his vocation. Because the Cardinal called him to task, his anger was kindled, and he tried his best to put a bad interpretation upon his words and deeds, attacking him while living, and slandering him after he had departed to a better life. Being in authority at Milan he tried to prevent Father Giovanni Pietro Stoppano from publishing a little work in praise of the Saint, and moved the Holy Office of the Inquisition against Fr. Francesco Panigarola because in his funeral sermon on his death he called him a saint. In the midst of his misdoings he was summoned to Rome, imprisoned, and came to a wretched end shortly after.

The other was a religious of the same order, who endeavoured to take away the Saint's reputation before men by accusing him of acting with a sinister intention. In his history of these times, when he had to speak of the plague, he asserted that the Cardinal had by his imprudence hastened on the pest, that he entered into the controversy on jurisdiction egged on by a spirit of ambition, that he was not wounded by the shot of the arquebuse, but that the bullet hit the wall and rolled beneath his feet; in short, he expended all the ingenuity of his malice upon the Saint. But God has said, *In memoria aeterna erit justus* (Ps. cxi. 7). "The just shall be in everlasting remembrance." Pope Sixtus V. put the matter into the hands of the Holy Office, so that all copies of the scandalous work were not only removed from the shops of the booksellers, but those that were found in private possession were corrected, the author being snatched away by death from further penalties.

Note on page 280.—" Catholics in England."

It seems from this passage that some account or life of St. Charles was circulated in England at the end of the sixteenth or beginning of the seventeenth century. Father Campion, S.J., certainly visited the Saint at Milan in 1580, on his way to England, and stopped with him some eight days, "discoursing before him every day at dinner." No doubt Fr. Campion would, before his martyrdom in 1581, spread abroad in England the report of St. Charles' sanctity, and probably leave behind him some account of it in writing. See *Simpson's Life of Campion*, and note at end of *chap. xxvi., book viii.*

CHAPTER XVIII.

THE SAINT'S BODILY APPEARANCE.

ST. CHARLES was somewhat above the common height, well built, and of a well-proportioned frame. Though plump in youth he wore himself away in later years by labours and austerities. In face he was rather long than otherwise, with broad and calm forehead, well-formed head, hair of a colour between chestnut and black, blue eyes, and large aquiline nose. His beard before he used to shave was brown, short, and not much cared for by him. He only begun to shave when he was thirty-eight years of age,[1] and then the wrinkles in his cheeks were seen, and the leanness and pallor characteristic of saints. He possessed naturally a good constitution, but owing to his continuous toils suffered from catarrh, and from erysipelas in one of his legs.

His prevailing temperament was sanguine, with a slight admixture of the bilious. In outward bearing, which, according to St. Ambrose, is an index of the mind, he was grave and composed, and nothing unbecoming was ever seen in his behaviour. His walk was

---

[1] In 1576, *vid.* Book iv. 10, vol. i. p. 439.

neither too slow nor too fast, and he never made an unnecessary gesture. He received every one with a cheerful countenance, never laughed outright, but used to smile with much grace and sweetness. He was sparing of his words, and seemed to labour from some impediment in his speech. Some thought he did so of set purpose, in order that he might have time to think before he spoke, so as not to offend in word. In giving audience he used to stand for the most part, or supported himself by a table or window-sill. He was endowed by God with a bearing which had in it something divine, and begot reverence in all who addressed him, so that no one could speak to him except seriously and in fitting manner. In his latter years he was somewhat bent by continual study and austerity, and consequently looked older than he really was.

It may well be said that in labours he had lived a very long life, and that in St. Charles the words of Holy Scripture were verified, " Being made perfect in a short space, he fulfilled a long time." [1]

[1] Wisdom iv. 13.

Book VIII

CHAPTER I.

OF THE VIRTUE OF FAITH IN ST. CHARLES.

GOD bestowed upon St. Charles an eminent degree of the virtue of faith—not only an illumination and knowledge, in the light of which he saw himself and the whole world as nothing, but also a burning desire that all men should attain to a true knowledge of God in the faith of Jesus Christ, and the bosom of the holy Catholic Apostolic and Roman Church, under obedience to the Supreme Pontiff, the Vicar of God.

He spared no labour, nor fatigue, nor cost, in order to spread the faith and to cast out every stain of heresy and schism, and never failed to prefer the increase of the faith to everything in the world and even life itself. Many have thought that the light that appeared at the hour of his birth betokened this zeal; just as the star of the Magi indicated the faith of those saints in the new-born Christ.

The effects of this faith were manifested even in his early years, when he gave himself up to the practice of good works in the service of God. As soon as he had a larger field of action, his zeal in spreading and defending religion grew more fervent. During the pontificate of his uncle Pius IV., in order to check the advance of heresy in Europe and to uproot it entirely if possible, he encouraged that Pontiff to bring the labours of the Council of Trent to a conclusion, and himself devoted especial care and solicitude to the undertaking, in spite of impediments raised up by Satan to quash the undertaking, which as we see and know has been greatly blessed. During two succeeding pontificates he left nothing undone in word and deed to uproot heresy. When he became Archbishop, what he had most at heart was to preserve his church from the least taint of error and to make it resplendent in purity of faith. From the very first he made the observance of the decrees of the Council of Trent his principal care, ordering all libraries to be examined, and every doubtful book to be cast out; forbidding the printing or introduction into his diocese or province of books suspected of heresy or contrary to good morals, directing that schoolmasters should be men of learning and good repute, and that they should pay more attention to teaching Christian faith and doctrine rather than to mere book-learning. When young men came into the Milanese state from heretical countries for study, he desired notice to be given of it, that they might have instruction in good morals and a Christian life; in like manner when any heretic had occasion to enter his diocese, the same notice had to be given, lest Catholics should be perverted; that a particular residence should be assigned to such persons, that they should not enter the churches except during sermons, and as to outward behaviour, at least, should set no bad example. When heretical soldiers were quartered in the state, he took infinite pains to guard his flock from infection, directing the parish priests to make reports of their conduct that any disorders might be checked at once, and forbade meat to be given them on fasting days, and all intercourse or intimacy with them. Several companies of German soldiers of heretical opinions being quartered one winter in the diocese, as it was known that they insisted on eating meat publicly on Fridays and other days, he laid a complaint before the Governor, who at once gave orders that they should not eat forbidden food, or give outward sign of heresy, under severe penalties. Moreover, he made a rule that all rectors and parish priests, in those places where there were soldiers, should not allow them to enter the churches, unless they first made a profession of faith according to a certain form in writing; and by this means he put a stop to public scandal. He took care to inform the King of Spain of what he had done, asking that no soldier of a different religion should be sent into Milan, as it led to heresy and dishonour to God among the people, and disturbances and revolutions in the state.

As he was not able to put a stop to the intercourse of his people with heretics, as in the Chiavenna and Tellina valleys which border on the Grisons, districts partly heretical, he visited those places himself, in order to prevent further loss, and to revive the faith. He was very careful that no harm should come to those of his flock who had dealings with heretics, or went where they abounded, and directed his parish priests to watch over them with great charity. Beside the passport or leave of absence necessary for visiting those parts, he required from such persons certificates of Paschal Confession and Communion, of hearing Mass on days of obligation and keeping the commandments of the Church ; in brief, positive proofs that they had lived as Catholics during the time they had remained abroad. As far as was possible, he refused to allow any of his people to take up their habitations in such parts, in order to prevent any danger to faith and morals.

For the same reason he published twice a year, at the beginning of Advent and Lent, an edict against heretics, to the effect that they and all suspected of heresy, all who read or kept prohibited books, should under pain of excommunication, *ipso facto*, be denounced to the Holy Office of the Inquisition, and prosecuted according to law.

He was most scrupulous in requiring the profession of faith and obedience to the supreme Pontiff from all beneficed clergy and all in holy orders, all preachers and confessors coming from other provinces, physicians, surgeons, schoolmasters, teachers of liberal arts and sciences, lawyers, proctors of the holy office, booksellers, and printers of books. He took means also to prevent any who were not good Catholics from holding such offices, in order that all danger to souls might be avoided. In like manner he directed that Christians should hold no conversation with Jews, or go to their feasts, entertainments, or synagogues, or hold any familiar intercourse with them.

By means of such precautions he governed his diocese without the least suspicion of error or false doctrine, and succeeded in banishing many superstitious customs of enchantment, divination, and magical arts, which tend to heresy. In the beginning of his episcopate these superstitions abounded, but by his exertions he gradually made the light of faith to shine with greater purity.

His zeal for the faith was so great that he ardently desired to visit Germany and France to devote himself to the conversion of heretics in those parts. As he never found himself able to go in person, he did all in his power to advance the faith by writing to Bishops and those who held temporal power, to beg them to defend and spread the cause of religion, and by entering into friendly relations with the rulers of countries infected by heresy so as to be able to do good by means of correspondence.

At Brescia in the time of his uncle Pius IV., being at table with several prelates and noblemen, when he was on his way to Trent to meet the two sisters of the Emperor Maximilian, one of the company happened to let fall some heretical expressions. As he corrected him, but without any effect, he immediately left the table, and wrote to the Holy Father begging him to do all in his power to rescue that gentleman from heresy. He was entreated to abstain from so extreme a course of action, but persisted until the culprit, who was a person very high in authority in the city, withdrew his words and repented of his error. The report of this strong measure soon spread abroad and was considered an act of heroism.

CHAPTER II.

OF THE VIRTUE OF RELIGION IN THE SAINT.

THE sentiment of reverence in him was so great, that when he uttered the name of God or heard it uttered by others, he always uncovered his head, and never spoke of Him except to His honour and glory. In order that His holy name should be revered by all, he enacted penalties against blasphemers and those who harboured them, or neglected correcting blasphemy. He reserved to himself the absolution of this offence, and begged all rulers and magistrates to use their best endeavours to banish it entirely from the mouths of those under their charge: and for this end he established a society of men with the particular object of correcting blasphemers by example and precept.

The Holy Scriptures he made his constant study, and had so great a veneration for them that he always read them kneeling with his head uncovered, in the latter years of his life on his bare knees. In his first Provincial Council a decree was made that no one should speak of the Holy Scriptures by way of jest or in useless conversation, much less for superstitious purposes, and all confessors, preachers, and directors were urged to make every effort to put an end to such abuse of them.

He had great devotion for sacred pictures, having many of them in his rooms. In his diocesan synods he enjoined reverence for them, and that they should be placed fittingly in the churches over the altars after being blessed by the Bishop with the proper prayers and ceremonies. He directed that all those that were old and worn-out should be burnt and the ashes buried under the pavement of the church, that they might not be trodden under foot, conformably to orders he had already made concerning vestments, altar linen, &c., books of Holy Scripture and other sacred things. He said Mass every day with preparation of vocal and mental prayer and daily sacramental confession, before he took any business in hand, and was wont to say, that it was not becoming in a priest to occupy himself about temporal things before he had celebrated holy Mass. It is not on record that amid his many occupations and the frequent journeys he undertook, that he ever omitted saying Mass one day, and that, when he was prevented so doing by serious illness, he received Holy Communion. At his confession every morning he always said the Our Father, Hail Mary, the Creed and the Ten Commandments, in obedience to the decree of one of his own synods to that effect. After Mass he remained some time before the altar in prayer, and then said Sext and None or other hours of the Divine Office according to the time. From this custom of his saying Mass every day some simple people naturally thought that all Cardinals and Bishops did the same. On one occasion when a Bishop was at Milan and frequently did not say Mass, but only heard his chaplain's Mass, a lady was so surprised that she asked if he were suspended.

He always recited the Divine Office on his knees, with his head uncovered and with particular attention, sometimes going into ecstasies through his great union with God: and used to read the whole Office without repeating any part of it by heart, to avoid any risk of making a mistake. He directed his clergy to do the same, and urged them to say the Office at the proper time and hour according to the use of the cathedral of Milan. He never failed to say the whole of it, except on the day of his death, and then he heard it said by Jerome Castano, his chamberlain, who recited it kneeling by his bedside.

He was most devout to the Blessed Virgin, having chosen her as his especial Patron, and had recourse to her with great confidence in every need. He reformed her Office and said it every day on his knees, and also the Rosary, even on his journeys; his custom being to meditate on the mysteries, when the way was long. On all the vigils of her feasts he fasted on bread and water, and when he heard the Angelus ring, he knelt down to say it wherever he might be, even in the mud, as I have seen myself; if on horseback, he would dismount to say it on his knees. Whenever he happened to meet the Blessed Sacrament carried to the sick, he would turn and accompany our Lord till He was borne back to the church and replaced in the tabernacle. Out of devotion to our Lady he dedicated an altar to her in his cathedral, and founded the society of the Holy Rosary there, obtaining from the Supreme Pontiff all the indulgences granted to that society in the church of the Minerva at Rome, and instituted a procession of Our Lady on the first Sunday of every month, as is now the custom. He presented to this altar a copy of the picture of the Annunciation at Florence, given to him by the Grand-Duke of Tuscany, Francesco de Medici. He directed that in all collegiate and parish churches the bells should be rung to assemble the clergy and people every Saturday evening to sing the Antiphon of Our Lady according to the season; that the priest when saying Mass and the clerk who was serving should bow their heads at her name, to honour her, and set an example to the people to do the same, and that her image should be placed over the door of the parish churches. He entreated his people to go to Communion on her principal festivals, and made it a rule that even soldiers should carry her medals about them, and say her Office every day. To all colleges, institutions, congregations, and confraternities that he founded, he gave the Blessed Virgin as their particular Patron, recommending that out of devotion her Office and Rosary should be recited.

He was also most devout to the saints, choosing some for his particular patrons and protectors in heaven, as St. Ambrose, whom he endeavoured to imitate in all his virtues, and the holy martyrs St. Gervasius and St. Protasius, who were citizens of

Milan, whose feast he placed in the calendar. He also decreed that the feast of the ordination of St. Ambrose, as principal Patron of the diocese, should be kept throughout the whole province, and that a commemoration should be made of him after our Blessed Lady and the Apostles in the Divine Office, that he might be recognised as the Patron of the Milanese Church. He also directed the observance of the festival of St. Barnabas, as founder of that Church, and of the glorious martyr St. Sebastian, who was also a native of Milan, and by another decree he appointed that the feast of the titular saint of every parish should be observed as a day of obligation by the parishioners, and he recommended them to fast on the vigil.

We have seen how devout he was to relics. It really seemed as if he had fixed his heart upon them, and had no other delight in the world, but in venerating them and urging his flock to do the same by his solemn translations of them, passing the whole night in prayer wherever there were relics or bodies of the saints, undertaking long journeys to visit them, and striving to obtain them wherever he could to enrich his church. He obtained many indeed from different places, especially from Ernest of Bavaria, Archbishop of Cologne, and the Duke, his brother.

The Saint himself, in answer to a letter of the Archbishop informing him that he had consigned the relics for which he had asked, to the care of Francis Cassina, a Milanese residing at Cologne, wrote as follows:—" I was glad to receive your letter of the

1st of July, in which you promise me the holy relics.
As nothing is dearer to me than the glory of God,
and devotion to those holy men who have shown
themselves brave soldiers of Jesus Christ, your kindness is highly prized by me, since it bestows upon
me the privilege of beholding, touching, and venerating the relics of the holy martyrs. I am eagerly
looking for Cassina with the treasure."

He generally wore hanging from his neck a little
cross filled with relics, which after his death came
into the possession of Father Ludovico Moneta, who
gave it to the Poor Clares of St. Barbara, that it
might be preserved with greater reverence. In his
life-time he presented another gold cross, which contained a piece of the wood of the true cross, to the
Abbate Giovanni Simonetta, when he went on a
mission to Spain. He used to wear also an Agnus Dei,
blessed by the Holy Father, which on his death was
taken from his neck by Bernardino Tarugi, one of
his chaplains, and afterwards given to Charles Emmanuel, Duke of Savoy, who made it a perpetual
heirloom in his family.

St. Charles made many decrees in his synods and
councils on the veneration due to relics; among
others, directing that they should not be kept in
private, but should be preserved in churches and
holy places. He set the example himself by making
a free gift of a precious shrine he had received in
Rome to the Church of St. Barnabas, belonging to
the Fathers of St. Paul. This shrine contained three
pieces of the cross of our Lord, two thorns from His

crown, a piece of His tunic, of His girdle, of the sponge, the pillar of scourging, of His cradle and manger, various relics of our Blessed Lady, of St. John the Baptist, the Apostles, and other saints, and is now one of the chief treasures of the Fathers. In order to prevent the removal of relics, he obtained a pontifical brief, forbidding their removal, under pain of excommunication, from any place in the province of Milan without the permission of the Supreme Pontiff.

He displayed his devotion in frequently visiting holy places and churches; when in Rome he used to visit the stations on foot, and walk long distances to the shrines of our Blessed Lady and others, both there and in Milan, praying before every altar. His piety was so great that he seemed unable to quit such places. He would usually remain five hours together in the chapel of the pillar at Santa Prassede in Rome, once he stayed all night in the catacombs of St. Sebastian outside the walls, and in the morning, it being the feast of St. Agnes, he went on foot to the church of that saint beyond the Porta Pia, where he said Mass and remained a long time in prayer, returning thence to Santa Prassede, after twenty-two hours' absence. We have seen how he went through the Forty Hours' Prayer, never leaving the church during the whole time; as he used to say, it was his delight to be in the church. He had a great desire to make a pilgrimage to the Holy Sepulchre and other places in Palestine, but having the charge of souls he would not give up residence to satisfy his devotion, nor would the Pope readily have given him permission.

He took great pleasure in his episcopal duties, and fulfilled them with such perfection as to surprise all who beheld him, so that they would remain with him in church all day long, forgetful of everything else, sustained by the delight and consolation they felt at seeing him celebrate the Divine Office with his Canons. His synods and councils he held with great solemnity, frequently as they occurred; at his fourth Provincial Council, twenty-seven Pontifical Masses and Vespers were said. When he approached the altar, or ascended the pulpit in his vestments, there was such a dignity in his manner as cannot be described, for he seemed more like an angel than a man. In the process of his canonisation Father Achilles Gagliardi writes as follows of him: "He breathed an odour of sanctity, and there went forth from him a harmony as of heavenly sweetness. I remember that frequently when I have been with him at synods or on solemn occasions, it struck me that the very sight of him would force even an enemy to exclaim like Balaam: How beautiful are thy tabernacles, O Jacob, and thy tents, O Israel! as woody valleys, as watered gardens near rivers, as tabernacles which the Lord hath pitched."[1]

He had so high an opinion of his episcopal functions that he would not neglect one for any consideration whatever, and would give up every other business for them, taking long journeys, travelling post-haste when at a distance in order to be present at these solemnities. Once when he was ill in bed, on the feast of Corpus

---

[1] Numb. xxiv. 5, 6.

Christi, he rose to join in the procession and carry
our Lord himself according to his custom, heeding no
suffering or inconvenience to do the work of God.
Another time when he was in the procession, the rain
came down in torrents and he was wet through, for those
who were supporting the canopy upset it unawares,
and poured down his neck the water that had accumu-
lated on the top, yet he remained to the end of the
Office without any sign of annoyance. So when he
preached, as he often did, quitting the pulpit in a
perspiration, he remained in the choir for the Divine
Office without rest or retirement. He was so particular in all matters of divine worship, that he noticed
and corrected the least defect by whomsoever committed, being desirous of the greatest perfection
possible. When he was one day giving Holy Communion, through the fault of one of the attendants,
the pyx nearly fell from his hands, and upset some
particles of our Lord's body upon the cloth beneath,
which grieved him so much, that it was difficult to restrain him from doing penance for the fault of another.
While he was occupied in these sacred functions he
would not be disturbed by anything whatsoever that
might happen. .

On one occasion when he was at his seminary, occupied in a sacred though not important function, a
messenger, who was eagerly expected by him, arrived
from Rome, yet, when informed of it, he would not
see him until he had quite finished what he was about.
The Bishop of Novara relates on one occasion that he
himself had to send word about important business at a

time when the Saint was preaching a sermon at a convent of nuns, but he paid no attention till he had finished, and then gave his answer. Considering it unworthy of the service of God to allow other matters to interfere with it, he therefore mortified himself by refusing attention to other matters although of importance. He discharged all these offices not only with the greatest attention, but also with the most perfect ceremonial in every place, even in the mountainous parts and among ordinary folk, for he had no regard to place or persons but only to the majesty of God whom he was serving; and if by chance anything necessary were wanting, he would rather omit the function than perform it with the least defect or imperfection. Neither would he allow its being done hastily or with any omission of proper ceremonies because it was late, or that there was much to occupy them; but he would have everything done completely and perfectly although it might take time. Hence it was that he would often be in the church from early morning until vesper time, and in the evening till far into the night, never showing any signs of weariness or bodily pain or want of attention, though he passed many days continually in the church occupied in serious matters and with constant fatigue; which was thought something superhuman and miraculous, especially as he took so little rest at night and mortified himself so much with fasting and penances.

He used his utmost endeavours to keep up respect and veneration for churches and holy places, by his decrees enjoining reverential behaviour and devotion

there, forbidding chattering, walking about, carrying
guns or arms, or other unbecoming things; desiring
women to veil their heads and to be apart from the
men, and men to wear cloaks and kneel on both
knees. He required all rectors of churches to see
that these regulations were observed, and to reprove
those who did not comply. To establish these rules,
he had clerks standing at the church doors to give
notice to all to obey them, and he took care to admonish the people himself as to their observance,
and would not tolerate the least irreverence in sacred
places. On solemn occasions and the principal feasts
he used to send his vicars and officials to the most
frequented churches to prevent disorderly conduct,
and to apprehend the disobedient and contumacious,
and had the streets around such churches barricaded
to prevent horses and carriages from disturbing the
people at their devotions. He would not allow
seculars to enter the choir with ecclesiastics, or approach the altars, and for this purpose he fixed iron
railings round, nor would he allow any ecclesiastic
to remain in choir without a clean surplice and his
choir habit. He likewise forbade the clergy and
sacristans to decorate the altars or perform any other
service without a surplice, and required them to bow
or kneel as they passed before them at all times. In
the same way he reformed the music and singing,
enjoining that all the singers should be ecclesiastics
and wear the surplice. He would allow no other
instrument in the church but the organ, and prohibited all such as are used for profane purposes as

unfitted for the service of God. He required exact obedience to these rules, granting to no one, however great a personage, permission to contravene them; so that great and small were alike obedient. On a report once arising that the King of Spain was coming to Milan, when he was asked whether he would allow him to enter the choir, "I consider," he replied, "that his Majesty has too much piety to wish to do so;" showing that he held the choir to be set apart for ecclesiastical persons and the ministers of God.

Page 298.—The Saint's spirit of devotion.

Mark Antony Bellini, Canon in Ordinary of the Chapter, writes of the Saint: "When I consider the devotion of Charles, I can only lift up my heart to God with the prophet and say, '*Lord, who will believe our report! to whom has the arm of the Lord been revealed!*'[1] He was always serious, always employed, always forecasting everything with so much faith as to make one despair of ever attaining to his spirit; he seemed always *so to run as to obtain*.[2] His life as a bishop was so ordered that one work led on to another, and that which would have seemed extraordinary in another person in him appeared to be only natural and proper. What has been said of a certain prelate may well be applied to him : 'He was one who did not look for peace and quietness, or pleasure, but ardently desired labour, gladly putting up with contempt; impatient of honour, poor in spirit, rich in the reward of a good conscience, humble in his expectations, but proud against the assaults of temptation. He was entirely given up to holiness, and breathed only prayer and contemplation. His only care was to speak or read of God : to those who were irreverent in the temple of God he was terrible. He was feared for his severity, but loved for his kindness.' O happy land that gave birth to such a son ! an advocate in heaven, an angel rather than a man."

[1] Isaias liii. 1.   [2] 2 Cor. ix. 24.

CHAPTER III.

OF HIS RESPECT FOR THE HOLY APOSTOLIC SEE AND THE ECCLESIASTICAL DIGNITY.

FROM his deep religious feeling sprung a high honour and respect for the Supreme Pontiff and the Holy Apostolic See, and for all orders of ecclesiastical persons. He recognised the Supreme Pontiff as the Vicar of God, and honoured and obeyed him as such, being greatly displeased if any one mentioned him without respect and veneration, and deemed it the chief error of heretics that they disobeyed the Pope, and spoke ill of the Cardinals.

When he himself named or heard others mention the name of the reigning Pontiff, he always uncovered his head out of respect. Once when he was celebrating Mass in the Pope's chapel at Rome, he refused to wash his hands in a gilt basin, saying it was not fitting in presence of the Pope. On another occasion in the church of Santa Prassede, the Fathers there had prepared for him a cushion which the Pope had used when he went thither: he had it taken away, saying it was not right that others should kneel on it after it had been used by His Holiness. One day when he was saying Mass in the Pope's oratory outside of Rome, His Holiness came to hear his Mass, out of devotion, he immediately sent away the two ministers who were serving him, and said Mass as a simple chaplain, out of respect for him.

He was always most obedient to the Supreme Pontiff, and to all his orders, executing them with all promptitude and submission. Observing that an intimate friend on certain occasions of need, when assistance that had been asked did not come quickly from Rome, would burst forth indiscreetly into improper complaints against the Pontiff, he reprehended him like a father in these terms : " Remember that in all things we must obey God, and that the Pope holds His place, whosoever therefore does not obey him, disobeys God : we must do what lies in our power to obey him, and we may then consider that whatever he decides is right." He acted in this way himself towards the Supreme Pontiff, who is the head of all, for he used to refer the proper cases to his judgment, taking his commands in good part as from God's own hand. He was never heard to complain of the Pope or his ministers in all the business he had continually to transact at Rome. He paid great respect also to all such ministers as representing His Holiness, and strove as far as he could to make others do the same ; and never failed to go to Rome every three years to visit the shrine of the Apostles according to the obligation of Bishops. In writing or speaking of the Apostolic See, he always added the title of " holy " speakihg of " the Holy Apostolic See," as its

supreme dignity and sanctity required: and sought
by every possible means to vindicate its authority
without human respect, heedless of any annoyance
he incurred by so doing.   Everything that he thought
would benefit the pontifical government, he laid
respectfully before the Pontiff, to the great advantage
of the Church in general   When any Apostolic briefs
were presented to him, he would uncover his head to
receive them, and kiss them with reverence.   If any
doubtful question of church-government came before
him, he always referred it to Rome, and yielded entire
obedience to all judgments from thence, because the
Holy Roman See was directed by the Holy Spirit.

He had great reverence for the office of Cardinal,
nephew of a Pope as he was himself, and prevailed on
his uncle Pius IV. to make rules to further its honour
and dignity.   By the example of his own life and in
other ways he greatly increased the consideration paid
to it; towards his brother Cardinals he was unassum-
ing and humble, though favoured by his uncle and of
great authority with him.   When resident at Milan
he paid them every possible honour; if he heard that
any Cardinal was coming to the city he would go to
meet him; if absent he would return without delay to
welcome him to his own house, with all reverence
accompanying him through the city on horseback or
in a litter, as he was not accustomed to use a carriage;
and with a holy violence obliging him to give his
blessing to the people, and for greater honour he
would invite the prelates and gentlemen of the city
to join in escorting him.   He strove to have the

dignity respected in his own person, by acquiring the virtue and sanctity fitting so eminent a rank, and so great a fire of love and zeal for the glory of God and the Catholic faith, as to be willing if necessary to shed his blood for it; he was wont to say of himself: "I wear this red garment to show that in case of need I have to shed my blood in the service of God and for the benefit of Holy Church." He wished to be considered by others not as Charles Borromeo, which he looked upon as the vile and base portion of himself, but as the Cardinal of Santa Prassede, in which capacity he received the honours conferred upon him as from God, bestowed upon the office and not upon himself.

Many were surprised to see on one side so great humility, and on the other such majesty that even princes were struck by it, and stood uncovered in his presence, though begged by him to cover their heads. When he was speaking in his own person, he placed himself below all, but when he spoke as Cardinal, he deemed himself above every other dignity inferior to his own, and was so tenacious of his office that in presence of princes his first consideration was how he should treat them without derogating from his dignity, as when he spoke with the King of France at Monza. Princes indeed of their own accord gladly showed him honour for his great sanctity. If it happened that persons of rank failed in this, he took notice of it, as was the case when a nobleman of distinction came to Milan, the Saint went to visit him and paid him the respect due to a prince, but not meeting himself with the treatment he expected as a Cardinal, he let his displeasure be known on the return of that personage to Milan, when he declined to visit him in person and sent Mgr. Seneca in his stead, giving him to understand in this way that the dignity of Cardinal was greater than he supposed. This was considered an act of heroism, in the face of a man of exalted rank.

He had no less respect for the office of Bishop, which he deemed as much above any worldly dignity, as the spiritual is above the temporal. He restored to them the title of Most Reverend, it being customary with some Cardinals at that time to style them Very Reverend only. When he heard of the arrival of a Bishop at Milan, he would send some of his household to meet him outside the city and accompany him to the cathedral where he was received by the Canons, and after prayers was taken to the rooms reserved for Bishops and waited upon by the Cardinal's own servants. When a Bishop paid him a visit, he went out to meet him, and at his departure showed him every mark of affection and esteem. While in Milan he would find him spiritual entertainment in visiting churches, colleges, and pious institutions, and ask him to preach and administer the sacraments, anxious that his own flock should derive benefit, and that the opportunity should not be lost, and he would have him bestow his blessing upon the people as he passed through the city.

He did all in his power to assist all Bishops by letters, advice, and favours obtained from the Apostolic See, and was careful that due honours should be paid them by princes. When once at the palace at

Turin with the Duke Emmanuel Philibert and his court, he was told that the Archbishop of the city was coming, upon which he rose, leaving all to go and meet him, in order to show the Duke the respect due to Bishops. Observing that the Archbishop had not his archiepiscopal cross carried before him when he entered the ducal palace, he told him that he ought to have it carried before him always, even in the Duke's own chamber. In the same way when St. Charles was walking in the city with the Duke in company with the Archbishop, he desired the latter to walk by their side, and on bidding him farewell would accompany him out of the room, though he had to leave the Duke alone.

On another occasion, in the palace at Ferrara, when the Saint was washing his hands before dinner, in company with the Duke Alfonso d'Este, he saw the Bishop of Ferrara offering a napkin to the Duke— which he forbade him to do, desiring him to wash and sit down with them, and at his departure he accompanied him out of the room, leaving the Duke alone. So at Rome when he visited Cardinals and princes, he would not take Bishops with him, as he did not think it fitting to leave them in the ante-chambers.

All ecclesiastics and regulars, as persons consecrated to God, were treated by him with similar respect and reverence. Those whom he knew to be leading a holy life, and were lovers of discipline and zealous for the salvation of souls, were cherished by him with great affection, and they had greater influence with him although they might be of low birth, than others who were of high rank and learning, because he looked to goodness of life more than great acquirements and noble lineage, when not found united to goodness. He chose his Vicars-General and directors of souls from the number of such zealous priests, although not distinguished for learning, and of low extraction, and preferred them to learned theologians who were wanting in discipline, though at the same time he set a high value on good birth when united to good morals. For the ecclesiastical state he had such respect that in speaking to priests, though of humble condition, he never uttered a word wanting in consideration or implying servitude, but treated all with due honour. He would not permit any menial office to be performed by those in holy orders, although of his own household, so also when he dismounted from horseback where no servants were in attendance, he would rather go about all day in his riding-boots than suffer an ecclesiastic to assist him. When he gave audience to them, he always remained standing out of respect. He also strove to inspire lay people with great esteem for the ecclesiastical state; and when any business had to be transacted between a priest and a layman, he could not bear to see the priest take off his hat while the layman kept his on. Once when it was hinted to him that it would be well to limit the ecclesiastical titles in his church, in the way the King of Spain had done in regard to secular honours, he replied that, although there might be a large number, it was better it should be so, to maintain the dignity of the clergy and accustom the people to hold them in proper estimation. Observing on one occasion that a priest, in imitation of himself, acted with more humility than was fitting, he pointed out that the authority he possessed was not in his own name, and should not be put in jeopardy by such behaviour; that the same argument did not apply to himself, because his dignity being joined to his person, his acts of humility did not diminish his authority but rather increased it, according to the words of our Lord, "He who humbleth himself shall be exalted."

Finally, he entertained a very marked respect for his confessor, considering that he held the place of God. When he took him with him in his journeys, especially if he were making the spiritual exercises, he used to visit his room before dawn to give him a light, bowing as he passed him on entering, and again on leaving the room, even though he were asleep.

Note on page 306.—His respect for the episcopate.

His brethren in the episcopate in their turn entertained a great respect for the Saint himself. Once when the Bishop of Ventimiglia, who wore a beard, on coming to Milan, was told of the synodal decree against beards, he at once summoned a barber and had himself shaved before calling on the Cardinal.

CHAPTER IV.

ON HIS REFORM OF DIVINE WORSHIP.

FINDING divine worship in a neglected state in the church of Milan, the Saint set himself diligently to restore it to as perfect a state as possible. He reformed the ritual, which was full of errors and imperfections, and not only provided for essentials in the administration of the Sacraments, but brought the observance of ecclesiastical ceremonies to a high state of excellence, thereby promoting the devotion of the people. From his great desire that the church should be distinguished for majesty of ritual, his first care was directed to the celebration of the Divine Office, teaching his clergy what ceremonies were to be observed, even to the smallest particulars, not considering anything unimportant that appertained to the worship of God, though it might seem so to ordinary people. In order that this service might be carried out with great exactness and majesty, he formed a society of learned men, who were to discuss and decide all questions of this kind, calling it the Congregation of Rites, after the one he had already established, with the Pope's permission, in Rome, for the benefit of the Church in general.

He appointed masters of the ceremonies in his cathedral, and taught the clergy of the city and diocese their use and practice by establishing the like office in all the Chapters of collegiate churches, in every parish, in the seminaries and colleges, and publishing them every year at the diocesan synod. In this way the use became uniform throughout the diocese, and seculars acquired a knowledge of what was right and proper. After the Saint's death, it happened that when a foreign Bishop sung Mass in the cathedral, he put his hand to his mitre as he was returning to the altar, out of respect to the Governor of the city, who was seated outside the railing of the choir. This gesture was noticed by a lady, who said that the Cardinal, when he had his mitre on, never did anything of the kind.

He reformed the Ambrosian Missal, and was particular in observing that rite himself, and reviving its ancient glory, and would not allow any deviation from it, on account of its antiquity and approbation by the Holy Apostolic See. He also founded a special congregation for this rite, and printed a little book of the ceremonies of the Mass in order that it might be offered in spirit and in truth according to the decrees of the Council of Trent, without avarice and simony. He abolished the abuse existing in some places of saying more than one Mass a day, and founded a fund for the maintenance of celebrating priests and chaplains, and for the offices and funerals of the departed, at the same time enacting that no vagabond, criminous, or illiterate clerks should be received into the diocese, that no one should be allowed to say Mass without previous examination and a written permission, that foreign priests must have testimonials from their own Bishops. He forbade any one to serve Mass except tonsured clerics wearing a cassock and clean cotta. He abolished the custom of celebrating in private Oratories, in order that Mass should be said only in public churches, and was so strict on this point that he would not allow a private Oratory even to the Governor of Milan himself, though permission had been obtained for it from Rome; in like manner, he prohibited Mass to be said outside churches, and removed all altars that had been erected for that purpose before the gates of churches. He exhorted all persons to hear Mass and receive the Sacraments at their own parish churches, in order to have the advice and instruction of their own pastor, and to assist at the holy sacrifice with reverence, piety, and devotion, that all public and scandalous sinners should be excluded as unworthy to be present. He corrected many abuses in early Masses that were sung; and in celebration of anniversaries of the titular saints of churches, which had become market-days and times for plays and profane revels rather than holidays, he forbade all impiety and desecration, and brought those who had before given themselves up to buying and selling, dancing and drinking, to spend their time better in hearing Mass and sermons, in receiving the Sacraments and other spiritual exercises. He would not allow watching in the churches at night, according to an ancient custom, on account of many disorders committed, and because the fervour of early Christian times no longer existed. He forbade the clergy having banquets on such days, as they had been accustomed to do, in order that they might without inconvenience remain in the churches, and give spiritual exercises to the people; and established the same good custom for all other days of obligation, forbidding at those times not only servile works and business, but also all profanities, games, balls, masks, tourneys, plays, mountebanks, and every other spectacle and idle amusement; instead of which he made it a custom throughout his diocese, to have the spiritual exercises, which occupied the people beneficially all day, during the festival. He was only able to put these regulations into practice gradually, amid much difficulty and opposition.

In the same way he reformed the manner of reciting the Litanies, and conducting processions, and restored the observance of the holy times of Advent and Lent, of vigils and ember days,[1] into which many abuses and improprieties had crept. He was especially careful to ensure veneration for the Blessed Sacrament of the Altar, and finding that the body of our Lord, in some few churches, was kept without due decency in certain receptacles in the wall, he decreed that the Sacred Host should be reverently preserved upon the high altar in all collegiate and parish churches and convents, with a lamp constantly burning, in tabernacles as handsome as possible, lined with silk, and with proper covers, beside the canopy

[1] See the " Acta Ecclesiae Mediolanensia."

to be placed over every altar. Neither would he have the Blessed Sacrament removed on any occasion of celebrating High Mass or solemn offices, considering it unbecoming to place His Divine Majesty on any other and inferior altar. He established the Confraternity of the Blessed Sacrament in every parish and church of the city and diocese, in order to provide for everything necessary for the altar, to accompany It to the sick, and to join in the processions which he appointed for every third Sunday of the month in the parish churches. These confraternities flourished during his lifetime, to the glory of God and the welfare of souls. As he found in Milan an ancient custom of the Forty Hours' Prayer, during which the Blessed Sacrament was exposed upon the altar of some particular church, and that the devotion was not well ordered, and that inconveniences sometimes arose, he gave directions that there should be an exposition of the Most Holy Sacrament in every church of the city in turn for forty hours, and thus revived the devotion of the primitive Christians among the people.

How he raised the rest of the Sacraments in the estimation of the people may be gathered from the decrees of his Councils and by the Ritual he published. He introduced improvement and reformation throughout, down to the slightest matters, in order that priests should administer them reverently in clean cotta and stole with preparation and prayer; that the confessions of women should be heard in the daytime only at the grating in the confessional, with something intervening to prevent their being seen; that when confessions of sick persons were heard the door of the room should be left open. He printed a book of advices for confessors, with the reserved cases and censures and canonical penances which were formerly in use. He would not allow priests to receive anything for administering the Sacraments, not even for almsgiving, to banish every shadow of temptation to avarice, and that the words of the Gospel might be fulfilled in them, " Freely ye have received, freely give." [1]

His efforts were especially directed to promote the fitting worship of God by the clergy in saying the Divine Offices. Rules were laid down by him for everything that was to be done, both for its recitation in private and publicly in choir, as to the proper times and ceremonies, the attention necessary, the choir-habit, and the most minute particulars. He had tablets containing these rules made to be hung in the sacristies, that all might see and know them, appointing *punctators*, or markers, in the collegiate churches and for the clergy, to note down deficiencies, the penalty of which was forfeiture of part of the daily distributions.

He reformed the Ambrosian breviary, with the assistance of learned men, and restored the ancient use, and directed all the clergy to say the Office according to this revised edition, and by this means increased the devotion and attention paid to its recitation. He printed an *ordo*, or calendar, for the regulation of the Office, and kept the feasts of the canonised Archbishops of Milan, to the number of thirty-one, with solemn rite.

As the houses of God, where He is worshipped

---

[1] St. Matt. x. 8.

and divine duties are discharged, were in a bad state, and had lost much of their ancient splendour, he took great pains to restore them and remove everything that was unbecoming, such as profane statues and pictures, military flags, and especially sepulchres and memorials put up aloft, and ordered the bodies of the dead to be buried underground. This he had carried out in the whole of his diocese, as well as in others that he visited, though it sometimes caused displeasure to persons concerned, yet he had more regard for God's honour than for gratifying the inclinations of men. He made also a thorough reform in every part of the church itself, and in the sacred vessels and church furniture, insisting especially on great cleanliness and order. That uniformity should be observed in the building of churches throughout the province, he published a book entitled "Instructions on Ecclesiastical Buildings," containing all directions necessary for the material construction, and appointed Father Ludovico Moneta to superintend all such buildings, with the title of Prefect of Ecclesiastical Buildings. In process of time all the churches of the city and diocese were either rebuilt or partially restored, and enriched with suitable church furniture, even in the villages and poor mountainous districts, as every parishioner tried to renovate and adorn his own church, and provide it with vestments, because the Cardinal had given orders to that effect in his visitation of the diocese.

The zealous pastor desired that churches, altars, sacristies, and everything in them should be kept in perfect neatness and cleanliness, and printed full instructions to be observed everywhere, and enforced by his prefects and visitors. In this way he restored divine worship throughout his extensive diocese and throughout the province to such a degree of splendour, that all were edified by it and gave thanks to God.

I will here quote the testimony of Father Achilles Gagliardi on this matter, referring to what he had seen with his own eyes. " His church fills every one with astonishment, and seems like the palace of Solomon, and the temple of Jerusalem." He also enriched it with many spiritual treasures obtained from the holy Apostolic See, to stimulate the devotion of his people, and make them visit the churches ; as we see in the seven churches of the stations indulgenced like those in Rome, so that Milan is called another Rome.

Note on page 312.—" *Foreign priests must have testimonials.*"

When St. Philip Neri, at Charles' earnest request, in 1575, sent to Milan two of his fathers, viz., Alessandro Fedeli and Pompeo Pateri, one of them was unprovided with the *celebret* enjoined by the decrees of the Council of Trent, and in consequence the Cardinal could not allow him to say Mass until he had procured it from Rome. See Capecelatro's *Life of St. Philip Neri*, vol. i. p. 488.

CHAPTER V.

OF HIS SPIRIT OF PRAYER AND CONTEMPLATION.

HE was so given to prayer that it seemed to be his food and delight. He spent many hours every day in mental prayer; and every night, except the few hours he allowed himself for bodily rest, he passed in study and prayer. If, however, there was any matter of moment either as regards the Church or the public welfare, he remained all night in prayer: so also when visiting places of great devotion, or on occasion of translating the relics of saints, or consecrating churches and altars, he spent the whole night in prayer. He frequently meditated on the Passion of our Lord, which had a singular attractiveness for him, and divided the subject into various points, and had a book printed with texts and pictures representing all the mysteries, to assist the memory, and place before the eye the matter for meditation. He made a large collection of similar meditations, three or four volumes of which were found after his death, some of which are now preserved in the library of the Canons Ordinary of the cathedral. In order to have a place of retirement for

prayer, he had a little oratory made with a small cell
adjoining to sleep in, under the roof of his palace, far
away from all noise and disturbance. He was accustomed twice a year to retire to some solitary place
where, free from the tumult of the world for a few days,
he would fortify his spirit with divine contemplation.
He then made a general confession of the time elapsed
since his last retreat, and returned to his duties and
good works with as much fervour as though he had
never done a good action before and was only beginning to serve God. He took care that his household
and his coadjutors in the care of souls should have the
same opportunity for spiritual retirement. He used to
go to the choir for the Divine Office on all feast-days,
and on the more solemn festivals would remain there
all day, with his mind so fixed in contemplation that
he seemed rapt in ecstasy : at times it was found necessary to shake him in order to bring him to himself
when he had to answer in the Office. When the choir-
office was ended, he would withdraw to an oratory
beneath the choir, called " Scurolo," or the " dark place,"
and there remain in prayer, and was always accustomed
to keep his hands joined from the intense application
of his mind. When riding or travelling on foot, if
not called upon to speak upon business, he spent all
the time in prayer, and his mind became so absorbed
in contemplation that he would not notice whether his
mule was going right or wrong, and he would even fall
off some times unawares,—as Mgr. Speciano, Bishop
of Cremona, testifies, in the judicial process of canonisation, that once he saw with his own eyes that when

the Cardinal was on his way from Milan to Cassano, he became so intent in prayer that, not minding the reins, his mule fell with him without his being sensible of it. On another occasion, when he was riding from Como, wishing to reach Milan by evening, he fell into a pit, under his mule, near Barlassina, and as it was dark his companions passed on some distance without finding it out. On turning back they found him silent in the pit; he told Mgr. Speciano that he was occupied in prayer. He was wont to pass whole nights in prayer in the Church of St. Ambrose at Milan, and in the Catacombs at Rome.

In his ordinary and frequent prayers he was evidently so united to God that even when he was occupied with business, though he was attentive to what was going on, his mind was raised to God, resting in Him, and abstracted from everything else. On this subject Father Gagliardi says in his attestation: " I cannot here omit relating what I have observed in him with astonishment, and there are plenty of witnesses to confirm what I say. During the time that he was doing business, with numbers of people, on the one hand, he was most attentive listening to all that was said, and entering fully into all matters in order to settle them to the satisfaction of all; while, on the other hand, it was clearly seen by the moderation of his words and gestures, that he was so united to God as to be more in the other world than in this, as the saying is. I have often reflected upon this, on seeing him do business, and he seemed to me to realise those words of St. Luke, " we ought always to pray and not to faint.'[1]   This seems to be an evident sign of the profound contemplation in which he was always buried."

Other persons who had the opportunity observed with astonishment the same power of abstraction in him, particularly during the latter years of his life. This degree of contemplation was acquired by his frequent prayer, to which he added a strict watchfulness over himself and his senses, avoiding every occasion of distraction, curiosity, and gossip about the doings of others, to all which he was, as it were, dead, and wished others to act in the same way.   So that we may truly say, his life was a perpetual and perfect prayer, for he was always walking in the presence of God with his mind raised to heaven.   By this means he reached a very high degree of perfection, in which he united the works of the active to those of the contemplative life.   He used to say, speaking of watchfulness over oneself, how necessary it was in a Bishop, in order that action should not hinder contemplation in him, as being always occupied in the administration of the things of God.

[1] St. Luke xviii. 1.

CHAPTER VI.

OF TEACHING CHRISTIAN DOCTRINE.

THE Cardinal on coming to his diocese found that heresy was spreading throughout Europe, and that it arose in great measure from ignorance of the faith, because pastors of souls had neglected the instruction of the young, and that this neglect in turn had caused a relaxation in good morals and Christian discipline. While occupied in offices of the pontifical government in Rome, he gave the charge of Christian doctrine to his Vicar-General, Ormaneto, to promote it in every way possible. There were then found in Milan about fifteen schools established by some good priests, which by his exertions were soon increased to thirty. The Saint on taking up his residence made a decree in his first Provincial Council, directing all parish priests and pastors of souls to summon all the children of the parish at the sound of a bell to meet in the afternoon of every Sunday and holiday of obligation to be taught Christian doctrine in the church. He then summoned before him all the parish-priests of the city, pointing out the absolute necessity of this work which was their proper office and duty, and ordered by the Holy Council of Trent, begged them to give all their energies to its discharge, and not to be wanting in co-operation with the lay workers and in founding schools and providing for their needs. Addressing the lay-workers in turn, he enlarged on the importance of training children in Christian discipline and the holy fear of God, and uniting together for the salvation of souls with an infinite reward promised by God; that his desire was to form a congregation of labourers for the care and charge of this holy work. He desired all preachers to recommend this confraternity of Christian doctrine, and to exhort fathers of families to take their children with them to church on all feasts, showing them that they were bound to know the doctrines of faith and to teach them to their families.

By these exhortations the Saint so inflamed the hearts of his people that in a short time he found a great number of persons of both sexes ready to join in the work. He did not fail to take his share in it, going sometimes to one church and sometimes to another to visit the different schools, begging them to persevere, and laying down rules for the steady progress of the work. He sent the most experienced and pious labourers into the various parts of the diocese with letters patent and especial faculties, even to the distant districts in the mountains, to found there schools in the same form and under the same rule as in the city, desiring all parish priests to give them every assistance, and to take particular care themselves to teach and exhort the people to come themselves, and make it a matter of conscience with fathers and mothers to bring their children. In this way he established schools of Christian doctrine throughout the diocese, even in the most remote valleys and mountains, in a short space of time.

When he afterwards made the visitation of his diocese, his first care was to visit these schools, encouraging those who laboured in them with much affection as brothers, and bestowing upon them favours according to his opportunities. These good assistants were so devoted to the work, that they thought nothing of fatigue, and patiently bore insolence and sometimes blows from the wayward and wanton, when they would take them away from gaming, idleness, and other evil habits. His priests he watched over himself, reproving those who were negligent and little disposed for the work, and in cases of necessity had recourse to penalties. On festival days, therefore, all the churches in the city and diocese were filled with men, women, and children, all teaching or learning Christian doctrine. On every side these good scholars and teachers were heard singing the praises of God in litanies, hymns, and psalms, to the great joy and consolation of all, especially in the villages and country places. There the people took so much pleasure in singing at home as a recreation the hymns and canticles which they learnt at these Sunday schools, that they gave up their dances and profane songs and worldly recreations, in which they had hitherto spent their holidays. In a short time, in places where even grown-up men but a

while before could not say either the *Our Father*
or the *Hail Mary*, even lisping children answered
with intelligence the truths of our holy faith, and
taught their parents what they were bound to believe and to practise as true Christians for their
salvation.

St. Charles seeing that the work thus begun was
making such wonderful progress in Milan and in all
parts of the diocese, desired to establish it in a permanent form. He determined therefore to form a
particular congregation of principal workers from
amongst the most experienced in the work, who
should be charged with the direction of the whole
undertaking. He gave them such rules as should
enable them to guide and govern the schools, so that
the work might not fail, even should it lack the care
and solicitude of the Archbishop and the parish
priests. This he did in the following manner :

He formed a primary congregation in Milan of
twenty-six men chosen from among the most prudent
and pious of the workers, elected yearly by their companions and confirmed by the Archbishop, who were
to fill the following offices :—One to be at the head
with the title of Prior-General; another under him,
Sub-Prior ; then two Visitors-General, two Discreets,
one Counsellor-General, one Chancellor, twelve Primary
members, and six assistants. For the more permanent
establishment of this confraternity, he afterwards made
it dependent upon the Congregation of the Oblates,
enjoining that the Superior General of the Oblates
should be its permanent Protector, and that the Prior

General and his Sub-Prior should both be priests of that congregation. Besides this, he ordained that six gentlemen of the city, under the name of Deputies, should be associated with the Protector in the care of the confraternity, and should aid it in all temporal concerns. To this body thus organised he entrusted the whole government of the schools of Christian Doctrine, enjoining that the officials should assemble together on every festival to consult and deliberate concerning the direction of the work, and of all the schools in the city and diocese, assigning to them the Church of St. Dalmatius in Milan as their own, in which to hold their meetings. He gave them rules made by himself, both for the general government of the whole work, and for the particular office of each of the general officials as well as for those of particular schools, instructing each what to do for the perfect fulfilment of his particular office in the most minute points. These rules are to be found in the " Acts of the Church of Milan."

The Prior-General and his Sub-Prior are to have the general government of the confraternity. The office of the Visitors is to found schools, either in company with the Prior-General or by themselves, when he is unable to attend, and to visit them together with the twelve primary officials, both in the city and throughout the diocese, to attend to the observance of the rules, to remove disorders, and to watch over the general progress and good government of the work. The Discreets assist the Prior-General with their advice in the regulation of the affairs of the society.

The Monitor is charged to watch over the conduct of the brethren, and if he find any of them to be guilty of any failing against the rules of the confraternity or good morals, he is charitably to admonish him in order to his amendment; and if this admonition prove fruitless, he is to give notice of the same to the Prior, in order that he may take more effectual means for the amendment of the person in fault. If he then prove incorrigible and refuse to set good example, he will be expelled from the society. The Chancellor takes care of the books, and notes down all things necessary for the conduct of affairs, the six assistants aid by their counsel in the general government of the confraternity.

Besides the above-named general officials, he established particular directors for each school, viz., a prior, sub-prior, discreets, monitor, chancellor, head-teachers, silence-keepers, peace-makers, infirmarians, fishermen, and those who accompany the Fathers. All these are distinct officers, but the most important are the fishermen, whose business it is to go about the streets breaking off games and other vain amusements on festival days, and bring persons to church to learn the Christian doctrine.

They are assisted by those who accompany the Fathers, viz., the Oblates or Jesuits, who visit the schools of Christian Doctrine on every festival day, setting forth the doctrines of our holy faith, and seeking to inflame the souls of their hearers with Christian piety by spiritual discourses. These companions traverse the city in the discharge of the same office of charity, putting an end to vain amusements, and bringing the idle to the schools to listen to the exhortations and instructions of the Fathers. It is impossible to describe the good effected by these fishermen, amounting in the city to the number of four hundred, and in the diocese to no less than fifteen hundred, all labouring in this holy work on Sundays and festivals. Hence we may conjecture what signal fruit they produce in souls, especially as inspired with fervent zeal for their neighbours, they go about collecting sinners and vagrants, inducing them by their exhortations to approach the Sacraments, to attend the churches, and to lead Christian lives.

In order to give more power and efficiency to the undertaking, and that the whole work should proceed in a uniform and orderly manner, the Saint laid down that on every feast-day after the school exercises the general officials and also the head officials of the other schools in the city should assemble in the church of St. Dalmatius, and in the presence of the Prior-General give a report in public of the day's proceedings in each school, of the numbers, of any disorders that might have occurred, or of any changes necessary in local arrangements. So that within the space of little more than half an hour the Prior-General and the whole confraternity obtained information of the state of each school and of its necessities, for which, after due consideration, the council of general officials were enabled to make proper provision.

He did the same throughout the diocese, establishing similar councils in the different parishes to preside over the schools of each parish, and to give a report from time to time, to the Primary Council in Milan, of the progress and the needs of each school, for which the Prior-General and the other officials were to provide in the same way. They were bound to visit all the schools in the diocese at least once a year, and to give an account to the Archbishop, in a full congregation, of the whole state and progress of the Christian doctrine, in order to provide for any necessities which might have arisen, with the order and commission of the Archbishop himself or his Vicar-General. This mode of government, devised by the holy Cardinal, is of such excellence, that one of the things chiefly desired by foreign prelates who visit Milan is to be present at this meeting at St. Dalmatius on a feast-day, as well worth while, and a work without parallel.

Out of the desire cherished by the Saint to draw all souls to God by the way of a truly devout life, he furnished these scholars of the Christian doctrine with many spiritual aids. First, he obtained divers holy indulgences from the Apostolic See, and moreover enjoined on them besides the perfect observance of the commands of God and the Church, fasting on certain days, and other acts of devotion, to confess and communicate at least once a month, giving a particular injunction to the parish-priests to see to the spiritual direction of these persons, that they might be fed upon the Word of God by the spiritual exhortations given in the schools on every feast-day by the above-named Fathers. He gave Communion to them all with his own hand once a year, appointing a general Communion in the cathedral on the 1st May, the Feast of St. Philip and St. James, a plenary indulgence being attached to this Communion. On this occasion he used to preach them a sermon, enkindling them to perseverance and the practice of good works, especially to zeal for the salvation of souls. By these means he caused them to advance so much in the service of God that many of the workers of both sexes attained to great holiness of life and a fervent spirit, that might be compared to that of the Christians of the Primitive Church. He therefore made use of many of them, although seculars, in other labours for the glory of God; finding them obedient to his slightest wish and full of filial affection towards him. On his part he loved them with the love of a father, and took especial care of them, as if they had been indeed his own children.

They were most prompt and skilful labourers in founding the schools of Christian Doctrine and carrying them to great perfection, instructing others also to follow the same path, so that many Bishops applied for their assistance to the holy Cardinal, on account of the great need in their dioceses of such a work. Among other prelates may be mentioned Cardinal Paul of Arezzo, Archbishop of Naples, to whom the Saint sent a certain Francesco Rinaldi, one of his chief workers, who was greatly esteemed by all, and did great good in that city.

So great indeed was the fruit of these pious labours that when the Saint passed from this present life, he left in the city and diocese seven hundred and forty schools under the care of two hundred and seventy-three general officials, 1726 particular officials; and the workers or labourers amounted to 3040, the scholars to 40,098.[1] By reason of its solid foundation and the rules left to it by its holy founder, the confraternity has not only persevered in this state, but has greatly increased, especially since the accession to the See of Milan of the illustrious Cardinal Frederic Borromeo, who both imitates his holy kinsman in other virtues, and follows him in his paternal care of this holy work which he zealously fosters (A.D. 1610).

[1] Vid. Acta Mediolanensis Ecclesiae.

CHAPTER VII.

OF HIS HOPE AND CONFIDENCE IN GOD.

As St. Charles had all his thoughts directed to God and never sought anything but His greater glory, so he had a firm confidence that every undertaking in which he was engaged would turn out well. In all his trials and needs he rested upon this as upon an anchor of safety; accordingly, in the most desperate cases, when friends of learning and experience had lost hope, he felt sure of aid from God, and he was not disappointed, although men of the world were surprised. For he used to say, that he who serves God with a pure intention, casting aside all self-interest and seeking only His glory, may always hope for success, especially at a time when, according to human judgment, there seems to be only failure; adding that human prudence can never attain to do the works of God, inasmuch as His service far exceeds the wisdom of man and depends upon a higher principle. He had recourse to God in all his undertakings by the particular means of prayer, with which he began, continued, and ended everything he did. The more important and difficult his undertakings

were, the more he prayed; if it happened that
matters were not only difficult but apparently desperate, he would not on that account cease to pray
to God, but would have recourse to more frequent
and fervent prayer, and to his private devotions he
added the public prayers of the church, of the clergy,
of nuns, and of the faithful. Hence it was that he
succeeded, amid the surprise of all, in so many great
undertakings, which to human judgment seemed impossible. I remember that once he urged me to have
confidence in God on every occasion, reminding me
that He never abandoned, even in the least important
matters, those who placed their trust in Him.

As a proof of this he related the following fact,
which had happened shortly before. His steward
had complained to him that there was no money
in the chest, and that he did not know how to
provide for the necessities of the household, begging
him not to be so liberal in alms-giving, because his
works of charity had reduced them to that extremity,
and concluded by wishing to know where he was
to go for money. The Cardinal made answer that
he must trust in God for help, but the steward was
not at all satisfied with that reply. Within a couple
of hours there came letters with a bill of exchange
for three thousand crowns from Spain. Handing it
to his steward, " Take this," he said, " man of little
faith; see, the Lord has not forsaken us." The
Cardinal said this was really the work of the providence of God, for he was not expecting the remit-

tance, nor was it due to him, for two months to come.

From the process of his canonisation it appears that at the time of his controversy about jurisdiction with the representatives of the King, many remarkable facts occurred, clearly manifesting the providence of God in protecting him. Among others I read the deposition of a well-informed witness, who states that when an outcry was raised against the Cardinal for his excommunication of the King's officers, the Governor, with some members of his privy council who were adverse to the Saint, often thought of carrying out rigorous measures against him personally, as they could hit upon no other means of thwarting him in his defence of the rights of the Church. Every time the council met to settle the matter, they changed their plans, not being able to resolve on doing anything against him, as if God Himself caused this wavering of their minds, and the sanctity of his life made them exclaim, as in Holy Scripture, " This man doeth many miracles."[1] They were much surprised themselves at not being able to come to any decision, because the same thing always occurred when they wanted to enter into any conspiracy against him.

When visiting the parish Church of Canobbio on Lake Maggiore, on his way from Trefiume to Cavaglio among the mountains, as he was passing a dangerous spot called the Rock of Crocina, his mule fell upon

---

[1] St. John xi. 47.

him on the verge of a precipice, at a risk of throwing him to the bottom. Humanly speaking, he must have perished, and it was considered a miracle that he was saved without injury.

Another time coming from Desio on a dark night when he was absorbed in prayer, he fell into a deep and narrow pit with his mule upon him, and being unable to move without danger, his attendants thought it would be necessary to kill the mule in order to extricate him. But that he would not allow, from his confidence that God would send him help, and the mule rose dexterously of his own accord without doing him any injury.

So great was his trust in our Lord, that after prudently deliberating upon undertakings which he thought would be to the glory of God, although others might judge to the contrary, he would enter upon them and carry them out successfully. In this way he did not hesitate to take long and difficult journeys in the cold of winter or the heat of summer, travelling day and night, crossing rugged mountains, venturing on stormy lakes and rivers, at the risk of health and other dangers, when it was for the service of God. His confidence in his Divine Master was so strong that his companions and attendants caught a portion of his spirit, for in all the dangers they encountered on rivers, lakes, and mountains,—and every one had his own share in them to relate,—no one ever perished; God assisting them in a miraculous manner when their case seemed hopeless, as happened to Giulio Omato and the Rev. Bernardino Tarugi, who both escaped death by a miracle,—Omato among the rocks of Camaldoli,[1] and Tarugi in the river Ticino.[2]

Girolamo Castano, one of his chamberlains, met with a similar accident about the beginning of June, 1581. During the Cardinal's visitation in the parish of Arcisato, he consecrated the church of Cuasso on the mountain, and while keeping his usual watch on the eve, before the relics which he had brought to place on the altar, he had his attendants by turns to pray with him all night. The next day after the dedication, he left for Varese, Castano riding on before with the archiepiscopal cross in his hands; the latter, through not having slept at night, was overcome by weariness and fell from his horse with his foot in the stirrup, the cross being caught in the branches of a walnut tree. The animal being alarmed started off at full gallop, dragging his rider over rocks and through woods for about half a mile; and when they expected to see him dead, or with broken bones at least, he was found in no wise injured, which was considered miraculous, as appears from his own depositions in the process of canonisation, and from the evidence of Mgr. John Baptist Guenzato, Bishop of Polignano, who was present, and had likewise kept watch with the Saint on the preceding night.

The greatness of the Saint's confidence in God is shown by his prudence in guarding against its opposite fault—presumption. He never exposed himself to danger unreasonably, and never put his hand to any extravagant undertaking or that would not contribute

---

[1] Book vi., chap. i.   [2] Book ix., chap. ii.

to the glory of God, or acted without deliberation and due care. On proper occasion he had recourse to human assistance, without, however, making it his chief reliance, but as subordinate to Divine Providence. This was manifested at the time of the plague at Milan, because, except in the exercise of the duties to which he felt bound as Archbishop and the Father of his people, he used every precaution in his own person and in the care of his companions. He often reproved them, when he saw that they placed themselves in danger of catching the malady, and warned them that they were not allowed to approach as near the sick as himself, or to do what belonged to his office of pastor. With every hope in God and confidence that assistance must come from Him alone, he did not refuse human remedies to relieve the sick and deliver the city from the contagion, but made use of them as in every other necessity. By thus avoiding the vicious extremes of despair and presumption, he preserved the middle course and the perfection of the virtue of hope.

CHAPTER VIII.

ON HIS LOVE OF GOD.

WE may judge of his love of God by the many works he did for Him, and from the clear evidence that they were not prompted by any mere human motive. His was not a love of sweetness satisfied with delights and spiritual consolations, but a strong and powerful love, urging him on not only to do, but also to suffer much for God without fainting. Nay, he felt every day more fresh for these labours than the day before, and knew no end, nor interval, nor slackening in doing and suffering. While his companions dropped to the ground under their burdens, he tired out all, and never gave the least signs of fatigue himself; the more he laboured day and night, the more vigorous he rose up, as if labour served to feed and strengthen him, and he never would break it off by recreation or amusement of any kind. Moreover, he never seemed satisfied with what he had done or suffered, but was always considering how he could do and suffer more — a proof that he was eager for martyrdom, as the Cardinal of Verona and others said, "martyrdom stopped short of him, not he of martyrdom."[1] His

---

[1] Vid. Book vii., chap. xv., vol. 2, p. 265.

friends could never prevail upon him to take any care of himself personally, not even after he had been shot at. When he suffered so much from the governors of the state, and saw his palace beset by soldiers, at such times he left all his doors open, and omitted none of his usual duties, often quitting the house to visit churches with few persons in company, and unguarded, leading men to suppose that he would not have refused to suffer death, had God permitted it— a sign of the purest love of Him that a soul can have in this life.

When he excommunicated the Governor of Milan by name, Baron Sfrondato, brother of Pope Gregory XIV., together with other chief men of the state, earnestly besought him to withdraw the excommunication on account of dangers that were to be dreaded, he remained firm in his purpose, and replied, "I am clothed in red in token that I am ready to shed my blood in the service of the Church." When the baron said that at least he should keep his doors shut for the safety of his person: "I do not care to do so," was his only answer, showing that he was ready to offer his life for the love of God.

His heart was ever burning with an insatiable desire for the glory of God, and he was always forming projects in his own mind to increase and spread His worship. He never thought or spoke of anything but of God and what related to His service, his great desire being to draw all souls and all the world, if possible, to His love. No miser indeed was ever so eager to heap up riches as he was to increase the honour and glory of his Lord. He was so ardent in his words, especially in his sermons, that it seemed as if he infused the living flames of this love into the hearts of men from the fire that burnt in his own heart, and drew the souls of sinners to God.

According to the opinion of his physicians and friends he could not have lived so long, considering his labours and sufferings, with the little food and rest he allowed himself, had not the love of God sustained and strengthened him, as his food and supernatural support. His countenance, though pale and thin, was always cheerful and serene, betokening his interior content and close union with God, and used to shine in a wonderful way on many occasions, according to the sworn testimony of trustworthy persons, and among them the Blessed[1] Philip Neri, a man remarkable for sanctity of life and for working miracles, who states that when St. Charles was speaking to him he seemed to have the face of an angel of God. The same effect was produced by his words, a certain joy and sweetness breathed from him that appeared to be something more than human, attracting and winning the hearts of all to him in a wonderful way, particularly when he spoke of God. His words addressed to others were blessed with such virtue that they ensured perseverance and patience in adversity; as we know by experience at the present time of many priests, religious and seculars, whose souls had been directed by him and always retained the love of virtue and discipline which he had implanted.

---

[1] Not yet canonised in 1610, when this life was first published.

His assistants were so encouraged by a single word from him as to do great things, and there was nothing too laborious for them if he ordered it to be done. The fatigues endured by those of his household, and their perseverance under them, were thought almost miraculous, the more so because they seemed to enjoy them, and lived in great gladness of heart in the midst of all their labours, as if the Saint had imparted to them his own spirit and interior joy by means of the love which united him to God.

What passed in secret between him and God is beyond words, for he was reserved and kept in his own heart the favours and graces bestowed upon him, so that no one could understand them. By many signs, however, the converse of his spirit with God might be guessed at, especially his remaining whole nights in prayer : for it is difficult for a soul to persevere in such exercises if not assisted by God in an extraordinary way with great spiritual sweetness and fire of love.

During the latter years of his life it was quite clear he ardently desired to leave this world and to be united to God in heaven. I remember a conversation I had with Giovanni Andrea Pionnio, one of his household, who was much beloved by him, when he told me that when he was with the Saint for many days during his visitation of his diocese, and conversing upon spiritual subjects, he had gathered that he greatly desired to quit this life, and offered up special prayers to obtain this favour from God, and that he himself thought that the Saint would not be with us long.

Mgr. Bascapè in his life of St. Charles relates that the Saint was once speaking about the years of his life which, he said, was drawing to its end, and that he asked Father Francis Adorno how old he was. When the latter replied, " Fifty years old," he exclaimed, " O father, is not it time to die ? " hinting that he had lived too long, and that he wished his own days might be few. It was observed that when he spoke of his death, he seemed pleased at the thought that it was not far off, yearning to be speedily united to God, the Supreme Good—as if he could not bear to be any longer separated from Him, so ardent was his love. He used to say that he liked to be present at the burial of the dead, because he was reminded of his own death and passage to another life, and he was glad to talk often about it as a subject in which he took great delight.

CHAPTER IX.

OF HIS LOVE FOR HIS NEIGHBOUR.

THE Saint gave the world an example of the perfect fulfilment of the precept, natural as well as divine, of loving our neighbour. His life seems to have been spent in nothing else but doing good to his neighbour, and was a constant exercise of works of mercy and charity. He was considered the universal Father of his people; orphans, widows, the bashful poor, the suffering, and sinners had recourse to him and were aided by him, because he had within him the bowels of compassion, which led him to devote himself and all that he had to their service without regard to any inconvenience or cost to himself. This is clear from his works of charity during the plague, but there are many instances of it in the judicial process of his canonisation which are not mentioned here.

His charity towards the sick was marvellous; he would go to their houses to visit them by day or night, especially if they were prelates or persons of distinction; sometimes rising from his bed when ill himself, as in the case of Alessandro Cremona, to whom he went though suffering from sickness, to assist him in making a good death. He exercised the same charity towards those of humble condition, especially if they led good lives, as in the case of the workers in the Confraternity of Christian Doctrine for whom he entertained great affection. Latterly, however, he was more cautious, for it was rumoured that the sick re-covered when he visited them, so every one was desirous of being visited by him in order to regain their health. When he heard this, out of humility, and to do away with that impression, he withdrew into retirement.

These services he was exact in rendering to his clergy, whom he loved as if he were their own father. He not only visited them when ill, but he also took care that they were well attended to, and were not in want of anything, although they did not belong to his own household. When they were getting better, or had suffered a long and tedious illness, he ordered them change of air, defraying the cost himself for those who needed it: some he would send to his country-house of Groppello, a very healthy place. His charity led him not only to take care of them personally, but also of their poor relatives, rendering them assistance in many ways, such as finding husbands for their sisters, as though in his charity he clothed himself, as it were, with their garments and necessities.

Trusting to this charity of their saintly Archbishop, not only the poor but also the rich and noble had recourse to him for advice in difficult cases, and left him satisfied and consoled. When any affliction or calamity visited Milan, St. Charles was the refuge of

all. Prisoners and those who were bereft of all other
aid, and grievous sinners who despaired of salvation
on account of their crimes, by his means were brought
back into the path of safety. His clergy as well as
the laity trusted so much in him and felt so sure of
his assistance that they feared no danger or mishap.

Strangers and foreigners also, when possible, he
was not slow to assist with advice and protection.
For example, when he was in Rome, during the
pontificate of Gregory XIII., a poor widow woman,
who was condemned to death for offences she had
not committed, but had confessed when under tor-
ture, despairing of every other assistance, sent to him
stating her case that she was to be put to death,
though she was innocent. He went to the Pope,
and obtained a re-examination of her cause, and being
proved guiltless she was liberated. At another time
an apostate monk, who had committed great crimes,
begged for his protection. To escape punishment
he had taken refuge among heretics in Germany,
where he remained some years, preaching against the
faith. At length, repenting of his guilt, and wishing
to be reconciled, he disclosed his wretched state by
letter to St. Charles, and begged him to plead for
him with the Apostolic See, although he did not
know the Saint except from report of his charity.
The Cardinal wrote to Rome in his behalf, but could
not obtain his pardon on account of the heinousness
of his offences. The apostate then came himself to
Milan, and placed himself without reserve in the
hands of the Saint, who on again applying to Rome

was directed to put him in prison in punishment of his apostasy. The Saint obeyed the order, not without regret, while the poor wretch remained some time in prison, and in the meanwhile the Cardinal departed to a better life. Contrary to all expectation the monk received a pardon, and it was considered that he had received this favour on account of the Saint, who had recommended his cause so earnestly.

Finally, his great charity led him to do many penances for the sins of his people, in order to turn away the anger and scourges of God. When a prelate begged him not to perform so much penance, " A Bishop," he replied, " is bound by his example to temper the bitterness of such penances, that his people may make trial of them as profitable to salvation." This was indeed a truly maternal affection for his flock; for as a tender mother softens food for her babe, so he devoted himself to an austere life of fasting and penance, in order to make them easy and lead others to follow his example. Nor did it fail to produce its effect; for in Milan, those who had not fasted, according to report, even in Lent, then began to do so from devotion, and with many fasting became almost a daily custom, and other practices of penance were adopted by the example of the holy Archbishop.

CHAPTER X.

OF HIS LOVE FOR HIS FLOCK.

I CAN without doubt affirm that the love which this Blessed Patron bore to his church far surpassed any human love, even that of a mother for her child, or a wife for her husband. He speaks of it himself in his sermon at his first Provincial Council, as in extent both a paternal and filial love, feeling unable to explain it except by using both comparisons.

This love of his possessed all the marks of a perfect love. In the first place, it was pure, without any admixture whatever of self-interest; for he accepted the charge neither on account of its dignity nor for its revenue, but only in obedience to the Supreme Pontiff, and from his ardent desire to improve its condition and knowledge of its needs. While he was pastor he sought nothing else but the well-being and salvation of souls; for this end alone he laboured and suffered.

His love was one and undivided, for although he had other dignities and honours,[1] he never placed his

---

[1] Among these were Grand Penitentiary, Arch-priest of St. Mary Major at Rome, Abbot of twelve Abbeys, Apostolic Legate, Prince, Count, Marquis, Protector of many kingdoms and religious orders.

affections upon them, though they might have procured him pleasure and aggrandisement, which are prized by the world. In order that these should not interfere with his love for the Church, his spouse, he voluntarily renounced them to the surprise of his friends, who tried to dissuade him from a self-denial so unusual, and in their opinion so unnecessary.

Again, his love was ardent, and allowed him no repose either by day or night, but like fire it was always burning, keeping him in continual watchfulness over his flock, always devising new helps, new remedies and new plans for the good of his church and of souls. All which may be seen in the " Acts of the Church of Milan," in the form of decrees, instructions, rules, and pastoral letters.

His love was unitive and bound him so entirely to his church that he could never leave it or remain away from it. When his elder brother, Frederick, died, his uncle, Pope Pius IV., was willing to make him head of the family, and to lavish worldly dignities upon him as he was sole heir to his father's estates. As his friends also persuaded him to quit the ecclesiastical state and to enjoy the grandeurs of the world, he took the resolution of uniting himself altogether to the spouse of his choice, the Church, and was ordained priest privately without informing his uncle. From thenceforth he yearned to go and reside at Milan, and often entreated the Pope's permission to do so. At last, to his great consolation, the Pontiff gave him leave; and in the address to his suffragans, before quoted, after saying that only obedience had withheld

him from coming sooner, he adds, " As soon as ever
I obtained permission I eagerly availed myself of it."
His motive was no greediness for wealth, nor any
desire of personal comfort and convenience, but solely
to do good, in the words of the prophet, " I will seek
that which was lost; and that which was driven away
I will bring again; and I will bind up that which was
broken, and I will strengthen that which was weak,
and that which was fat and strong I will preserve."[1]

When it is considered that a nephew of the Pope,
in the prime of life, on the pinnacle of earthly
grandeur, having the reins of government in his
hands, gladly withdrew from that position in order
to devote himself to the care of souls, it must be
acknowledged that only a great love could have
dictated such a course.

After the death of his uncle, although the succeeding Pontiffs wished him to assist in the general
government of the Church at Rome, he would not
remain there, having a fixed determination to reside
in his diocese. Whenever he was absent from it,
it seemed as if he were in bonds, so great was his
desire to return to his proper sphere. Hearing that
the Supreme Pontiff wished to assign to him the
visitation of some churches beyond the limits of
his province, he begged to decline the commission
on the plea that to watch over his own diocese was
quite enough for him. He only visited the bishoprics
of his own province, which he felt bound to do as
their Metropolitan, and the Swiss and Grisons dis-

[1] Ezechiel xxxiv. 19.

tricts, on the confines of his diocese, in order to drive away the infection of heresy. He always tried in this way to avoid absenting himself from his See; not even the defence of his rights of jurisdiction could induce him to leave it. Latterly, when his diocese had been brought into a good state and every want provided for, he was willing, in his zeal for the extirpation of heresy, to visit the countries beyond the mountains, but was prevented by death.

When bound to go to Rome, either for the election of the Popes or for the visit of the *Limina Apostolica*, he was always thinking how soon he could return; and during his short stay there, his own church was the great subject of his meditations. Though absent in body, he was present in spirit and affection, never failing to do all in his power for its benefit, having its necessities ever imprinted on his heart. When he was once obliged to go to Rome during the controversy about his jurisdiction, and his adversaries spread a report that he was not coming back any more to his diocese, he said he would rather resign the office of Cardinal than abandon the church of Milan, although he had so much to suffer there. His example was productive of much good, for several Bishops were led by it to observe the rules of residence; and others resigned their Sees, because in their cases he put the decrees in force.

His love was so strong and powerful that it moved him to do and to suffer in a wonderful way, so that men said the same of him as Paulinus did of St. Ambrose, in his life of that Saint, that after his death many Bishops together would not be able to do what he had done by himself; according to others, he alone had done more than all his predecessors in the See for four hundred years past.

His works were continual prayer; five or six hours' study a day; giving audience daily for three or four hours; besides which he used to receive petitions while walking through the streets of the city, where he used to say he liked to go on foot, as it gave every one an opportunity of speaking to him. He spent many months of the year in his visitations, penetrating into the recesses of mountains and valleys where no Archbishop had ever been before. When the roads were too difficult he either put iron spikes on his shoes, or he crept on his hands and knees, in order not to fall over the precipices. He insisted on visiting every church in person, and seeing his flock face to face, although he had to go to wild and desert places on foot and in the heat of summer. He consecrated more than three hundred churches and altars; in the space of eighteen days he was known to have consecrated fourteen, spending eight hours continuously in each function, beside keeping vigil all through the preceding night, and fasting on bread and water the day before.

The administration of the Holy Sacraments was a continual and unceasing work with him, especially that of the Holy Eucharist. He purposely avoided celebrating in his private chapel in order that he might give his people an opportunity of receiving Communion from himself in the churches where he said his Mass; and he used to say that a Bishop should always celebrate in the presence of his people, and only make use of his oratory in case of necessity.   In this way he used to give Communion to great numbers every day.   When he went anywhere out of the city he usually had a general Communion; for when people heard of his arrival, on any day and at any time of the year, they prepared themselves by confession for receiving Holy Communion at his hand; and it was observed that once he gave Communion in one day to as many as eleven thousand persons.   On great festivals and days appointed for general Communion in the city, he used to be occupied in this duty from early morning till vespers in the afternoon without intermission, except when saying Mass.

His sermons were frequent, and prepared with great care.   During his visitations he preached two or three times a day, and was continually performing episcopal functions, such as attending processions, conferring holy orders, clothing and professing nuns, translating the bodies of saints, holding diocesan synods and provincial councils, to all which he devoted much time, celebrating them with full ceremonial, with mind intent upon them, and preaching sermons of considerable length.

He held councils and consultations daily on the affairs of his church, and some times he had two or three to attend on the same day.   Of his ordinary business he drew up a diary for himself, noting down from day to day and week to week what had to be done; in which is found such a multiplicity of matters to be dealt with, that, humanly speaking, it seems impossible that one man could take the whole in hand.[1] He had another diary of spiritual matters distributed throughout the year, embracing all the pious societies and congregations, the hospitals, confraternities of Christian doctrine, prisons, and different classes of persons, to whom he gave particular supervision by visits, preaching, and administering Holy Communion, now here, now there, an ever-recurring labour, in order to keep up the fervour of their spiritual life. In addition to these ordinary duties he had extraordinary business from Rome and other parts of the Christian world, and many persons came to consult him on difficult questions, not ecclesiastics so much as secular princes. From all parts and all kinds of persons he received and answered great numbers of letters, some of which, comprised in thirty-one volumes, are preserved in the library of San Sepolcro; and always replied to every letter by whomsoever written to him. He was ever occupied in devising new means of benefiting souls, new decrees for maintaining discipline, and new adornments for churches. Never satisfied with what he had already done, he was devoured with a desire for improvement both in himself and in others. When we consider all his occupations and labours, they form such a mass of business that, in the opinion of eye-witnesses, it was far beyond the power of one man to deal with such an accumulation.

His labours in the reformation of bad habits, in the introduction of discipline, and in the defence of his

---

[1] See Appendix for this diary.

jurisdiction, have been already told. He could not bear to hear it said that a Bishop was idle. When a Bishop in his province wrote to him that he had little to do, he sent Mgr. Antonio Seneca to him though he was sixty miles away to show him his mistake, and wrote him a letter in which he enumerated all the duties of a Bishop, after each one as he specified it, repeating, " Has a Bishop then nothing to do ? " He deemed such language utterly unworthy of one who had the charge of souls and the administration of a diocese.

When he officiated at the funeral of Bishop Bosso of Novara, he was told that the Bishop's death was owing to his labours in the visitation of his diocese. " So a Bishop ought to die," he replied, " in the service of his Church." " A Bishop," he used to say, " has as much to do as he can wish to have ; he will find enough, if he is diligent and does his duty ; little, if he is careless and negligent. He cannot discharge his obligations if he studies his own convenience and what is beneficial or injurious to his health. If the people make little progress in serving God, it is the Bishop who is in fault, because he is negligent of the things of their salvation."

His love was communicative or bountiful, prompting him to divest himself of all he possessed—the furniture of his house, his bed, his clothes, and even his life itself, to bestow it upon his flock. It made him value souls more than everything else in the world, and himself besides. He prized his church more than the rank of Cardinal, for he was ready to renounce that dignity for its sake, and he only accepted it because it invested his See with greater authority. He placed it above the Papacy, we may say, because he preferred it to the high position he held in Rome in his uncle's time; above his own honour and reputation, as he did not care what the world, or those who do not understand the service of God, said of him, when he was undertaking its reform; above relations, as he gave them up for its service; above hereditary estates and lands, so much valued by mankind; above himself and his own life, as he proved during the plague when he exposed himself to every danger of death. His love for his church indeed far surpassed his love for his own life, and passes understanding, as is shown by Father Francesco Panigarola, afterwards Bishop of Asti, who in the funeral sermon he delivered over the Saint says of him :—" Once when he was describing the love a Bishop ought to have for his church he said, ' Even if one is possessed with the desire of dying for it, I consider that there are many other degrees of more ardent love, and to attain to them must be the pastor's constant aim.' "

CHAPTER XI.

ON HIS LOVE FOR HIS RELATIONS.

His detachment from flesh and blood was marvellous, for he manifested no particular affection towards his nearest relatives, except such as is required by charity; beyond that he would not go, and they had no more influence over him as relations than strangers, although they were persons of distinction, living in the same city, where he had an opportunity of seeing them and hearing about them every day. His rule was to visit them once or twice a year, as he did in the case of the Countess Margaret, his aunt, a pious lady. When they were ill he paid them great attention, and gave them every spiritual assistance to make a good death. This he did for his uncle, Pope Pius IV., Count Frederic his brother, and Francis Borromeo his uncle, and attended their funerals; also for Cesare and Ottavio Gonzaga, and others, because charity required it of him. Occasionally he would be present at the marriage of relatives, as when he united his cousin Isabella to the Cavalier Girolamo Visconti, and was present at their nuptial banquet; so also when a relative of the Verme family was

married to Ottavio Speciano, he considerably dimin
ished the expenses by ordering a moderate banque
in order to set an example in the city and avoid th
excess common on such occasions. He introduce
reading at table, and preached with great unctic
on the proper way of celebrating marriage in
Christian manner, in order to have a reason fo
officiating at the ceremony. He baptised Giovann
the son of Count Renato, and took charge of the educa
tion of his cousin Frederic, now Cardinal and Arch
bishop of Milan, and showed his affection to relativ
by many other offices of charity, which was so purifie
in him as to suggest the manner, time, and persons
be benefited.

On the other hand he would make no effort to serv
relatives for their own sakes, any more than if the
were strangers, unless he were bound in charity to d
so. For this reason he would never appoint any
his relatives to any office about himself or elsewhe:
in his diocese, much less would he grant any favou
through their means, and was so strict on this poin
that they used to have recourse to pious persons i
order to obtain his patronage for themselves. H
avoided also particular friendship with them; whe
they attended his receptions he behaved towards the
exactly the same as towards other gentlemen with
out regard to kindred. Although Count Frederic Bo
romeo wore the cassock, was modest of behaviour, an
had made great progress in learning and virtue, yet h
never showed him any mark of particular affectio
and would not invite him to stay in his house. A

he was unwilling to grant his relatives any favours
himself, so he also refused to interest himself with
others in their behalf.   They ran indeed some risk of
losing what they had through being connected with
him : at the time of the controversy about jurisdiction,
he was deprived of his property on the rock of Arona,
and threatened with the loss of other estates — yet
nothing would induce him to appeal to the King of
Spain for its restoration.

Year by year the income of his patrimony was
devoted to works of charity ; a portion, however, was
set aside to defray certain payments incurred for
church purposes which before had been usually charged
upon vacant benefices.   At his death he left nothing
to his relations, but made sundry bequests to friends
and members of his household; his own writings
in manuscript he left to Mgr. Francisco Bonomo,
Bishop of Vercelli, rather than to his cousin, Frederic,
who might have been supposed a more fitting person
to inherit them on account of family ties.   When he
resigned many rich benefices, he left to relatives for
whom he had great affection no interest in them whatever.   When visiting his estates, especially Arona his
birthplace, he preferred to lodge in the humbler dwellings of ecclesiastics rather than at his family seat or
those of his relatives.   After the year 1575 he give
up the use of his surname Borromeo, with the permission of the Supreme Pontiff, and adopted instead
Santa Prassede, his title as Cardinal.   In his pastorals
also he omitted his family name and arms and made
use of the likenesses of St. Ambrose and the martyrs

St. Gervasius and St. Protasius for crest and supporters. In this way he could truly say with the Psalmist, " I am become a stranger to my brethren, and an alien to the sons of my mother." St. Laurence Justinian followed the same rule, as he thought that detachment from family ties was more efficacious than any other means for gaining the good-will of his people and urging them to good works, and that he could not with a safe conscience bestow church revenues, which were left to feed the poor, upon relatives to be spent in worldly pomp and luxury.

Just in proportion as he did not lavish affection upon relatives, was he desirous of rendering them every aid for the salvation of their souls and of removing every obstacle in the way of their spiritual progress. There was at one time a proposal to bestow a Bishopric in the province of Milan upon a relative, but he put a negative upon his appointment from a scruple of conscience, because he did not see in him the necessary qualities. When the candidate and his friends made some complaint, he openly disclosed to them his reasons. From his childhood he evinced this liberty of spirit and zeal for religion, and when his judgment was matured, he would not allow his father to administer the revenues of his abbey of Arona, because it was against his conscience to use such funds in the maintenance of the household. When he sent Ormaneto as his Vicar-General to Milan, at the time when he was with his uncle Pius IV. in Rome, among other matters, he commissioned him to see that proper discipline was observed in communities of nuns as regards talking and intercourse with secular persons, and bade him begin with the convent in which were his sister Corona and his two aunts, sisters of Pope Pius IV. It may be supposed that such a mandate was considered a novelty at that time.

It was his wish that ecclesiastics especially should be imbued with this spirit of detachment, and be on their guard against yielding to this affection for relations lest they should do anything unworthy of their vocation. He cautioned his priests not to be on too familiar terms with them, considering that such intercourse causes the mind to deviate from that rectitude of intention in the service of God which is looked for in them, cools the fervour of charity in the exercise of good works, and even leads them to actions contrary to their life and profession.

He gave them his own case as an example, saying that though he visited his relations as seldom as possible, he never did so without feeling his fervour somehow cooled, and his strength in the service of God weakened. The requests of relatives, he used to say, ought to be well weighed in the balance by ecclesiastics lest they should be inclined to grant them in an unsuitable manner, and they ought to be ready to refuse improper petitions with fortitude and resignation to the will of God. He warned them to mistrust any particular friendship with kinsfolk, as the bond of relationship had a strong tendency to enervate the mind and obscure the judgment, and in fine to make the worse appear the better course.

In like manner he forbade his clergy to live in the houses of lay people, in order to keep them from intimacy with their kindred, on account of his desire to teach them to prefer the service of God to flesh and blood. He himself went before them like a burning light, and observed such strictness in this matter, that he scarcely seemed to acknowledge relatives unless compelled to do so from charity, although with others he was liberal and munificent.

CHAPTER XII.

ON HIS LOVE FOR HIS HOUSEHOLD.

IN the management of his household, which is a matter of great importance to a Bishop, the Saint has left an example of great prudence. He generally had about a hundred persons in his house, of various nations, and of different qualities and conditions, because he required many officers and administrators in the government of his diocese. They nevertheless lived together in great order and union of charity, as if they had been brothers; and he, although he was their lord and master, treated them like a father in his love for them, making no distinction between greater and less, but dealing with every one according to his merit. As we see a single lamp giving light to many persons, so there grew up in the hearts of all a spirit of union, in which they loved one another and lived in fraternal charity, illuminated and set on fire by the living flame of love which burnt in him, their head and father.

John Baptist Possevino of Mantua, who was in the service of the holy Cardinal when he passed to a better life, in his account of the life and actions of the Saint, gives the following testimony in his fifth chapter.

"Whoever entered the household of this servant of God had to cast aside every vain and unworthy motive, such as the desire of obtaining benefices or pensions, to be entirely resigned to the will of God and of his master, to be prepared to do anything, and to be resolved to live in humility and charity with every one without singularity of any kind. It was wonderful indeed to behold the order and charity that reigned in so numerous a family, among persons differing so much from one another. Of the hundred persons in the house—gentlemen, officials, and servants — there were scarcely three from the same country, but some were from one city, others from another, a difference of origin frequently the cause of strife. We can only believe that the prayers and holiness of their master brought this blessing on the house. As all were witnesses of his humility and unwearying labours, so they endeavoured to prefer their neighbour in honour, according to the admonition of St. Paul.[1]

"Duty was fulfilled so exactly, that though all lived together in the same house, it sometimes happened that they did not become acquainted with one another for months, because they shunned idle talking and private meetings. After dinner and supper, when pious books were read, and silence observed, after prayers had been said in common, every one withdrew to his own occupations. The

[1] Rom. xii. 10.

Cardinal loved all belonging to his household not as servants, but as sons and brothers; and though he would not have men serve him with a view of receiving benefices or stipends, yet he gave every one what was necessary for clothing, and defrayed the expense in advance, as he enjoined a particular style of garment.   But beyond this, if it was necessary for any to go home on duty, he paid all travelling expenses, which he also provided in the case of those who entered his service from a distance."

To enter into practical details, the Saint took care that all his household should be well served.   From time to time at meals he would have the bread and wine from their tables brought to him to ascertain if all was according to his orders.   Those who were persons of condition, occupied for the most part in study and mental work, were well attended to by his own inspection of their rooms.   His kindness to them when ill cannot be expressed in words, for he both visited them himself, and placed them under the care of the infirmarian and physicians.   When any were too old or too infirm for work, he did not discharge them, or send them to the hospitals, but maintained them till death, although of humble condition, as in the case of a groom whom his steward intended to dismiss, but the Cardinal gave orders that he should remain with allowance of his usual meals and wages, and exemption from work.   When he was away on journeys, he made it a rule to take more care of his attendants than of himself, taking the worst and leaving the best for them in the matter of beds, food, and such like.   On his way back from Switzerland, he one evening arrived unexpectedly at a town on Lake Maggiore, and not finding beds for all at the inn, he slept himself upon a table, to accommodate his attendants, and took nothing but bread, leaving them some fish that had been procured. Once during his visitation in the mountains of Morterone, he was surprised by heavy rain on his way through nearly desert places, and took shelter in a priest's house, where there was only one bed. When it was time to retire, he took the bed out to his people, saying, " Take that, my children, and go to sleep," and went without one himself. Mgr. Bascapè tells us that, when with him on visitation at Brescia, he himself fell ill, whereupon the Cardinal immediately came to see him in bed, and being afraid that he was not warm enough, he had the coverlet from his own bed given him. Cesare Pezzano, a Canon of St. Ambrose the Great, in Milan, deposes, in the process of the Saint's canonisation, that when he was attending him as notary during his visitation of the Mesolcina valley, he suffered considerably one night from a catarrh ; and the Cardinal hearing of it, rose from his bed, and asked him to describe his malady, and to relieve him had his head raised, when his illness ceased, as he himself thought, miraculously. Similar instances of his charity to those about him were of frequent occurrence, exceeding even the love of parents for their children. He displayed great patience in bearing the natural imperfections of those of his household, from his desire that they should feel one for another, and was always careful to banish dis- sensions and ill-feelings from among them, that they might be united together in charity, the bond of Christian perfection. They might truly say that in him they had a high-priest[1] who had compassion on their infirmities; who, though rigid and severe with himself, was full of compassion and kindness for them, and took every care of their bodily and spiritual welfare.

The honour and respect he paid to every one according to his station was beyond all praise, for when some whom he employed in writing or studying did not rise at the proper hour in the morning, so far from being angry with them, he would go and call them up himself, and light their candles; and if he had to pass by rooms where others were asleep, he would use every precaution not to disturb them, even taking off his slippers for that purpose. He endeavoured by every means in his power to banish all self-love and personal interests from the hearts of those who were in his service, that they might live with him as sons and brothers. Those in whom he discovered any inordinate affection he reproved like a father, and offered to provide not only for their own wants, but also for their relations, if they had any in need. In some instances where they had sisters to be married, or who wished to be nuns, he provided them a dowry himself, and was displeased if they were unwilling to make their wants known to him. He thus embraced all in his paternal charity with the desire that they should walk in the way of perfection, and imitate, as far as possible, the primitive Christians who had but " one heart and one soul."

[1] Heb. iv. 15.

CHAPTER XIII.

ON HIS ZEAL FOR THE SALVATION OF SOULS.

His great vigilance in watching over souls made him a continual resident in his diocese, and prompted him to direct all his parish priests to do the same. He took care, accordingly, that every parish church should have a resident priest, and that every single soul should be cared for, requiring all to take an account once a year of the state of souls under their charge, and know each individual by name. This account was then forwarded to him for his own information, as were also reports which he obtained from monthly meetings of the parish priests of the city and diocese, which he set on foot to be schools of discipline, to ascertain the state both of priests and people. The rural deans of the diocese and the prefects of the city had to take note of all spiritual and temporal wants, and include them in the same report.

Above all it was his wish that particular care should be given to souls when they most needed it, viz., at the hour of death, when the devil makes every effort to drag them to perdition, and that parish priests should be present to assist the dying, to defend them against temptations, and help them to make a good end. He was always ready himself to visit the sick when in danger of death, especially his priests and the Bishops of his province, and would undertake long and fatiguing journeys for this purpose. As he saw what a consolation it was to souls at the hour of death to be visited by their pastors, he obtained from the Holy Father for the Bishops of his province the privilege of granting a plenary indulgence to the dying on visiting them and bestowing the Episcopal blessing, and in this way moved them to perform this act of charity.

He also devised a way of making every father of a family the priest and pastor of the souls of his own household, by directing parish priests to hold meetings of such persons to point out to them their duties of keeping all their family in the fear of God and guiding each individual soul in the way of salvation, and requiring from them an account of their observance of these rules. He used to enlarge on the value of a single soul, since it is worth more than all the treasures of the world, as the devil well knows, who is so eager for its damnation. One single soul, he said, was worth the continual care of a pastor. On one occasion when he was begging a Cardinal, who held a bishopric, to reside in his See, the latter excused himself on the plea that his diocese was but small and could easily be managed by others. The Saint, extremely grieved to find a prelate without any pastoral zeal, made answer as follows, " One single soul is worthy of the presence and guardianship of a Bishop."

When he found among the mountains and poor districts souls far from any pastor, where in their poverty they were not able to maintain a priest, he was much distressed, and used to long to be a simple priest himself, in order to minister to them, and would have gone willingly among the wildest mountains, and endured every privation for that end.

One of his motives for founding the congregation of the Oblates was, to have priests free from every obligation of residence to be sent at his will to such places where spiritual assistance was needed. The particular end of their institute was the salvation of souls, and he shows in the constitutions which he gave them, how great was his desire that their hearts should be on fire with a holy zeal for souls; which are so precious in the sight of Jesus Christ, who did not refuse to shed His precious blood to redeem them, so that there is no greater or nobler office upon earth than for a man to devote himself to the salvation of souls, wherein he becomes a fellow-worker with God Himself.

In the Bishop of Novara's life of St. Charles it is related that once at the seminary of the Canonica he gave certain points of meditation from the Gospels on this subject to some candidates for admission, requiring them to repeat their meditation the next day in order to ascertain their spirit and vocation. While engaged in this holy exercise, he turned to the Bishop who was present, earnestly exclaiming: " Oh ! if I were not as I am, how willingly would I place myself under obedience to a good Bishop to be sent whither he pleased to save souls without fixed dwelling or stipend, or heeding inconvenience or fatigue."

This zeal he did all in his power to infuse into his priests, as shown by the decrees of his synods and by his sermons which he preached with heart all on fire with love. In the third sermon of his eleventh diocesan synod he placed before his clergy the example of St. Catharine of Sienna, in whom this zeal was so ardent, that she offered herself to God to suffer the pains of hell, in order to save souls that were on the way thither, exclaiming, "Oh! zeal worthy of imitation by all Christians! Oh! if we could understand what it is to deliver a soul from hell, I doubt not that many of you would become Oblates this day, and not only go cheerfully to the mountains, but risk any danger in the hope of saving at least one soul. How beautiful are the feet of those who preach the Gospel of peace. No wonder that holy virgin of Sienna kissed the ground that had been trodden by preachers, because they were fellow-labourers with Christ. There is nothing more pleasing to God than to be helpers of His Son, and to be willing to undertake the charge of saving souls. Our holy mother, the Church, rejoices in nothing more than in those who bring souls again to spiritual life, thereby despoiling hell, defeating the devil, casting out sin, opening heaven, making the angels glad, glorifying the most Holy Trinity, and preparing for themselves a never-fading crown."

He was not satisfied with seeing his priests full of this desire for the salvation of souls, but endeavoured to inflame the hearts of laymen and seculars with the same zeal. In the rules he gave to the workers in the confraternity of Christian doctrine the following words occur:—"The workers must be very zealous for the salvation of souls, purchased by the precious Blood of our Lord Jesus Christ. This zeal will be found in them when every one makes every effort possible to prevent the loss of souls ransomed at so great a price."

When he found any one zealous for his neighbour, he felt grateful and much beholden to him. To such persons, although of low condition, he more willingly granted favours than to those of high station, who were devoid of this spirit of love.

His zeal was also manifested by his pastoral care in healing the wounds and infirmities of sin. He took great pains to obtain information by means of his coadjutors and clergy of all who were leading bad lives, that he might provide for their salvation by withdrawing them from sin and guiding them in the way to heaven. He could not endure the thought that even one soul should perish, and his charity towards sinners had reached such a height that he would take charge himself of the most abandoned and those beyond ordinary remedies; and then with prayers, admonitions, and penances, he would bring them to change their lives, and keep watch over them, until they were confirmed in well-doing.

I remember that when I was prefect of one of

the six districts of the city, he gave me a note of all who had been leading sinful lives in that part; on inquiry I found that all by his means were mending their ways and doing better.   He made no exceptions of persons or conditions, but extended his care to every soul in need: and possessed a wonderful tact in winning souls at all times and in all places, like a skilful fisherman, who fills his net with every kind of fish.   He sought to gain all to God, to benefit all, whether prelates or princes, rich or poor, without considering whether they belonged to his diocese or not, because his ardent desire to save souls urged him to win all who came in his way, and to incite them to devotion by giving them rosaries, pious pictures, and spiritual books.   Hence he used to preach continually, and administer the Sacraments wherever he went, even beyond his province.   When he was travelling in the mountains, if he met with any of the poor mountaineers, he would stop and speak to them of spiritual things, instructing them in those truths of which they were ignorant.   In some places he would gather a number of poor children together and teach them Christian doctrine, giving each of them a little reward to encourage them to learn it. When he was once visiting the Leventina valley on foot, seeing a poor boy sitting near a wretched hovel at some distance from the road, he went up to him, and with great charity stayed to teach him to make the sign of the cross, and to say Our Father and Hail Mary, although he was covered with dirt and brought up among cattle.   His charity was so ardent that he could say to God with truth : "The zeal of Thy house hath eaten me up." [1]

Hence it was that he underwent such toils in his visitations of the mountains, and took so careful an account of the state of souls in the city, administering Holy Communion, and preaching frequently, and going from place to place, at one time to the College of Doctors, at another to the Lawyers. One day he would assemble the Magistrates, on another the Canons, on a third day the parish Priests and Chaplains. To-day he attended the oratory of one pious confraternity, to-morrow he visited the church of another, the convent chapels and pious foundations, preaching the Word of God to all according to their state and condition, entailing continual labour upon himself on account of the numerous institutions which he had either founded, restored, or reformed, in order to enable every class to serve God and lead a spiritual life. He was the first guide and director of all, and it was wonderful how he found time for all his works and undertakings. He noted down in his diary the particular spiritual occupations and functions of each day throughout the year. His zeal extended to all parts, and strove to benefit every country as far as he could by letters and friendly intercourse. He wrote to Bishops and Archbishops to bring them to reside in their Sees, and to hold their synods and visitations ; to the Supreme Pontiffs begging them to provide for the needs of the Church, to send visitors, to found colleges

[1] Psalm lxviii. 10.

and seminaries for the training of Priests, and in this way benefited every part of Christendom.

Thus, at the time of his death, out of the wilderness of the diocese and province of Milan, heretofore full of abuses, corruptions, and sins, he had made a spiritual garden, and had brought it to such perfection, that Cardinal Paleotto called it a "heavenly Jerusalem" in a sermon preached at San Nazaro in Broglio, in the year 1582, when administering confirmation. " O Milan," he said, " I know not what to say of thee, for when I consider thy holy works and thy devotion, I seem to behold another Jerusalem, thanks to the toils and labours of thy good Pastor."

The clergy were so reformed that strangers thought all the Milanese priests belonged to strict religious orders, and the people were so devout that their good example spread to neighbouring countries ; as the Duke Emmanuel Philibert of Savoy said to St. Charles, " Your Eminence has wrought so much spiritual good among your people, that even those beyond your diocese reap the benefit."

CHAPTER XIV.

HIS LOVE FOR HIS ENEMIES.

IT was the will of God that His servant should not live without powerful enemies during almost the whole time of his residence at Milan. He knew, however, how to reap much benefit from them, by loving those who hated him, and by doing good to those who persecuted him, as was the case of the Frati Humiliati and others, who caused him much trouble and suffering.

He gave an especial proof of this love in the person of one of his principal enemies, who had gone to Rome as ambassador in the name of the city of Milan in the year 1580, and afterwards falling from his high estate into a needy condition, was summoned to Spain by the King to render an account of himself. He had recourse to the Duke of Terra Nuova, then Governor of Milan, for his good offices, but the Duke told him he could not do him much good, and that he had better apply to the Cardinal, as the King had a great esteem for him. Hesitating at first on account of his own unworthiness, and the trouble he had caused the Saint for so long a time, he was obliged to trust to his charity, and to ask some mutual friends to intercede for him. The Cardinal replied that he had always loved him personally, and hated only his vices, and would grant him any favour, provided he amended his life and lived in the fear of God. Encouraged by these words, the man confessed that he had ceased to be a public sinner, promised amendment for the future, and asked pardon for his misdeeds. I myself was present, and was astonished at the charity of the Saint, knowing the great trials he had long endured at the hands of this man. With great humility St. Charles embraced him tenderly, as if he had been a dear friend, and with joy like that of a father welcoming a prodigal son on his repentance. He gave him letters of recommendation to the King, and to show his confidence in him gave him authority to receive a sum of six or seven thousand crowns, bequeathed to the great hospital of Milan from the revenues of the principality of Oria. This favour would have been of great assistance to his suit with the King, had not a sudden death put an end to his days.

The Saint was indeed wonderfully pleased when he could show his enemies some mark of affection; if he occasionally had recourse to strong measures against them, it was either because he felt himself obliged in conscience to do so, or that he wished to use every possible means to save their souls.

On another occasion, after excommunicating the mayor (Podestà) of Varese for having imprisoned a priest, he refused to give him absolution when he had admitted his mistake and promised satisfaction; for on account of the importance of the case and as an example to others he decided to refer the matter to Rome. However, as the Grand Chancellor pleaded in behalf of the mayor, at his entreaty the Cardinal withdrew the appeal in order to show that although he had disagreed with him on the question of jurisdiction, yet he bore him no animosity and was glad to do him a favour. Being on visitation at Bergamo, he summoned Cesare Porto, the Provost of Varese, and gave him authority as follows:—"I was not willing to absolve this man, but the Grand Chancellor has begged me twice to do so. Though since his excommunication we have not been on terms of friendly intercourse, as he himself now asks for absolution, I am willing to grant him the favour as a proof of my good-will towards him. You will, therefore, absolve him by our order."

He used to show the same marks of affection to all in whatever way they offended him, in proof that he entertained no rancour, but every good feeling for them.

There was a parish priest in Milan, of untoward disposition, who was not pleased at the reforms made by the Cardinal in ecclesiastical discipline, and found it difficult to comply with his regulations. Finding he was forbidden to have a banquet on the anniversary of the dedication of his church, in defiance of his pastor, he invited some friends like himself who had no regard for discipline, to dine in a garden in the suburbs, where beside drinking to excess they made game of the Cardinal and ridiculed him with improper words and gestures, spending the whole day in dissolute amusements. The outrage was so great that it was bruited about the city, as a scandal that ought to be punished. The Saint was grieved at the bad example and breach of order; but as it was an offence against himself, he took no further notice beyond summoning the priest, and reproving him in a fatherly manner so as to bring him to an acknowledgment of his fault. Overcome by these kind words, he threw himself on his knees, confessed his misdemeanours, and received forgiveness from the Saint.

CHAPTER XV.

OF HIS FATHERLY WARNING AND ADMONITION.

ONE of the greatest effects of the blessed Cardinal's charity was his way of helping and improving his neighbour by fatherly admonition. He was so moved to compassion when he found souls laden with sins, that, like a second St. Ambrose, he grieved over them as if the guilt were his own, and allowed himself no rest till he had done what he could to deliver them. I remember that on being informed of some offences committed by ecclesiastical persons, he was pierced with grief at the injury they had done themselves, and the bad example set to others. He exercised great prudence and charity in his admonitions, for although he could not tolerate wrong-doing, he was anxious in casting it out to preserve reputation, especially in the case of those who had the charge of souls; he used to say, that when a priest has lost his good name, he will not hesitate to commit fresh sins, and then loses the respect of his people and all power of benefiting souls. He kept such faults secret as far as he could, and in order to correct them, would give them paternal admonitions in private, and would sometimes keep the culprits shut up in his own house, with fasting and discipline. If the occasion of sin were found in their own parishes, he sent them elsewhere for a time until it had been removed; or he gave them another sphere of duty, to take them away altogether from every occasion of wrong-doing, without publishing their sins and miseries, and thus both cast out the sin, and preserved the reputation of the sinner.

He obtained such influence in this way, that there arose a great carefulness in many to avoid displeasing him by misconduct or vice. At the time of his death it was manifest that he was much beloved by his priests, who were inconsolable at his loss, as having lost a true father, and not likely to find another Archbishop like him, who could compassionate their infirmities, and to whom they could with confidence disclose the wounds and needs of their souls.

He made use of various methods of correction according to circumstances, in one way or another convincing culprits of their guilt, and moving them to acknowledge their sins though committed in secret and without witnesses. In one case he would express great compassion for the sinners, in another he would plead their good intention, and lay the blame on human frailty; in pointing out their faults to those who were delicate and sensitive, he would accuse himself of his own imperfections, regretting that he had no one else to do that office for him, and with great dexterity he would lay his hand upon their wounds and heal them, without pain. He never failed to

admonish all who needed it, and was even more
ready to perform this act of charity for princes or
prelates than for others, as he knew that they had
few or none to tell them the truth; and his words
produced signal effects in amendment of life and conversion of obdurate sinners.   When it was known
that Cardinal Borromeo was coming, then every one
looked to himself to see if there was anything which
would not be approved by him, so much so that
even the bakers in the chief cities, when he went
thither, gave loaves of better weight in order to escape
reproof.

I will here relate two instances of the way in
which he converted sinners.   In a certain town of
his diocese there lived an ecclesiastic who had grown
old in sin, to the public scandal of the inhabitants.
The Cardinal on going thither was informed of the
evil example he gave.   He accordingly sent for him
and privately admonished him as a father, and dismissed him without imposing any penance.   The
people who were expecting some great demonstration
were ill satisfied; but finding that the priest made
an immediate and total change in his life, were filled
with wonder, thinking it quite miraculous that a
single expostulation should produce such an effect.

In the same diocese, in a valley near the Protestant
parts of Switzerland, lived a layman who was leading
a very bad life, an enemy to the Church and ecclesiastical persons, and given up entirely to drunkenness.
When taken seriously ill he made a will in which he
left directions that when he was near his end wine

should be poured down his throat till he breathed his last. He recovered, however, and returned to his bad habits; and the Cardinal being then in that part of the country on his visitation, had a conversation with him in private for about an hour, reproving him for the bad life he was leading. His words had such an effect upon the man that he altered his habits, tore up his impious will, and lived thenceforth a better life and persevered till death.

He thus effected the reformation of sinners more by means of charity than strict justice.

CHAPTER XVI.

OF HIS HUMILITY.

THE light vouchsafed by God to His servant, in which
he despised and resigned all the honours of the
world, retiring into private life in order to serve
Him better, is a clear proof that he possessed within
him a fund of humility, a virtue which is as rare as
it is highly praised. He entertained in his heart
such sentiments of self-abasement and contempt for
the world, that when his uncle was elected Supreme
Pontiff, he would not leave Milan, except at his
command, because he had determined to wait on God
alone. When he was raised to the dignity of Cardinal,
as the Pope's favourite nephew, he remained firm in
this resolution, although to please his uncle he accepted
ecclesiastical preferment, yet honours never made him
change his mind, but He used them only for the
greater glory of God, to assist his uncle, the Pontiff,
and to effect reform in the Christian commonwealth.
When his uncle offered him other honours, such as
the post of Cardinal Camerlengo, and when other
dignities were awaiting him in case of his resignation
of the ecclesiastical state, he absolutely refused them

and when he could no longer discharge his responsibilities with satisfaction to himself, without any ulterior motive he resigned them altogether into the hands of the Supreme Pontiff.   It was the general opinion that he would have resigned the Cardinalate itself as well as the See of Milan, only that he considered that in those offices he was furthering the salvation of souls.

Although he had been enriched by God with so many spiritual graces and supernatural gifts, and his works have shown him to be a saint, yet he acknowledged himself to be but a vessel of impurity, full of every imperfection, and was much displeased when no one told him of his faults. When he had an opportunity he would beg his friends to point out his offences and failings, and used to have spiritual conferences with pious persons, in which they disclosed each other's faults, in order that he might be made aware of his own imperfections. As he thought that those of his own household might not speak as freely as he wished, he used to beg of foreign prelates to do him this kindness, as in the case of Mgr. Sega, Bishop of Piacenza, afterwards Legate in France, and Cardinal, whom he humbly begged, as one zealous for the honour of God, to point out everything that he thought required to be amended in himself. When any one had the charity to apprise him of any defect, he was much obliged, and returned him many thanks. Two priests of his household were appointed by him to take note of all his actions, and freely tell him of his faults.

He observed great reserve in regard to the gifts

which God bestowed upon him; for although he was
in spirit united to Him, and had, it is believed, much
familiar intercourse with Him, yet he concealed all
His favours and graces. He chose himself a secret
place under the roof of his palace, far away from other
rooms, that no one might see or hear him when he was
communing with God. He was much displeased when
he heard virtues ascribed to him, such as abstinence
and severe penance, as he sought to conceal them as
far as possible, in order to dispel the idea that he was
a saint. In his external actions he avoided everything
like singularity, unless from the motives of Christian
prudence or the duty of setting a good example.
Although he was enlightened and experienced in spiritual things, he would not take it upon himself to dictate
to others in such matters. His desire being to save
souls, he always tried to give advice and admonition,
but in such a way that he never seemed to be teaching, but rather wishing to learn, especially when
addressing Bishops or Prelates. He never praised
or mentioned in conversation anything he did himself,
unless he wished to obtain the opinion of others. He
showed no self-complacency in what he did, and when
his acts were praised by others was displeased if the
credit of them was attributed to himself.

When he made the solemn translation of the body
of St. Simplician, in the presence of many prelates
and a great multitude of people, after the master of
ceremonies congratulated him upon it as more successful than anything that had before been seen in
Milan, in order to put him to silence, he replied,

"You seem satisfied with very little." To another person, a stranger, who was saying that he could not imagine how he could do so much, he answered, "One ought not to consider the work so much as its imperfections, and how much is not done at all."

It gave him great displeasure to see the people acting towards him as if he were a saint, as when they touched his vestments with their rosaries and the like; yet they would do it stealthily without his perceiving it, and would take the opportunity when he was giving Communion, for then his mind was quite intent upon the sacred function. During his visitation of the church of Cortenova, in the Sasna valley, in the year 1582, the people all rose, as if moved by an impulse of devotion, to touch his cope and mitre, which were in the hands of his attendants, with their rosaries. When he perceived it, he blamed them for allowing it.

From the same motive he forbore to give his blessing to those who were possessed, from a doubt, as he said, whether they were not feigning all the time, and would feign also to be delivered; and because he could not endure the noise and uproar they made at his appearance. Once when he was preaching near the Porta Tosa, in Milan, at the solemn blessing of a cross, two women possessed by evil spirits screamed and howled so loudly that it was quite unbearable. He then turned to give them a blessing, that they might not interrupt the sermon; when the spirits were instantly silenced, to the surprise of all present.

Although he was always doing great things, he thought himself that he had done nothing, that he was an unprofitable servant, and did not correspond at all with the grace of God. Accordingly, if he happened to meet with any contempt or mortification, he bore it with pleasure. From his early years, when his companions used to make game of him for his devotions, or because he would not join in their amusements, he never appeared to care for their ridicule, but smiled as if pleased at it.

When Pope Gregory XIII. thought of sending him as legate to Spain, a prelate of authority dissuaded his Holiness from so doing, saying that Cardinal Borromeo would not do for such a post, as he stammered. The Saint on hearing it, said, "He is quite right; he told the truth." He used to say that he ought to be struck dumb in the pulpit for venturing to preach when he had neither grace nor talent sufficient for the sacred duty. He suffered a slight several times in his own cathedral from a preacher of one of the Regular orders, who publicly spoke of him in his presence as wanting in prudence, and much more, which the people themselves would not tolerate; but he himself quietly accepted the mortification.

It was his custom not to depend upon his own opinion in matters of importance, but to seek the advice of others. For this purpose he formed many councils for the administration of affairs, every member of which was free to give his opinion, in order that the best course under the circumstances might be followed. If he considered that his own opinion was

the best for the service of God and the business in
question, he always gave his reasons for his belief
in such a way as to satisfy all. Hence it was that
all who beheld his modesty and humility in council
profited much by his example as a living pattern of
virtue. The bright influence of his humility was
reflected upon all around him, in his dress, his house,
and even his furniture. I say his dress, for although
in his outer garments he wore what was proper to his
dignity as Cardinal, he avoided everything like ornament and vain decoration, as he delighted in simplicity
himself, and wore underneath garments such as the
poorest would not wear. In his own room he wore
garments so poor and common that he was taken to
task for it by his friends, to whom he would reply,
that he did not want better; these were his own, the
others belonged to his office as Cardinal and not to
himself, whom he took to be only a poor beggar. He
delighted in this humble simplicity so much that
although his ordinary habit was stained with oil that
had been spilt upon it from a lamp he kept burning
in his room, his chamberlain never could induce him
to change it or have a new one, though they found
various pretexts to persuade him to do so. In the
process of his canonisation, the Rev. Bernardino
Tarugi, one of his chaplains, deposed, that when they
gave a poor man, for the love of God, some clothing
which the Saint had left off, it was found to be so
tattered and torn that the man would not take it, and
thinking they were making game of him went and complained to the Cardinal himself, to his secret amusement.

In his palace no ornament whatever was allowed, neither painting nor sculpture nor other embellishment; his rooms were plain and without tapestry; in furniture and plate and the like he was also as plain and sparing as possible. In order that everything should correspond and breathe humility, he removed some fine paintings that had been placed in the palace when he came from Rome, as he liked to see plain white walls. He also removed the arms and name of his family, which had been painted in various parts of the palace, and put in their stead paintings of the Blessed Virgin Mary and St. Ambrose, patron of the city. When he saw that in the new house for canons, which had been built at his expense, next to his palace, the arms of the Borromean family had been carved, he was not pleased, and ordered them to be removed, which was done except with some very high up which escaped his notice. He said the Archbishop of Milan, and not Charles Borromeo, had erected these buildings. In like manner he forbade any memorial of himself or his family, according to a bad custom, to be put on vestments or sacred vessels which he gave to churches, or on those which were made for his own use; and wherever he found them he had them removed, forbidding the same to others by a synodal decree, as improper and savouring of pride and ostentation. If he saw his likeness anywhere, he was annoyed and ordered it to be taken away. He would not allow his name to appear in the volumes which he published containing his councils and other works in the reform of his diocese, which he simply entitled, " Acts of the Church of Milan." He gave up also using the surname Borromeo, from a motive of humility to conceal his noble origin, though the contrary effect followed; for the means he adopted to hide his name and reputation have raised him to honour and greatness, the fame of his sanctity being spread throughout the world, dreaded by the powers of hell, venerated by men and angels, thus fulfilling the divine oracle, " He that humbleth himself shall be exalted." He took such delight in this feeling of humility, that although he had so numerous a household, he would not be served in private by any one, but waited on himself; he liked himself to wait upon his attendants, and used to light their candles for them at night, and would willingly have rendered them any other service had it been consistent with his dignity as Cardinal, for he considered himself the least of all; was pleased to talk with poor people, and willingly sought their society and simple manners.

In the year 1582, when he was visiting the Sasna valley and the Bergamese district, a wild part of the country with very poor inhabitants, as he was descending a high mountain by a narrow path, he met a silly man, a beggar, barefoot and not able to speak, who nodded his head to him at a distance, and coming up with smiling face offered his hand. The Cardinal stopped to receive his salutation with pleasure, and returned it with a friendly grasp, as if they had been near relatives who had not met for some time. As he was passing through Cremeno he was met and accompanied by the people in procession; on finding himself in the midst of them, he began to join in their litanies, and sing the praises of God like one of themselves. Although these incidents may appear trifling, yet taking his high office into consideration, and his humility withal, we can see in them acts of merit and virtue.

He displayed the same humility in choosing the houses of the poor to lodge in, and always declined the invitations of the rich when he could, and went to the houses of the priests, the poorer and more inconvenient they were, the better he seemed to like them. While he was visiting upper Macagno on Lake Maggiore, he was suffering from fever which had seized him some days before, but paid little attention to it, and continued the duties of his visitation as usual; as, however, he became much worse, he was obliged to take to his bed. As the parish priest's house was not habitable, he went to lie down in a wretched room of a poor man, whose few chattels hung upon poles round the bed. It chanced that Mgr. Giovanni Fontana, now Bishop of Ferrara, went to see him, and finding him in bed in such a poor place without any attendants, was so moved that he could not say a word. The Saint cheerfully begged him not to take it ill, for he was very comfortable, much more so than he deserved.

St. Charles was always much pleased to serve the poor at table, and to wash the feet of the pilgrims in holy week, and performed these offices not as mere ceremonies but out of devotion and humility.

When in Milan, he always went out on foot,

although it might be raining, and the streets were muddy, and would have no retinue either at home or abroad; and used to take but few persons with him, as all his household had their duties and occupations. He conducted himself in so unpretending a manner, that some, who knew little of God's dealings and of the lives of the saints, took scandal at him like Pharisees, and said that he lowered the Cardinalate, complaining of him to the Supreme Pontiff, Pius V., who, being a saint himself, found nothing in his behaviour but what was worthy of imitation instead of reproof, and used to quote him as an example to the Cardinals, as a good model for them to copy. The wise men of the world, incapable of this virtue and void of illumination, considered it as a defect, but the Saint tried to make them understand that the true dignity of the ministers of God does not consist in worldly show and ornaments (which in certain cases, however, are not to be despised), but in virtue and holiness—the true adornments of him who has been consecrated to God—which exalt him in His sight and the estimation of the truly wise. From his desire to see this spirit in prelates, and to induce his own clergy to follow the path of the saints, he had often in his mouth exhortations to cast aside vanity and take pleasure in simplicity, and many decrees to this effect are found in the records of his councils. He never failed to take notice where he perceived worldly ornament and display in Bishops; and on one occasion when he saw a

Bishop wearing smart stockings, he took him to task, saying that a Bishop should be conspicuous for good example, and not for finery.

The spot which he chose for his burial shows the perfection of his humility, for it was in the common part of the church, most frequented by the people, in order that he might be remembered in their prayers, especially by the devout female sex, according to his own words in his epitaph.

Lastly, the very demons themselves testified to the Cardinal's humility by their abhorrence of it. Once when he was entering a church with the long train of his robe on the ground, a woman, who was possessed, unable to endure his presence, began to make an uproar, and exclaimed, "Oh that I could but put a little pride into that train!"

CHAPTER XVII.

HIS MEEKNESS.

THE Saint's meekness was equal to his humility, for God granted him from his birth the singular privilege of never being prone to anger, so that even in his childhood he was never known to give way to passion, however he might be crossed either by servants or strangers. He was so patient and quiet, that he was thought by some persons to be almost stupid. It was related by his servants, that when he was a student at Pavia, they never saw him show the least sign of anger, although of an age when it is difficult to subject the mind to reason. He could not, however, endure or conceal his displeasure at anything wrong, especially in his own household, but reproved and corrected with great calmness and gravity. This virtue increased with his years, and was practised to the end of his life in an exemplary manner, being particularly seen in the reformation of his diocese, when the devil stirred up nearly all the world against him to hinder his plans, and to destroy the fruit of his labours. In the midst of great opposition he never said or did anything in anger, or showed any perturbation of mind, but governed himself with prudence, and having a perfect command over his passions, referred all crosses to God, reaping merit from them by bearing them meekly, and treating both enemies and evil-doers with gentleness.

He went once to visit one of the principal convents of nuns in the city, whose direction he had placed in the hands of secular priests instead of regulars. As he proposed to enter the enclosure, the nuns became turbulent, because they did not like the reforms he had made, nor the change of directors : so running to the door, with impertinent and even violent behaviour, they stood in the way of his entrance. Neither in words or actions did he show any sign of anger at this insult, but returned home without inflicting any penance, or treating them with severity. He purposely left them time to acknowledge and repent of their mistake, for he could not allow such a bad example to pass without correction. The nuns were shortly very sorry and asked his forgiveness, and behaved with obedience afterwards.

He often bore with great calmness disrespectful and offensive words from laymen of low condition, whom he never slighted, but with kindness overcame their stubbornness, and led them to do what he wished. When giving audience he never displayed indignation or anger, though he often had to do with those who were troublesome and insolent, especially in the beginning of his reforms. At times I was myself present on such occasions, and must confess to giving way to impatience at his gentleness, which appeared to be excessive. In the controversies about his jurisdiction he not only forbore from complaining or speaking ill of his opponents, but would not listen to any murmurs against them from others, and used to change the conversation when the facts allowed of no excuse. In correcting actual faults and shortcomings he blended meekness with zeal, like the good Samaritan in the Gospel, who poured oil and wine into the wounds of the sick man. In the case of opponents he showed that he had at heart both the good of their souls and the credit of their names. One of his household seeing some lampoon written against the Cardinal, tore it down and showed it to him. He, however, merely glanced at it and threw it into the fire without further thought about it.

In the year 1579 a certain ship-captain, Giorgio Longo, who had been condemned to the galleys for some offence, informed Mgr. Cesare Ferrerio, Bishop of Savona, that there was a conspiracy to kill Cardinal Borromeo. The Bishop much distressed immediately despatched a messenger with proofs of the plot to Girolamo Visconte, a cousin of both of them. As a relative he laid them before the Cardinal early the next morning. The Saint, however, threw them in the fire without opening them, with these words: " Signor Cavaliere, I am much obliged to you for your kindness, and I beg you will thank the Bishop of Savona in my name, as I shall also myself. I do not wish to know of any one who has ill-will against me, because I am going to say Mass shortly, and do not want my peace of mind to be disturbed."

Whilst he was solemnly blessing his own house, during the plague, there came a report of the murder of one of the chief persons in the city, a relation of his own; notwithstanding, he heard about it without a word, and continued his duty with calmness.

In ecclesiastical functions his gentleness was extra-ordinary. Always wishing to carry out the ceremonies with as much perfection as possible, there were daily mistakes occurring to try his temper, owing to variety of places, persons, and offices, but in setting matters right, his mildness was a subject of general remark. When saying Mass once, while on his way to Rome, instead of wine there was given him oil, which he discovered on consuming the chalice. Apprising the server of the mistake, with perfect composure he con-secrated afresh without disturbing the congregation.

In giving orders he showed the same gentleness, and so far from giving occasion of annoyance to others, usually calmed the spirits and softened the hearts of those who were in any way perturbed. His manner was so tempered by meekness that he seemed to entreat and exhort rather than to exercise authority. When he saw that any one had a difficulty in perform-ing what he had to do, and was consequently backward and stubborn, he did not use harsh or severe words to ensure obedience, but used to say, "God will help you," "Let God do it and you will do it well;" and by words like these he made such an impression that no one would ever oppose him. He was accordingly served willingly by all, and they would undergo any fatigue in the fulfilment of duty, however difficult it might be, and sometimes at the risk of life, as in the time of the plague, and in his labours of charity among the heretics in the Grison district. After an exhortation at one of his synods, so many priests offered to go to those parts to assist in saving souls, that he could not gratify the desire of all to join in the laborious work.

In bearing the defects and failings of those of his household and servants, he was patient of any mishap to himself personally, without showing any sign of displeasure. One of his assistants, a man of birth, had remarkable defects in his address and manner of speaking, and used to give way to impatience in word and action at the slightest cause, not only to others but even to the Cardinal himself, who, however, always treated him with gentleness, out of consideration for his learning, and as a trial of his own patience. When others in the house urged that something ought to be done in order to put a stop to the annoyance, the Cardinal used to say in excuse, that it was a defect of nature and not of will, and that it was better to bear his behaviour with patience, as he had many good qualities. He gave him two hundred crowns a year during his lifetime, and at his death left him a pension charged upon his estates.

On the other hand, it was a great consolation to see the obedience and affection rendered to the Saint by his clergy and people, and how they considered it a great favour to do anything for him. In the latter part of his life all were so attached to him that no one was found to go against him, owing to his virtues and the meekness of his words. In the controversy about jurisdiction, serious accusations were sometimes brought against him, and he was declared to be wanting in loyalty to the King of Spain, so that his friends began to be alarmed; he did not alter, however, his behaviour towards those who were plotting against him, but always treated them with kindness, by which they were so overcome, that they changed their minds, through mistrust of one another, and uncertain what charge to bring against him.

One rare quality he possessed in the courage he displayed under almost insupportable trials, for he was always so composed that he was never seen to be angry or depressed, nor could his most intimate friends discover in him any sign of perturbation except that he used sometimes to scratch his nose with his finger.

Finally, his meekness not only secured peace in his household by preventing all disputes and pacifying those inclined to strife, but also brought about the recovery of property which had been illegally taken away from the Church, and induced private persons and others to contribute generously to the building and restoration of churches, and to other works of piety.

CHAPTER XVIII.

DENCE IN DIRECTING AND ADVISING OTHERS.

lence was so great, that even in the pontificate
uncle, Pius IV., it was called by experienced
s and princes more than human, as passing
:hat of men.   Though some were found who
:d him imprudent in resigning his benefices,
is election of Pius V., as also in endangering
during the plague ; it is clear that such
were actuated by worldly feelings only, and
motives, at variance both with the Christian
stolic spirit.
us in his long residence at Milan that his
: was most manifest, surprising even those
l daily experience of it in all the business
. he was engaged, particularly in the councils
. the more delicate matters were discussed by
earning and experience, for by the inspiration
rness of his judgment he solved difficulties,
ich no one else, however experienced, could
escape, directed as he was by the interior
:ion of God to avail himself of the best
f assistance.   He never undertook anything

of importance without having recourse to three things, viz., prayer, fasting, and counsel. His own prayers were fervent and continual, and when engaged in business of importance, he begged for those of devout persons and of his clergy and people. It would seem that he both depended entirely on God and set no value whatever on human assistance; and entered so deeply into consultation and co-operation with others as to cause some surprise. He was anxious that his diocese should be governed in as perfect a manner as possible, in order to be a model to others. He always revised again everything that passed through the hands of his officials, however learned and experienced they might be; and he had always something to add or to correct in the light of his understanding, in which he was excelled by none. Nothing was allowed to be published except that which had undergone every correction, in which he was both prudent and laborious, devoting himself to the examination of all documents, advising by word of mouth, and writing himself, when necessary.

Two communities of regular clergy petitioned him to make over to them a church adjoining one of his colleges, as he had the power to make the grant from the Pope. One of the communities begged a certain prince to interest himself with the Cardinal in their behalf. The Cardinal would not make any decision until he had laid the matter before his council, who considered it would be better for the service of God to give the church to the community that had not made use of any influence to obtain it. Accordingly, he refused the prince the favour, although he would have been glad to oblige him.

There was a serious difference between a convent of nuns and a nobleman who had an adjoining property, on account of a wall of separation, the latter defending his presumed rights in a very determined manner. The Cardinal, to put an end to the discussion, went himself to visit the spot, and found the nobleman stubborn in maintaining his own opinion. The Saint, seeing that the nuns had right on their side, with prudence and tact set to work to convince him, and at last succeeded. Like instances were of daily occurrence, and suffice to show the prudence he exercised in all his transactions.

Wise and cautious as he was in temporal affairs, he exercised, if possible, greater prudence in spiritual matters, in the direction of his own soul and those of others. As to his own soul, he always followed the advice of his confessors, and endeavoured to prove the spirits if they were from God, before he trusted to them, and never allowed himself to be carried away by a false zeal in any matter whatever. As to austerities, he never attempted anything he was not able to carry out, nor did he reach his high degree of penance without advancing step by step [1] towards it.

He would not readily believe in the sanctity of any person, although commonly reputed a saint, unless assured of it by proofs that could be relied upon, as he well knew that the devil is wont to transform himself into an angel of light, in order to deceive the

---

[1] Vid. chap. xxi. p. 415.

unwary who are wont too easily to believe in every spirit.

During the latter years of his life, there was a young woman in Milan who, though mixing in the world, seemed to devote herself entirely to the service of God in the state of virginity. In course of time people began to believe she was a saint, and many had recourse to her, and among them persons of consequence, to ask her advice and to obtain graces from God by her means, as her penances and austerities were bruited abroad. The Cardinal did not wish to approve of this until he was sure of her spirit, and commissioned Father Francesco Adorno to ascertain whether it came from God. The latter, being led astray by her, although he was a man of learning and experience, reported well of her. The Cardinal, however, was not satisfied, and wished to have more certain proofs and further examination by placing her in a convent; but as he was called away from this life, his determination was not carried out. In time she was discovered to be an impostor, leading a carnal life under the cloak of sanctity, and giving scandal to the whole city—an example well worthy to be noted and followed by all pastors of souls.

When we consider the observance of his many decrees, his reform and discipline of his clergy and people, his rules and institutes for the furtherance of Christian life, the manifold instructions found in his printed works, we cannot but be filled with wonder at the skill and prudence bestowed upon him by our Lord for the edification of the Church.

The prudence of his counsels is clear from results. Not only had private persons recourse to him, but princes, and the Supreme Pontiffs themselves, consulted him in difficulties; because they found from experience that his counsel was not only well weighed and efficient, but likewise had something more than human in it: as St. Pius V. said, when he had entrusted to the Cardinal the management of a matter in which the honour of persons in high position was at stake, "Truly Cardinal Borromeo has the Spirit of God with him."

In offering advice he spoke but few words, and those entirely to the point. As an instance, when one of his chaplains begged him for some instructions for gaining heaven, as he had come from a distance to devote himself to his service for that end, and not from any human motive, he gave him the following advice: "Whoever wishes to make progress in the way that leads to God must be always beginning, that is, he must always endeavour to serve God with the same fervour as if he were making a fresh beginning every day; he must always walk in the presence of God, and make Him the end of all his actions."

In these words appears to be contained the whole discipline of the interior man in the spiritual life.

CHAPTER XIX.

ON HIS FORTITUDE AND CONSTANCY.

SOME evidence of the undaunted spirit of St. Charles on all occasions has been already brought forward. When in times of danger others were filled with fear, he alone who was threatened by the blow, was firm and unmoved. Even death itself, last and most terrible blow of all, had no power to alarm or quell his heart. It was said, at the time when he was shot, that his freedom from fear in so great a risk was a greater miracle than for his linen rochet to be changed into a shirt of steel. At the time of the plague, when from fear of death the mother forsook her child, and the wife her husband, he seemed heedless of death, and went about in search of the plague-stricken to prepare them for their last end. While his assistants, men of merit and courage, had a dread of entering the rooms where such were lying, he went fearlessly to their beds and gave them the sacraments himself. It is well known to all his friends that, in the greatest dangers, when the whole city was in a state of terror, and he was warned of plots against his life, with a smile he bade them not to be afraid, as if

ould spring . up to defend him. Whatever
ight threaten, he never would forsake his
ut was resolved to die rather a thousand
e used to say that he suffered more from a
discipline committed by a priest than from
tion of many temporal princes, and that he
l the least harm done to the Church, more
the tribulations in the world were to over-
elf or his family. He possessed such strength
iat it appeared to increase in the midst of
; while others, though courageously disposed,
panic-struck as it were in the thick of the
fence it was that he succeeded in all his
igs, and with invincible constancy gained
r over all his difficulties, though they seemed
ery day.

thers manifested their inward feelings by out-
s, turning pale or red, with joy or sadness—
ich cannot be concealed—in him there was
, for his manner never varied. The different
ices and accidents of the world, however serious
t be, had no power to affect the stability of his
his latter years he had great peace and tran-
nd met with no opposition whatever, as all
iim unhesitating obedience. The devil then
new warfare for him in the heretical country
sons, which he willingly undertook from his
ire to do them good. In that enterprise he
ite, deterred by no expense or difficulties,
s he was on Christ the rock, whom he strove
in his zeal for souls. As a Bishop he

strove to love Christ crucified, and to keep His image engraven on his heart, and in this way attained a strength of mind that rendered him invincible and willing to shed his blood for the salvation of those for whom He died. This is the mark and touchstone of the good pastor, which distinguishes him from hirelings, engrossed in self-love and afraid of every trouble, —who flee when there is no danger, and are frightened when there is nothing to fear, overpowered by the least difficulty, while the true pastors lay down their lives for their flocks.

This constancy and stability of mind in the Cardinal was considered by worldly men who are entirely opposed to the Spirit of God to be stubbornness and an obstinate adhesion to his own way of thinking. This impression arose in great measure from his determination to have the decrees of the Council of Trent carried out, without yielding to the devices of opponents and entreaties of the world. He had himself brought that Council to a successful conclusion by stimulating the zeal of his uncle the Pope. When he had made up his mind to put any good design into execution, not all the power in the world could change him. To these two virtues, his prudence and his fortitude, we owe the reform of his diocese ; by the first, he foresaw and provided all the necessary means ; by the latter, he put them into practice to be observed by all of every condition and quality, notwithstanding all the opposition he encountered, as if all the powers of hell had been leagued against him.

CHAPTER XX.

HIS PATIENCE IN TRIALS AND SUFFERINGS.

THOSE who were intimately acquainted with him called his life a long and slow martyrdom, not only on account of the penance he voluntarily performed, but also from his sufferings during life, and the infirmities which God permitted to afflict him. In the midst of his daily labours he showed an unconquerable patience in bearing all crosses, accepting them as pleasures, in imitation of many other saints who rejoiced in the trials and torments of this life. He had such patience in bodily pain and sickness that at times he seemed almost beyond the power of feeling and suffering. Every one saw that while he was suffering from fever he continued his usual labours and penances, as if nothing ailed him, and kept his complaint concealed as far as possible. It was a saying of his that he who had charge of souls ought not to take to his bed until after a third attack of fever.

One summer he went on his visitation to the Travaglia valley, and the parish of Canobbio— mountainous districts with difficult roads—by Lake

Maggiore, when he had seventeen attacks of tertian fever without ever interrupting his duties, going on with his visitation even when the attack was at its height, so that he was seen to be at one time shivering with cold, at another time burning with heat. He consecrated the church of the Capuchin Fathers at Canobbio, although his fever was raging, preaching a long sermon outside the church, that all might hear him, bearing both the heat within and the scorching sun outside. He generally made the visitations of his diocese during the three hottest months, and after finishing one went straight on with another. As it was usually after mid-day when he ended, in order to lose no time he rode off at the hottest part of the day without any shield from the sun's rays. If he had to pass through wild craggy districts, where there was no road for horses, he would go on foot, suffering so much from perspiration that his clothes would be wet through. When he reached the end of his journey, instead of changing his garments, which he might have done, he would go straight to the church, say some prayers, preach, and begin the duties of the visitation, as if he felt no fatigue. If he were wet through with rain, or from crossing streams, it would be all the same to him; he would immediately set about what he had to do. Once when visiting the church at Settala he passed through a stream so deep that he was wet to his waist, yet he would not on that account delay going to the church, but without drying himself or changing, he would begin his duties. He always rode rapidly, travelling great distances, day and night. Urged on by his ardent spirit, he longed to reach the end of his journey, in order to be at work again. His journeys in this way were made much more laborious, taking as he did no rest nor refreshment, except such food and sleep as were absolutely necessary, according to his austere habit. In consecrating churches, cemeteries, and other functions, when the ceremony required it, he remained with his head uncovered, exposed to the sun's rays in the intense heat of noon; and as this happened frequently, he became quite sunburnt.

He endured cold with the same patience, and on journeys as well as at home, never allowed himself to go near the fire or to wear furs or gloves, and would ride out in the depth of winter with nothing on his hands, when everything was covered with ice. His hands would become so chapped, that blood would gush from them, and when his attendants begged him to have some compassion on himself, and keep them covered, on account of his dignity at least, he refused to do so, from the wish to suffer for the love of God : neither would he listen to them when they urged him to wear warmer clothes, seeing that he was shivering with cold.

I will here narrate what Mgr. Francesco Panigarola said on this subject in the funeral oration of the Saint: "He never spent any of his income upon himself personally, except for the little bread and water that he ate, and the straw he slept upon. When I was with him in the Mesolcina Valley, a rough part of the country, on going to him once at night, I found him studying in a torn dressing-gown of thin black cloth, I begged him to put on a warmer garment and not perish of cold. He replied with a smile, Suppose I have no other, and want nothing else; my other garments belong to my dignity and not to myself: as for me, I am satisfied with this garment both for summer and winter, and will have no other as long as I live."

When he had strangers with him, he would occasionally join them at the fire, but not to enjoy the warmth, for he would remain at some distance, or turn his back to it. Giulio Petruccio, one of his chaplains, one day complained of his austerity, because he would not allow his bed to be warmed. The Saint replied that to study bodily comfort was giving way to sensuality: "There is a better way for not finding the bed cold than warming it, and that is to go to bed colder than the bed itself." He knew this from experience, and, moreover, never used to eat anything at night, and had only a little straw for his bed, and for his covering also. As men of the world try to avoid suffering and become attached to every comfort, he, on the contrary, avoided every comfort, and sought for greater suffering and bodily affliction.

Once when he had retired for prayer to one of the cells he had built for spiritual exercises in the seminary of the Canonica, it being the rainy season, Castano, his chaplain, begged him to leave the place, because the water was coming through the roof and wetting him through, but he merely obtained leave to put a plank above the bed, which did not even shelter him from the wet. He preferred to remain in that state of discomfort, although there were plenty of comfortable rooms in the seminary that he might have occupied; showing that he felt pleasure in these sufferings, and testifying to his hatred of himself, and close union with God.

On one occasion when he was staying in the house of a Bishop of his province, he heard the sound of musical instruments while at table; whereupon he found fault with his host, saying that a Bishop ought to avoid everything that delights the senses. At another time, seeing a priest, one of his household, drink between meals, he made the remark that, by yielding to the sensual appetite, he would make himself a slave to it, the next day he would drink again at the same hour. The priest excused himself, saying he was only washing out his mouth, but the Saint rejoined, that to do so was sensual also, and that he ought to mortify himself, and would do better to suffer thirst. He practised this self-denial himself, for he never drank between meals, not even a little water when fatigued in hot weather.

At the time of the plague in Milan he used to join in the processions when there was ice upon the ground, and he would go barefoot, because his feet would then be cut and blood would flow, as if he delighted in shedding it, for the love of God. It was the same when he had a wound in his foot, and walked in the processions three successive days without applying anything to heal it. Nor would he remain indoors when the nail had afterwards to be cut off, and he met with a fall in consequence, and dislocated a bone in his hand, which was very difficult to set again, the surgeon being more troubled than his patient.

CHAPTER XXI.

ON HIS SPIRIT OF PENANCE AND AUSTERITY OF LIFE.

WHAT struck the world with astonishment was the austerity and penance which the Saint practised in the midst of all the anxieties and business of his diocese. He had reached such a degree of perfection in the latter part of his life that he fasted almost daily on bread and water, except on feast-days, when he made some addition, but took neither meat, eggs, fish, nor wine. During Lent he gave up the use of bread, and lived upon dried figs and boiled beans, and during holy-week on lupines alone, and had only one meal a day the year round.

At night a straw mattress served him for a bed, with a straw bolster and coverlet of the same, hempen sheets, coarse and rough as they came from the loom. Until the time of the plague he used to sleep upon bare boards, with a blanket; but at the request of the Bishops in two Provincial Councils, he made some relaxation in his austerity, and out of obedience made use of a common folding bedstead, with straw mattress, placed against the wall. Next to his body he wore a coarse hair shirt, which is now venerated in the

Great Hospital at Milan, and has been mended in several places from being much worn. Besides this he had another, which was divided into several pieces at his death. He used the discipline so severely throughout the year that marks of it were found on his body after his death.

He reached these degrees of penance step by step, increasing them with prudence from time to time, and inflicting on his body only what it could bear. As he had been brought up tenderly, he acquired the virtues befitting a Cardinal and Archbishop by practice, and attained in the same way to mortification and corporal austerities. Beginning with easy fasting, he increased it day by day till he habituated himself to great abstinence. Never satisfied with the standard which he had reached, he always strove to multiply his austerities. Thus not content with fasting on bread and water, his lenten fare was lupines and figs, and he would have tried a severer diet could he have hit upon it. It was his set purpose never to stand still in the spiritual life, but to be always advancing till his last breath. So he never let a good resolution drop, but increased in fervour until he could go no further, desiring "to be dissolved and to be with Christ," our Lord opening the gate at last and admitting him into His heavenly kingdom.

The best proof that he was guided by discretion in his penances is, that he was never owing to them unable to perform his duty, or so ill as to be prevented continuing his labours in the service of God. At the end of his life his strength was equal, or but little inferior to what it had been in his prime. As the cares of his diocese increased, his bodily strength grew in proportion, so that he was never overpowered by them. I may assert indeed with truth, that in his austerity he did not suffer from indisposition as formerly, but he used it as a means of keeping under his body. When any one begged him to work less hard, and to moderate the severity of his life, he would reply that he felt all the stronger for it, and that when he was a young man in Rome, he could hardly bear even a light hat upon his head in the hot season, while now he could wear a berretta and his Cardinal's hat in the greatest heat without inconvenience; moreover, that our Lord gave every one strength according to the burden he had to bear, and to His own pastors grace and strength to do their duty, when they have a good will and a pure intention.

In order to avoid any taint of sensuality mingling with his austerities, he would not have any particular pains taken in the cooking or selection of food set before him. He ate the common bread, whatever was set before him, and always drank water which was often turbid and bad ; and when his attendants would have boiled it to make it better, he would not allow it, as a kind of indulgence or sensuality, saying that true virtue consists not only in resisting gratification of the senses, but also in repressing those pleasures altogether —not so much in refusing to indulge the senses, as in taking delight in their mortification. When he went into the poor mountain districts nothing delighted him so much as when no bread was to be had, and he was obliged to eat chestnuts and drink milk, and to sleep upon benches and boards. In the warfare which he waged with his body—to which he refused all pleasure—he had gained the victory, and had brought his sensitive appetite into entire subjection to reason and spirit, and thus neither ate nor slept but in obedience to their commands.

Besides the little sleep he took in general, at the times when he had any unusual amount of business, as in his Provincial and Diocesan Councils, and his translations of the relics of the saints, he either slept very little, or merely took a little rest in a chair; which he liked doing, as he used to say there were generals who were so vigilant in time of war that they never lay down in bed, but only slept in a chair, and quoted his uncle, John Joseph de Medici, as an instance. "Hence," said he, "a Bishop who has the direction of souls, and fights against the legions of hell, ought not to be less watchful than a general in worldly warfare." To maintain this watchfulness gave him perhaps more trouble than anything else in this life, for he was naturally much inclined to sleep, and his body, wearied by his continual labours, needed more rest than he allowed it; and having to use violence in this way, there arose in him a continual struggle between body and spirit. Although he had the inferior part in subjection, yet he was never able entirely to overcome his strong propensity for sleep, notwithstanding his struggles against it. "As to his great austerities during the whole course of his life," says Father Gagliardi, "I refer to the testimony of those of his own household, who being with him day and night, had full knowledge of them. They were also well known to the world at large, who wondered at them as excessive, but almost all great saints have chosen the same path. Let me say that I have remarked, in his austerities, a great discretion presiding over all. I used to admire one thing in him, which few perhaps have observed, that besides doing great violence to himself by his austerities, in order to make the victory over his passions easy, and to acquire the habit of virtue by frequent acts of it, God was pleased that nature should so far have the upper hand as not to allow him this facility, but obliged him always to use violence to himself, as in abstaining from sleep. Through the power of divine grace he never relaxed, but kept his vigils with assiduity and perseverance, showing that he took pleasure in such violence, however long it might last. He never discovered any means of dispensing with this struggle, and never relaxed his watchfulness over this enemy, whose power he always felt within him. It has seemed to me to be a wonderful way of seizing the prey from the hands of the enemy without destroying his power, of conquering without subjugating him, and of enjoying a mode of doing violence to self, of which we have few examples even among the saints of antiquity."

This struggle against sleepfulness was manifest to all, as an enemy that was perpetually troubling him ; but at the same time it was noticed that he never suffered himself to be overcome by it. When he was so far overcome by nature that he seemed as if he were asleep, still he was so far on the alert that he heard everything, and could give, for instance, an account of what the preachers said in sermons, and noticed if they made any mistakes, just as if he were the most wakeful of all. The last time he was in Rome, he used to go sometimes to hear Father Francesco Toledo, afterwards Cardinal, and on one occasion he appeared to be fast asleep all the time, when a prelate said to Francesco Bernardino Nava, then present: "If I were Cardinal Borromeo's confessor, I should bid him sleep at night for his penance, that he might keep awake in the daytime, especially at sermons." It chanced that the Saint had a Cardinal and others to dine with him that day, and in conversation began to speak of the sermon, and gave a minute account of it, at which his brother Cardinal and those who had seen him asleep were much surprised. Some who saw him fighting such a hard battle pitied him, and recommended him to take a little more sleep; one person gave him the opinion of a spiritual Father of great authority, who said that he ought to have at least seven hours' rest in order to keep in health and to bear fatigues; to which he replied, that the Father did not understand it was a Bishop he was speaking of. I remember that in a conversation with me on this subject he said that he certainly felt it a hard struggle with nature to avoid sleep, but when he considered his duty to God and the Church, he was able to overcome every difficulty.

It gave him much trouble to see that his austere

mode of life was not approved of, as many advised him to abstain from so much penance, lest he should shorten his life ; and others wrote to him begging him to mitigate his austerities, among whom was the Archbishop of Valencia, in Spain, Father Luis of Granada. One of his intimate friends wrote also to Pope Gregory XIII., complaining that if his Holiness did not prevent it, the Cardinal would soon put an end to his days, as he could not survive under the weight of so many toils. A letter from his Holiness forbidding his austerities reached him in the beginning of holy week, 1584. During that Lent he had eaten dried figs, but had begun to take only lupines, but that diet he gave up immediately out of obedience to his Holiness. To others, as to the Archbishop of Valencia, before mentioned, he quoted the example of many saints who had used similar austerities, as follows : "It is unnecessary to remind you of holy men like St. Nicholas, St. Chrysostom, St. Spiridion, and St. Basil, who, although Bishops of large dioceses, persevered in continual prayer and fasting, and yet reached a good old age."

By these examples he wished to show that he could conscientiously, without risk of shortening life, continue his usual penances, and that even if it should please God to call him away soon, he should consider it a great favour, from the desire he had to offer up his life for the love of God in the service of His Church. He said the same in another passage of his letter to the Archbishop, as follows : " We ought to esteem it our greatest gain to spend our strength and our lives, which we must sooner or later lay down, in the service of the Church for which Christ died. No one, much less a Bishop, ought to be hindered by anxiety about health, or by fear of death, from the discharge of his duty, which is more important than any other consideration."

Although this austere life of the Saint was not approved of by all, as beyond human power to endure, yet it seems to have been pleasing to God, that in a time of great sensuality he should set an example in order to recall the pastors of souls in particular from the pursuit of pleasure and gain to the true discipline of the spiritual life. Our Lord therefore manifested by many signs and miracles that his servant's mode of life was most pleasing and acceptable to Himself, although not understood or approved of by all men.

CHAPTER XXII.

OF HIS CHASTITY.

RLES had so great a respect for the ecclesias-
,it, which he had worn from his childhood,
 avoided the smallest act of levity that was
ng his vocation, although not a matter of sin.
re all things, and at every period of his life,
most careful to preserve his heart and soul
ery stain of impurity which he hated and
 as contrary to the angelical virtue required in
:ical persons who are the living temples of God
rnacles of the Divinity and Humanity of our
Lord.   He was on his guard, therefore, against
ought, word, and deed, that might soil him with
ı of such sin.   Although the devil laid snares
 as he did for St. Thomas Aquinas and St.
 and introduced into his chamber young
o tempt him at the most dangerous time of
·ertheless by divine grace and the protection
ıgel guardian he preserved his purity, so that
opinion of all who were intimately acquainted
. that he lived and died a virgin.   Georgio de
; guardian in youth, who had been an eye-

witness of his whole career, bore testimony to it; and the same declaration was made on oath by others who had served in the Borromean family, who had known him from childhood, and in after years. It is also confirmed by Mgr. Bascapè, Bishop of Novara, in his life of the Saint, where, speaking of his young days in the time of Pius IV., and of the strict guard he kept over his purity, he says: "He never was known by any one to have even an evil inclination contrary to this virtue, and more than once freed himself from snares set to entrap him."

During his episcopate his manner of life was so well known that all Milan could testify to his innocence and purity; but those of his household, in daily intercourse with him, who could not but be well informed, deposed upon oath in the process, that he kept himself so far from every stain that he could not bear to hear anything like an impure word uttered, in order to avoid the risk of any taint. If he was obliged to speak upon such subjects, he never allowed an impure word to pass his lips, but used circumlocution where he could, or Latin words, and would have others do the same. On one occasion when a religious who was employed in some office about him, in explaining a certain case not only mentioned persons but also the sins in common terms without any respect whatever, he reproved his want of delicacy, and dismissed him from the office he held, and desired his superiors to admonish him. It is the testimony of his personal attendants that he was so modest in dressing and undressing that they never saw any part of his body un-

; when they were taking off his stockings he
ay the coverlet over his legs, and used to wear
at night as a protection. When visiting one
household who was ill, and observing that he
his bare arm when the physician felt his pulse,
e departure of the latter the Saint blamed him,
that it was contrary to modesty to allow any
the body to be seen. He dreaded the occasions
of falling into sin so much, that, favoured as he
God with many graces, he always kept his body
ction and punished it by fasting and penance.
always avoided conversation with the female
l would only speak to a woman, even near
s, in a public place, and in presence at least of
nesses, and observed the same rule even with
ntess Margherita Trivulzia his aunt, of mature
l great piety. On one occasion when he was
g to the Marchioness di Melegnano, the wife
ousin, in the presence of Moneta and Castano,
er left the room for a while, for which the
everely reproved him, and would not accept
ise he offered, viz., that Moneta was there and
y was a relation. He made it a rule indeed
) speak to any females, not even his relations,
n case of necessity. When he was in Rome,
er Anna, the wife of Fabrizio Colonna, wished
im, yet though she was his sister and a woman
piety, he avoided interviews with her; and if
ited to speak to him, she had to go to the
s to find him.
)bserved also great caution with nuns, and

never went to their convents except on business, taking especial care not to speak to them in private, and only for their spiritual benefit; if he had to speak to any nun in private, he took with him two priests, and never entered the enclosure unless accompanied by chaplains of mature age, one of whom was generally Lodovico Moneta. He was so circumspect that on finding that one of his household was writing a diary of his daily acts, and had put down that he had been to a convent of nuns without stating the business which had taken him there, he gave him a reproof, saying, that it was not proper to write down that a Bishop had entered a convent without mentioning his reason for so doing, and forbade him to continue the diary.

His interior purity and innocence were so great, that they shone brightly in his face: all who looked at him felt a mortification of sense and passion and drawn to the virtue of holy chastity. God gave him such influence that he led many of both sexes to embrace a single life, of men, some entering the clerical state or a religious order; many observing perpetual chastity in their own homes, while others joined a celibate society founded by himself under the name and protection of St. Maurice. He not only filled existing convents with nuns, but formed new communities, as the Ursulines, who spread nearly over the whole diocese, and the Society of St. Anne for widows, who served God in great purity of life under a rule. These results may be considered as the fruit of the Cardinal's example, which induced so many of every state and condition among his spiritual children to practise the virtue of chastity.

CHAPTER XXIII.

ON HIS PURITY OF CONSCIENCE.

GINNING from his earliest years to love and fear
d, to practise virtue and avoid sin, St. Charles, when
came to the full use of reason, did not allow divine
ce to lie idle in his soul, but strove to live in
ity of conscience. He applied himself to prayer
l self-examination, and frequently approached the
raments with self-denial and watchfulness over
iself so as to avoid the least occasion of sin. He
de such progress, that whereas at first he went to
afession and Communion once a week, he afterwards
at every day. Thus by degrees he acquired the
iit of continual prayer, and at first examined his
iscience once or twice a day, but in time attained
such perfection that he not only made an examina-
a of every particular action, but took care that
acts should be accompanied by all the conditions
essary to make them fruitful and give good example.
used to weigh well every word he uttered in order
, to enter into useless conversation, or incur other
lts. Those who were intimately acquainted with
a for many years deposed upon oath that they

never heard him utter an idle word: which is a remarkable testimony when his continual conferences and discussions are taken into account, as well as his daily occasions of falling into sins of the tongue. He entirely banished from his mouth all kinds of jokes and jests, and avoided vain and useless sayings and mere matters of curiosity: so that all his speech was about God or His service. As this holy custom of his was well known, no one spoke to him except upon business or things spiritual. To this he added another rule to be observed, which was never to lose a moment of time uselessly, so as not to have to accuse himself in confession of having wasted his time. These two things were admired in him, as having been noticed in but few servants of God; that plunged as he was in business and intercourse with the world, he should have so governed his tongue during the nineteen years of his active episcopate, that no one could say he had uttered an idle word or wasted a moment of time. He was so anxious, moreover, to spend his time fruitfully, that when he could, he would do two things at a time, such as making notes or studying at meal-times, which he did generally when fasting on bread and water. When in company with others, there was always during meal-times pious reading to which he paid great attention. He always read the Holy Scriptures, his constant study, on his knees, and used to be seen in tears, moved by the sacred subjects he was contemplating, and thus at one and the same time he would be eating, studying, and meditating. He used to read, or had some one to read to him, while his hair was being cut. During his journeys, he generally prayed or studied, for which purpose he had a bag of books sent on before. The hour after dinner in order to employ it to good purpose he spent in giving audience to his Vicars-General and others, as not being a time for serious occupation of mind. In the distribution of his time, there was none set apart for recreation and relaxation of mind, which is commonly done even in strict religious orders.

As he had perfect control over his senses and governed his passions conscientiously, he was never elated by prosperity or depressed by adversity; never too lively or too sad, but preserved great equanimity under all circumstances. He was so sedate and circumspect in his actions, as to avoid any movement that might be noticeable as a defect; for instance, he sometimes gave audience leaning against a window, but was never seen to look into the street, whatever might occur there; nor would he look about him when walking either alone or with others, considering it unbecoming to the gravity of a Bishop. He would never allow himself to be seen, except by his chamberlains, if he were not in his Cardinal's dress, in order to keep up his dignity, and he never left his private rooms in the morning except in his ordinary habit as ready to say Mass, for before Mass he never gave audience to any one unless on very urgent matters. He usually kept silence from the time of night prayers till after his Mass the next morning, out of reverence to that Divine Mystery.

In his every word and work he breathed sanctity

and kept watch over his slightest actions, as he considered any failing to be of importance in a Bishop, not merely on its own account but because of his person, which ought to reflect a bright example of virtue. Being once asked by a man of mature years why he would not listen to the news of what was going on in the world, which many who have the charge of important affairs would do as useful for them in their office, he replied that it was not fitting in a Bishop who should be engaged in meditating on the Divine law, and not in curiosity about worldly things. Wishing to point out how necessary it was for a person dedicated to God to be recollected and grave in all his actions, he quoted the example of St. Ambrose, who would not admit a young man into the ecclesiastical state because he observed something careless and unseemly in his gait. He used to censure his priests if he observed any deficiency in gravity of manner or outward bearing, and he effected so great a reform among ecclesiastics in his diocese, that they came to be greatly respected by seculars, whereas before they were a bye-word on account of the bad example they set.

He was so careful to avoid the least stain of conscience that he never took in hand anything of doubtful matter without first taking counsel whether there was any risk in it. As to the many faculties he asked from Rome in matters dependent on the Supreme Pontiff, he always begged for larger powers than necessary. When any business came before him in which there might be any scruple involved, he either

to undertake it, or made himself quite certain
incurred no sin himself in so doing.

e it was that in all important matters he ob-
he opinions of learned men, or referred them
upreme Pontiff at Rome. He was particularly
about ecclesiastical funds, as having to render
account of them to God. I remember on
asion when he spoke to me on this subject,
that he had to keep an account of every
, in order that he might not be called upon
Judge at the Last Day. He divided his into three parts, the first part for the support
household, the second for the poor and the
f hospitality, and the third for the benefit of
ese. He had all his accounts minutely noted
nd when he held his provincial councils he
them before his suffragan Bishops, as of pro-
at did not belong to himself, who had been
ed only as an administrator by God. His
rs acknowledged that they learnt much from
essions, from the illumination of his conscience
lustre of his virtues. Such was the testi-
f Father Francesco Adorno, a man of great
ce in the spiritual life, as also of Griffith
Canon Theologian of the Chapter, who was
essor in ordinary.

when he was giving Communion in the city
ia, through the fault of the server, who knocked
him, one of the consecrated Hosts fell to the
at which he was so grieved that he fasted
ek as a penance, and abstained from saying

Mass for four days, and would have denied himself longer, had not his friends given him to understand that he was inflicting punishment on others, who were thus deprived of hearing Mass and receiving Communion, rather than benefiting by a self-inflicted penance for no fault of his own. Besides the Sacramental Confession which he made every day, he used to go through an examination of conscience, and a General Confession once or twice a year, when he made the spiritual exercises, washing out with his tears the stains he had contracted through human frailty during the year, and he persevered in this holy practice to the end of his life. Many, both of clergy and laity, were induced by his exhortations to imitate his example in this, and found by experience that meditation on the things of God, away from the world, is the surest means of illuminating the soul, and bringing it to recognise the folly of departing from Him, the fountain of all good, beguiled by the love of vanities here below.

Finally, the Saint was on his guard, not only against sin, but also, as far as lay in his power, against all those imperfections and natural defects that are allied to sin, because he knew that they diminished the brightness of the soul and destroyed the cheerfulness of spirit by which progress is made in holiness. He attained indeed to such purity of conscience that those who had constant intercourse with him did not venture to approach or speak to him if they felt the stain of any sin upon their souls. One of his Vicars-General used to go to Confession

efore he sought an audience of him, thinking, not
ithout good reason, that from his great purity he
w into the interior of hearts.

Thus reverence for him increased in the hearts of
en in proportion as they knew him intimately, and in
ose of his household and the principal persons of the
iocese, on account of the sanctity they saw growing
1 him day by day.

CHAPTER XXIV.

ON HIS UPRIGHTNESS AND SINCERITY.

His fear of God and hatred of sin made him so just and upright that neither respect for princes, nor the favour of friends and relations, nor promises or threats, had any influence over him to make him swerve from justice and honour. He was very circumspect in granting favours, for although he was kind-hearted and affectionate, and glad to please every one, yet his upright mind made him firm in refusing anything that was not just, or might interfere with the good discipline of the diocese. He was most strict in adhering to the decrees of reform, and would never dispense with them, even when there seemed to be good reason for it in matters of slight importance, as he used to say " every little helps," " in the end comes downfall." He insisted himself on the exact observance of every rule, however unimportant it might seem, and inculcated the same spirit in his Vicars-General and officials, and thus succeeded in establishing good discipline everywhere. Obedience to his decrees was required from all, and no exceptions were made in favour of great persons, for it gave him great pain when he saw prelates yielding for no good reason and without hesitation to the demands of the laity. At one time a banker at Milan had been arrested for debt, but on his way to prison contrived to escape from the officers of justice and took refuge in a church. His creditors, being in authority, got leave from Rome to remove him from the church to be tried before the secular court. The Cardinal, however, prevailed on the Pope to withdraw the permission, as having been granted without sufficient reason.

When he was reforming the discipline of cloistered nuns, a lady belonging to one of the principal families of Milan begged him to allow her to enter a convent in order to see her daughter who was seriously ill. As it appeared to him that such a concession would be prejudicial to exact observance of the rule, he refused her the favour in the following terms: " The consolation to you would be but for a moment. If you in your position will render a cheerful obedience to the decrees, it will be of great assistance to me in exacting observance of the rule, as I shall be able to make use of your example in requiring strict obedience." By this answer the mother was as satisfied as if her request had been granted. By adopting similar gentleness in his dealing with others, and by reasonable answers, he reconciled them to his policy, although their petitions were refused.

In his ecclesiastical courts he exercised great watchfulness over his deputies, in order that strict justice should be rendered to all. For this purpose he published " Regulations of the Ecclesiastical Court of

the Archbishop," containing all the rules for the ordering of a church court, and prohibiting everything that
might hinder the administration of right and justice.
He forbade all judges and officials to receive money
or any other gift, however small. He would not place
natives of the city in those positions, in order that
no blood-relationship or personal interest or human
motive might lead them from the paths of uprightness.
In this way he maintained in the diocese a school and
tradition of ecclesiastical discipline for future time.
He reaped himself the fruit of his exertions, and
witnessed exact observance among the clergy, greatly
promoted by the example of their fellow-citizens in
their own order.

He was careful to prohibit the members of his own
household from favouring or interfering in matters of
justice.   In order to provide another safeguard for his
tribunals, beside his own care and vigilance, he entrusted
the Visitors-General of the city and diocese with their
supervision.   He often visited the prisons himself
together with the judges of his courts to satisfy himself about the trials and treatment of prisoners, and
thereby greatly helped the administration of justice;
for if he discovered any negligence or failure in any
of his deputies, he took care to remedy it; and dismissed them from their office if necessary, as he did
in the case of one who had accepted a bribe.

As he was held in high esteem by the supreme
pontiffs, by kings and princes, many persons had recourse to him for favours and assistance.   He paid,
however, no attention to such requests if he did not

find them just and reasonable. For instance, when in Rome, he was once earnestly entreated with tears and supplications by a mother to take up the cause of her son, who was in prison, and likely to be condemned to death. Although he was moved to compassion by her affliction, he could only comfort her with kind words, as he found, after inquiry, that it would not be right to interfere with the execution of justice. He acted with so much candour and sincerity towards all that he never entertained them with flattering promises, as courtiers are wont to do, but always plainly declared his mind. Thus, when he could not grant a favour he said so openly, and gave his reason for refusal, in order to satisfy the petitioner, thinking it contrary to his profession to do otherwise. At first, when he was in the service of the Pontiff, his uncle, he gave in to the custom of the Roman court, and used to make promises to all who applied to him, without considering whether their demands were worthy of attention; but finding this practice to be faulty, and that frequently it was not right to grant such requests, he proceeded more cautiously, and only promised what he knew he could fulfil, and this rule he afterwards observed with persons of every condition. Thus, when improper requests were made, he acted with charity, and recommended that such matters should be left alone, especially when he saw men running the risk of sin. Hence his word was more trusted than any bond, and all who obtained a promise from him felt certain of its fulfilment, for he never failed them. He was equally sincere with persons of rank, and the Pontiffs themselves, openly giving them his opinion, and never allowed himself to be influenced by any human respect.

He was eagerly consulted on important matters by princes and exalted persons, because they felt sure of fair and just treatment from him. This was shown by Cardinal Henry of Portugal, who succeeded to that kingdom on the death of King Sebastian, his nephew. When the Portuguese nobles considered that the direct line ended in the Cardinal, and that there would be great troubles in the kingdom through pretenders if he died and left no heirs, they begged him not to hesitate to take a wife, and to petition the Supreme Pontiff for leave to do so, as he was in priest's orders. Cardinal Henry, together with the nobles of the kingdom, knowing the influence the Saint possessed with his Holiness, Gregory XIII., wrote to him to ask for his good offices with the Pontiff. To St. Charles it appeared not to be right to grant to one who was a Priest, Archbishop, and Cardinal, permission to marry —as a bad precedent in the Church, and likely to lead to great disorders—even to ensure the peace and welfare of the kingdom. The Saint openly declared this opinion, and cited the examples of kings and others in the world who had observed chastity in order to be more pleasing to God ; that it was not right to abandon the high dignity of the ecclesiastical state to take a wife in order to secure a successor to a kingdom where lawful heirs would not fail to be found. Should he wish to satisfy his subjects, it would be sufficient to state the facts to his Holiness, without begging for a dispensation, but waiting for his decision, and submitting to it as ordained by God. St. Charles also gave his opinion to the Supreme Pontiff, and the result was that the dispensation was not granted, and the Cardinal persevered in the ecclesiastical state until his death, when the kingdom of Portugal fell to the Crown of Spain.

The Saint held truth and sincerity in so great esteem that he could not endure flatterers. He would not keep them in his house, nor have anything to do with such persons, in order to escape the danger of being deceived by glozing words; and he was desirous that all his own deputies and officials should act with the same sincerity and speak their minds freely. I remember being once present at a conversation between him and one of his functionaries on a matter of business, when the latter said, "I will tell your Eminence candidly what I think on this matter." To which he replied, "Then do you not always speak candidly? Be assured you will not be my friend if you do not speak candidly with your lips what you feel in your heart." He went on to show the hypocrisy of such persons, and the punishment they deserve as the cause of many evils; on the other hand, the inestimable value of candour and sincerity in those who profess to be Christians, who are called upon to give counsel in Church and State.

CHAPTER XXV.

OF HIS LIBERALITY AND MUNIFICENCE.

THE virtues of this great servant of God were so eminent and reached so high a degree of perfection that it is not possible to say which was the greatest and held the first rank. His familiar friends made the same confession, that they could not discern which shone forth brightest where all were resplendent. When Francesco Besozzo was writing an account of him in his history of the Archbishops of Milan, he recounted all the virtues that shone in his predecessors, and found those of more than five and thirty saints united in St. Charles.

He was devout to God, assiduous in prayer, charitable to his neighbour, and munificent in promoting the glory of God. In spending upon himself he was sparing, but always most liberal in laying out his wealth for others, as far as he felt himself allowed to do so. Had not his generosity sprung from the true spirit of Christian liberality, he might have been called prodigal and profuse in expenditure, instead of what he really was, a magnificent despiser of worldly riches. Indeed a man of rank in a letter to

Pope Gregory XIII., on the death of the Saint, said that "in him ecclesiastical liberality had perished."

He left many examples of his liberality in Rome, where he rebuilt churches, and expended large funds on his titular of Santa Prassede. As Archpriest of Santa Maria Maggiore he presented the church with silver candlesticks of great value, besides plate, tapestry, and similar gifts to other pious institutions in that city. His palace and gardens at Rome he gave to Marc Antonio Colonna. When he dismissed eighty persons, gentlemen and servants of his household at one time, he remunerated and perfectly satisfied all.

With a great spirit of liberality he prevailed on his uncle, the Supreme Pontiff, to incur the large expenses necessary for holding the Council of Trent, sending many legates and nuncios to Germany and other parts, in order to bring it to a successful issue. Although the Pope complained of the great outlay, his nephew urged that in order to finish the work of the Council and save an infinite number of souls, all the money in the world was as nothing.

Another great undertaking was the church in the baths of Diocletian, now called St. Mary of the Angels, which he persuaded Pope Pius IV. to erect, together with the Carthusian monastery adjoining. When legate at Bologna he gave himself and collected large sums for the building of public schools. In Rome he was conspicuous for his private beneficence to cardinals and prelates of little means, and for rewarding the merits of artists and literary men much beyond their expectations.

In Milan he provided many churches with all suitable and necessary furniture, and aided in the repairing of poor churches, presenting them with sacred vessels and vestments according to their needs and the urgency of petitioners. For the building of the great seminary, he sold some valuable tapestry. In other parts of his diocese from whence he derived certain revenues, on the petition of the Syndics he spent them upon the churches of the district. To the cathedral he presented precious tapestry of silk embroidered with gold, large silver vases, and many vestments to the value of many thousand crowns. For the canons ordinary he built a beautiful house with a subterranean passage leading to the cathedral, and another building for the minor canons and clergy, in order that all who served the cathedral might live close at hand. He devoted a part of his own revenues to increase the stipends of certain of its benefices, besides maintaining twelve and sometimes fifteen canons in his own house free of expense like brothers. He entirely rebuilt the Archiepiscopal palace with the chapel, stable, and prison, as they now stand.

He brought from Rome and elsewhere many priests and students for the service of his diocese, and provided them with outfit and stipends; the latter he maintained till they had finished their studies and taken their degrees. At his colleges and seminaries he provided poor students with books, clothing, and everything needful to enable them to pass with honour. He introduced many religious communities into Milan, among them the Congregation of the Oblates and other pious institutions, and furnished them in the beginning with everything at his own expense. At Pavia he built the Borromean College, which, in the opinion of those qualified to judge, is one of the most magnificent edifices in Italy. In Gropello, belonging to the diocese, he erected the church presbytery and country-house of retirement for the Archbishops, which has now been finished by his cousin Cardinal Frederic Borromeo. He also made considerable additions to the buildings of the great seminary at the Eastern gate of Milan ; to the house of Canons at the Porta Nuova, where he also erected a house for spiritual exercises, after the model of a Capuchin monastery ; to the college of Nobles, and to the three diocesan seminaries.

He spared no expense in organising his ecclesiastical court, and in appointing pious and learned men to the various offices, and made this See, which before his time had been left to the charge of a single Vicar-General, a pattern and example to other dioceses. To all his officials he gave good stipends with their food, all necessary furniture for their rooms, servants, books, and medicine and attendance when ill, in order that they might be free from worldly cares to devote themselves generously to their duties.

On one occasion he ordered his accounts to be made out to ascertain whether he had a balance or not ; on finding that he was only three hundred crowns in debt he did not seem pleased, and said, "It is a greater honour for a Bishop to be in debt than to have money in the bank, and an Archbishop of Milan ought to be ashamed of owing less than three thousand crowns."

He immediately gave an order for a white pontifical vestment of that value for the cathedral; and by such examples many ecclesiastics were moved to great liberality in rebuilding and furnishing churches and dwellings attached to their benefices.

To princes he showed the same spirit, in making them gifts of objects of piety, and to those in his service; when they quitted it he used to make them presents over and above their stipends. At the time of the plague many resigned their offices from fear of death, but he did not let them go without such gifts, in some cases amounting to two hundred crowns apiece. At the time of the controversy about jurisdiction he spared no expense neither at Rome nor Milan in defence of ecclesiastical immunity, consulting the most learned men, and sending delegates and couriers in addition to his ordinary agents, expressly to attend to that business. In like manner, large sums were expended on the embassy of Father Charles Bascapè to Spain; in obtaining bulls and privileges for different churches and pious institutions founded or assisted by him; in donations for services rendered in Switzerland for the propagation of the faith; and in the maintenance at Milan of the tribunal of the Holy Office, the Father Inquisitor of which had a pension of two hundred crowns a year.

It was his desire to see this liberality practised by all his officials who had the management of his temporal affairs, and dreaded to find avarice showing itself in them. Hearing that his steward was too exacting in his demands for money to meet the expenses of the household, and that he was making contracts which, though not unjust, did not set a good precedent, he gave him a public reproof, because he thought that not only a Bishop himself, but all who acted for him, should be entirely free from all inordinate affection for earthly things, in order to avoid discrediting his office and marring the work of gaining souls. Such an impression was made upon the steward, that he fell ill, it was thought in consequence of the reprimand, and died within a few days.

The Saint had a great abhorrence of controversy and litigation about temporal affairs, and preferred to incur loss himself rather than go to law when he could do so without prejudice to his successors in the diocese. Thus in the beginning of the Pontificate of St. Pius V., hearing that his agents had begun a lawsuit against a Cardinal about a sum of twelve thousand crowns a year, the revenue of an abbey, and that as the judges of the Rota had already decided some points in his favour, a successful result was anticipated in all; he withdrew altogether from the case and gave up his rights and claims to any share in the property; in his own words, "from a wish not to distract his thoughts from the things of God, nor to continue a lawsuit with a colleague in a matter where his own private interests were concerned, involving others in trouble and litigation;" thus setting more value on his neighbour's peace of mind than on any worldly advantage. His action in this suit was highly praised by the Pope and Cardinals, as giving a good example of moderation.

It is evident, therefore, that this virtue was well regulated in him, and was joined to a conscience which never allowed him to go to extremes, but with a single intention led him to the love of God and his brethren. He was never liberal in spending money upon frivolous or useless matters, to gratify taste or sensual pleasure, or even for the advantage of his family : for though he erected many buildings, he never placed one stone upon another, or spent a farthing for the aggrandisement of kindred. He used to say that a Bishop is only the steward, not absolute master of his revenues, and that he cannot expend them liberally upon superfluities or worldly things, but that he is bound to lay them out in the service of God. When he found that from his acts of liberality there arose in his mind a suggestion of self-complacency not altogether reasonable, he always took the opportunity of mortifying himself, in order to attain to a perfect standard of virtue. When a well-dressed stranger once asked an alms, it occurred to him to bestow a large bounty to show his liberality, but recognising in this a feeling of self-complacency, he mortified himself and gave him a sixpence,[1] the smallest sum he usually allowed himself to bestow in alms.

[1] Un quarto di giulio.

CHAPTER XXVI.

OF HIS HOSPITALITY.

THE Saint held the virtue of hospitality in high esteem, as especially befitting a Bishop and commended by the Apostle St. Paul. He kept open house not only for the poor but for pilgrims and strangers of every sort and nation. One of his household was Prefect of the guest-chambers and charged to take particular care that all Cardinals, Bishops, Prelates, and their representatives, who passed through Milan should be made welcome to his house. Information was sent from the inns when such persons arrived, and they were received with their horses and attendants. Since many Bishops came to Milan, either passing through or from a wish to learn how the Cardinal managed his diocese, they were welcomed with great kindness, and those who desired it had every opportunity afforded them of profiting by their stay. He kept them with him for months, took them on his visitations and to the meetings of his different congregations, to his diocesan and provincial synods, showed them his colleges and seminaries with their rules and mode of governing them, and to do them honour asked them occasionally to officiate at ordinations, the consecration of churches and altars, confirmations, and the profession of nuns. If they were poor pilgrims, he gave them money and a horse to take them on their way, to some he also gave clothing, as he had occasion in the case of Bishops from distant countries who were not well provided, on their way to and from Rome, being desirous that they should receive due respect. When they were ill, he had every care taken of them. In the year 1576, a Bishop who came from the other side of the Alps fell ill and died at his house. The Saint administered the last Sacraments with his own hands, assisted him in making a good death with all possible charity, and finally gave him a funeral proper for a Bishop at his own expense.

He was well pleased to have opportunities of receiving princes and secular persons in his house, in order to practise the works of mercy in giving them good counsel and example. Among these were Andrew Bathory, nephew of Stephen, King of Poland, who stayed with him twice with a retinue of more than fifty persons; Pietro Gaetano with five and twenty, when on his way to the war in Flanders; Count Annibale Altaemps; the Gonzagas with numerous escorts, and others. On such occasions the principal men of the city were invited to meet them; and they were received with every honour at bed and board, but without display, their treatment never going beyond the bounds of ecclesiastical simplicity. He received all his guests, even great lords, in the common refectory, where spiritual books were read during the repast, as he was anxious to bring this good practice more into use especially at the tables of Cardinals and Bishops, and owing to his authority the custom was adopted by many.

Visitors from the Swiss Cantons and the Grisons were welcomed with marked affection by the Saint, who wished to re-establish Catholic faith and discipline in the parts where heresy had crept in. With them he used to take food which he usually denied himself, and even wine sometimes, to adapt himself to their customs, in order to win them over to God, whence he could say with the Apostle, "I became all things to all men, that I might save all."[1]

Attracted by his liberality, poor strangers and pilgrims used to come to him in great numbers— Germans, Flemings, English,[2] Scotch, and others, on

---

[1] 1 Cor. ix. 22.

[2] In May 1580, Goldwell, Bishop of St. Asaph, Dr. Morton, Penitentiary of St. Peter's, Fathers Campion and Parsons, S.J.; four Marian priests of the English hospital, viz., Dr. Brumberg, William Giblet, Thomas Crane, and William Kemp; Ralph Sherwin, Luke Kirby, Edward Rishton, priests; Thomas Bruscoe and John Pascal, lay students, the first fruits of the recently erected English college; Ralph Emerson, a Jesuit lay brother, and another not named, were received into his house at Milan by St. Charles, and kept there for eight days. Sherwin preached before him, and Campion discoursed every day after dinner. "He had," says Parsons, "sundry learned and most godly speeches with us, tending to the contempt of this world and perfect zeal of Christ's service, whereof we saw so rare an example in himself, and his austere and laborious life; being nothing in effect but skin and bone, through continual pains, fasting, and penance; so that without saying a word, he preached to us sufficiently, and we departed from him greatly edified and exceedingly encouraged."

After the visit of these pilgrims, St. Charles wrote to Agazzari, the President of the English college at Rome :—"I saw and willingly received those English who departed hence the other day, as their goodness deserved, their way to Rome, seculars as well as ecclesiastics. Milan being conveniently situated on the road thither, there were sometimes as many as thirty or forty in his house, going to the colleges founded by Gregory XIII., for the benefit of those countries, to return thither after being ordained priests, to labour for souls. These both going and returning generally availed themselves of the Cardinal's hospitality, and were helped on their way by him when they lacked means, and furnished with every assistance for the promotion of the faith in their native lands.

As the Saint's liberality became more known, his hospitality increased ; many of the nobility and gentry came on purpose to consult him and ask for spiritual assistance. Although having so much to occupy his mind he was always informed by the guest-master every day about all strangers who were in the house, and never omitted to pay them every attention according to their condition. Notwithstanding a great number of guests, the house was always quiet, and order was kept as if there was nobody more than usual, the same discipline

and the cause for which they had undertaken their journey. If in future your Reverence shall send any others to me, be assured that I will take care to receive them with all charity, and that it will be most pleasing to me to have occasion to perform the duties of hospitality, so proper for a Bishop, towards the Catholics of that nation. Milan, the last day of June, 1580."

St. Charles always showed a partiality for the English exiles. Bishop Goldwell was his suffragan in January 1565, and accompanied him on his entry into the city. Dr. Owen Lewis, Archdeacon of Hainault and afterwards Bishop of Cassano, was his Vicar-General at this time. William Gifford, afterwards Archbishop of Rheims, was his chaplain. His ordinary confessor was Griffith Roberts, a Welshman, and Canon Theologian in the Chapter.[1]

[1] *Simpson's Life of Campion*, p. 111. Records of English Catholics.

being observed in the guest-rooms as was usual among his own household.

The Cardinal was always glad to invite his visitors to join in the spiritual exercises of the house, viz., the prayers, the points of meditation given out every evening in the chapel, and spiritual conferences, in order that Bishops and prelates might be led to observe the like rules in their own houses. At Rome he used to practise the same hospitality; in his residence at Santa Prassede, in 1575, the year of the jubilee, he entertained visitors from Milan, Switzerland, and the Grisons.

At one time the guests in his house became so numerous, and the quantity of provisions for his table brought into Milan was so large, that the collectors of the customs thought that there was some fraud practised, and laid a complaint before the tribunal of the royal revenues. The magistrates begged the Cardinal to see that the customary dues were not evaded, as it was not possible that such an amount could be consumed in his house. The Saint heard them attentively, and ordered the household accounts to be brought for their examination. Upon a minute inspection of the expenses daily incurred for the household and for strangers, it was found that as many as three hundred of the latter had been received in a single month. All suspicion of fraud was thus removed, and the magistrates were much edified by the liberality of the Cardinal.

At one time his stewards finding that the expenses were very great, and that it was impossible to meet them with the income at their disposal, in addition to the abundant alms that were distributed and other extraordinary expenses, brought their difficulties before the Cardinal, with a complaint of the daily increasing number of guests. The Saint called a meeting of the officers of his household to consider the matter, explaining to them on one hand the expenditure required, and on the other the merit and advantage gained by such hospitality, finally asking what was to be done. After various suggestions, he put an end to the difficulty by saying that " it was best to exercise hospitality, because God in His goodness would provide the means." What he had said before to the commissioners of revenue when they hinted that it would be well to put some limit to his hospitalities, he repeated to the steward of his household in the following words, " It is the duty of a Bishop to be hospitable, and to seek to take away or diminish that obligation is to do nothing less than to deprive him of his most precious crown in the sight of God and men."

He was so far from wishing to lessen his expenses in this respect, that during the last year of his life he increased them, for he then gave orders that all the ecclesiastics of his diocese who came to Milan should be received in his house. He had the maintenance of good discipline so much at heart that he was always seeking for means to further it. As he had done everything to promote it in their churches and houses by means of spiritual exercises, by insisting on simplicity in food and clothing, and the like, he was anxious that the same rules should be observed when they came to the city. In order to avoid every occasion of evil, that they might live according to ecclesiastical rule, he forbade his clergy to lodge at inns, and provided a guest-house for them, with every requisite, near his palace. In this he placed a staff of well-qualified men-servants, under good management, so that they lived in the observance of rule, with spiritual reading at meal-times, and had nothing to pay, except for their food, which was a great advantage for the rural clergy. Towards the end of his life he determined to pay all expenses himself, and gave orders accordingly to the steward of his household, Mgr. Antonio Seneca, who opposed the plan on account of its expense. "He had now determined," replied the Saint, "upon this course. The clergy, by this bounty, would become more obedient, and as they did not come to Milan without good reason, they would not stay longer than was absolutely necessary. Being thus removed far from every danger, they would learn from the discipline of this house how to live in their own homes, and would be able to teach their flocks the same observances. He should thus have, as it were, a synod continually sitting, with many opportunities of benefiting the souls both of priests and people. And that, finally, it would lead them to practise hospitality to each other throughout the diocese."

So powerful was the example of the holy Pastor that this custom has now become the rule, the clergy being everywhere welcomed into each other's houses, and in some places innkeepers are forbidden to receive priests.

The Saint had but just made these regulations for hospitality, when our Lord called him to receive his reward in heaven.

CHAPTER XXVII.

HIS CONTEMPT FOR EARTHLY THINGS AND LOVE OF POVERTY.

ɛ Saint greatly impressed the minds of men by
wing clearly that he esteemed all worldly riches as
hing, so that it could be said of him that he had
the smallest affection for them. Although he
d in the world, in the midst of riches and earthly
adeur, yet his life was not inferior to that of a
igious who by solemn vow embraces holy poverty;
ight even be called more perfect, as manifested by
voluntary renunciation of so many benefices and
tes, and of so much wealth, which he looked upon
he dust of the earth. He had so little regard for
iey, that he would not touch or look at it, except
in charity obliged him to carry it about him for
s to the poor; he would not allow it to be treasured
in his house, as unbecoming in a Bishop, and pre-
ed to be in debt rather than to have money in
d.

)ne day a sum of forty thousand crowns was
ight to him in payment for the principality of
ι, which he had sold. He would not so much as

look at the money-bags, but withdrew to another room, and when the legal formalities were completed distributed them among various pious institutions.

Another proof of his contempt for the things of this world, was the little store he set upon his own hereditary estates and castles that are so much thought of by men. When he was deprived of the fortress of Arona, the key of the northern frontier of the state, he could never be induced to apply to the Spanish King for its restoration, and hearing that Pope Gregory XIII. intended to appeal in his behalf, he begged him instead to use his authority in defence of the rights of his See.

Nothing was clearer to his friends than that he had not the least attachment to anything he possessed, but had such an aversion for them that he could not bear to hear them spoken of. When his steward had to speak to him on household affairs, the only time he would discuss them was when he was riding outside the city, and it was almost necessary to force him to speak on such subjects. It was observed that he did not care to visit palaces, beautiful gardens, and the like, even by way of recreation; but if chance or business led him to such places, he would not so much as raise his eyes to look at them. I remarked this myself once when he spent a day at a villa of Mgr. Alessandro Simonetta, a great friend of the Saint, who had served the Holy See in different capacities. It was a delightful place ten miles from Milan, with large and beautiful gardens and walks, fountains and fish-ponds, situated in a plain, but diversified with

s and flowery vales, formed with wonderful art,
t pleasant and picturesque. The Cardinal was
ight through these gardens on purpose to give
pleasure, but all to no purpose, for he would
even turn his head to look at the beauty of the
e; once only he turned to me who was beside
and said, " This is a fine place." He then went
ight to his apartments, and did not leave them till
next morning when he went to say Mass in the
tory in the grounds; he then returned home with-
turning aside for any of its attractions.

Vhen he was at Caprarola, a beautiful place belong-
to the Farnese family, he went straight to the
ns prepared for him, and never left them to look
he fine buildings or delightful gardens. He put
ilence a prelate who begun to praise the magni-
nce of the villa with the words, " We have to build
·lasting habitations and to seek a dwelling eternal
he heavens." [1]

Vhen it was said to him that he ought to have a
len for recreation and fresh air at his palace, like
; of the Bishop of Vigevano, he replied : " A Bishop's
len ought to be the Holy Bible."

'assing on one occasion through Bagnaja, near
erbo, he was asked by Cardinal Gambara to stay
his palace, and was taken by him through his
itiful gardens. He was invited first to look at
thing, then another, but occupied by very different
ights, he made no reply; at length being still
d with questions, " Monsignor," he said, " you

[1] 2 Cor. v. 1.

would have done much better in building a convent for nuns with the money you have lavished upon this place."

With thoughts like these St. Charles, full of a holy conviction of the nothingness of human things, attained to such a state that, as was said by Father Francis Panigarola in his funeral sermon, "he took from his wealth only what a dog has from his master—bread, water, and straw:" thus it was his habit to take of the things of this world bare necessaries only, and of those as little as possible.

Though his house was frequented by princes and prelates, he would not on that account introduce any kind of worldly pomp or luxury in the decoration of their apartments. He wished them to understand that at the courts of Cardinals and Prelates, men may practise the virtues of poverty, humility, and contempt for earthly things, and at the same time maintain the splendour of their ecclesiastical dignity. His guests were more edified by these considerations than if his palace had been adorned with tapestry and costly furniture; and the people of Milan were so impressed by it, that when they saw prelates acting otherwise, they took scandal.

He was so great a lover of poverty that when he found his purse at a very low ebb he was glad to suffer its consequences, and especially to find himself obliged to send and collect alms for the poor when his own means were exhausted. He would willingly have asked alms himself from door to door for the love of God, had his office allowed him to do so. He had the

same wishes at Rome at the height of his grandeur,
for which he cared nothing; and with an income of a
hundred thousand crowns was entirely detached from
riches, and would not allow them to accumulate, but
spent them so liberally upon the Church and the poor
that he was always in debt.

This spirit of contempt for worldly things was engraven on his heart, and he earnestly desired to imbue
his clergy with the same disposition to follow the
Apostolic life, as he hated avarice in them more than
any other fault, and could not endure to see those
who had been consecrated to God desirous of possessing riches, as showing a sordid spirit, and a mind
unworthy of their vocation.

By his decrees he banished divers abuses of taking
money and gifts for the administration of the Sacraments.   He wished his clergy to act from charity, and
not from motives of interest, and took to task all those
whom he found too eager to amass money, even among
his suffragan Bishops, as shown by the following
incident :—

An abbey in another diocese falling vacant, a Bishop
sent a special courier to him to ask his interest with
the Supreme Pontiff that the benefice might be bestowed upon himself, as the income of his See was
small.   St. Charles replied, that in the spiritual needs
of his diocese he would assist him in every way possible, but as to increasing his revenue he would not
say a word, since it was not a matter of necessity;
that his predecessors, some of whom were saints, had
lived upon the income of the See, and that he might

still do the same, adding that the abbey had been founded with another end and aim. He quoted the example of St. Augustine, who begged God to banish from his heart the desire of earthly riches, as powerfully withdrawing the mind from the love of God, and alienating him from spiritual and heavenly things.

He finished his letter by saying that the Bishop might have made a better use of the seventy crowns he had given his courier by spending them upon the poor or on the needs of his church, and so benefiting others as well as his own soul.

CHAPTER XXVIII.

OF HIS ALMSGIVING.

From his early years the Saint felt great compassion for the poor; it might be said he inherited the virtue from his fathers, as it increased with his years. His bounty in Rome, as the Pope's nephew, was great, and abounded still more in after years. After the death of his brother, finding that a large amount of valuable property, statues, antique medals, and paintings had been left behind by him, he sold them without reserve, in order to give marriage portions to poor girls with the proceeds. One morning he assembled a hundred maidens and sent them in procession to Santa Maria Maggiore, where he said Mass, after which, passing before him two and two together, each one received from him her marriage portion. He then sold part of his plate and distributed the money among pious institutions, saying, with the example before him of his brother, dying in the prime of life, that it was foolish to lay up treasure here below where it perishes; far better, according to the Gospel, to lay up treasure in heaven, where it may be enjoyed for all eternity.

On going to reside in his See at Milan he found that many pious institutions stood in need of support; to assist them he sold a quantity of plate and valuable furniture in Rome, Venice, and Milan, to the amount of thirty thousand crowns, which he distributed among them. He also effected a sale of his principality of Oria in the kingdom of Naples for forty thousand crowns. In the apportionment of this sum, Mgr. Caesar Speciano, then the steward of his household, added in by a mistake two thousand crowns more than he had at his disposal. On finding out his error and mentioning it to the Cardinal, in order to make the requisite deduction, he was not allowed to do so, as the mistake was in favour of the poor. So that they benefited to the amount of forty-two thousand crowns. He set aside in addition a regular almsgift of two hundred crowns a month to be divided among such institutions, and appointed as his administrator one of his chamberlains, Giulio Petruccio of Sienna, a man according to his own heart, and very liberal to the poor, the Cardinal having ordered that he should have all he required for their wants. When the procurator often made complaints about his distribution of alms, the Saint paid no attention to them, but said the poor must be attended to when they were in want.

He had also another private almoner to inquire into the necessities of the bashful poor and assist them in secret. He also by the Cardinal's orders was supplied with all the funds necessary for the maintenance of a number of poor persons who were ashamed to beg, chiefly widows and young girls. Occasionally he had to provide for the necessities of people of rank who had fallen into poverty, among whom was Tomaso da Marino, Duke of Terra Nuova. He never sent a poor man away without an alms, and in the absence of his two almoners used himself to carry a purse; since he did not think it right for a Bishop, who is the father of the poor, to allow any one to depart without assistance. Thus the poor had three purses always open to them, while for the service of his house there was only one.

Virginia della Rovere, the widow of his brother Frederic, in her will bequeathed to him a sum of twenty thousand crowns in discharge of certain debts, which sum the Saint immediately transferred to pious institutions, without keeping a farthing for himself. When it happened that the poor were in extreme necessity, as in the time of the famine in 1570, and of the plague in 1576, he considerably increased his alms, also when pious institutions or private persons were in any need. As he never reckoned what money he had in his purse when it was a question of alms, nor consulted the procurator to know what funds were available, relying entirely on Divine Providence for what he required in alms-giving, he often reduced his household to great straits. The procurator wishing to prevent this, begged him to put some limits to his bounty and not to reduce them to such extremities, to which he rejoined, "that as charity had no limits, alms-deeds as the effect of charity should be unlimited." When it happened that there was no money in the house for alms, he used to send to rich persons in the city, there being always a few who would assist him in such a necessity. In the time of the plague it was an edifying sight to see gentlemen going from house to house with bags on their shoulders, like poor beggars. He was wont to have recourse to God in prayer to help him, and had marvellous answers to his petitions, for bags of money were often brought to him, even secretly, by those who did not wish their names to be known. He only reserved for himself his pension from Spain, and devoted the proceeds of all his benefices to alms-giving. When his friends hinted that he had exercised a mistaken liberality in past times, and now had better opportunities of laying out his money well, he replied, that he who gave both the tree and its fruit did much better than he who gave the fruit without the tree. During the plague Mgr. Seneca, his procurator, finding that there were then some sixty or seventy thousand poor people dependent upon him for alms, said that he would have done well if he had kept the sums he had given away, as he would be able to assist so many more. He replied, "that he did not at all repent of having freed himself from much responsibility to Almighty God, and was glad to have relieved himself of the trouble of having superfluous riches, and that a Bishop ought to be content with the endowments of the Church his spouse."

In fine his charity towards the poor was so great that he was often reduced to straits in respect of food and clothing, though satisfied with the barest necessaries, a little bread and water for food, some straw to sleep upon, and the poorest raiment, from his love of

ie spirit of poverty for himself and larger alms for
is neighbour.   When they would sometimes make
im new and better clothes, he would not wear them,
ut used to send them to the Poor Men's Hospital.
[is attendants had great difficulty in inducing him
o put on new stockings or other garments under his
abit as Cardinal, although those he had were all
orn out, so much did he rejoice in holy poverty.   At
is death, he set the last seal to his charities by
cknowledging himself the father of the poor, and
iaking them his heirs, leaving all he had to the great
Iospital of Milan; indeed he would willingly have
equeathed to them his patrimonial estates had it
een permitted by law to do so.   But Divine Provi-
ence did not fail them, for after the payment of all
is debts, there remained a large sum for the Hospital.
)thers were led to imitate his example in this, lay-
ien as well as ecclesiastics, among whom were Cardinal
.gostino Cusano, and his successor in the see of Milan,
rchbishop Gaspar Visconte.

CHAPTER XXIX.

AMONG the gifts bountifully bestowed by our Lord upon the Saint was his love of learning. From his childhood he had a great inclination for letters, and went at the age of fourteen to the university of Pavia, where he applied himself to study with great application and earnestness, heedless of almost all recreation for his body, so that he became seriously ill. When, through the mercy of God, he recovered, he joined to his love of learning a greater spirit of devotion and piety.

When he was in Rome engaged in the most important affairs of the Pontifical government, of which he was the main support, as he was not able to study during the day he used to encroach upon his time of rest at night. He founded the celebrated Academy of the "Notti Vaticane," or "Vatican Nights," a society of learned and religious men, who discussed moral science and sacred literature, in order to avoid idleness and to encourage the pursuit of knowledge. Out of this academy came men who were afterwards distinguished as Bishops and Cardinals.

Mindful of the office to which God had called him—the cure of souls, he applied himself diligently to the study of philosophy and scholastic theology, and in order not to encroach upon the time devoted to affairs of state, often gave but two or three hours to sleep, a wonderful instance of self-sacrifice in one so young and highly placed. He always devoted a set time to prayer, which he never omitted whatever might happen, for it was the will of God that he should set an example to pastors of souls that how much soever they may be occupied, they should never omit the holy exercise of prayer and meditation, as the most efficacious means of arriving at perfection in all their works.

When he went to reside in his diocese, he constantly studied the Holy Scriptures, the Fathers, and ecclesiastical history, generally devoting three or four hours a day to the duty, even when he was engaged in visitations of his diocese or province. For this purpose he used to take with him on his journeys two cases of books, with sliding compartments, that he might be able at once to put his hand on the book he wanted. He used to say that study ought not to interrupt the work of the diocese, which should take precedence of study itself; that men ought to love learning more, the higher the position they hold, but that such hours only should be given to it as remain after all duty has been well done. His learning is sufficiently shown in his sermons, pastoral letters, and the decrees of his various councils and synods. He did not, however, neglect other branches of study, and was wont to say that he who does not strive to gain some knowledge of everything is scarcely worth his salt. I have heard him give learned discourses upon moral philosophy, to which he had devoted much time, subtracted from his hours of sleep. He never at any time neglected reading and meditation, but daily devoted himself more and more to both; so much so, that in the latter years of his life, he spent six entire hours in preparation before he said Mass.

In the acquisition of knowledge he was so quick that he was said to devour books, and would look through a whole page at a glance as it were. His object was not merely to become learned, but to find the best way of doing good to the Church and his neighbours, to restore discipline and save souls. He left his clergy and people a rich collection of decrees and instructions full of wisdom and of the Spirit of God in printed books and manuscript sermons,[1] among which is a "storehouse for pastors,"[2] collected from the Holy Scriptures and the Fathers for the use of priests, wherein we see reflected his burning zeal for the salvation of souls.

From his love for study sprung the high esteem in which he held learned men, whom he favoured in every way and preferred to benefices and ecclesiastical dignities; to this zeal for learning we are indebted for the erection of the public schools of Brera, the founda-

---

[1] Giussano adds "furnished with admirable *trees*," i.e. probably analytical and synoptical tables.

[2] Preserved in the Ambrosian Library of Milan founded by Cardinal Frederic Borromeo.

tion both of colleges and seminaries and of prebends in churches of the city and diocese, and for his decrees for the furtherance of learning among his clergy. He was in truth the restorer of learning, which had been almost extinct in his diocese. Before he came to the See, the ignorance of the clergy was so great that scarcely any one read or understood the Latin language : now by his means, benefices and prebends are filled by good jurists and theologians. He is therefore deservedly called the father and restorer of learning and discipline in the city and diocese of Milan.

CHAPTER XXX.

HIS PRACTICE IN THE BESTOWAL OF BENEFICES.

As to bestow benefices rightly is one of the greatest responsibilities of a Prelate, and tends especially to promote the salvation of souls and good discipline among the clergy, the Cardinal was very careful to avoid mistakes or cause any prejudice to candidates.

Since the Holy See had given him full powers as to all benefices in his diocese, to secure himself against going wrong he first closed the door against every human interest, and would not allow himself to be influenced by the solicitations of any one, however powerful he might be, or however closely related to him, from the great risk of simony, injustice, and other sins. He was known to be so fixed and determined on this point, that no one dared to ask of him any favours whatever for another, since they knew well that it would tend to injure the person recommended. Moreover, he would not confer a benefice on any one by way of stipend for services, as he did not think it was right to use for that purpose " the patrimony of Christ," the name he gave to the revenues of the Church. He is not known ever to have conferred a benefice on this ground, or to have assigned any payment from a benefice to any of his household or officials. Their services and merits he amply rewarded in other ways, either with annuities, presents, or pensions out of his own patrimony, as appears from his last will and testament. He had a great dread of charging benefices with pensions, because he objected to any one deriving benefit from a place in which he did not labour, and because it injured the churches, which could not be well filled when their funds were diminished. Again, because their occupants could not dispense the charity which they owed to their flocks, and it was contrary to the pious intentions of those who had founded or endowed such churches, viz., that their incomes should be given to those who discharged the duties, and not to those who did not serve them. He used to say that a Bishop did not possess the episcopal spirit if he attempted to impose such charges upon benefices with cure of souls, and that he could only do so with good conscience in the case of those priests who have laboured long in their office, and by age or infirmity are incapacitated from further duty.

He laid down these rules for himself and recommended them to his brother Bishops in his Provincial Councils. The smaller titles or benefices also he never gave away from favour or for the satisfaction of others, but when vacant he either conferred them on poor collegiate churches, or on parish churches, for assistant priests, where there was a large population, or united them to other benefices when the latter did not provide a sufficient maintenance for those who held them, or he presented them to qualified persons as a title for orders in his diocese. In case of the promotion of such persons, he required them to resign their first title, for he had great objection to anyone holding more than one, even though the duties were compatible and might be discharged by one person, considering that ecclesiastics were bound to keep themselves aloof, not only from avarice, but even from the smallest attachment to earthly things, in order to be worthy of the love and service of God. It was his endeavour to revive the ancient rule and discipline, that every one should hold but one benefice, of which he set the example himself in resigning all that had been conferred upon him except his archbishopric, and by that means more easily prevailed upon his clergy to obey his decrees. This spirit gained such ground that ecclesiastics who had more than one benefice, were looked upon as wanting in discipline and the fear of God, and begun themselves to be ashamed of being pluralists, since at the synods they had themselves called as holders of one benefice only, and in this way the Saint had proofs of a better mind spreading among them. He was always anxious to assist good candidates for holy orders who were poor and had not the means of studying; and used to confer on them the small benefices, which enabled them to prosecute their studies, and provided his diocese with good priests.

He entertained a great horror of the custom introduced into the Church by those who, in presenting to benefices, merely sought to provide for an individual without regard to the benefit of the flock, which for various reasons might require incumbents of greater prudence, learning, or sanctity. In conferring benefices he always had recourse to God in prayer, in order that he might come to a just decision for the good of souls. When he reflected on the great extent of his diocese, he used to say that he needed many assistants in order to fulfil the various functions of a Bishop, in preaching, administering the sacraments, and making visitations. To supply these needs he founded the congregation of the Oblates, and conferred the canonries and benefices of his cathedral and other churches on men of talent who would be able to assist him in his diocesan duties. He observed the same rule in bestowing the minor benefices, canonries, and chaplaincies on those who could not only fill the offices well, but also assist in hearing the confessions of the people, in directing convents, and in other works of the cure of souls. "A good Bishop," he repeated, " ought not to bestow a benefice for the advantage and interest simply of the person to whom he offers it, but for the good of the Church and the salvation of souls. By this means only could he prevent the malpractices of those who, having got a living, charged it with a pension for themselves and then transferred it to nephews or other relatives who possibly were not able to discharge the duties :—a lamentable kind of traffic in benefices." In his appointments to vacancies he tried to put the right person in the right place —to ascertain the inclinations, temper, and character of those whom he promoted, in order that there should be no unfitness for the special duties of the post.

He once intended to promote to the office of Provost of a Chapter a certain official, who had been a long time in his service.   From intimate acquaintance he knew him to be much attached to his own opinion and somewhat stubborn, and that, in consequence, he might, if well disposed, be of great assistance in the furtherance of discipline or on the contrary greatly injure it, as head of a Chapter.   After reflecting upon it for a fortnight and offering up prayers to God he consulted with his chief advisers, sent for the person and addressed him as follows: " Could I be assured of two things, I should have the greatest possible pleasure in conferring this office upon you: first, that you will not resign it in favour of any one else; next, that you will always do your best to assist the Archbishop of the diocese in the observance of ecclesiastical discipline." To which the other replied: " As to the first, the law of Christ binds me to it, for it is not lawful to dispose of the fruits and enjoy them at one and the same time—to accept the benefice and then to resign it: as to the second point, I would pray God to take me to Himself rather than permit me to hold this office in a spirit of opposition to the discipline and reform in which I have assisted you so long."   The Saint was much encouraged by his answer, and conferred the dignity upon him to his own advantage, and that of his successors.

In this way he selected the most worthy priests for all offices and benefices with the cure of souls, and in conformity with the decrees of the Council of Trent, made all such appointments by *concursus*, or competition, to which he invited those priests whom he thought to be fit candidates. His clergy on their part had such confidence in their pastor that they left all to his good pleasure, well assured that a prelate so enlightened by God would not neglect the deserving, and that those who solicited promotion or canvassed for it proved themselves unworthy and devoid of the ecclesiastical spirit. When he found those who served God out of pure love, and followed his own example in the refusal and resignation of benefices, the Saint felt great consolation because he saw there the hand of God. As he was afraid that he was not carrying out the decrees of the Council of Trent in nominating the clergy for the *concursus*, he referred the question to Pope Gregory XIII., according to his custom where he had any scruple about his mode of acting. The Pontiff commended the moderation of the clergy who had profited so much by the example of their pastor and sanctioned all his procedure.

He had a note-book in which he took down the names of all his clergy who were eligible for the cure of souls, those from his seminaries and colleges forwarded by the rectors, and those in the city and diocese prepared by the spiritual Prefects and Visitors. He divided them after examination into four classes, according to their knowledge and acquirements: the first class comprising those who had made great proficiency in learning, who were promoted to the principal offices and dignities: the other classes embracing those who were inferior in qualifications down to the fourth, on whom he conferred the charges of least importance. He admitted no one to priests' orders who had not gained a place in one of those classes.

When he had to provide for a vacant post, and no one offered himself or was eligible, he summoned the Visitors and Prefects of the city, and after discussing the needs of the particular place and the persons suggested for the vacancy, their theological degrees, age, prudence, moral character, and bodily health, then proceeded to elect the fittest person. Although he had a good knowledge of every ecclesiastic in his diocese, and could call them all by name, yet he never made appointments of himself only, but always took counsel with prudent persons, thinking it quite as necessary to have advice in this matter as in making synodal laws and decrees. When candidates had been thus nominated, all were then examined and the appointment made accordingly, to the consolation of those who were chosen in this way, as elected by God, without any thought or effort of their own.

After being approved by the Synodal Examiners he confirmed the appointment as follows:—"My son, we have not given a benefice to you, but we have given you to the Church; your obligation is, with holy solicitude, to correspond to the duties of your office in the service of God and the salvation of souls. In our visitations of your church, and of yourself, we shall diligently inquire into your conformity and obedience to the decrees of the Holy

ncils.   As prescribed in our synods, we shall
e a pastoral letter to your people in testimony
our piety, religion, and charity.   Go in peace,
may God be with you."

Then young priests did not possess any great
, he gave them places of less responsibility in
beginning, and kept a watch over them; if they
well, he presented them to more important
ges, provided they did not ask for them.   In
way he filled the more important churches with
ified priests, who had already done their work
and deserved promotion, and inspired others
courage to persevere and attend diligently to
duties.   Those who were not promoted applied
iselves to their studies, with a certainty of being
rded according to their merits, avoiding license,
devoting themselves to industry and good habits.
observed the same rules with the members of
household and officials, whom if deserving he
lled among his clergy and appointed to higher
is when he had become acquainted by experience
their character and deserts.   On returning from
visits to Rome he usually brought back with
many ecclesiastics, and he also received them
other parts, and after making trial of their
nments and dispositions in his colleges and else-
re, received them into his diocese, if he found
obedient to discipline, or, if otherwise, dismissed
L

ence it was that the diocese was well served and
inistered with great order and union among the

clergy, so that there never came before his court suits in the matters of resignations or changes of benefices and the like. All placed confidence in the paternal care of the holy Cardinal, and gave no thought to self-interest, but devoted themselves to the observance of order and rule. The Saint used to say, "that the best way of establishing true ecclesiastical discipline is to banish from the minds of priests avarice and ambition, the cause of every kind of corruption; to be guided by merit only, and to provide for churches, not for individuals, in all appointments to benefices."

To crown the charity of the Saint in all his promotions, he allowed no charges to be made for letters of induction, except a small fixed sum for writing and copy, not exceeding a crown, however rich the benefice might be.

Book IX

CHAPTER I.

OF THE MIRACLES WORKED THROUGH THE INTERCESSION OF ST. CHARLES.

To attempt a mere enumeration of the graces and miracles obtained through the intercession of the Saint would be an impossible task. Indeed, there is hardly a family in Milan which has not been visited by the wonder-working hand of the Cardinal. Not only his own diocese but many parts of Italy and other distant kingdoms bear witness to his miracles. Processes were formed in Milan, Pavia, Cremona, Piacenza, Bologna, Pisa, Monferrato, and Poland. In the Cremonese process alone, drawn up by Caesar Speciano, Bishop of that city, we find no less than sixty recorded cases of miracles, and all of importance. The attestations of miracles wrought at the burial of the Saint were upwards of a thousand signed by the persons themselves on whom they were wrought before the Vicar-General of the diocese. The thousands of paintings of the miracles, the great number of waxen *ex-votos* in the cathedral, those in silver

ounting to ten thousand three hundred and fifty in
mber, set like a fringe round the dome, and covering
marble pillars, force the beholder to acknowledge
it the miracles of St. Charles are beyond reckoning.
A few of these have been selected from the sworn
timony in the authentic processes drawn up in
lan and elsewhere by the authority of the ordin-
es for the canonisation of the Saint. They have
en divided into six classes; first, those worked
ring the life of the Cardinal; next, those that
curred at his death; thirdly, those wrought by
iyers; fourth, those that occurred after his burial;
fifth and sixth class, those worked by means of
tures, garments, and other things used by him.

CHAPTER II.

THE terrible risk the Saint ran from the shot of the arquebus has been already related in the Second Book. When St. Charles visited Henry III., king of France, in the territory of Monza, in the year of our Lord 1574, there met him a young married lady (who desired her name not to be mentioned) who had fallen into a grievous state of weakness, occasioned, as far as could be discovered, by the acts of sorcerers and evil spirits. She suffered from constant disturbance of the digestion and disquietude of mind, accompanied by melancholy. She fancied she had swallowed some thorns that always tormented her, and impeded her breathing. She shuddered in the presence of priests and even of her own mother, and when in church could not bear the sight of the Most Holy Sacrament at the elevation in the Mass, and threw herself into various irreverent attitudes. Having endured this malady a long time without having received any assistance from the various medical remedies employed or from exorcisms, upon hearing that the Cardinal was in Monza, she came in the assured hope of being

ored to health by his blessing. And with this
ct, when she heard that he was passing near her
lling, she went out into the street, and kneeling
n the earth got his blessing, and with it thought
received a potent medicine, since she felt herself
ned of strength, and her digestive organs relieved.

then gradually recovered her strength, and her
.th in an instant, without there remaining to her
remnant of her complaint.

.t the close of the plague of Milan, Margherita
tua, wife of Francesco della Guardia, goldsmith,
seized by severe fever and other maladies, that
ed more than six months without any favourable
l, although she employed during this time every
ible remedy. Nay, rather ever growing worse,
was finally so reduced as to be only skin and
e; and she could not turn herself in bed, to which
was confined all this time, and had to be moved
l the sheets; the physicians themselves had given
up as incurable. Being in this wretched condi-
, she many times entreated her husband to obtain
her the Cardinal's benediction, in which she re-
ed great confidence, being sure of gaining her health
eby. He, being well acquainted with the Car-
l, informed him of the bad state his wife was in,
begged him to give her his blessing. The Car-
l promised to bestow upon her his blessing when
assed her house in procession the following Sun-
which was Trinity Sunday in the year 1578.
Saint, on his way to visit the hospital church
ae Mendicanti in the Borgo di Porta Vercellina, in

passing before the sick woman's door (whither she had caused herself to be carried) in the Street of the Goldsmiths, halted for a while· and blessed her with the sign of the Cross, and immediately Margherita found herself strong again, and all pain removed from her back. With very little assistance she ascended the stairs, and finding herself restored to health, returned no more to her bed, but, after taking refreshment, sallied forth from her house and went on foot for a mile at least without assistance along the entire course pursued by the procession, to obtain the plenary indulgence granted those who visited on that day the said hospital. After this she had no other ailments, unless twice or thrice a slight attack of fever of no considerable consequence.

Giovanni Pietro Stoppano, an oblate, now archpriest of Mazzo in the Valtellina, was grievously attacked at St. Sepulchre's by fever, which at last became so acute that he was reduced to the last extremity, and the physicians reckoned him a dead man. The Cardinal, much grieved at the threatened loss of this good priest, transferred him to his own house; serving him with his own hands in his bed with all charity and humility. He also heard his confession and gave him the last sacraments, seeing him at death's door. When on the point of yielding up the ghost, just when the Saint was praying for him, his health was restored to the surprise of every one, on account of the unmistakable character of the miracle. Lodovico Settali and Giovanni Battista Silvatico, two of the principal physicians in Milan, who had charge of the patient, deponed to the case in the process as a certain miracle, besides other witnesses.

Giovanni Battista Berretta of Milan was seized from childhood with a flux of blood from the nostrils, that issued in large quantities six or seven times a day and during the night, for at least the space of two years continuously, without any remedy giving him relief. Whence the poor youth was given up for dead (the more so as an uncle had died of a similar complaint), and had not strength to stand upon his feet owing to the extreme weakness occasioned by such a loss of blood. Reading of the woman in the Gospel who was cured of an issue of blood after twelve years' duration, by touching the hem of our Lord's garment, he formed an assured hope that he would yet recover if he could touch the Cardinal's robes, on account of his being a holy man. Full of this faith, he reverently touched his garments on the second of the Rogation days, about the year 1581, when he was entering in procession into the Church of St. Nazaro in Brolio, and was instantly cured at the hot time of day when the malady was wont to be at its height.

When St. Charles made the visitation of the three valleys belonging to Switzerland, in going from Polegio to Iragna in the valley of the Riviera, on the feast of the Assumption of our Lady, 1581, he had to cross the river Ticino, which was much swollen by previous rains. The Cardinal crossed safely with his attendants, having as guide the Cavaliero Giovanni Baptista Pelanda, a native of the country. The Abbate Bernardino Tarugi, visitor of these valleys, with a Notary,

Giuseppe Cavaliero by name, being the last to cross, were so frightened at the swollen tide that they let their horses drift down the stream into a deep place, in which they would assuredly have been drowned, as they were up to their necks in water. Seeing this, " They are lost," said Pelanda to the Saint ; " God alone can save them." The Saint then turning himself towards them, joined his hands in prayer, and with his eyes raised to heaven, blessed them with the sign of the Cross ; and immediately the horses, as if they had wings, sprung out of the water on to the river bank, and they were miraculously saved from their perilous position.

A youth of about fifteen years of age, son of a poor widow of the parish of St. Simplician at Milan, was troubled by evil spirits for more than a year and a half, and although he had been exorcised from time to time by Father Pio Camucio, a monk of the Cassinese Congregation of St. Benedict, the exorcisms were nevertheless of no avail. Finally, whilst preparing for the translation of the relics of the saints of the above-mentioned church, this Father, having a great opinion of the sanctity of the Cardinal, advised the young man to obtain his blessing on the occasion of this translation, saying, " The Cardinal is a holy man, and I hold it for certain that he will have power to drive out the demons." The young man took this good advice, and throwing himself on his knees at the feet of the Saint, on the 29th day of May, in the year 1582, besought his benediction, and immediately upon receiving it, fell in a faint to the ground, and

r afterwards suffered any disturbance from the
ts.

here was in the convent of nuns of St. Martha at
n, a devoted servant of God, Bianca Lucia Caima,
for a long time suffered from a disorder in the
which troubled her greatly, and endangered her
;, being considered incurable by the surgeon who
ided her, since no remedy benefited her. The
dy proved to be a fistula, from which there was
pious discharge, accompanied by decayed matter,
h all but completely obstructed her sight, and
pelled her many times to keep her bed. One morn-
in the year 1584, this nun heard the Mass of
Charles in her monastery, and inspired by God,
ed the following prayer :—" O God, I beseech Thy
ne Majesty to be pleased to grant me cure of this
of mine, by the merits of Thy servant, if he is
saint we take him for." When she had made
request, she found herself in an instant healed,
t she would not publish the miracle until after
leath of the Saint.

any other cases might be related of cures when
Cardinal visited the sick, such as were those of
cello Rincio, Giovanni Paolo Balbo, and Ferrante
aro, who were cured, the first two of grievous
dies, and the third of a mortal wound received at
ito ; of the Marquis Philip d'Este, who was healed
dangerous vomiting of blood ; of Ferdinand de
ici, the infant Marquis of Melegnano, restored
moment as it were from death to life by a
paid him by the Saint at Melegnano. It was

declared upon oath by Domenico Missalia, rector of the Church of Mezzana, that in his presence the Cardinal, when on visitation, refused Holy Communion to a native of the place, Buschino by name, knowing by intuition that he was not fasting. When the provost spoke to the man on the gravity of such an offence, he found what the Cardinal had learned by the Spirit of God to be the exact truth.

CHAPTER III.

A PIOUS teacher of the confraternity of Christian doctrine, prioress of the School of St. Mauritius in Milan, named Constantia Rabbia, had her right arm disabled for many years, so that she was unable to make any use of it, and was obliged to have it always attached to her neck by a bandage, as incurable. When she heard of the Cardinal's death, overcome with grief through the love she bore him, she began to bemoan herself, and to say "Poor me! I who am aged, disabled, and useless in the world, remain alive, and this holy man is dead, who did so much good to the Church and to his flock. I will pay a visit to his remains, as I trust, if I can touch them with my bad arm, it will be cured by the mercy of God." With this confidence, she went to the chapel where the body of the Saint was lying, and prayed to God, through the merits of His servant, to be healed, touching the body with her disabled limb, and at the same instant was completely cured. Full of joy, she went home, and found she could use it as well as the other in hard work, such as washing clothes, cutting wood, and similar tasks, and that it remained strong and whole till her death.

Ottaviano Varese, a´ Milanese nobleman, much devoted to the Cardinal, found himself confined to bed for three months, together with a constantly recurring tertian fever, which the physicians, unable to cure, pronounced dangerous, or at least taking a long time to cure. When the sick man heard to his great sorrow of the death of St. Charles, and bewailed his inability to pay him at least the homage of accompanying him to the grave, holding for certain that he had gone to heaven, and, commending himself to the intercession of the Saint, he begged for deliverance from his malady, was immediately cured, and was able to attend the funeral of the Saint.

There were in Milan certain pious women who entertained a singular devotion to St. Charles, and went to hear him say Mass and preach wherever he went, and to receive Communion almost daily at his hands, amongst whom was a lady, Ursula Besozza by name, who having refused earthly wedlock, had given herself up entirely to the service of the Celestial Spouse, leading an exemplary and spiritual life in her father's house. God, in order to try her by bodily suffering for her greater merit, permitted her (through long remaining on her knees in prayer) to incur a great weakness in one knee, which became inflamed, and in process of time much swollen, and so painful that she was unable to bend or rest it on the ground. At the death of the Saint she wept for him as a father, saying many prayers for his blessed soul, and followed him to

e grave, desirous not to leave him as long as she
uld see him.   On her return home, feeling no pain
her knee, she found it all sound, the swelling and
flammation having disappeared, while she was intent
prayer for her blessed pastor, without her having
much as asked this favour of him.   She recognised
is cure as wrought by the infinite mercy of God
rough the intercession of the departed Saint, and
joyed freedom from infirmity to the time of her
ath.

CHAPTER IV.

MIRACLES THAT OCCURRED AFTER THE DEATH OF ST. CHARLES.

1. ABOUT the year 1585, a year after the death of the Cardinal, Sister Euphrosina Balcona, a poor Clare of the Convent of St. Barbara in Milan, a devout servant of God, was troubled for a year by a weakness in her left knee, which was inflamed and swollen, so that she was unable to put it to the ground, or kneel even at Mass. She suffered much, and had begun to despair of any remedy, as she found no benefit from them. Whilst she was at church one day saying the Divine Office, seeing all the other sisters upon their knees, and feeling great trouble at not being able to follow their example, she set herself with great confidence to pray to St. Charles, for whom she had a great devotion, to obtain her cure from God. Suddenly she found herself saying to herself, " Kneel down, for you have obtained the grace." She did so, and found that she could kneel without any pain, and that the limb was quite sound. When the Divine Office was over she went to her cell full of joy, and never suffered any inconvenience afterwards.

2. At Pinzano, near Milan, lived a poor countryman named Domenico Provaso, who had suffered from dropsy and fever for eight or nine months. His whole body was swollen and yellow, so that all who saw him were moved to compassion. He was long confined to bed in much pain and weariness, as he was not able, on account of his poverty, to go to physicians. When about to betake himself to the hospital, he was advised to have recourse to the intercession of the holy Cardinal to obtain his recovery. He made a vow to say every day of his life two " Our Fathers " and two " Hail Marys " in memory of the Saint if he obtained his cure. On beginning to fulfil the vow he was sensible of a notable diminution of the malady, and found himself free from fever; and in the course of fifteen days the whole swelling left him, and the bad colour and every other token of disorder, and he found that his original strength of body was miraculously regained, and his previous condition of perfect health. This happened about the year 1591.

3. Sister Archangela Gussona, a poor Clare of the Convent of St. Barbara, mentioned above, had been ill fourteen years with a flux of blood, through the opening of a branch of the portal vein, and although she had taken a great number of remedies they had not done her any good. Losing all her strength, she grew daily worse, and expected from hour to hour to be taken away suddenly, on account of the great quantity of blood that she lost. One day in August 1600, finding herself very ill, she threw herself on the ground before the Most Holy Sacrament, and prayed earnestly to St.

Charles to obtain her cure from the Lord, if it were
good for her, vowing, if she recovered health, to take
him as her especial advocate, and to fast upon bread
and water upon his vigil for the rest of her life.
When she had made the vow she felt a wonderful
joy in her heart, accompanied by a firm confidence
that her prayer had been heard, which was a clear
proof that she had received some grace. Not only was
her malady removed, but she received such strength
that she set herself to work at her usual tasks, and
returned to the observance of the rule as she had done
before her illness. One of the witnesses examined in this
case was the physician, Cesare Bergamio, who attended
the sick woman, and judged her cure miraculous.

4. Agnes Giezzi, a lay sister of the Convent of
St. Catherine of Brera, in Milan, was most devoted to
the Cardinal on account of his having assisted her to
become a nun, and recommended herself every day to
his prayers. She suffered from hernia for nearly ten
years without obtaining any relief. As the malady
increased she knew not what else to do than to
pray to her holy patron more earnestly that our
Lord would give her strength to support it. One
evening in October 1600, she went to bed with
a pain so keen that she could get no rest the
whole night through. Near morning, being unable
to bear it any longer, she sat up in her bed and
earnestly prayed to God and our Blessed Lady to
have compassion upon her, and send her assistance
in her extremity. When she had made this prayer,
she laid herself down, and falling into a doze saw

the Cardinal shining in glory like the sun. He consoled her, and said that she would not suffer any more from that infirmity, and disappeared. At the same moment the servant of God awoke full of joy, as if she had been in Paradise, and finding herself cured, she arose and disclosed the miracle to the Mother Abbess and the rest of the sisters. Quite restored to health, she thenceforth discharged all the duties of community life.

5. John Baptist Brasca, a youth dwelling in the suburb of the Ticino Gate at Milan in the year 1601, suffered from fever, swelling of the body, and other ailments, which increased to such a degree that he was reduced to the point of death, being insensible, his eyes fixed, and his teeth clenched together. From the middle downwards he was cold and dead, and his relations stood gazing upon him to see when he breathed his last, and held him for dead, so that they had already got ready his winding-sheet and warm water to wash his body for his burial. At that moment it came into the mind of Francesco Brasca, the sick man's father, to recommend him to St. Charles, as a holy man who had done many wonderful works. Lifting up his heart to God, he implored Him, through the intercession of the Cardinal, to restore an only son to one who had already lost seven. Scarcely had he made this request when his son recovered his senses, opened his eyes, took food, and quitted his bed altogether in three or four days, and on the eighth was as strong as ever. This occurred in the month of March 1601.

6. Barbara, daughter of Julius Bonaccina, an advocate of Milan, about the month of April 1601 had a serious disorder in her right eye, for which no cure could be found. There issued from it an acrid humour that eat away her cheek, and finally the girl lost her sight. When she had suffered about four months, her mother induced her to pray to the Saint for her cure. Whilst they were saying their prayers together, the girl's sight was suddenly one night restored, and she arose in the morning with her eye so bright that, as her father affirmed on oath in the process, it seemed like an eye sent her from heaven.

7. Sister Angela Antonia, of Seni, a nun of the Convent of St. Agnes in Milan, when about seventy years of age, found herself troubled by a catarrh that took away all her strength. She was unable to dress herself or take off her clothing unassisted, much less to stand or walk, and was therefore compelled to spend great part of her time in bed. When she had suffered for eight years, always going from bad to worse, and deemed incurable by the physicians, she was restored to perfect health in an instant on Saturday morning, the 16th of June 1601, by a vow she made to St. Charles of reciting a rosary in his honour for five days, morning and evening. On the fifth day she obtained a cure to the great joy of the nuns, who went into their chapel and sung the *Te Deum laudamus* in thanksgiving.

8. A young gentleman of Ferrara, who had no devotion to the saints, found himself at Milan on the

course of a journey in the month of October 1601, and seeing in the house of Francisco Moghino, a beneficiary of the cathedral, a portrait of St. Charles, he took the priest to task for setting store by the picture, and uttered certain bad words, blaspheming the Saint. Moghino warned him that he would meet with chastisement for having uttered scandalous words against such a saint, and as he refused to withdraw them, he was presently laid up with a very severe fever, which put him in peril of death. Moghino then visited him in bed, and persuaded him to confess the sin he had committed, and induced him to make a vow, and ask the Saint for restoration to health. Having thus acknowledged and shown his sorrow for his fault, his illness took another turn, and he entirely recovered, and afterwards confessed that Cardinal Borromeo was a great saint.

9. There lay sick at Molena, in the parish of Incino and diocese of Milan, Isabella Porra, a young woman of a respectable family, suffering from a disease unknown to the physicians, who could not make out whether it was consumption or some other malady; and as she grew worse in spite of medicines, was finally considered incurable. After two years' continuance of her malady, she could only lie bent up in bed, growing weaker daily and nearer to her end. When she was about to draw her last breath, a brother of hers who was a priest, Pellegrino by name, seeing her dying, made a vow to take her to the tomb of St. Charles, and place a wax candle of six pounds weight there, to obtain her restoration to health. Presently

there was such an amelioration in her condition that the next morning she arose from her bed, and in two or three days was able to leave the house, sound and well. This occurred on Thursday, the 18th of October, 1602.

10. Virginio Casato, Doctor of Laws of the College of Milan, had suffered five years from colic pains that often assailed him so sharply as to bring him to the point of death. About the month of August, 1602, when the pain was more acute than usual, he had recourse to St. Charles, and promised to place a silver tablet on his tomb, should he be delivered from his malady. Straightway he fell asleep, and saw in a dream the Saint kneeling before a crucifix, in prayer for him. In an hour's time he awoke, free from all illness, filled with great consolation, and never suffered again from the malady, even although he was not so careful in his way of living as before.

11. Angelica Landriana, a Poor Clare of the Convent of Santa Prassede, in Milan, suffered from dropsy for more than nine years. Her stomach was swollen, and pained her so that she could not bear to touch it. She had also severe aches in all her joints, and a constriction of the chest, so that she could hardly utter a word. When she tried to speak she felt such rumbling and gurgling in the stomach, that she could scarcely hear herself speak, and could not breathe, except with great exertion, from asthma, which threatened her life some time or other. She was reduced to such a state of weakness that she was unable to walk without assistance. She was in conse-

quence placed in the infirmary, and was discharged
from the observance of the rule, and given up by the
doctors. Her sufferings made her so restless that she
became a burden both to herself and to the sisters
who attended on her. As God had wrought some
miracles in the convent through the intercession of St.
Charles, she also began to recommend herself to him,
although it seemed impossible that she could be cured
of such an inveterate malady. When she had persevered about three months in prayer to him, and
was not heard, as if angry with the Saint, she
betook herself to St. Raymond and St. Hyacinth,
who had shortly before been canonised, saying to St.
Charles that others would aid her since he, her father,
would not attend to her supplications. In the meantime she heard an inward monitor bid her not desist
from devotion to St. Charles. She began again and
persevered in importunities to him. At length on the
Vigil of the Nativity of our Lady, in the year 1602,
she heard in like manner a voice that said to her, " Go
to the refectory, and join in the community life." It
appeared to her impossible to do so in such a bad
way as she was. Several times during the night she
heard the same voice urging her to go to the refectory,
and also the morning of the feast in the church whilst
she was hearing Mass ; it seeming as if there were
force put upon her, the voice declaring that such was
the will of God. Accordingly she disclosed all to the
Mother Abbess, that she might do nothing without
obedience to her, and the Father Confessor also, with
their permission. At the dinner hour she left the

church and went to the refectory, where she had scarcely set her foot when her malady left her in a moment, and the colour came back to her cheeks. She sat down at table with the other nuns and ate with appetite, and from that time was able to keep the rule, hard as it was. Besides this, by a special grace, there was bestowed upon her by God such a gift of devotion and interior spirit, that she became like an angel, altogether filled with the love of God, and a surprising degree of conformity to His Divine will; together with a most ardent love of the holy Cardinal, on account of his having obtained for her these favours from God.

12. John Baptist Podio, a Milanese boy about eight years, wishing to draw a bucket of water from a well, on the 4th of December, 1602, fell into it head first, and went down to the bottom, where he buried himself in the mud. He called upon the Blessed Virgin and St. Charles, to whom he used often to commend himself, and found himself miraculously borne about an arm's length above the water, without any effort of his own. With his hands resting upon one side of the well, and his feet upon the other, he was then drawn out in safety. The wooden bucket only suffered injury.

13. In the year 1602, two Fathers of the Society of Jesus, Alfonso Vagnone of Piedmont, and John Baptist Porro of Milan, went to the Indies to preach the Gospel to the Gentiles. These Fathers had a particular devotion to St. Charles, and took with them some pictures of him and relics of his vestments.

They embarked at Genoa, going by way of Barcelona, and when they reached the Gulf of Lyons there sprang up a tempest, with a wind so boisterous as to carry the waves sky high. The storm growing worse and worse brought the vessel into danger of shipwreck. When the water was up to their knees in the vessel, the very sailors accounted themselves lost. When the Fathers saw themselves in this peril they had recourse with confidence to the intercession of Cardinal Charles, and together with the whole ship's company prayed to him, and promised to keep a fast for their preservation. In an instant the wind ceased and the sea became calm. All of them then fasted the next day, in honour of the Saint and fulfilment of the vow made.

14. Count Emmanuel Philibert Rotario Severino, Grand Equerry of the Duke of Savoy, was lying in danger of death in Turin, about the month of December, 1602, through a severe attack of fever, that returned many times a day, with pains and vomitings; he suffered moreover from retention of urine, which physicians and surgeons tried in vain to cure, leaving the poor man for dead. Seeing himself without human aid, he had recourse to the assistance of heaven, praying St. Charles to succour him in his need, and made a vow to go and visit his tomb if he recovered his health. The malady then began to subside, and in sleep while all thought him a dead man he seemed to see a certain ray of light that gave him life; and at that moment the bladder was relieved, and the fever ceased in the presence of physicians and surgeons, who

considered the cure miraculous. The Count came then to Milan to fulfil his vow, and to offer at the sepulchre of St. Charles, two silver tablets, a heart of gold, and his cross as knight of St. Maurice of Savoy. He moreover drew up a formal deposition of his cure for the process of canonisation.

15. A master builder of the name of Domenico Brusatore, dwelling in the Porta Vercellina at Milan, entertained a devotion to St. Charles, and began immediately after the death of the Saint to say a Pater and Ave in his honour every day, and kept a portrait of him in his house. It happened in the year 1603, about the beginning of July, that whilst he was erecting a building for Donato Toso at Molinazzo, outside the Porta Vercellina, he was wont to retire for repose at mid-day in a church dedicated to St. James; and one day when he was asleep there, on the predella of an altar, St. Charles in pontificals appeared to him, and bending towards him said, " Brother, go hence, for the church is about to fall." The builder awoke full of terror, still seeming to behold the Saint who urged him to flee. Leaving the church in haste, some persons who saw him, pale as death, inquired of him what had happened. When he related the vision, they would not believe it, not giving credit to it. " What ! " said they, " the church going to fall, not it ! " It seemed sound and strong, and no external tokens threatened a downfall. As he held fast to what he had said, they all turned to look at the church, and at that instant it crumbled to the earth before them, the bell tower falling exactly upon the spot where

Domenico would have been lying, so that if he had remained in the church he would have been buried beneath it.

16. A remarkable miracle was wrought by St. Charles in the city of Pavia, in May of the year 1604, John Baptist Tirone, a child five years old, son of Bernard Tirone, of the parish of St. Theodore, having fallen into the river Ticino in full stream. The child in falling called upon the Saint, who took him in his arms and bore him more than a hundred yards in a quarter of an hour, on the swollen waters, without his suffering any injury, until a boatman, Bernardino by name, swam out into the stream, took him from the arm of the Saint, and carried him to the bank. A great number of people ran to see this marvel, and although the Saint was seen only by the child, it nevertheless appeared to all an astonishing thing that he was not drowned, and that he skimmed the waves so long a time like an empty cask or a bird, the more because there were eddies and whirlpools that would have drawn down a man, even if able to swim well. It was recognised as a miracle, when the mother of the child, running up to see what had happened, began to weep, the child answering: "Do not weep, mother; keep quiet, for I am alive; it is the blessed Charles who has helped me, and kept me up, from being drowned in the river." And when he reached the house he said the same words in reply to Bernard his father, showing him with his finger a picture of St. Charles that they had in the house, before which the child was wont to

recite a Pater and Ave every evening upon his knees, adding: "It was the blessed Charles who helped me and kept me from drowning by supporting me with his arm." And he was able to say that his deliverer was a fine tall man in a red habit; and that when the boatman took him from his arms, the Saint ascended to heaven.

17. Still greater than this was another miracle wrought by the Saint the same year, 1604, in giving sight to one born blind, an event that took place on this wise. Whilst the Cardinal was visiting the sick in the huts at the Porta Romana at the time of the pestilence, he found a plague-stricken woman pregnant at her full time in one of the cabins, with a little boy at the point of death by her side. He consoled the afflicted woman, said the last prayers for her dying boy, and when she had brought forth a female child baptised her with water from a fountain near at hand. As the child was as black as a coal, on account of having been born of a plague-stricken mother, he had her reared on the milk of she-goats, kept for such cases. When this girl had come to a marriageable age, she became the wife of Philip Nava of the parish of San Giovanni in Conca, and on the sixteenth of October gave birth to a male child with closed eyelids, upon opening whose pupils there was found no sign of eyes, their sockets being full of foul matter, that was so abundant that it had to be cleansed every quarter of an hour, or otherwise his cheek would have been eaten away by it. On the second day after his birth, two tumours arose on his forehead, each of the size of half an egg, which much disfigured him and

casioned sorrow to his parents, as they knew that
human remedy could restore the eyes of one who
is born blind. Therefore they did not use any
edical treatment, beyond cleaning away the fetid
atter with a cloth steeped in water. The mother had
great devotion to St. Charles as her particular patron,
d gave his name to her son in hope of his assistance.
e tenth day of November, which was the twenty-
th since the birth of the child, the mother finding
m in worse condition than ever, filled with grief, put
m in the arms of a young woman, her stepdaughter,
med Isabella, as she wished to light the fire to dry
e swaddling-bands for the child. Recommending
rself to the Saint with tears in her eyes, she begged
m, as he had wrought so many miracles for others,
work this miracle also for her son, and give him
ght, since out of devotion they had given him the
me of Charles. Whilst she was making this prayer,
little daughter of hers, four or five years old, Clara
name, knelt upon the ground, and began to say:
O mother, mother! the Blessed Charles has given
s blessing, and little Charles has opened his eyes."
e mother turned immediately to her boy and saw
m with sound and good eyes, without any sign or
ark of infirmity; they all filled with joy knelt down
return thanks for so great a favour. The mother
ent to the tomb of the Saint to repeat her thanks-
ving, and took with her her son with an offering of
o silver eyes, the little girl remembering that the
rdinal was clad in crimson when he made his
pearance in the air, and was able to show the way
which he gave the boy his blessing.

CHAPTER V.

MIRACLES WROUGHT AT THE TOMB OF ST. CHARLES.

GIOVANNI GIACOMO LOMAZZO, a gentleman of Milan, entertained little or no affection for the Cardinal, because he had excluded the first Sunday in Lent from the Carnival, and cancelled certain standing payments to some workmen of the cathedral, who did not deserve them. Blinded by passion, he went so far as to murmur against him publicly, and censure his acts. Although frequently taken to task by his friends, he nevertheless did not cease to give vent to complaints, and persisted in his ill-will, even after the death of the Cardinal, although he perceived that all held him to be a saint. God allowed this man to suffer from a severe attack of erysipelas in the legs, which became so ulcerated and painful that he might have described himself as having his purgatory in this life. He was reduced at last to so bad a condition, after five years of suffering, that he could hardly support himself on his feet. Being advanced in years, he was only able to leave his house for a short distance, even with a stick. A great quantity of matter constantly issued from his wounds, which defied the remedies of the best physicians and surgeons in Milan. The night of the Vigil of St. Thecla, the 22nd September, 1587, he suffered such pain in his limbs that he was unable to obtain any rest; full of impatience, he arose from his couch in the morning earlier than usual, and went limping with his stick to the cathedral, which was near, to hear Mass. As he knelt at the tomb of St. Charles, a sudden access of pain having come on, he cried: "Oh, most blessed soul of Cardinal Borromeo, if thou art now in heaven, and enjoyest eternal happiness with the saints, I humbly pray thee to obtain for me, from Almighty God, the use of my limbs and my whole body." When he had made this prayer, seeing a Mass about to begin, he went to hear it, and when it was over he found himself sound and well. He threw aside his stick, filled with astonishment and infinite thanksgiving. He returned home to impart to his wife and family the miracle that had taken place in his person. Taking off his shoes and stockings, he showed that the wounds which they had seen little more than a half-hour before fetid and full of decayed matter, were cured and made sound, with scarcely any mark or scar left. The poor old man then shed such a torrent of tears that he could not utter a word from remorse, at having murmured against the Cardinal; and to unburden his conscience, he summoned those with whom he had been wont to speak against the Saint, told them of the miracle that had taken place, and showed them his limbs whole. He drew up an authentic account in writing of all that had happened, in the order of its occurrence, that the memory of it might be perpetuated; which manuscript has since been used in the process of canonisation.

2. Antonia de Geroni of Torre Vecchia, fourteen miles from Milan, being harassed by evil spirits, and maimed by them in the thigh and right knee, could hardly move, and was only able with much difficulty to take any food. As no medicines were of any avail, she prayed to God to assist her in her poverty, being unable to work to gain her living. In this prayer, there came to her the inspiration to have herself taken to the tomb of St. Charles, in the hope that he would free her from her maladies. She was taken to Milan in the month of July 1594, by one of her uncles in a car. On her arrival at the tomb, she fell to the earth in a swoon; two hours after, having returned to herself, she rose to her feet, and found that God had delivered her from her lameness, from the evil spirits, and from every other malady. She rendered due thanks to God, and to her holy intercessor, and returned to her dwelling on foot, in good health, in which she continued during the three years that she survived.

3. An Ursuline nun of Milan, whose name is advisedly suppressed, was troubled by cruel assaults of a demon, who tried her with a thousand immodest lures, appearing to her frequently both by day and night in visible form, now as a handsome young man, again as a friar, or a priest. As the nun, who prayed to God, made a courageous resistance, according to the advice of her ghostly father, the tempter frequently proceeded to blows and violence to gratify his lustful

intent. The poor nun was so afflicted by all this that life was a burden to her, and she prayed God that He would deliver her from her long and perilous martyrdom, which she had now suffered continuously for four years. Her confessor, who did not know how to assist her, exhorted her to recommend herself to St. Charles, and to visit his tomb. This she did, and having gone there five Fridays, the last day, which was the Vigil of the Annunciation of our Lady, the 24th of March, 1601, whilst she was eagerly entreating aid from the Saint she heard a voice, which said to her : " Go home, daughter, for thou art delivered from all thy affliction ; " which filled her with an infinite joy and consolation. And she then found, in fact, that this voice was not a dream, because from that hour the demon never again appeared to her.

4. A serious infirmity, occasioned by small-pox, manifested itself in the eyes of Martha, daughter of John Ambrose de Vighi, in Milan, in the ninth year of her age. The humours flowing into her eyes gave her extreme pain and greatly impeded her vision. The malady went on increasing for the space of six years, so that she lost her sight, and remained blind without hope of recovery, it being necessary to lead her about by hand. When the poor girl, at the age of fifteen, had been about seven weeks in this state, believing that she would never again see the light of heaven, she heard say that the Cardinal wrought many miracles, and this gave her hope of having help from him ; chiefly because he appeared to her three or four nights in a dream, in purple robes, with a red beretta upon his head, and told her to go

to his tomb and her sight should be restored to her. She related these visions to her mother, Flaminia, who had her taken by her mother-in-law, Camilla, to the tomb of the Saint on a Friday morning in the month of June, 1602. Having stayed there three hours in prayer, whilst stooping to kiss the stone placed over the tomb, she received her sight, so that in raising her head she saw those present perfectly; and to her joy found her eyes as good as they were before the setting in of her malady.

5. Angelo Monte, dwelling near the cathedral square in Milan, had a daughter, Margherita, who was lame in both feet, the soles being bent inwards towards the legs, and the upper part of the foot used as the sole, and they were, moreover, knotted together like two clubs in a monstrous manner. The girl grew up until the age of six in this state, her parents being unable to find any cure. Milizia Verga, mother of the child, hearing of the great miracles of the Cardinal, full of hope of obtaining the cure of her daughter, sent her to visit his tomb and light a candle there, when behold! her right foot was made straight. The girl, assured that a complete cure would follow, returned and lighted candles again there, and thus the other foot was straightened in the same way, nor did there remain the smallest token of her previous defect. This was in the month of June, 1601.

6. In the month of October 1601, Giacomo Antonio, son of Venturino Taveggio of Bruzzano, near Milan, fell dangerously ill, of a complaint that swelled his stomach out of measure, rendering it as hard as a

ne, with pains so sharp that he was brought to
ith's door.   The poor father, who was present, seeing
it there was no longer any hope of his son's life,
ommended him to St. Charles, and made a vow to
:e him to his tomb if he recovered.   Suddenly the
.lady took a turn, the disease left him, and when the
her carried him the next day to the tomb of the
int, he was entirely restored to health with manifest
ns of a miracle.

7. In the following month of November, 1601,
:re came to the shrine Francesca de' Crespi, an
suline nun of Vigentino, near Milan, who was
own and valued by St. Charles during his lifetime,
account of her spirituality and fear of God.   For
e years she had suffered from the falling sickness,
1 once, when engaged in prayer, she was overtaken,
ling to the ground half-dead, when the Saint
peared to her, vested for Mass, and giving her his
:ssing, exhorted her to be patient, because God
uld always give her something to suffer.   He assured
r of deliverance from her disorder, as she should
ver more be troubled by it.   The nun recovered
isciousness in about a quarter of an hour, filled with
much consolation that she could not refrain from
.rs ; she forthwith disclosed what she had seen to
other member of the community, and from that
ie began to keep the fasts as well as to eat and
.nk as she could not do before.   Though she suffered
more from the falling sickness, other disorders gave
r opportunities of exercising patience as the Saint
:dicted.

8. Francesco Cuniolo, a page of Alessandro Secco, a juris-consult of Milan, when twelve years of age had suffered for five years from stone, with such pains as almost to kill him, especially at the changes of the seasons; the malady increasing, and no remedy giving him relief, the surgeons determined to use the knife. Whilst waiting for the operation, the boy had recourse to prayers to St. Charles, promising to visit his tomb for eight days, and to keep a candle burning there, in hope of cure. On the seventh or eighth morning he obtained the favour he requested, the stone having miraculously disappeared, although it was at a change of season, when the malady usually increased. This occurred in the month of October, 1601.

9. Girolamo Baio of Albairate, near Milan, had for four years been a paralytic, deprived of motion in all his limbs, and was like a corpse in appearance, being only able to move his tongue. He had consequently to be fed and carried like a child, and was so wasted as to look like death itself. No medicine availed him aught, and his disorder was adjudged incurable by physicians and surgeons. There came to the ears of this poor invalid the fame of the miracles of Cardinal Borromeo, and he kindled with the desire of recommending himself to him. On making a vow to have himself carried to his tomb, he found himself on a sudden so much better, that he began to be able to move his hands, which gave him the hope of obtaining a complete cure, if he could accomplish his intent; he was taken thither in a litter, made for the purpose, and on entering the cathedral he found such strength

miraculously restored to his limbs that he raised his
arm and doffed his hat.   On reaching the tomb he felt
yet greater benefit, and gradually recovered his strength
and original state of health, in the month of June,
1602.

10. Father Sebastian of Piacenza, a Capuchin, had
for the space of twenty-four years so serious and
capricious a malady, that the physicians owned that
they had never seen a similar case, some calling it
a falling sickness, others a palpitation of the heart.
He was tormented by fits, that seemed almost to
pass beyond the bounds of nature, no part of his
body remaining free from spasmodic movements, by
which it was agitated with such vehemence that the
poor man dashed his head, hands, and feet against
the wall, not being able in any way to check himself,
the fit lasting three and four hours; and if his hands
or head were touched, the pain increased.   This
shaking and concussion of the body made him at
times gnash his teeth like a soul in torment, the
fits attacking him as often as six times a day, leaving
him senseless and out of his mind.   After having
been attended for a long time by many physicians
in various cities and places, and having taken in
vain a great number of remedies, it was pronounced
to be an unknown malady, for which no remedy
could be found.   The good Father hearing of the
miracles wrought by the Blessed Cardinal, went to
visit his tomb, on reaching which he remained for
some time hesitating whether he ought to pray for
entire recovery or for patience in enduring his suffer-

ings, as he had found by experience that they always increased after asking for the intercession of the saints. He felt himself urged to pray to the Saint for recovery, and when he had done so, he felt such consolation that he was sure his prayers had been heard. Accordingly, he became so strong and well that he immediately resumed his fastings and penances, in which he has persevered to the present time, St. Charles having appeared to him in sleep, and assured him that he had heard his prayers and delivered him from his malady.

11. Beatrice, daughter of Antonio Francesco Crespi, silk merchant in Milan, was attacked by disease in the right breast, penetrating to her shoulder, accompanied by such pain that she had difficulty in breathing. A great wound penetrated into her body, a quantity of corrupt matter issuing from it, with such violence as to extinguish a lamp. Hence this girl, at the age of fourteen or fifteen, was crippled in her right side, her very bones being out of their proper place. The physicians and surgeons not being able to discover any cure, she grew continually worse, till she was not able to move in her bed, in which she had lain for five months; and it appeared certain that she would die, because there was such an abundance of matter issuing from her shoulder, and from the corrupted parts, that not being able to discharge itself completely by a silver tube placed in the wound, the poor girl had to spit it out by her mouth, with sickness and an intolerable stench. The father of this girl conceived a great hope that the Cardinal Charles

ıld restore her to health, and made a vow to send
three Fridays to his tomb on foot to pray for this
our.   Despite her being in the state already de-
.bed, he sent her thither one Friday in August,
ɔ3, accompanied by a servant, in order to assist her
walking and taking rest, so as to reach the tomb of
Saint on her feet.   The vow being thus fulfilled,
girl gained such strength that she went herself
the tomb to say her prayers, and returned home
l, with the wound miraculously healed, so that the
·er tube fell out of it, and she recovered her natural
dition of health.

ı2. Domenica, daughter of Pietro Nabone, of
·argna, in the mountains of Porlezza and diocese
Milan, was deprived by illness of speech and
:ion, so that she was like a corpse, except that
breathed and had not lost her eyesight.   In this
dition she continued for fifteen months, applying
ɑy remedies without any benefit, and was reduced,
ɔugh long continuance of the malady, to nothing
skin and bone.   The rector of the Church of
·lezza induced the father of the girl, when about
ılve years of age, to take her to the tomb of St.
ırles and to recommend her to his prayers.   He
ɔrdingly put her into a basket upon the back of an
and took her to Milan, about the 10th May, 1604.
ıen she had been twice carried to the Saint's tomb
was cured, so that she was able to return home
foot.

ı3. Giovanni Battista Marone, of the parish of St.
:hael, in Milan, had a daughter Giovanna, who,

upon being set free from her swathing-bands, was discovered to be lame, without proper use of feet and legs, and having the joints of those limbs so loose that she could turn them inwards, and throw them up to her shoulders before and behind, so that it seemed as if they were attached by the skin only without any bones. Being thus unable to keep herself upon her feet, she moved from one place to another by jerking herself upon her haunches along the ground, with a piece of leather beneath her. In this condition she grew to the age of four, her parents being unable to find any cure for her, on account of her having been born so affected. When the child heard her mother Veronica say that she would take her to the tomb of St. Charles, she began to show great joy; and some of the servants of the house teasing her, and saying to her that it was a shame for her to go to the tomb of the Saint, sitting in that way upon the ground, she answered them that she would soon go on her feet, being certain that she would be cured. Her mother, therefore, had her carried thither in July, 1604, and herself accompanied her; and when she was placed on the ground at the tomb, she made an offering of a black velvet dress. Whilst Francesco her son was saying Our Father and Hail Mary for the child, she began to pray herself to the Saint, and feeling her limbs knit together, she raised herself from the ground, and getting behind the enclosure of the tomb, full of joy on account of the strength she had gained, began to call out, "Mother, mother, I am on my feet," showing her that she had actually the use of them, and that St. Charles had cured her as she hoped. Having thus regained the use of her limbs, she succeeded in two or three days in learning to walk, which before she had never been able to do.

14. In August, 1604, there came to the tomb Giulia Milliavacca, of Pavia, who had suffered from quartan fever six years, and in the fifth year found herself also possessed by spirits. She sought the aid of Saint Charles, and obtained release from the fever; and as the evil spirits still remained after many sacrifices had been used in vain, she paid another visit to the shrine on St. Bartholomew's Day, and before she left was completely delivered from her affliction.

15. Margherita de Simoni, servant of Doctor Ottavio Bonamico of Pavia, was sick of a fever, and having in the course of eight months taken many medicines which did her more harm than good, discovered that she was possessed by evil spirits. Having made frequent use of exorcisms without any improvement, through hearing of the cure of the aforesaid Giulia she came to visit the tomb of the Cardinal, where, having invoked his assistance, she found herself delivered both from the fever and the evil spirits, on the Feast of the Decollation of St. John the Baptist, August 29, 1604.

16. Antonia, daughter of Michael Ughetti, of the parish of St. George in Milan, owing to illness, laboured under so great a weakness in the loins and back that she could not without assistance raise herself on her feet if she were lying down or sitting. This malady lasted for four years together. She was one

night inspired with the thought that if she visited the tomb of St. Charles, she would be cured. With this hope she went there early in the morning of the 27th day of October, 1605. On reaching the shrine, not venturing to kneel down from her fear of not being able to get up again, she heard an interior voice bidding her kneel down, as she would find no difficulty in rising again. She then knelt down, and having said two rounds of the Rosary to obtain her recovery, still doubtful as to whether she would be able to rise, she took hold of the iron rail surrounding the tomb; but the voice bid her rise without assistance, because her prayer had been heard. Making the attempt, she found herself entirely delivered from that infirmity, and from that time enjoyed the use of her limbs.

I may mention, in conclusion of this chapter, that Julius Cæsar Coiro, a jurisconsult of Milan, went to visit the tomb of the Saint in company with Giuseppe de Regi, on the 20th of Octobor 1601, in the evening, when they both became sensible of a fragrant odour, like violets in spring-time. They were much astonished at this, and inquiring for its source, found that it could only come from the tomb itself. Doctor Coiro deposed himself to this circumstance in the process of the canonisation of St. Charles.

CHAPTER VI.

MIRACLES WROUGHT BY MEANS OF PICTURES OF THE SAINT.

WE have already spoken of the veneration paid to pictures of St. Charles even before his beatification, not merely by the common people, but by princes and great men in all parts of Christendom; and not without reason, as God has wrought miracles by means of them, notwithstanding that these portraits differ not a little from his real appearance, no one having succeeded in exactly representing him, because he never would sit for his likeness. Some of them, indeed, are exceedingly inexact, and very far from resembling him.

1. I will first relate some wonders wrought on the 15th of June, 1601, by means of a little picture of the Saint possessed by the nuns of St. Agnes at Milan. Sister Radegunda Poliaschi, of that convent, who had one of these pictures, gave orders for it to be covered with glass, to keep it with greater care, as the portrait of a great friend of God. When taken in at the convent the glass was seen to be overspread with a thick film, so as to obscure the whole figure of the Cardinal. When one of them endeavoured to remove it she was not

able to do so, either with her pocket-handkerchief or tunic. Whilst many of them were standing looking at the picture, the film cleared away from the glass, and rising through the air, and then gently sinking, left on the glass the figure of a heart; it then rose again and settling on the picture in three separate parts disappeared, the glass remaining clear and transparent. The nuns were much astonished, not knowing what these signs might mean. The miracle of Sister Angela Antonia de Seni the next day,[1] and at the end of eight days the occurrence of two other miracles made them believe that they were indicated by the picture, and that the heart signified the paternal affection that St. Charles ever bore to their convent, for which, during his life, he had such regard that he, by authority of the Holy See, took the direction of it from the Regulars to himself, in order to bring it into a better state of discipline and observance. This reform he effected, to the great benefit of the souls of these servants of God, although at first they were averse to such a change, and resented it, from not being aware of the benefit they would receive. This was perhaps the meaning of the film that covered the picture of the Cardinal, viz., that the holy intention of the Saint and the advantage they would derive from the change of direction were hidden from them.

2. Sister Candida Francesca, a professed nun in the convent of St. Agnes, was overtaken by an attack of fever that occasioned her pains in different parts of her body, with strong epileptic fits, that contracted

---

[1] Vid. chap. iv. 7.

right leg at least three inches, and so weakened
that she could neither stand nor walk, but was
ipelled to lie constantly in bed, and it was neces-
ɿ for her to be carried by two or three nuns when
had to move, and she was hardly able to sit on a
ir. Cramp, weariness, faintness, and unconscious-
ɕ came upon her; and this weakness lasted more
n twenty months. Though she was under the care
the principal physicians of Milan, yet she got no
ef, and was looked upon as incurable. A serious
ɪck of fever then ensued with a troublesome cough,
ch took away her voice, so that she could hardly
heard by her confessor. Hence it was the opinion
he physicians that she had only a few hours more
ive. Hearing of the miracle that had taken place
the person of Sister Angela Antonia of the same
vent, she entertained the hope that she too might
ɪin her cure from the holy Archbishop. She
refore sent the chaplain to his tomb to pray for
, and it was observed that at the very hour that the
ɛst was praying for her the cough left her and the
ɛr diminished, although the pain in her crippled
b and in her breast and head so increased that she
ught herself dying. Thinking that her end was
ɪe from the severity of the attack, as she had near
bed the picture of St. Charles, spoken of above,
had herself carried to the little altar to ask his
yers upon her knees; but being unable to support
self, just as if her legs were made of tow, she was
en back to bed, where on Friday, the 22d June,
ɔɪ, as she was holding the picture in her hand,

with her eyes fixed upon it, she begged him for restoration to health. After having said an Our Father and a Hail Mary, with a lively hope of receiving help from the Saint, she felt a fresh current, as it were, running through her veins, and especially in the crippled limb, that gave her internal consolation, and at the same time she was sensible of an extension of her knee-joint and cessation of pain. Her body at the same time regained its vigour, so that she left her bed to run to the church and return thanks to God, not remembering in the joy of her heart that she was clad only in her night-dress; but on being reminded of this by the sister who waited on her, she put on a tunic, and so went barefoot from her cell to the church, where all the nuns assembled with glad voices and tears of joy to sing the *Te Deum* round the cloister, in company with their sister, so happily restored to health, who then proceeded to visit every part of the convent, even to the topmost dormitories, finding herself stronger than she was before her sickness. She immediately began to observe the rule and carry on the work of the convent, as God bestowed upon her a strong interior spirit of courage and love. These graces she has ever since employed to the glory of God, her own benefit, and that of the community.

3. Two days after, viz., on the 24th of June, there followed another miracle in the neighbouring convent of St. Maurice, wrought upon the daughter of Bernardo Casato, a physician of Milan, Paola Justina, who had been eight years and a half confined to bed by paralysis of the arm, thigh, and right leg—half, in fact, of her body—

so that she could not move without assistance, or even raise herself to a sitting posture in bed, having completely lost all power of motion and sensation; so that if she were pricked with needles in those parts she felt no pain, and no blood flowed, just as if she had been dead. Her affected limbs exhaled a fetid odour; one leg was longer than the other, with no sign of circulation in it. She suffered also from headache, falling sickness, and fits, in which she hit herself with such fury that two strong nuns could not hold her. Three or four of the best physicians of Milan attended her as though she might have been a queen or empress, as they themselves deposed upon oath in the process, and they could not have done more. Having heard of the two miracles wrought at the convent of St. Agnes, she began to recommend herself to the Cardinal, and having his picture brought to her room, she made a vow, and determined, with the permission of the Mother Abbess, to give clothing to some poor women in imitation of the abundant alms bestowed by St. Charles. On the Festival of St. John the Baptist she was carried to the church in firm confidence of obtaining her cure. When she prepared to received Holy Communion, she was unable to raise herself up to the grill at which Communion was given. It therefore became necessary for the priest to enter the nuns' choir to administer to her. She was then carried back into the cell of a lay sister, the thought having suggested itself to her that the Saint would heal her in a cell and not in the church. Upon entering it, the paralysed arm gave a crack as if the bone had been broken across. Having been carried back to her bed, she continued full of hope of recovery. About ten o'clock of the same day, supported by two nuns, with the picture of the Saint before her, she applied it to her face, making a short prayer with great eagerness of mind. Immediately her strength was restored to her, with wonderful interior consolation. Finding vitality restored to the limbs that had been dead and torpid, and that her leg had recovered its natural dimensions, she rose upon her feet and went into the church to return thanks to God, all the nuns assembling there with tears of joy to sing the *Te Deum*. Little by little the blood returned to her veins; some small degree of weakness remaining in her feet and arm, which soon gathered strength. And she then learned again the Our Father and other prayers, which had escaped her memory owing to her maladies.

4. Cancer attacked the left leg, from the knee to the ankle, of Aurelia degli Angeli, wife of Antonio Cabiato, of the parish of Santa Maria Beltrade, in Milan, who had holes in her knee a finger deep, and a large one in her heel, from which three pieces of nerve were removed. Her leg became so putrid that the barber cut away from it pieces of flesh so fetid that he himself all but fainted. The sick woman endured this infliction for more than three years, together with constant fever, remaining great part of the time in bed, and no medical treatment availed her, for she grew worse and worse. Her malady being reckoned incurable, it was thought

that she could not last much longer. She began then to recommend herself to St. Charles, as she had a picture of him in her chamber, beseeching him that, as he had wrought other miracles, he would deign to hear her also. She made a vow to visit his shrine, and to burn a wax candle there, and felt herself much better, seeming to be raised from death to life. This was about two o'clock on a day in the month of June 1601, and the following morning she found herself as well as she ever was. The fever had ceased, her wounds were cleansed and healed, and, moreover, her limb, that had shrunk from contraction of the nerves, grew to its original length. In two or three days she became quite strong and well, with evident token of a miracle.

5. Clara de Boccoli, wife of Giovanni Tomaso Bordigallo, of Cremona, suffered from severe pains in the head, accompanied by fever. She became so ill that she kept her bed constantly, without being able to lift her head from the pillow, owing to her pains, and her sight had grown very dim. She could not taste her food, and was, in a word, as bad as could be, deriving no benefit either from the corporal or spiritual remedies that were applied. Finding herself one day, after two months' suffering, at death's door, she sent to summon Father Giovanni Antonio Gabuti, a clerk-regular of St. Paul, superior of St. Vincent's Church, who used to heal the gravest disorders by blessing the patients with a medal, upon which was imprinted the likeness of St. Charles. She was blessed by him with this medal, imploring the

intercession of the Saint with special prayer, and obtained deliverance from her malady on the 3d of August 1601, rising from her bed in half an hour stronger than she was before her illness.

6. A poor old woman of Cremona, aged sixty, of the name of Catarina de' Bignoni, owing to a severe shock she had received from a fall, was so maimed in body that she could not stand on her feet nor walk without assistance, as the bones of her left side were paralysed. The remedies she took did not benefit her, and in despair she considered herself as incurable. Having heard of the miracles wrought by the blessed Cardinal in Cremona by means of his pictures, she felt for three nights a strong inspiration to get herself blessed with one of these medals in order to recover her health. One morning in August, 1601, she went limping, supported by two crutches, to the Church of St. Vincent, where, having confessed her sins with humility and true confidence in the intercession of the Saint, she blessed herself with a medal stamped with his image, belonging to the Father Superior mentioned above, and in the very act of benediction she seemed to feel a great joy and a loosing of her whole frame, so that she raised herself to her feet without pain or difficulty, and leaving the crutches, without which she was before unable to move a step, in the hands of the Father Superior, she went stoutly twice round the church, and rendered due thanks to God and the holy Cardinal for her restoration, and afterwards returned home in good health, to the astonishment of her neighbours and acquaintance.

7. Sister Maria Elizabeth de' Borghi, professed nun of the Annunciation in Cremona, was for the space of twenty-two years subject to severe hysteric attacks, with convulsions two or three times a day, of such vehemence that the united strength of many persons was not sufficient to keep her in check, and no remedy could quiet her. She was reduced to such a state that she understood nothing, and could not frame an answer to any questions. Her body swelled, and became like death, the physicians concluding that the malady was beyond remedy, as she had never derived any benefit from an infinite variety of medicines during the long time that her illness had lasted. The fame of the miracles of St. Charles having reached the ears of the patient, she began to entertain a devotion towards him, and to recommend herself to his intercession, asking him for her restoration to health, if it were for the good of her soul; and she made, moreover, a vow to offer him an image of wax, and finally was blessed with his image by the Father Superior of St. Vincent's, when she felt an inexpressible joy, as if she were an altogether different being; and the pains that she had suffered three days continuously ceased, and she was completely cured. This was on the Assumption of the Blessed Virgin Mary in the year 1601.

8. The same year at Bologna occurred the following four miracles in the convent of St. Mary of the Angels:—The prioress of the convent, Sister Agostina Bonfilia, had suffered for two years severe pains, and it was the opinion of the physicians that she had internal ulcerations, and that the malady was incur-

able, because no medical treatment ever benefited her. With much faith she had recourse to the intercession of St. Charles, and was blessed several times with his image by the Mother Vicaress. At the last benediction she felt within herself much interior consolation, and was cured.

9. Sister Angela Lodovica Gozzadina, Mother Vicaress of the convent, suffered for a year from a troublesome headache, with disorders of the stomach and body, that troubled her much, as she was not able to join in the exercises of the community; she had come to the point of giving up drugs, because they did her no good. She then had recourse in prayer to the Cardinal Charles, and on being blessed with his image, there entered into her heart a wonderful sense of joy, and she was cured: so that she went to the Church the same day to the Divine Office, and was not any more troubled.

10. Sister Jacoba Bocadella for six and thirty years suffered from hernia, accompanied by much pain. Having never found any cure, she was freed from her infirmity and cured by having herself thrice blessed by the Mother Vicaress with the medal of St. Charles, while she invoked his aid, no sign of her malady remaining upon her.

11. Sister Serafina Minganti, fifty years of age, had suffered from childhood with headache, so that she could not hear or say the Divine Office in choir, and could speak only with difficulty. Her malady continually increased, so that at last she fell for two months into troublesome fits, with contraction of the nerves and faintings, so

that at times she did not know where she was. The physicians finding it impossible to cure her, her malady was judged incurable. She was told by the Prioress that if she were blessed with the medal of Cardinal Borromeo she would be cured. As owing to the severity of her malady she could not apply her mind to prayer, she went over to the choir, where she heard Mass. After praying to St. Charles to obtain from God her restoration to health, she was blessed with the medal and recovered.

12. Anastasia de Maggi, in Milan, had been for thirty-six years harassed by evil spirits, that gave her so much trouble that her life was a constant martyrdom. During that time she never found any relief, though she had frequent recourse to exorcisms, and to the intercession of various saints, making for this purpose many journeys on foot to holy places. She at last recommended herself to St. Charles, and made a vow to visit his tomb every day for fifteen days, and to say there a Rosary and five Our Fathers each time. After practising this devotion for eight days, on Friday evening the 23d of November, 1601, whilst she was in her house at prayer before an image of the Saint, the demon tormented her so that she fell half-dead to the ground, and after having lain there the space of two hours, she arose free, and has never since been troubled.

13. Angela Paola Bottigella, wife of Giovanni Paolo Emanuele, apothecary in Pavia, was afflicted with gout, accompanied by fever, with such severity that, of all parts of her body, she could only move her tongue. After eight or ten days of this suffering, at

the time when the pain was very great, she turned to a picture of St. Charles hanging near her bed, whilst Lelio Francesco de Medici, her son, was reading to her the life of the Saint. Fixing her eyes upon it, she earnestly prayed the Saint to obtain for her from God the power at least of joining her hands together in prayer, like his own in the portrait. This she said because she was then unable to use them at all. She then felt a certain faintness, as if all her powers were failing her. Afterwards there came upon her a wonderful consolation of spirit, and all her pain and malady ceased. Finding herself well, she rose from her bed, and having returned thanks to God and the Saint her intercessor, she began to go about the house, and perform her duties as if she had never been ill.

14. Melchior Bariola, of Chignolo, in the district of Pavia, when about five years of age, suffered so badly from hernia in his left side, that his life was despaired of. He had been taken by his father, Jerome, in vain to all physicians and surgeons of Milan, Pavia, Piacenza, and Lodi, but grew worse instead of better. One day his mother Agnes leaving him in bed until evening without the band that was used for him, the boy suffered so severely that she found him at the point of death, swollen up like a balloon, with his intestines gone down to his knees. The poor mother having done all she could without avail, seeing him in extreme pain, about seven o'clock at night on the 18th of April, 1602, knelt down before a picture of the servant of God, to which both she and her son had great devotion, being accustomed to

ay a special prayer before it every day. She implored
he Saint to intercede with God, either to take her son
rom the world, as she could not endure seeing him
suffer so much, or else to obtain his cure. When she
had made this request the child fell asleep, and
waking after three hours full of joy, called his
mother and said, "Mother, are you asleep?" When
she had replied in the negative, he added, "Do you not
know that our Cardinal has cured me?" And when
she inquired how he had done it, he put his hand on
his side and said, "He did it so with his hand on
which he had the glittering ring," showing how the
Cardinal had touched him. The mother took the
candle and found the boy quite well. Think of the
joy she felt, and the thanks she returned to God and
to the blessed Cardinal for such a favour! The boy
told how the Cardinal, in his red robe with his beretta
upon his head, had appeared to him in a dream, when
he touched and healed him.

15. Gianuario Foresti, apothecary in Bergamo, had a
son on the 13th of February, 1604, who was subject
to a falling sickness, owing to fits that attacked him
soon after his birth so severely that the nurse, from
her experience of such maladies, thought that the child
would be unable to walk, and told the father so,
bidding him have patience. The sixth day the usual
fit came on, turning him quite black in the face, and
was so severe as to deprive him of life, his father and
mother and a third person seeing him give up the
ghost, and change to the colour of one dead. They
touched him after he had expired in various parts of

the body, and found him quite cold, with the tokens of actual death. The father, who was very devout to St. Charles, and kept his picture in his chamber, knelt before it, and entreated him with great fervour that he would raise his dead son to life, making a vow to go on foot and visit his tomb and pray there, in firm confidence that God would grant his request. Finding that the child was really dead, he went to a shop to get the wax for his burial, and then renewed his entreaties to the Saint, repeating the vow; and such was his faith, that God restored his son to life, to his joy and consolation. He came to Milan to fulfil the vow, where he had the miracle registered in the process. Although the child was dead only about two hours, the circumstances are such as do not permit doubt of the miracle, because at his birth he was so weak that the nurse held it certain that he would never be able to walk, and afterwards the witnesses saw him fall into his usual fit, and presently yield up the ghost in the very same way that his father and mother had seen their other little children die. These are the words of the father, who, as being a man of judgment practising the trade of an apothecary, may be believed to have had acquaintance with similar attacks:—" *When the said child was in the arms of my wife I saw him expire, and he remained without feeling, without life, and deprived of his natural colour, like a daughter of mine who died a little before with the same symptoms.*" These are the words of the mother:—" *I saw that the said child was half-dead, turning grey and black, but in a short time he became pale and dead, and departed this life, and I saw him draw his last breath just as I have seen two others of my children die ; and I touched the nose, feet, hands, and pulses of the said child, and I found that he was cold and without sensation"* A matron, Jacoba de Aldegani, deposes to the same effect in the process, saying that she saw him die and draw his last breath, being quite cold and frozen. Moreover, the boy after this attack suffered no more, and became so robust that he seemed to exceed the ordinary strength of his age, as if supernatural strength had been given him by Heaven.

CHAPTER VII.

MIRACLES WROUGHT IN POLAND BY MEANS OF A PICTURE OF ST. CHARLES, EXTRACTED FROM THE PROCESS DRAWN UP BY THE APOSTOLIC NUNCIO IN THAT KINGDOM.

1. A SEVERE illness attacked the Countess Anna Miskowski, of the family of the Marquis of Mirow, and wife of John Branicki, Count of Ruiscza, captain of Biec and Niepolonicze, near Cracow in Poland. She entirely lost her natural strength and the use of her hands, which were inflamed and contracted so that she was unable to make use of her fingers, being on that account obliged to be dressed and undressed, and have even her bread cut by others. Beyond this she suffered severe pains that allowed her no repose night or day, and she often desired that God would call her to Himself rather than permit her to endure so intolerable a punishment. The malady was considered incurable, because during the space of eleven years she had tried many remedies, procured not only from Poland, but from Italy and other countries. Though she had recourse also to prayer to God and to the saints to whom she was particularly devoted, nothing

l her any good, but she became worse. Therefore
ere remained for her nothing further to do than to
ay God for patience, which she did with many tears.
happened then that her servant, Giovanni Rinaldi,
nt to Bologna, his native place, upon business, and
on his return to Poland a portrait of St. Charles
is given him by Sister Felice Riaria, a nun in the
nvent of Corpus Domini, to take to the Countess, in
e hope that she might by its means get her hands
red. She received it with reverence on her knees,
d having placed it in her chamber, said her prayers
fore it when much troubled with the pain in her
nds, in hope that the Saint might aid her, as
e had heard of his sanctity from those who had
own him in life. At the end of six weeks, on the
stival of All Saints, in the year 1604, having been
acked by the pains in the hands with more severity
an usual, she prostrated herself, with abundance of
irs, before the picture, uttering these words, " Holy
rdinal, pray for me ; I am unworthy to be heard ;
tain for me, a poor sinner, mercy from my
sus ; I fear by impatience in my pains to bring
wn on myself the anger of God." Hardly had
e finished this prayer when she felt all pain
ddenly cease, and the contracted fingers regained
eir powers. She immediately acquainted her hus-
nd with the signal favour she had received from St.
arles ; and the report rapidly spreading through
e district, such was the concourse of people to see the
raculous picture of the Saint, that to satisfy their
votion it was placed in the parish church dedicated

to the Ten Thousand Martyrs in the chapel of St. Anne, with two silver hands in memory of the miracle. Many persons from other parts, afflicted by various infirmities, betook themselves to the servant of God for aid before his picture, and were heard by him with a succession of graces, in which the King himself had a share, as the Queen wrote to His Holiness Paul V., as may be seen from the following letter, written by the auditor of the Apostolic Nuncio to Monsignor Antonio Seneca, Bishop of Anagni :—

Letter of Giovanni Maria Belletto, Auditor of the Apostolic Nuncio in Poland, to Monsignor Antonio Seneca.

"Most illustrious and reverend Lord, I send your most reverend Lordship a copy of the letter which the Queen of Poland has written to His Holiness in the matter of the canonisation of the Blessed Charles, towards whom the people of this country, so far as I can understand, continue to manifest daily greater devotion. The King himself also having been during the past months grievously afflicted with toothache without finding any cure, was recommended to the prayers of the Blessed servant of God by the Queen, without cessation of the malady. Recourse was made to him a second time by the Queen, together with the lady who had been cured of the numbness in the hands. Whereupon his Majesty having turned on his bed, fell asleep and awoke cured of his pain, for which he returned thanks to God and to the Saint.

Wherefore I, who have a particular devotion to the blessed Cardinal, have brought this matter to the knowledge of your most reverend Lordship, who served him upon earth and now venerate him in heaven. Wherewith I humbly kiss your hands. From Cracow, 10th May, 1608."

The following is the letter from the most Serene Lady Constance of Austria, Queen of Poland, from which the devotion entertained in Poland for St. Charles, and the miracles there wrought by him, may be understood:—

"Most Holy and Most Blessed Father, kissing the blessed feet of your Holiness, I recommend myself humbly to your prayers. For some time the sanctity of the Blessed Carlo Borromeo, Archbishop of Milan, approved by many miracles that followed his death, has been celebrated in this kingdom, and the report continues to increase and spread especially among those who implore his aid in these distant parts. It would take too long time to record the numerous examples of it that occur here. I have myself recognised his intercessions as displayed towards the King, my husband, who a short time since made public acknowledgment of having received a cure of a severe malady from the Blessed Charles. Knowing, moreover, that this holy man when alive used to bear a particular affection towards our house of Austria and to the Polish nation, I frankly confess that I have such a veneration for him that I should be glad, in union with all Christian people, that the Catholic Church should inscribe him in the catalogue of the saints, as precious in the sight of God; and for this end, therefore, I beg to make my humble supplications, in order to join with the majority of Christian princes, whose devotion leads them to urge the same request to your Holiness, sure as I am that you will be happy by your decree to raise to the altar of the Church the holy Cardinal, whom you have known in life as a great light of the Apostolic College and of Italy. For the rest, I desire your Holiness a long and prosperous life, and recommend myself to you in the Holy Sacrifice and the prayers you offer up to God. Given at Cracow the 22d April, 1608."

Pope Paul V. having heard of the miracle of the Countess Anna, desired that it should be formally drawn up. Letters were therefore sent to Monsignor Francesco Simonetta, Bishop of Foligno, Apostolic Nuncio in that kingdom, with orders to collect the necessary proofs. The following miracles with their proofs were added by that prelate:—

2. The blessed Constanza of Mirow, sister of the Countess, and of the Grand Marshal of the kingdom, a nun in the convent of St. Agnes in Cracow, had an infirmity in her eyes that almost entirely deprived her of sight. Although for a whole year every possible remedy was applied to her, she never gained any benefit. Having heard of the miraculous recovery of her sister, she went herself with great faith and hope to visit the picture of St. Charles in the Church of the Ten Thousand Martyrs. Whilst she was engaged in earnest prayer to the Saint, her sight was completely

restored to her. In memory of this she placed two eyes of silver as a votive offering on the picture.

3. Adrian Lubowicki, a gentleman of Skontinki, was deprived by illness of the faculty of speech. After having for a long while taken various medicines to no purpose, he heard of the miracles that had taken place before the picture of the Saint, and accordingly went with faith and devotion to visit it. Whilst on his knees before it, he miraculously recovered his speech, in evidence of which he made an offering of a figure of silver.

4. Marina, wife of a blacksmith of Niepolonicze, about the Christmas of 1606 having given birth to a child, had a severe attack of fever accompanied by dropsy, so that her face and body were swollen to a monstrous size. In this condition she continued six months, and at last was at the point of death. Having recommended herself to the intercession of the blessed Cardinal Borromeo, she became better, and was taken to visit his picture, and recovered her health, returning to her dwelling without any assistance, to the astonishment of her neighbours. This occurred on the Feast of St. Anne, the 26th July, 1607.

5. Albert Krupiella of Niepolonicze had suffered for five months great pains in his head and body. As his malady increased and no cure could be found, he paid a visit to the picture of the Saint, and was healed.

6. Sophia Ligocka, a lady of the household of the Countess Anna, fell sick of a tedious fever that lasted the greater part of a year, and no medical treatment

did her any good. She was cured after the Countess had prayed to St. Charles for her restoration to health.

7. Elizabeth, wife of Sigismund Miskowski, Marquis of Mirow, Grand Marshal of Poland, in the year 1606 suffered so much from toothache during fifteen days that she thought she should go mad or die of it, as she was not able to rest either by day or night. Having had recourse to human remedies without success, she made a visit to the picture of the holy Cardinal and was cured.

CHAPTER VIII.

MIRACLES WROUGHT BY MEANS OF CLOTHING AND OTHER THINGS USED BY THE SAINT.

VEN in his lifetime the clothing and other articles
sed by the Saint were held in reverence. The people
ed to touch his vestments with their rosaries and
eep the sticks he had carried in his journeys, and
hey were wont to look upon the rooms in which
e rested at night as sacred; as was done by Signor
Luzzago at Brescia and Count Paolo Camillo Marliano
it Pogliano, who made an oratory of the room which
:he Cardinal had occupied in his house, as he thought
t unbecoming that the chamber which had been honoured by the presence of such a saint should be used
'or profane purposes. He decorated it with paintings,
ind put up the following inscription :—

QUID MIRARIS SACELLUM EX CUBICULO EFFECTUM.
P. CAMILLUS MARLIANUS ET JULIA MARTINENGA
OPTIMA ET AMANTISSIMA EIUS UXOR
REVERENTIAE CAUSA ERGA B. CAROLUM
ILLUD COMMUTARUNT NE PROFANUM HABERETUR
QUOD OLIM TANTUS ANTISTES IN OBEUNDA DIOECESI
NOCTURNA COMMORATIONE CONSECRAVIT.[1]

---

[1] " Marvel not to see a chapel instead of a guest-chamber.
P. Camillo Marliano and Julia Martinenga, his wife,
have reserved from profane use
and dedicated to the Blessed Charles
this room, in which that great prelate lodged
during the visitation of his diocese."

Some persons also used to preserve the knives which he had used and the bread which was left at table as a cure in sickness. Others, even in his lifetime, kept his garments with great devotion as precious relics, as well as articles that had in any way touched his body, his tomb, or any likeness of him.

Even heretics, from their high opinion of his sanctity, have busied themselves to obtain and preserve objects of this kind in memory of him. Sigismund Curtius, a Lutheran of St. Gall, being once in the house of Ambrogio Fornero, saw in the hands of the latter's wife a little bag stained with blood, that she had found in a stocking of the Cardinal when mending it after his return from the pilgrimage to Turin.[1] When he heard that this bag had been beneath the foot on which the barber-surgeon had performed an operation, Curtius begged for it with great importunity. "What do you," said the lady, "who are a Lutheran, want with it?" "I have a great devotion," replied he, "for this man, whom I consider to be a saint on account of the good works which I have myself seen him perform, and have heard of from the testimony of others. In memory of him I wish to keep this article stained with his blood." He accordingly obtained and kept it as a precious treasure.

Many persons held in great veneration holy water that had been blessed by him, and preserved it to use in sickness, because it was found to have great virtue not only against sorceries and evil spirits, but also in healing bodily infirmities. It has been taken even into

---

[1] *Vide* Book V. chap. v. vol. 2, p. 39.

Spain by persons of consideration. A single example of cures wrought by such blest water is here given.

1. Ursula Cavalla, a noble lady of Milan, had a daughter, Catherine, who, at the age of a year and a half, suffered from soreness and eruption. After the malady had continued the space of six months, and no cure could be discovered, it was then miraculously healed by the application of this holy water.

Such relics are not held in great estimation by the common people only, but also by kings and princes. The Catholic King, Philip III., preserves with great reverence a small portion of the Saint's hair-shirt, which Father Diego de Torres of the Society of Jesus brought him from Milan; his wife, Queen Margaret, keeps as a treasure a chasuble that was sent her by Cardinal Frederic Borromeo. Her mother, Maria, Archduchess of Austria, possesses part of an alb used by the Saint, which she was so anxious to obtain that she wrote to the Archpriest of the cathedral to ask for it, and expressed herself extremely grateful for the favour. Frederic Borromeo presented the rochet in which the Saint was buried to Carlo Emanuelle, Duke of Savoy, who, in token of veneration, received it publicly in the Metropolitan Church of Turin, in presence of the Apostolic Nuncio, the Archbishop of the city, and of all his court, and placed it in the same repository over the high altar, in which are preserved the most holy winding-sheet of our Lord and the body of the glorious martyr, St. Maurice, Captain of the Theban Legion, in order to give it an honourable place. No less token of reverence was exhibited by Christiana,

Grand-Duchess of Tuscany, for one of the pontifical gloves in which the Saint was buried. When Cardinal Frederic sent it to her, she received it in the presence of her court all upon their knees. It was then given to the princes her sons to be kissed; and she exhorted them to have St. Charles as their special patron, and placed it on the altar of her oratory in a beautiful casket.

The Grand-Duke Ferdinand, her husband, esteemed the relic so highly, that he told the Abbate Giovanni Battista Besozzo, who brought it, that he valued the gift more than the addition of another province to his states.

Foreign princes also have been conspicuous in reverence for the Saint, and all memorials of him. At Gratz, in the year 1607, the Archduke Maximilian of Austria, brother of the Emperor Rudolf, in the presence of several princes of Germany, presented the Archpriest of Milan cathedral with precious vases of silver in return for a small portion of one of the albs formerly used by the Saint.

His brother cardinals and prelates, it need hardly be mentioned, valued and treasured up these relics in proportion as they remembered him well in life, or were acquainted with the still recent traditions of his sanctity. Cardinal Cæsar Baronius knelt down to receive a stole that had belonged to St. Charles when presented to him by Marc Aurelio Grattarola, the superior of the Oblates of Milan, and would not touch it, but struck his breast as unworthy even to hold so precious a relic in his hands.

Pope Paul V. himself, when he conferred the See of Anagni on Mgr. Antonio Seneca, hearing that the rochet he was putting on the Bishop-elect had been one used by the Saint, kissed it with great devotion, and preserved with equal reverence a portion of the alb in which he was buried, presented to him by the same prelate.

As persons in high places are not in general easily moved to value such objects, we may without doubt conclude that God has been pleased to show that Charles was a man after His own heart by inspiring them with such veneration for him, and bestowing the power of driving away disease and infirmity on mere contact with things that he used.

A few instances of this may be here cited.

1. Maddalena, wife of Ottavio Bonamico, an advocate in Pavia, was seized with the pains of premature child-birth, from which she suffered for twenty-four hours without alleviation or power to bring forth her offspring. Almost driven to despair, one of the Cardinal's stockings was brought to her, which she took into her hands while she devoutly asked his prayers, and forthwith without difficulty gave birth to a female child, who survived a day and was baptized. This occurred about a year after the death of the Saint.

2. Clementia Aresa, wife of Prospero Crivello, of Milan, was near her time of child-bearing, when she was attacked by pains so severe that she gave herself up for dead. The infant lay transversely in her womb some twenty days, and she did not feel any quicken-

ing, and the ordinary time for bearing was past. Hence the midwife herself held the case desperate, but Clementia, full of faith, placed upon her body a shirt of St. Charles that her husband kept as a relic, which had worked miracles already in cases of child-bearing and sickness. A boy was brought to birth, but with head black and swollen, and other signs that he had not long to live. They therefore baptised him immediately, and gave him the name of Charles, in memory of the circumstances of his birth. The child survived and completely recovered from his disorders. This happened the 18th day of June, 1588.

3. Clara Mondui, wife of Giacomo Filippo Calerio, was with child in Milan, in the year 1593, and in great peril of life, because for eight days she found no rest. Her body swelled to such a degree that she seemed ready to burst, and her skin yielded in several places; thinking she would assuredly die, she recommended herself to the intercession of St. Charles, one of whose letters[1] was brought to her by her husband, who placed it on her neck, in hope of assistance from him who wrote it. As she knelt down to say a prayer, she gave birth, without difficulty, to a male child, whom the father had to wrap up in his own mantle, as there was no time to call for other aid.

4. I cannot here pass over in silence the cure wrought in myself, unworthy as I am, in July, 1600, by means of the holy Cardinal's hood, which I have ever held in veneration, as a relic of a saint.

---

[1] This was written to Girolamo Arabbia, Canon in Ordinary of the cathedral.

in bed afflicted by gout, from which I have
[many years, in the joints of my right hand.
in was increasing from the humours flowing
nto the parts, and at last became intolerable.
ig the assistance of God, of the Blessed Virgin,
the saints, I bethought myself of this treasure
I had in the house, viz., the Saint's hood or
L I placed it with faith on the hand, and at
st touch my pains began to abate, and soon
ceased.   For three days the humours descended
il, and yet I was free from pain, a manifest
of favour bestowed by God by means of the
y which others also have been aided in sickness.
tance, a lady of the parish of St. Carpoforo, of
y, had been lying with extreme pain and at the
 life three days and three nights in childbirth,
t being able to bring forth her offspring. She
t forth her child without any pain, when this
ad been placed upon her by her parish priest,.
meo Alchisio, then its possessor, from whom I
rds obtained it.
Dorothy, wife of John Baptist de Rè, of Pavia,
ick of fever, accompanied by severe pains, and
ger of death, applied to her body the stocking,
mentioned, of the Cardinal, with the fulfilment
ow made to him.   She recovered her health, to
at joy and consolation.   This happened on the
ay of May, 1601.
Sister Candida Agudi, a poor Clare of Santa
le, of Milan, had been three years and five
s upon her bed sick of a tertian fever, which

seemed incurable, the physicians, considering her case desperate, merely tried to keep her alive. She was reduced so low that she could not lift up her arm for the physician to feel her pulse. She looked like a skeleton, and had the smell of a corpse. Her skin, at the same time, was peeling away from her flesh, owing to putrefaction. In her last days, convulsions setting in, the last Sacraments were administered when she had almost completely lost her voice, and was not able to raise her head to receive the most Holy Eucharist. Being about to breathe her last, a poor old garment which had belonged to the Saint[1] was put on her while she asked for his prayers, making a vow to fast upon bread and water on the day before his anniversary. By means of miraculous strength from heaven she blessed herself with the garment, and rose from her bed, restored to health, and rid of her complaint. She went into the church to return thanks to God and say the "Te Deum" together with her sisters, who shed tears of joy to see the marvels wrought by God in their convent at the intercession of their own founder. From that time forward the nun thus cured was able to keep the rule. This occurred on St. Peter's day, 1601.

7. In the same convent, Sister Beatrice Besana had spit blood for many years, and was brought so low that she could hardly move in her bed, in which she had lain two years and a half. She was not able to say the "Our Father," and indeed could hardly utter

---

[1] Called by himself "his own" *la sua veste*, as distinguished from that of his office. It had been given to the convent by Fr. Lodovico Moneta after the death of the Cardinal. See vol. ii. pp. 388, 411.

ι word, and had been given up by the physicians, but
was cured by applying the same garment to her breast
and recommending herself to the intercession of the
Saint in the beginning of July, 1601. She was afterwards able to keep the rule, from which she had been
excused for many years.

8. Mansueta Crivella, lay sister of the Convent of St.
Augustine in Milan, for four years suffered from fever,
with pains in the head and stomach, and from weakness
of sight. The physicians could do nothing for her,
and despaired of her recovery. On the 21st of July,
1601, she heard that a handkerchief of the Cardinal's
had been brought into the convent for the benefit of
another sister who was sick, and knowing that the
Saint was wont to work many miracles, she said
within herself, "If I could have this handkerchief,
and apply it to my stomach and my head, I think the
Blessed Charles might cure me." She went to the
cell of the other sick woman to fetch it, but not being
able to get the handkerchief, she took the paper in
which it was wrapped and placed it in faith upon her
stomach, making a vow to fast on the vigil of St.
Charles, to keep his feast as a holy day, to recite on
it the office said by the lay sisters twice, and to have
a Mass said in honour of the Saint. She went to bed,
slept well during the night, and in the morning rose
perfectly well, and began to do her work in the convent
with new strength.

9. Francesca de Crespi, of Vigentino, previously
mentioned,[1] was attacked by a severe fever which

---

[1] Vid. p. 510.

brought her to the point of death, having lost her speech, and taken nothing for three days. Bernardino Borrone, the parish priest, having come to give her the last Sacraments, took from a reliquary hanging on her neck a piece of the Cardinal's beretta, and cutting off some threads of it gave them to her to drink in a spoonful of broth. Though a short time before the sick woman had not been able to take anything, yet she swallowed this relic without any difficulty. Those who were present recommended her to St. Charles with special prayers, and afterwards the priest anointed her, finding a foul sweat upon her like a corpse. When Francesca had taken the relic, she found herself strengthened internally, so as to be able to move without assistance, and her speech was restored to her so that she made the responses to the priest, who was anointing her. When she had received the holy unction she felt no pain, asked for food, and was ready to get up from her bed ; but as the priest would not allow her she sat up, quitting it altogether the next day in good health. This took place on the thirteenth day of October, 1601, an anniversary which Francesca always commemorated in honour of the miraculous grace she received.

10. Giulia di Ada, wife of Ludovico Busca, of Milan, in the year 1601, was afflicted by pains in the side and stomach, accompanied by vomiting, having tried in vain various remedies for three or four days. A hair-shirt of the Cardinal's, that was preserved as a relic in the great hospital of Milan, was placed on her stomach. As she invoked his assistance, she felt her

pains removed, a sensation like so many stings taken from her body, and her strength restored in the course of three-quarters of an hour.

11. In the month of March, 1602, Ursula Sarona Cassina, of Milan, was suddenly attacked by colic pains with such vehemence that they drove her beside herself. Although all possible remedies were applied to her, they nevertheless did not mitigate her disorder. However, when she placed upon her breast some relics of a vestment belonging to St. Charles, after begging for his prayers she was freed from her ailments.

12. Sister Joanna Francesca Mendozza, a nun of St. Martha in Milan, had a cold and headache, by which she was so tormented that she could get no rest, feeling as if her head would burst. She could not bear her head to be touched even by a thin veil. All the part affected was so icy cold, that everything applied thereto, however hot, became cold as ice. She could not stand upon her feet; her sight was dimmed, and it was with extreme difficulty that she took food. The malady lasted many months, and became so much worse that she was considered at the point of death; the nuns began to watch over her as a dying woman. Two slippers of the Cardinal's were brought her, and placing one of them upon her head, seat of the malady, on the 18th of April, 1602, with full confidence in the Saint, to whose prayers she had recommended herself, she kept it there for half an hour, and was rid of her disorders. When it was taken off it was quite warm, as if it

had been before the fire, whereas things that were
warm were chilled after contact with her. This good
servant of God found herself so well that she rose
the same day from her bed, as if she had never
been ill.

13. Father Angelo Cerro, a Capuchin of the
Milanese district, had come to Milan to preach the
Lent of the year 1602 in the cathedral, and being
overtaken by gout in the right foot, fifteen days before
the time for beginning his course, he gave notice that
arrangements should be made for another preacher,
because when this malady came upon him, he was
for the time so indisposed as to be unable to undertake such work. Being then in bed with his foot
inflamed and swollen, a mozetta of the Cardinal
was brought him, with which, after asking for his
intercession, he blessed his foot three times overnight.
In the morning he found himself quite recovered.
He then preached the whole Lent with much benefit
to souls.

14. A young daughter of Paul Areso of Milan,
in the month of May, 1602, lay sick in Bollate
of acute fever and stitch in the side, and grew so
much worse that the physician gave up all hope of
her life. The parish priest, John Baptist Samaruga,
visited her, and seeing her dying, placed upon her
a beretta of St. Charles, which he had by him, and
kneeling down, with the people of the house, they
all invoked the Saint. Immediately the fever left
her, and the child was completely cured.

15. Cornelia Grampi, a nun of sixty-five years of

age, of the convent of Santa Maria Valle, in Milan, was attacked by rheumatism in her knees and legs, so that they seemed to be made of ice, and she was not able either to kneel or to go upstairs. She had suffered for two years without alleviation of her disorder, and had besides a bad place of forty-seven years' standing in one of her breasts. On the last day of May, 1602, the mother abbess blessed her twice with a mozetta of the Saint, the first of which cured her breast, and the second delivered her from the rheumatism with a pleasant warmth that gave new life to her limbs and relieved her of all pain.

16. John Baptist Porta, a juris-consult of the Milanese College of Law, fell into a fever accompanied with vomiting and disinclination to food. As the best physicians tried their skill upon him in vain, he began to prepare for death. In the month of May, 1602, a waistcoat and beretta of the Cardinal's were brought and placed by him on his stomach with great confidence in the merits of the Saint. Directly the fever was 'stayed, his stomach at rest, his thirst quenched, and he gradually recovered from his weakness, with gratitude to the holy intercessor who had obtained from God so miraculous a recovery.

17. Oriana Parolina had an intermittent lameness in her left leg whilst in the Convent of the Nuns of Cantù for education, so that every three or four days she was not able to use it, and had to be carried from place to place. She grew much worse in the beginning of February, 1603, the inflammation ascending up to the knee. The nuns had recourse to the intercession of

St. Charles, and placed upon the limb a letter written by him, which they preserved as a relic, when the young woman instantly recovered.

18. Apollonia Ridolfa, a lay sister in the convent of St. Catherine of Brera, in this city, had suffered twelve years continuously from fever, with constant pain in the head, inflammation in the arms, legs, and body, and a tumour in the stomach. For six months she could not retain food in her stomach, and was compelled to eject it with other unwholesome material, being thus thrown into a state of great prostration. The sick woman spent most of her time in bed, and the last six months was there altogether, with constant nausea, and then discovered herself to be possessed by evil spirits; remedies being applied in vain. At last a waistcoat of the Cardinal was placed upon her on the Vigil of the Most Holy Trinity in the year 1603. After having first recommended herself to his intercession and that of the Blessed Virgin, she received aid; the demon being unable to endure the presence of this garment tormented her terribly until ten o'clock at night, after which he let her rest, and whilst she dozed she saw the Blessed Virgin clad in blue, with a lily in her hand, enter her cell together with St. Charles in white pontificals. Our Blessed Lady give her the lily to smell, and the Cardinal bade her rise, and putting his hands upon her head, commanded the demon to depart from her, after which they both blessed her and departed. When she awoke, she found herself kneeling upon the ground, to her great astonishment, because she was in bed when she fell

asleep; and she smelt the perfume of the lily the whole morning in her cell. Delivered from evil spirits and cured of her malady, she raised herself to her feet filled with joy, and went to the church with the rest of the nuns, it being the hour for matins, to sing the Te Deum in thanksgiving to God for so great a miracle. What adds greatly to this miracle is that Sister Apollonia received from God, together with her recovery, greater strength both in body and soul than she enjoyed before her sickness, the Lord bestowing upon her a very interior spirit. It is now seven years since this happened, during which time she has continued to enjoy good health.

CHAPTER IX.

A REMARKABLE MIRACLE THAT OCCURRED WHEN THE BODY OF ST. CHARLES WAS VISITED BY ORDER OF THE HOLY APOSTOLIC SEE, WITH A SHORT SUMMARY OF OTHER MIRACLES.

THE Right Rev. Filippo Archinto, Bishop of Como, and Claudio Rangone, Bishop of Piacenza, having been delegated by the Holy Apostolic See to draw up the process of the life and miracles of St. Charles, after they had completed the examination of witnesses, on the night of the sixth day of March, 1606, according to the orders they had received, visited the body of the Saint in his sepulchre; they found it compact and in many parts entire, with the flesh palpable, and without bad odour, notwithstanding the damp had penetrated into the tomb, so as to waste away in several places the leaden coffin itself, although well enclosed in another coffin of thick planks. The precious treasure was consequently soaked through and through, as if it had been lying in a ditch. It was surprising that the bones had not rotted away in the long interval of twenty-two years since the body had been buried. The vestments were partly rotten, but the winding-sheet upon the body itself was nearly whole, a clear token that the putrefaction proceeded from the external damp and not from the body itself. It was noticed that whilst the rotten vestments were in contact with the body they yielded no bad smell, but when separated from it, they emitted a foul odour. The body was then clothed in fresh pontifical vestments and replaced in a coffin of cypress, splendidly adorned, and the tomb was reconstructed as the old one was falling to pieces owing to the damp.

The winding-sheet being divided into many parts, a small portion of it came into the hands of a Milanese lady (whose name is not mentioned for obvious reasons), who had suffered for many years from the power of the devil, by whose arts there was formed in her womb a monster so horrible that the like has never been heard of; I who have had certain information upon the whole subject, assure the reader, that as I have never read or heard of such a case, I am dismayed by the mere thought of it as entirely beyond human help. The unhappy woman looked for aid only to the Divine mercy and the intercession of St. Charles, to whom she was wont to recommend herself. A small piece of the winding-sheet having come into her hands, she swallowed it wrapped up in a piece of wafer, in certain hope of receiving her cure. Nor was such expectation vain, for although at first she felt a terrible suffocation in her throat, yet it dispelled all the devices of the devil, the monstrous growth resolved itself into liquid matter, which was discharged in great quantity, leaving her extremely faint and weak but filled with joy and consolation at finding herself entirely freed from all disorder, with restored health and strength which she regained on March 23d, 1606, and has by the grace of God retained to the present day.

Daria Erata, of the parish of St. Satirus in Milan, was for a long time possessed by evil spirits, which were not driven out by any exorcisms. Her aunt placed upon her a handkerchief that had touched the body of St. Charles at the time of his death. The evil spirit, not being able to bear it, after having uttered many cries departed; the young woman immediately fell to the ground in a fainting fit, from which she rose up entirely freed and in good health.

Cecilia Litotti, a nun of the convent of Santa Grata of Bergamo, had been insane for two years, and was kept by the nuns under restraint. A mozetta of the Saint was put upon her, and after his assistance had been invoked, and a vow made in common by all the nuns of the convent, she was miraculously cured.

Margaret, wife of Simon Spinelli, dwelling in the Brisa district of Milan, had been in the month of August, 1601, five days in the pains of child-bearing. Her infant at last died in her womb, and she herself was on the point of departing this life when a piece of the hair-shirt of St. Charles was applied to her, and with the assistance of the women who attended her she gave birth to a male child, in so putrified a state that it seemed to have come from the tomb.

In October of the year 1602 there lodged in the Archbishop's palace at Milan, Monsignor Paolo Tolosa, of the regular clerks of St. Paul, Bishop of Bovino, lying ill of fever with severe fits, when sent by Clement VIII. as Apostolic Nuncio to Turin. Believing that he would presently end his days, he recommended himself to the Blessed Charles, with a promise of some offering, the Saint appeared at his bedside in his habit as a Cardinal, with rochet and mozetta, and spoke as follows: " *You will not die of this malady, but your illness will be a long one; it is reasonable that you begin your mission by the way of the cross.*" These words came true, for the fever lasted forty days, and he did not get well till after ten months.

Susanna, daughter of John Ambrose Tettamanzo of Caratto, in the diocese of Milan, fell with such violence upon the corner of a chest that she ruptured herself internally, and lost a great quantity of blood, which began to flow about the Ave Maria on the 7th December 1602, and continued for fifteen hours continuously without it being possible to stop it. Brought to death's door, at the suggestion of her father she made a vow to go on foot to the tomb of St. Charles, and offer there two wax candles if by his assistance she got well, when she recovered immediately.

Doctor John Aluigi Leone of Cabiaglio in Valcuvia, in the diocese of Como, had a son, Melchior Giovanni Giacomo, who at the age of twelve months was seized with small-pox, worms, and falling sickness, and became so bad that he was in danger of death, having been two days without being able to take any milk, when on the point of expiring he was taken with a fit on the 10th March, 1602. His parents expected him to die, notwithstanding their vows and prayers to God, and to the

Blessed Virgin in his behalf. His mother holding him for dead, took him in her arms, and carried him before a picture of St. Charles, which they kept in the study along with other pictures of Our Lord and of the Blessed Virgin. She and her husband knelt down with their five daughters, in firm faith and hope, and with tears invoked the Saint for the life of the child; when behold! he miraculously awoke as it were from sleep, and began on the instant to suck at his mother's breasts as usual before his illness. He suffered from no more fits, but in three days was restored to health. What is more wonderful is that the child shows a remarkable intelligence, for when three years of age he began to say that he wished to serve God in the ecclesiastical state, and all his tastes and pleasures are fixed upon imitating the priest in celebrating the sacred mysteries, and singing the praises of God.

Salvadora wife of Battista de Panizzi of San Pulo, in the district of Bergamo, had been possessed by spirits for a year, with such maladies in her body that she was unable to rest, and had no strength left for her work. Food made her sick, and her complexion turned yellow. As no kind of remedy proved beneficial to her, whether corporal or spiritual, at last she prevailed upon her husband to take her to Milan, in the month of August, 1603, to visit the tomb of the Cardinal, where she went two days to pour forth her prayers, which at last prevailed, and she returned home freed from evil spirits, and from every other malady.

Camilla, daughter of John Baptist Limido, suffered for two years from dropsy, being much swollen and in a very bad way. Her father had her treated with every care and diligence, but nothing did her good. At last he had recourse to the intercession of St. Charles, and made a vow to offer her dresses at his tomb. On her recovery a shirt of the Saint was placed upon her, when she immediately felt better, and in eight or ten days entirely recovered, without applying any other remedy. This happened in the year 1604.

Vittoria Festi, a professed nun in the Convent of St. Susanna in Rome, had suffered from a severe cold in the head more than four months, together with toothache, which did not allow her to rest day or night. Her head seemed to be pierced with needles, and she was unable to endure the least thing upon it, however light. No medicine did her good, but rather increased her suffering. On recommending herself to the Blessed Cardinal, and making a vow to recite in his honour an Our Father, Hail Mary, and the prayer Hail Holy Queen, every day for a year, her health was restored her on the day she made it, viz., the fifth of August, 1604.

Hercules Perego of Giussano had sciatica for fourteen years in the left leg, which was considered incurable, the leg having been two years as it were dead, with so much pain that at times he almost sunk under it. He was often confined to his bed from the severity of the complaint, and at last, becoming much worse, took to it for many days. He then had recourse to the holy Archbishop, and immediately felt better, which gave him hope of being able to make a pilgrimage to his tomb, to obtain his complete recovery. In three days he went thither on horseback, and was so much benefited that he left his crutches behind him. Health and strength were thus restored to him in the month of March of the year 1605.

Catharina Sarona, of the parish of Santa Maria Porta in Milan, was confined to her bed by fever and catarrh. On the third day of November, 1606, the vigil of the feast of St. Charles, she recommended herself to him with much fervour, vowed him an offering, and obtained her cure, the Saint visibly appearing to her, and blessing her. She rose the same day from bed, so that the physician who attended her said that so sudden a recovery was a manifest miracle, considering the severity of her malady.

Monsignor Antonio Seneca, now Bishop of Anagni, having suffered for two years from dizziness and headache, became during the last six months so much worse that he was often obliged to take to his bed. He was not even able to go about the house without the support of two persons. When confined to his bed in Rome, at a crisis of his malady, he read an account of the miracles of St. Charles, and prayed very earnestly, that as he had obtained from God so many graces for others, he would restore health and strength to him also, if it should be for the greater glory of God and his own salvation, in order that he might employ himself for the good of Holy Church. At the same time, if he obtained this favour from him, he made a vow to fast upon bread and water upon the vigil of the Saint. His prayer was heard, and he was entirely rid of his malady.

CHAPTER X.

OF MANY SPIRITUAL GRACES WROUGHT THROUGH THE
INTERCESSION OF ST. CHARLES.

To the before-mentioned corporal works of mercy
wrought by God, through the merits and intercession
of His servant Charles, there might be added a great
number of spiritual works as having frequently
occurred and being much more highly esteemed.
Being unable, however, to give the reader that
certainty that belongs to the former that are set
down in the process, and proved by the testimony
of many witnesses, I must pass over the latter, as
they are, for the most part, either secret or unfit
to be brought to the knowledge of all, and shall
only relate a few of unimpeachable authenticity,
which may be told without offence.

Paola, daughter of Battista and sister of Hermes
Visconti, knights of Milan, had been married to
Pomponio, brother of Agostino Cusano, Cardinal of
the title of SS. John and Paul, and having proved
by experience the vanity of the world, was inspired
with the holy intention of becoming a poor clare
in the monastery of Santa Prassede, choosing in this

matter as father and guide the Blessed Cardinal her Archbishop, into whose hands she gave herself entirely. Three months after the death of her husband he placed her in the convent, gave her the habit with his own hand, and in due season admitted her to make her vows as Sister Francesca. Whilst he lived he watched over her with particular care, recognising in her a valiant woman, as was shown by the proficiency she acquired in virtues, and the observance of the rule of her convent. She several times held the office of Abbess, with the whole weight of responsibility upon her shoulders. After St. Charles had passed to a better life, she was overtaken by severe illness, which reduced her to so weak a state that it was not without great difficulty that she could keep the rule at all. This much afflicted her, not so much on account of her bodily sufferings, in which she rejoiced with resignation to the will of God, as because she was obliged to relax discipline in herself, and was disappointed in her design of serving God as perfectly as possible. While troubled by these anxieties and by temptations of the enemy of souls, there appeared to her one night in sleep her protector St. Charles, in whom she had great confidence, in pontifical vestments, accompanied by a great company of saints; one of whom, St. Thecla, for whom the Saint in his lifetime had a special devotion, he took by the hand and drew forward, saying to Francesca, "Would you rejoice? Weep first as she has done." And he disappeared. Upon awaking she was filled with consolation, remembering that these words corresponded with what God had vividly set before her when He first called her to the state of perfection, viz. that the Cross is the ladder to heaven, in imitation of Jesus Christ the head and the saints His members. Thence she acquired such strength and vigour that, in all her infirmities and troubles, instead of the weariness that they are wont to bring, she felt great contentment and relish. She has confessed that the effect of this vision, which remained stamped upon her mind, is that not only do bodily comforts give her no pleasure, but they rather occasion her weariness and disgust, so that she can hardly bring herself to enjoy those that are necessary for life, and to keep up her strength for the Lord's service; a great grace which she knows is the result of the intercession and protection of her holy Father and Pastor.

A citizen of Milan who was much devoted to St. Charles, was in prayer in his chamber, when a young woman, a servant of the house, came in to make the bed. The devil tempted him to sin with her, and made so severe an attack upon him that after having resisted a little while, he surrendered to it; and rose with the intention of complying with that most evil suggestion. Whilst he was going towards the young woman, lo, suddenly there appeared before him the Cardinal in his pontificals, with so stern a countenance that filled him with shame and terror, and delivered him from temptation and the sin he was about to commit. This happened about the year 1588, four years after the death of the Saint.

In the year 1601 there was in Milan a man over

fifty years of age, who from his boyhood had given himself like a beast to the vice of lust, and from having been plunged in it for forty years, had acquired a most confirmed habit of sin. But coming to a better mind, and acknowledging his evil course of life, he determined to amend it; and yet found great difficulty, as if the habit of sin had become engrained in his nature, and he did not know how to accomplish his good purpose. He had recourse to fasting disciplines and other penitential exercises. Moreover, he sought the aid of confessors, and recommended himself to the prayers of many religious persons, but all in vain. Ultimately he came into the hands of a confessor, who, after having given him many remedies to no purpose, exhorted him to seek the aid of St. Charles at his tomb, through the experience he had of those who had been benefited by so doing. The penitent obeyed and received from it such abundant grace that he was wholly delivered from all temptation and inclination to lust, as if he had been a "piece of wood" (to use his own words), and, in addition, received an exceeding fervour of spirit that led him to spend the rest of his life in great penance for his past sins.

The same year in Salò, on Lake Garda, there was a man of honourable condition, who had lived for twelve years in the carnal sin of concubinage, and had refused to listen to his relations and friends, and the warnings of his ecclesiastical superiors. A daughter of his, an Ursuline nun, being much troubled by her father's bad life, moved by an interior inspiration knelt before a portrait of the holy Cardinal, which she kept in her chamber, and with earnest prayers, accompanied by many tears, besought the Saint to save her father's soul. Her prayers were heard, for her father determined of his own accord to amend his life, and the following day dismissed his mistress from the house, and made a beginning of a Christian life, and persevered, to the consolation of his daughter, who sent to Milan an attestation of this signal favour, with a picture as a lasting memorial.

Another person had given herself up to a devil, and had constant intercourse with it for many years. She then recognised the state of perdition in which she lay, and wished to abandon the diabolical practice, but not being able to do so through the constant assaults and violence of the enemy, began to despair of her salvation. She recommended herself, however, to the Saint, and after having prayed to him with many tears, her entreaties were heard, and she was delivered from all molestation of this infernal monster, and lived afterwards a devout and spiritual life.

Others also have acknowledged their deliverance from most harassing temptations of lust, both by calling upon his name in prayer and by carrying about them a small portion of his hair-shirt. Great benefit has been derived in these days from the recollection and tradition of his virtues; for in those who have known him it seems that he has power to keep them in the fear of God, and to make them persevere in the way of salvation which they learnt from him. Moreover, the many graces and miracles that he constantly works greatly encourage persons to amendment of life, devotion, and frequentation of the Holy Sacraments. Whence it is thought that he now in heaven helps in the salvation of souls just as much as he did while upon earth, because the corporal works of mercy wrought by his merits are accompanied in almost every case by spiritual graces.

In bringing this history to a close, I have to express to my sorrow that my skill has not been equal to clothe fitly in words the virtues of the Saint. So far from giving any idea of the perfection of his sanctity, this work, such as it is, can be but a rough sketch rather than a finished portrait.

Nathless I turn myself to you, O holy Pastor, praying you, for whose sake only I undertook the task, to excuse all my imperfections; my object being that your deeds should be had in remembrance to the glory of God and the benefit of Christian people. Be, I entreat you my advocate in heaven, as you were my Pastor and loving Father upon earth, and obtain for me from the Lord the grace to follow the path of salvation which you have pointed out by your example and precept, that I may, after this brief life, see you in the heavenly country, where you enjoy with the saints the eternal happiness you have won.

DIARY

OF THE

AILY WORKS OF ST. CHARLES AT WHICH HE WAS
PRESENT IN PERSON WHEN NOT PREVENTED
BY MORE IMPORTANT BUSINESS.

———•———

WEEKLY.

MONDAY.

he congregation of the holy office of the Inquisition. The congregation of the tribunal. The chapter of the fabric of the Cathedral
and that of the great Church of St. Ambrose. The congregation
of discipline of the clergy and people.

TUESDAY.

he congregation of regular discipline of nuns. The spiritual congregation of the seminary and of the colleges.

WEDNESDAY.

ermon in the oratory of San Sepolcro. The congregation of the
tribunal.

THURSDAY.

he congregation of the temporal administration of the seminary. The
congregation of the penitentiary.

FRIDAY.

he temporal congregation of the Swiss college. Sermon in the oratory
of San Sepolcro.

SATURDAY.

he chapter of the Hospital of Mercy (Pietà).

SUNDAY.

he Divine Office in the Metropolitan Cathedral.

MONTHLY.

The congregation of parish-priests and chaplains of each region of the city and vicariate of the diocese.

The congregation of rites (twice a month).

The visitation of the archiepiscopal household (famiglia).

The congregation of the college of nobles.

The congregation of the Hospital of Mendicants.

The congregation of the Oblates of St. Ambrose at San Sepolcro and in the four *consortia* of the diocese.

The congregation of the studies of the clergy.

The congregation of the peace-makers for the prevention of law-suits.

The congregation for the care of ecclesiastical property.

The congregation of the fathers of families for teaching them to bring up their Households in the Fear of God.

ORDINARY FUNCTIONS OF THE YEAR.

JANUARY.

1. The Circumcision.
6. Epiphany.   } Pontifical Mass, with First and Second Vespers.
20. St. Sebastian.

The congregation of ecclesiastical discipline in preparation for the general congregation of the clergy.

The general congregation of the clergy according to the 27th Decree of the Fourth Diocesan Synod, in manner following :—

Jan. 2. The congregation of the chapter and clergy of the Cathedral, with a sermon by the Archbishop. Examination as to Divine Worship, the recitation of the canonical hours, discipline of the choir, studies, spiritual chapter and observance of ecclesiastical discipline.

Jan. 3. The congregation of the canons of all the collegiate churches of the city, with sermon and examination as above.

Jan. 4. The congregation of parish-priests, with sermon and examination, and scrutiny as to the administration of the Holy Sacraments and as to the cure of souls.

Jan. 5. The congregation of chaplains, with sermon and scrutiny of matters concerning their state of life.

Jan. 6. The congregation of the inferior clergy, with sermon and scrutiny as above.

Monday in the week following :—

. The congregation of all regulars who hear confessions, with sermon and scrutiny as to their state and duties.

The congregation of the secular doctors of law and their college, with communion and sermon on doing their duty uprightly.

The congregation of physicians at San Sepolcro, with communion and sermon as above.

The congregation of advocates of both civil and canon law, in the *scurolo* of the duomo, with communion and sermon.

The congregation of select parish-priests, sitting in private to examine into the state of discipline among the clergy and the observance of the synodal decrees (to sit at least four times a year).

FEBRUARY.

The congregation for the fulfilment (riduzione) and execution of legacies.

The blessing of the candles on the Feast of the Purification of our Blessed Lady.

The preparatory meeting before the congregation of Vicars-Foran on the business of the Diocesan Synod, and the reports of the Vicars-Foran.

The congregation of Vicars-Foran, according to the 47th decree of the Fourth Synod, to be held on the Tuesday before Septuagesima Sunday. The Vicars-Foran give their report on the state of the diocese and of abuses to be remedied by synodal decrees.

The visitation of the congregation of the Oblates of Saint Ambrose.

In Septuagesima Week.

Visit to the seven churches by the clergy and people of the city each day of the week.

Devotions (oratorj) in the church of the Oblates at San Sepolcro every day except Saturday, with a sermon by the Archbishop each day.

In Sexagesima Week.

A general communion in each of the six regions of the city on different days, with a sermon by the Archbishop on each day.

Devotions at San Sepolcro as above, with sermon by the Archbishop each day.

The spiritual exercises in all the collegiate and parish churches, to keep the people from profane pastimes.

In Quinquagesima Week.

A general communion in the cathedral, with plenary indulgence.

A general communion on the week-days, times and places fixed beforehand.

Devotions at San Sepolcro, with sermon by the Archbishop each day as above.

A general procession to Santa Maria delle Grazie on the Wednesday, with sermon by the Archbishop on the way of visiting the churches of the stations for gaining the holy indulgences.

Examination of those who present themselves for orders, with general review of all the ordinandi, and sermon by the Archbishop on the way of receiving orders in a worthy manner.

The holy ordination.

Solemn Vespers on the first Sunday of Lent.

MARCH.

Visitation of the convents of nuns and of the societies of other pious women.

Second general ordination of Lent, with examination, review, and sermon as above.

Lenten sermons every day.

APRIL.

General visitation of the archiepiscopal prisons.

Blessing of the palms on Palm Sunday.

Pontifical Mass and Vespers on Holy Thursday and Saturday.

Blessing of the font.

Ordinations, with examination and review as above.

Pontifical Mass and Vespers on Easter Day.

MONDAY IN LOW WEEK.

Congregation of all the prefects of the city and Vicars-Foran, according to the 46th decree of the Fourth Diocesan Synod, in preparation for synod.

Congregation for the execution (riduzione) of pious bequests, in preparation for the next synod.

Visitation of the seminaries and of the Swiss college, with examination and recognisance of all the students.

TUESDAY IN LOW WEEK.

Congregation to arrange the synodal decrees of the next Diocesan Synod.

MAY.

THREE DAYS BEFORE THE SYNOD.

Congregation for the examination of documents, new decrees, and other provisions for the synod aforesaid.

THE DAY BEFORE THE SYNOD.

Congregation of Vicars-Foran for an exact scrutiny of the state of the city and diocese, and for the furtherance of discipline in the clergy and people.

THE THREE FOLLOWING DAYS.

Synod, with sermon by the Archbishop on each day to the assembled clergy, on the business of the same.

MAY 3.—FEAST OF THE INVENTION OF THE HOLY CROSS.

Pontifical Mass, with First and Second Vespers.

General procession of the Holy Nail to the church of San Sepolcro on the same day.

ASCENSION DAY.

Pontifical Mass, with First and Second Vespers.

JUNE.

Different congregations on the visitation of the diocese.

Appointment of the visitors for the six regions of the diocese.

Diary.

PENTECOST.
of the font.
Mass, with Vespers, on the vigil and day of the feast.
ration of the Sacrament of Confirmation each day in appointed
ches of each region, with sermon each day by the Archbishop.
ion of the ordinandi, with sermon.
rdination on day appointed.

CORPUS CHRISTI.
Mass, with First and Second Vespers.
rocession of the Most Holy Sacrament.
ongregation of the Oblates of St. Ambrose.
ongregation of all the clergy of the city on different days, as in
nonth of January, according to the 27th decree of the Fourth
san Synod, with sermon by the Archbishop each day.

THE ROGATION-DAYS.
ies on the three days, with fast; sermon by the Archbishop on
day.

JUNE 19.—FEAST OF SAINTS GERVASIUS AND PROTASIUS.
Mass, with First and Second Vespers.

ST. JOHN BAPTIST AND SAINTS PETER AND PAUL.
Mass, with First and Second Vespers.
visitation of the diocese by the Archbishop, together with the
al visitors.

JULY.
isitation of the diocese—(*continued*).

Y 2.—FEAST OF THE VISITATION OF THE BLESSED VIRGIN.
n to the seven churches.

JULY 28.—FEAST OF SAINTS NAZARIUS AND CELSUS.
Mass, with First and Second Vespers.

AUGUST.
isitation of the diocese—(*continued*).

AUGUST 10.—FEAST OF ST. LAURENCE.
Mass, with First and Second Vespers and procession.

AUGUST 15.—THE ASSUMPTION OF OUR BLESSED LADY.
Mass, with First and Second Vespers.

SEPTEMBER.
of the seminaries and the Swiss college, with examination of
nts.
of the college of nobles and of the students resident.

NATIVITY OF OUR BLESSED LADY—PATRONAL FEAST OF DUOMO.
Mass, with First and Second Vespers.

SEPT. 23.—FEAST OF ST. THECLA.

Pontifical Mass, with First and Second Vespers.

Examination of the ordinandi, with sermon.

General ordinations of September.

OCTOBER.

Examination of the state of all the clergy.

General congregation of the studies of the clergy, and of the matter to be read in the next year. Appointment of ecclesiastics for lectures delivered throughout the year by theologians and canonists of the chapters and in the college of Brera.

NOVEMBER.
ALL SAINTS' DAY.

Pontifical Mass, with First and Second Vespers.

Nov. 3.

Sermon of the Archbishop before the senate and magistrates.

Visitation of the churches, hospitals, and pious institutions of the city.

Congregations of all the clergy of the city, as in the month of January.

DECEMBER.

Visitation of the city—(*continued*).

FEAST OF THE ORDINATION OF ST. AMBROSE. DEC. 7.

VIGIL AND ANNIVERSARY OF CHRISTMAS DAY.

FEAST OF ST. STEPHEN.

Pontifical Mass, with First and Second Vespers.

EXTRAORDINARY FUNCTIONS THROUGHOUT THE YEAR.

Consecrations of bishops, abbots, and abbesses.

Ordinations *extra tempora* by apostolic indult.

Consecrations of churches, altars, chalices, and bells.

Benediction of sacred vessels and vestments, crosses and pictures, clothing and profession of nuns.

Blessing of arms and banners.

Consecration of knights by authority of the Pope or the Grand Master.

Promotion to the doctorate of the students of the seminary or of the Swiss college, by apostolic authority.

Procession of the Holy Rosary on the first Sunday of each month.

Procession of the Most Holy Sacrament on the third Sunday of each month.

Sermons every Friday in commemoration of the Passion of Our Lord. ——

General communions at colleges, convents, and societies of pious persons.

Congregations of the schools of Christian doctrine.

ORDER OF VISITATION.

Winter.—Visitation of the city.

Spring.—Visitation of the convents of nuns.

Summer.—Visitation of the diocese.

Autumn.—Visitation of the seminaries and colleges.

Every three years, celebration of the Provincial Council, together with the various congregations held in preparation for the same.

INDEX.

PRINTED BY BALLANTYNE, HANSON AND CO.
EDINBURGH AND LONDON